Introduction to Group Workflow, and Workgroup Computing

Introduction to Groupware, Workflow, and Workgroup Computing

Setrag Khoshafian
Marek Buckiewicz

John Wiley & Sons, Inc.

New York • Chichester • Brisbane • Toronto • Singapore

Publisher: Katherine Schowalter
Senior Editor: Diane D. Cerra
Managing Editor: Micheline Frederick
Text Production & Design: North Market Street Graphics

Designations used by companies to distinguish their products are often claimed as trademarks. In all instances where John Wiley & Sons, Inc. is aware of a claim, the product names appear in initial capital or all capital letters. Readers, however, should contact the appropriate companies for more complete information regarding trademarks and registration.

This text is printed on acid-free paper.

Copyright © 1995 by John Wiley & Sons, Inc.

All rights reserved. Published simultaneously in Canada.

This publication is designed to provide accurate and authoritative information in regard to the subject matter covered. It is sold with the understanding that the publisher is not engaged in rendering legal, accounting, or other professional service. If legal advice or other expert assistance is required, the services of a competent professional person should be sought.

Reproduction or translation of any part of this work beyond that permitted by section 107 or 108 of the 1976 United States Copyright Act without the permission of the copyright owner is unlawful. Requests for permission or further information should be addressed to the Permissions Department, John Wiley & Sons, Inc.

Library of Congress Cataloging-in-Publication Data:

Khoshafian, Setrag.
    Introduction to groupware, workflow, and workgroup computing / Setrag Khoshafian, Marek Buckiewicz.
       p.   cm.
    Includes bibliographical references (p.).
    ISBN 0-471-02946-7
    1. Work groups—Data processing.   I. Buckiewicz, Marek, 1947–   .
II. Title.
HD66.K495   1995
658.4′036′0285—dc20
                                                              94-43221
                                                                   CIP

Printed in the United States of America
10 9 8 7 6 5 4 3 2 1

Preface

Information prophets speak of connection. The computer is the means by which many of us pull ideas together and organize information. Once, only a few were able, with difficulty and time, to access and converge information resources for the purpose of creative invention; today, using networked computers, the many can search for and discover interrelationships of increasing complexity. Technology presents a potential platform from which humanity can take a quantum leap in intelligence, creativity, and achievement.

There are pitfalls. The temptation to invent the future in terms of the past is immense. We tend to define the tomorrow within the limitations of yesterday. Society has inertia. Decision makers who "earned their spurs" on the basis of obsolete ideas and fading paradigms resist change.

The idea of connection applies not only to the interrelation of pieces of information but also to the interactions between people. New technologies will change our sense of identity and behavior as well as our sense of shared space and how we work together within that space.

Collaborative computing is changing how information moves and is managed in business. Emerging "groupware" environments enable workers to collaborate through internetworked computers and interact freely in order to achieve common purpose.

There are challenges. Although the internetworking of computers is inevitable, it has not yet been widely adopted for business collaborations. Groupware faces cultural challenges in organizations with rigid business practices.

What does it do for me? is the question, demanding pragmatic answers. For a business to remain competitive, the average office worker and business executive must be educated about both the costs and the benefits of automating information management for collaborative work.

There is a great deal of confusion about collaborative computing. The scope and domain of collaboration spans simple home offices, companies, widely distributed enterprises, even entire countries or continents. Emerging connectivity and software technologies are realizing the potential of collaborative computing across geographically distributed offices.

Politicians promise equal opportunity information highways that, through high performance fiber optic cables, could carry video, phone conversations, and computer information. The intent is to provide access to huge electronic libraries, and through the ability to exchange data almost instantaneously, to afford "collaboration" and free exchange of information between researchers, schools, hospitals, universities, and private businesses.

But the highway is a poor metaphor. What is being built is more like a shared space that can accommodate an immense public. Perhaps the great task of our time is to discover, invent, and evolve how to interact within this great electronic, almost global space.

WHAT IS GROUPWARE?

Any computerized system which enables groups of workers to collaborate for some common purpose or task can be labeled as groupware. Groupware has unfortunately been associated with limited function sets for automating some work activities. It is more than that.

Groupware helps people work together. Groupware encompasses many systems and concepts. Groupware products are sometimes identified by features such as calendars and electronic meeting support. These features support collaborative work, however, any system that helps collaborative and cooperative work can be characterized as a groupware product.

Groupware draws on two important industry trends:

(a) Collaborative Team Work: Mid-level managers are being replaced by teams and work groups. Hierarchical management structures are being replaced with flatter, "democratic" organizations. Responsibilities are increasingly being delegated to individual work group members. The prevailing paradigm where consideration and decision is the prerogative of a manager who then delegates specific execution activities to the staff is becoming replaced by a model which diffuses intelligence, creativity, and responsibility throughout the team. Management tasks are being accomplished by groups.

(b) Downsizing: Difficult economic conditions have caused organizations and businesses to downsize. Downsizing means that the same task must be accomplished by fewer people. Downsizing also means a migration from mainframe systems to Local Area Networks and client/server architectures.

We are in the midst of a trend with tremendous possibilities for exchanging and interchanging information. If knowledge is power, then groupware empowers workers by providing an avenue for creativity, access to huge warehouses of information, and, most importantly, a means for collaboratively working with their peers.

AND WHAT IS WORKFLOW?

Organized businesses have policies and procedures which can be captured in forms which can then be filled, processed, and authorized by various workers. Workflow systems help to automate the processing of policies and procedures in an organization. While different products define workflow in different ways they all provide alternative solutions to the same problem: How to automate the flow of information.

Workflow systems have their roots in document imaging systems and electronic mail. E-mail systems allow for the interchange of text messages across LANs and WANs spanning cities, states, and continents. Many workflow systems use E-mail as a transport layer for messages. There are many different approaches for designing workflows including scripting languages and graphical design tools. Workflow tools are often used to implement reengineered business processes.

ORGANIZATION OF THE BOOK

This book is an introduction to groupware, workflow, and work group computing. The primary audience for this book is the worker who would use groupware. A secondary, albeit important, audience is the decision maker who would reengineer a concern by introducing groupware systems and philosophies. We seek to educate, inform, and motivate information workers and executive management about emerging systems which promise real benefits for business.

Chapter 1 presents an overview of the components of groupware systems and their respective benefits, especially for organizations which attempt to revitalize their business processes and organizational infrastructures.

Groupware is not a single technology but rather an aggregation of integrated existing technologies, including graphical interfaces, object orientation, routing, concurrent sharing, more advanced pattern recognition, and more. The question is not so much which technology is a subset of a groupware system, but how can any technology be used for collaborative work.

There are many categories and taxonomies of groupware. Chapter 1 presents groupware products along the primary dimensions of document-based communication, high-volume transaction-based communication, and organizational communication, as well as along the two (almost) orthogonal dimensions of object representation and collaboration. There are many aspects of object representation and modeling in applications, databases, and multimedia. There are also many aspects of collaboration in client/server architectures, document management library models, e-mail and messaging, workflow, and synchronous groupware solutions.

We also discuss the traditional academic groupware taxonomies along the Time-Space continuum. The four quadrants of these orthogonal dimensions include: Same Time/Same Place; Same Time/Different Places; Different Times/Same Place; and Different Time/Different Places.

Chapter 2 introduces the various objects that are used (or "operated upon") in a collaborative work groupware system. Coworkers collaborate on objectives and objects. These might be business goals, tasks, or products presented in various graphs, tables, documents, and spreadsheets and organized in folders.

This chapter discusses some of the most important object types used in groupware systems such as documents and information types for collaborative authoring, sharing and concurrent accesses, annotation, commentary, or authorization. We provide a very brief overview of the basic concepts and advantages of object orientation; in particular, how objects encapsulate both structure and behavior. The structure of objects is represented through object attributes and content. Behavior deals with operations users can perform on objects.

Brief descriptions of most of the application types used in groupware products are provided as well as additional object types including multimedia and especially, forms.

Graphical user interface (GUI) is evolving into a document-centric environment in contrast to the current application-centric paradigm. Although this transition is subtle and for most users transparent, this conceptual shift is momentous for software and system design, especially for groupware.

We briefly describe two document standards: OpenDoc (CILabs) and OLE 2 (Microsoft). Users can create compound documents containing parts from applications which are standards compliant.

We also discuss hypermedia, a generalized concept of containment, emphasizing the differences between hypermedia and compound documents. Finally, we discuss issues raised by the concurrent sharing of the object types.

Chapter 3 explains client/server architectures and their application to collaborative computing. This chapter also discusses LANs, WANs, file servers, database servers, and miscellaneous other server types or services, including FAX servers, video servers, and messaging servers. We also touch on advanced topics such as distributed database construction and concurrency control strategies.

Chapter 3 also discusses versioning and the check-out/check-in models for manipulating objects concurrently. Among the many models of cooperation, one of the most basic is the "library" or check-out check-in model. Workers collaborate by checking documents in and out for processing. Since only one copy is maintained, all modifications are coordinated.

The two fundamental approaches to exchanging messages and collaborating on tasks are point-to-point messaging and workflow. Point-to-point messaging is similar to electronic mail routing.

Chapter 4 discusses messaging and the most successful groupware application category: E-mail. Electronic messaging systems were the first systems to provide significant advantages to workers dispersed geographically. We discuss the main components from front-end graphical user interfaces and mail enabled applications to various back-end implementations. This chapter discusses directory services, messaging databases, and directory services as well as overviews of emerging messaging standards such as MHS for transport, MAP and VIM for API, and X.500 for directory services. We close this chapter with a preview of emerging "smart" mail features being incorporated into next generation e-mail and messaging products including features such as rules, multimedia, and digital signatures.

Chapter 5 presents the emerging workflow systems for collaborative computing. Workflow systems track message routes and maintain an audit trail of the various jobs performed by various workers. Workflow systems attempt to directly capture the information "manufacturing" processes in an organization or to present business policy or procedure while automatically "logging" all actions. Thus if the objects of collaboration (the document, charts, spreadsheets, etc.) are the data of a computerized collaborative system, the programs which manipulate the data are presented through workflows.

Workflow organizes processes in corporations into nodes which represent people, devices, applications, or other processes, and links which represent the routing of documents, requests, instructions, and commands. Workflows can be designed by using scripting languages and graphical design tools. Workflow systems may be flexible or constrained by some orthodoxy or particular model of human interaction, corporate organization, and work processing.

The chapter discusses three types of workflow: ad-hoc, administrative, and production. The chapter also discusses basic workflow concepts including graphical workflow tools, workflow status, work queues, workflow rules, case, groups, roles, retraction, iteration, and project management issues.

We report recent trends in standardizing workflow systems and interoperability. We close chapter 5 with an overview of next generation workflow architectures in client/server environment.

Chapter 6 looks at electronically enhanced meetings and collaborations. First we examine scheduling and time management tools that help workers to get in synch: Personal Information Managers, and Group calendars. Next we discuss decision support tools for meetings that take place at the same time and in the same place. These tools, which enhance group dynamics without fundamentally changing how we interact, are rapidly gaining market acceptance.

Next we examine tools that permit us to meet and interact in ways and in situations that previously were not feasible. People who aren't together can combine the information portions of themselves using tools for synchronous and remote meetings: whiteboards, shared editors, teleconferencing, and videoconferencing. Information-rich distance interactions depend heavily on underlying hardware, standards and, enabling technologies: CPUs, DSPs, RISC, communications hardware, multimedia support, and high-bandwidth network infrastructure.

Chapter 6 closes with a look at some human factors involved with Computer Supported Cooperative Work including a brief discussion of virtual teams, virtual corporations, and MUDs (Multiple User Dimensions) as possible models for workgroup collaborations. Finally we develop the concept of Organization Memory first introduced in chapter 1.

Whereas chapter 6 considers the human factor of collaborative technologies, chapter 7 focuses on the social impact of these technologies.

All of the opposition to groupware is not from entrenched middle managers and tenured bureaucrats. Some Luddite suspicion remains even at the grass root level. Some see "reengineering" as a euphemism for massive layoffs and groupware as the agency which makes workers redundant. To them, groupware is the looming shadow of Big Brother, technology is a lever for perpetuating class advantage.

A more positive vision for the millennium is one of collaboration and team work. Cooperation, collaboration, democratization, empowerment, and team work are becoming the essential ingredients of survival within an increasingly competitive environment. Prophets have hailed the electronically interlinked social mass forming around the globe as the Second Coming; an aggregate Messiah.

Writing about an emerging technology has a built-in time lag. Given the production cycle and lead times of hardcover publishing, groupware, especially in the volatile areas such as videoconferencing that are primed for a quantum leap, will have evolved even further into previously uncharted territory.

Where we are going is anybody's guess. The vote hasn't been taken and the fat lady has not yet sung. There are, however, some interesting possibilities that look good at this time.

As groupware evolves the time/place taxonomy becomes irrelevant. Light weight notebook computers, pen or other input driven computers, wireless LANs, cellular modems, and other communication devices can provide the means for direct sales teams, field service, law enforcement, and emergency units to function as integrated collaborative units any time at any place.

As workflow gains market acceptance it appears to be destined as a means for process-intensive organizations to coordinate teams of teams. Much research work into group process still remains to be done before workflow can be effectively orchestrated and extrapolated across large scale and complex projects.

Team rooms which provide a variety of resources for decision support and group collaborations are becoming increasingly popular. The idea of building virtual team rooms in cyberspace has captured the interest of some researchers. There appears to be a lot of opportunity for creative innovation in the design of shared spaces, both virtual and real.

As the scope and reach of team interactivity mediated through computer and communications technology evolve beyond the physical boundaries of space and time, the bounding elements will become cultural. Having transcended geography and time, bridges could be built to hurdle borders and transparently reconcile the diverse social protocols, assumptions, practices, and norms.

Japanese industry revolutionized manufacturing with the simple concept of Just-in-Time provisioning. The advantages afforded by the ability to diffuse novel procedures and resources throughout a business organization quickly become overwhelming in a complex and competitive environment. The ability to reconfigure an aggregation of human skills and resources depends on the extended concept of just-in-time learning.

Perhaps the most seductive vision of groupware technologies is the idea of a "window to anywhere". A generation has been weaned on the mass media. We easily accept our electronic windows as founts of information and vicarious experience. The question is, what will we do when the constraints imposed by an aging infrastructure are removed and the virtual spaces of the information highway become a reality available to the many? How will we interact with each other when our monitors become electronic windows to anywhere and anyone? What will you say?

ACKNOWLEDGMENTS

We express our appreciation to the many individuals and organizations that made this book possible.

First and foremost, we thank Aulene, Silva, and the children (Nishan, Jonathan, Shahan, and Nareg) for their patience and support.

We would like to express our gratitude to all the companies who provided us with demos, support materials, and answers to our questions. In particular, we acknowledge Portfolio Technologies, Reach, FileNet, Collabra, Lotus, Delrina, Plexus, Action, Silicon Graphics, Criterion, and others for their readiness to help us with the necessary technical materials and information.

Finally, we would like to thank our project editor, Micheline Frederick, for her patience and perseverance, and Diane Cerra and Terri Hudson, both senior editors at Wiley, for their trust and continued support.

Contents

1

INTRODUCTION ... 1

Understanding Technologies, Products, and Corporate Needs ... 2
Categorizing Groupware Applications ... 4
Organizing Humans ... 6
Groupware: Evolution or Revolution? ... 7
    First-generation Groupware ... 9
    Second-generation Groupware ... 10
Groupware: An Evolving Technology ... 12
    Blueprint for Adopting Groupware ... 12
        Enhancement Technology ... 14
        Design First ... 14
        Groupware: Here, There, Everywhere ... 14
LAN and WAN: Backbone for Groupware ... 15
    Large System Groupware ... 16
    Local and Wide Area Networks ... 16
Groupware and Computer-supported Cooperative Work ... 17
    Defining CSCW ... 19
    The Human Dimension of CSCW ... 19

Groupware and Business Process Reengineering 20
   Reengineering 21
      Combining Several Jobs into One 21
      Empowered Workers Make Decisions 21
      Reduces Checks and Controls 22
      Empowered Workers, Empowered Managers 22

A Brief History of Groupware 23
   Client/Server Foundation 24
      File Servers 24
      Database Servers 24
   From Sharing Files to E-mail 27
   In the Beginning There Was Text . . . and Then There Was Hypertext ... 27
      Memex 28
   Computer-supported Cooperative Work 29
   Group Decision Support Systems 30

Object Representation and Collaboration 30
   The Vertical Dimension 31
      Advanced Database Models 32
      Multimedia 33
   The Horizontal Dimension 33
      Client/Server Architectures 34
      Check-out/Check-in Document Management/Library Model ... 34
      Routing Models 34
      Workflow 34
      Team and Organizational Communications 36

Collaborative Work 37
   The Individual 37
   The Small Team 38
   The Enterprise 39

Information Overload 40

Organization Memory 41

Time and Place Interactions 44
   Same Time/Same Place 46
   Same Time/Different Places 47
   Different Times/Same Place 48
      Kiosk 49
   Different Times/Different Places 49

The Challenges and Problems of Groupware 50
   Uniformity in Product 51
   Too Much Structure or Too Much Work 52
   Challenging and Flatting Organizational Infrastructures 52
   Unfair Distribution of Tasks 52

Lack of Support for Exceptions and Nuances in Human Interactions	53
Resistance to Change	53
Summary	53

2

OBJECTS OF COLLABORATION — 55

Defining Objects	57
Editing And Viewing Objects	58
Overview of Compound Documents	58
Launching or In-place Editing	59
Standards for Portable Electronic Document Exchange	60
Collaboration on Objects	62
Object-Orientation	63
Customization	64
Customizing Behavior	66
Objects and Groupware	67
Typical Applications	68
Word Processors	69
Spreadsheets	69
Presentation Packages	69
Personal Databases	69
Corporate Databases	70
Accounting	70
Forms	70
Image Editors	70
Graphic Packages	71
Forms	71
Form Design Editing	73
Query By Forms	75
Forms in Document Imaging Systems	76
Indexing	78
Forms and Groupware	78
EDI	80
Compound Documents	83
OpenDoc	86
Document- or Content-based Model	86
Parts	86
Part Handlers	87

Editors and Viewers	88
In-place Editing	88
Frames and Layout	88
Linking	88
Storage	88
Run-time	89
Compound Documents in Collaborative Environments	89
OLE 2	90
Compound Documents in OLE 2	90
OLE 2 Architecture	91
Component Object Model (COM)	91
OLE 2 Storage Model	92
Embedding Objects	92
Viewing Components	93
Linking and Monikers	93
OLE 2 and Distributed Objects	93
Multimedia Objects and Groupware	94
Defining Multimedia Data Types and Objects	94
Hypermedia	98
Hypermedia Documents	100
Links	102
Linking Strategies	102
Hypermedia and Groupware	103
Containers	105
Cabinets	105
Folders	105
Other Collections in Groupware Applications	106
The Many Faces of Sharing	108
Referential Sharing	108
Location Transparency	109
Concurrent Sharing	111
Summary	113

3

CLIENT/SERVER ARCHITECTURE AND COLLABORATIVE COMPUTING   115

Defining Client/Server Architectures	115
Fine-grained and Coarse-grained	116
Object-orientation and Client/Server Architectures	118
Component Computing and Client/Server Architectures	120

Networking	121
Local Area Networks	122
Cabling	123
Topologies	123
Networking Protocols and Standards	125
The Physical Link (Layer 1)	126
The Data Link (Layer 2)	126
The Network (Layer 3)	126
The Transport (Layer 4)	127
The Session (Layer 5)	127
The Presentation (Layer 6)	127
The Application (Layer 7)	127
Data Transport Protocols	127
Internetwork Packet Exchange	127
Sequenced Packet Exchange	128
Network Basic Input/Output System	128
Advanced Program to Program Communications	128
Transmission Control Protocol/Internet Protocol	128
Network Operating Systems	128
Security and Authorization	130
Wide Area Networks	131
ATM	132
Frame Relay Service	133
Switched Multimegabit Data Service	134
SONET	134
ISDN	135
Client/Server Architectures: File Servers	136
Partitioning Functions in a Client/Server Architecture	137
Client/Server Architectures: Database Servers	138
Functions Performed on Database Server Nodes	139
Distributed Databases	141
Approaches for Developing Distributed Databases	142
Bottom-up Integration	144
Top-down Distribution	144
Characteristics of Distributed Database Systems	145
Distributed Concurrency Control	146
Distributed Transaction Management	146
Two-phase Commit	147
Replication and Distributed Databases	148
Change Management	148
Check-out/Check-in of Objects	150

xviii ■ Contents

Other Servers and Services for Collaborative Computing	154
Video Servers	154
Data Throughput	155
Data Storage	155
Response Time	155
Fax Servers	157
Messaging Servers for E-mail Transport	158
Summary	158

4

ELECTRONIC MESSAGING AND MAIL SYSTEMS   160

The Popularization of E-mail	161
E-mail and Organization Memory	162
Various Categories of E-mail Software	163
The Many Purposes and Advantages of E-mail	166
Client/Server E-mail Systems in Internetworked Architectures	167
Client Application	167
The Server Components	168
E-mail Transport	169
Directory Services	170
The Message Database	171
Standards and Common Mail APIs	171
MAPI: Messaging API	172
CMC	174
Simple MAPI	174
Extended MAPI	175
VIM: Vendor Independent Messaging	176
Functions of the VIM Interface	176
Transport Standards	177
NetWare Global MHS	177
X.400	179
Internet and Simple Mail Transport Protocol (SMTP)	180
Interconnecting E-mail System	182
Address Books for Users and Groups	182
Directory Services	185
X.500	186
Mail-enabled Applications	186

Message Content and Structure … 188
The Problem of Copies … 191
Folders and Cabinets for Organized Messages … 191
    Organizing Messages by Users … 191
    Filing Messages … 192
Smart E-mail and Advanced Electronic Messaging … 193
    Filters and Rules … 194
    Beyond Mail … 196
    Multimedia and E-mail … 196
    Document Annotations … 197
    Message Types … 198
    Notification and Receipts … 199
    E-mail Security … 200
        Cryptography … 200
        Confidentiality, Authentication, and Integrity … 201
        Digital Signatures … 202
    E-mail Workflow Support … 203
Topics and Message Threads … 204
Summary … 206

5

WORKFLOW: COMPUTER-SUPPORTED COLLABORATIVE WORK PROCESSING … 207

Workflow in Document Imaging … 211
Taxonomies of Workflow Systems … 214
    How Much Programming Is Required? … 217
    Message Based and Server Based Workflow … 220
    Empowering Users … 221
    Types of Workflow Technology … 223
        Transaction or Production Workflow … 223
        Ad Hoc Workflow … 224
        Administrative Workflow … 225
Assisting Work Processing … 226
Controlling Workflow … 227
More Than Flow … 230
Object-oriented Workflow … 231

Object-orientation 233
    Abstract Data Typing 233
    Inheritance 234
    Object Identity 234
    Object-oriented Features of Workflow Systems 235
Workflow Features and Concepts 240
    Graphical Workflow Definition 240
    Process Definition and Activation 243
    Tracking, Status, and Statistics 243
    Work Queues 245
    Cases 245
    Group and Roles 246
    Retraction 247
    Rules and Conditions 247
    Notification 247
    Suspense or Rendezvous! 248
    Iteration 249
    Workflow and Project Management: The Importance of
        Schedules and Status 249
Examples of Workflow 249
    Hiring Process 250
    Purchase Requisitions 251
    Trading: Research and Purchasing 252
    Quality Assurance and Production 253
Workflow Standards 253
Workflow Architectures 254
Summary 257

6

ELECTRONIC MEETINGS (EMs)   259

Basic Principles 260
The Reality of Work 260
    Working Definitions 261
Building a Collaborative System 262
Synchronous Local Meetings and Collaborations 263
    Time Management and Scheduling 263
        Personal Information Managers (PIMs) 264
        Group Schedulers 266
        Enterprise-wide Group Scheduling 267

Contents ■ xxi

- Advanced Scheduling Features — 268
- Security and Access Privileges — 269
- Lists and Notes — 270
- Notifiers and Alarms — 270
- Scheduling a Meeting — 271
  - Workgroup System Integration — 272
- Scheduling Summary — 272
- Synchronous Local Meetings — 273
  - Meeting Categories — 273
  - Synchronous and Colocal Meetings — 273
    - Computer-enabled Meeting Rooms — 274
    - Electronic Meeting Support Systems — 275
- Synchronous and Remote Meetings — 277
  - Teleconferencing — 277
    - Desktop Teleconferencing — 278
    - Electronic Virtual Meeting Rooms — 278
    - Voice Mail — 278
    - Faxmail — 279
  - Conferencing Software Features — 279
    - Developing Options — 279
  - Information Centered Meetings — 281
    - Anonymity — 281
- Meeting Tools — 282
- Distributed Meetings — 282
- Meetings Summary — 284
- Working Together: Collaborative Authoring — 285
  - Collaborative Technology — 285
  - Meetings vs. Authoring — 286
  - Interactive Editors — 286
  - Participatory Design — 287
    - Whiteboards — 287
    - Brainstorming — 288
    - Videoconferencing — 288
      - Standards — 292
      - Product Snapshots — 295
- Hardware Infrastructure — 301
  - Next-generation CPUs — 301
  - Cable Television — 302
    - Smart Servers — 302
    - Set-top Box — 302

Contents

The Digital Signal Processor (DSP)	302
Multimedia Conferencing	303
The DSP Deluge	306
Hardware Summary	307
The Human Factor	308
Shared Workspace	309
wb	309
Mscrawl	310
MultiDraw	310
Xspy	310
Awareness in Shared Space	310
Awareness in Collaborative Writing Systems	311
Quilt	311
PREP	312
GROVE	312
Mechanisms for Awareness Information	313
Problems with Information and Role-restrictive Approaches to Awareness	313
Problem #1	313
Problem #2	314
Problem #3	314
Shared Feedback	314
ShrEdit	314
Awareness Summary	317
Shared Feedback: An Alternative Approach	317
Semisynchronous Systems	317
Summary of Shared Space Awareness	318
The Architecture of Conversions	319
Action-coordination Systems	319
The Virtual Corporation	321
The New Corporate Model	322
Less Is More	322
Flexibility	322
Excellence	322
Globalism	323
Opportunism	323
Speed	323
Technology	323
Life Goes to the Movies	324
Loss of Control	324
Technology Leaks	324
Loss of Power	324
The Hollow Corporation	325
Accountability vs. Responsibility	326

Reengineering Industry	327
Facilitation	328
MUDs	329
MOO	330
Xanadu	330
Organization Memory	331
Summary	333
User-interface Principles	334
Grades of Proficiency	334
Ease of Communication Between Domains	334
User Programmability	334
People Support Services	334
Open Systems	334
Development of Methodologies	334
Coevolution of Roles, Organizations, and Technologies	335

7

CONCLUSIONS — 336

The Social Impact of Technology	337
New Ways of Aggregating Resources	338
The Nature of Enterprise	339
Groupware Technologies	339
Groupware Categories: Chapter 1	340
The Human Factor	341
Evolution or Revolution?	342
First-generation Groupware	343
Second-generation Groupware	344
Time and Place Dimensions for Categorizing Groupware	344
Objects of Collaboration: Chapter 2	345
Editing and Viewing Objects	345
Portable Electronic Document Exchange Standards	345
Compound Documents	346
Hypermedia	346
Collaboration on Objects	347
Client/Server Collaboration: Chapter 3	348
LANs	348
WANs	348
File Servers	349
Database Servers	349

Electronic Messaging: Chapter 4 349
    E-mail and Organization Memory 350
Workflow: Chapter 5 351
    Three Types of Workflow 351
    Workflow and Groupware 352
    Workflow Systems 353
    Components of Workflow 353
Electronic Meetings: Chapter 6 353
    Personal Information Managers and Group Calendaring Systems 354
    Synchronous Meetings 355
    Distributed Meetings 355
    Organization Memory 356
EPILOG 356

REFERENCES 357

INDEX 361

1

Introduction

We are what we do. We draw, for better or worse, much of our individual and group identities from what we do to earn a living; from our work.

Few ideas captivate audiences so readily as those that deal with teamwork and collaboration. Cooperation, collaboration, and teamwork are essential to the survival of any organization. Employees as well as upper management recognize the importance of teamwork and collaboration to the successful conduct of a business. Working together is a fundamental requirement for building and sustaining a strong and healthy organization.

For many of us, working together is the basis for much, if not most, of our social communion. Most of us affiliate with a variety of different communities, some based on geography, genes, history, beliefs or interests; some are workgroup communities.

It is, therefore, startling to realize that, until recently, the one sector of business where the computer industry had not made a serious dent was in the area of collaboration. Actually, though, this should not be so surprising. Human interaction is complex; there is a great deal of nuance, and many variables including background, education, culture, and religious belief affect human interactions. Furthermore, until recently, large companies and organizations have tended to rely on more traditional authoritarian, hierarchical, and bureaucratic models of management. The dire economic conditions of the late 1980s and early 1990s are forcing both large and small companies and organizations to adopt a flatter, more democratic and team-oriented model of social organization.

Groupware is an enabling technology that addresses the vast areas of collaboration, human-computer interaction, and human-human interaction through digital media to bring substantial improvement and transformation to organizations. Groupware builds upon the latest advances in information technology, utilizing and building upon local and wide area networking as well as all recent advances in software and hardware technologies to achieve both communication and collaboration goals.

Because groupware encompasses so many technologies, it is hard to estimate its actual market size. By most accounts, however, the groupware market will become one of the fastest growing industries of the decade. Some estimate that groupware will be a $10 billion industry by late 1998. This estimate could, however, be misleading since many products can be characterized as groupware or can be used as building blocks for other groupware products. Groupware applications tend to use and integrate many other technologies. It is possible to think of groupware in the most general terms as the ultimate system for utilizing and integrating most existing software and hardware systems to enable collaborative work. Many of the information technologies that are integrated into groupware products and systems are explained in this book, concentrating primarily on technologies that are currently popular in groupware applications. Almost every major technological advance of the past decade has paved the way for groupware.

Figure 1.1 illustrates the four main categories of information technologies which are used to build groupware: multimedia interfaces, communication and information sharing technologies, object-oriented technologies, and artificial intelligence. There are, of course, many overlaps. Furthermore, not all technologies are used as frequently or pervasively in current groupware applications. Some of the very important technologies used in most groupware applications include graphical user interfaces (GUIs), multimedia, and object orientation. Artificial intelligence, especially pattern recognition, is becoming increasingly important but currently has limited prevalence in groupware applications.

Technologies that enable routing, networking, communication, and concurrent sharing are also extremely important to groupware. As internetworked PCs and workstations demonstrate increasing advantage in terms of price/performance over mainframe systems, the words buzzing around organizations and rocking MIS departments are *client/server architectures* for *downsized solutions*. Internetworked workstations, through client/server architectures and involving local as well as wide area connectivity servers (file servers, database servers, fax servers, messaging servers, and so on) provide resources and information sharing to PCs and workstations acting as client nodes. Since groupware deals with connectivity and sharing, almost all groupware products are built on top of client/server architectures. Client/server is a concept so fundamental to groupware that an entire chapter (Chapter 3) of this book is dedicated to it.

UNDERSTANDING TECHNOLOGIES, PRODUCTS, AND CORPORATE NEEDS

Whether adopting groupware products or planning to, an understanding of these technologies is crucial to success. Information managers need to assess the cost/effectiveness of the groupware solution depending on the type of work processing being adopted. There are many groupware products and some will be more suitable and affordable to different organizations and purposes than others.

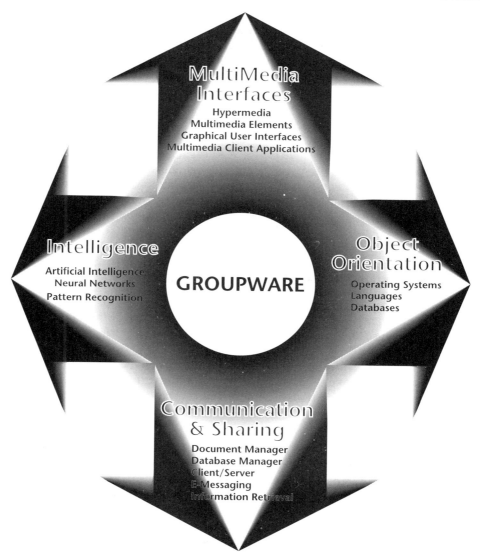

Figure 1.1 Technologies in groupware.

Many types of products can be characterized as groupware. In fact, any system that helps co-workers collaborate or enhance their teamwork efforts and achieve common goals can be characterized as groupware. Personnel and information officers and the overall leadership in the organization need to decide which are the groupware solutions or products most suitable for their needs given the organization's infrastructure, philosophy, and culture.

It is extremely important to assess organizational needs and to match the most appropriate groupware system to the identified need in order to achieve an overall improvement in quality and productivity. Although this is a very common sense "design before implementation" principal, it is often ignored—especially with products that deal with collaborative computing (that is, groupware). The result could be detrimental not only for the particular groupware product that failed to deliver on the expectations of the managers adopting the product, but it could stiffen corporate resistance toward other groupware solutions. Therefore MIS managers and decision-makers in general need to be very careful, when adopting a groupware solution. They must rigorously analyze the collaborative needs of an organization *before* choosing a workgroup solution. While in-depth research and preplanning are critical in the long term for the successful implementation of any groupware solution, there are currently few universally accepted standards and many possible strategies. By introducing the wrong product, users can be frustrated and discouraged from subsequently adopting any groupware solution.

CATEGORIZING GROUPWARE APPLICATIONS

This chapter will present a number of taxonomies and categorization systems for groupware. Figure 1.2 illustrates the three main categories of groupware applications. The figure also indicates which chapters cover these primary concepts.

Document and forms-based groupware: When collaboration and communication involves documents, application files, and forms, the most relevant broad categories of groupware applications include e-mail, workflow, and document management. Typically (but not always), these applications "group-enable" existing object types such as documents and forms.

Transaction-based high-volume information management groupware: When communication and collaboration involves high volumes of record retrieval, or transaction-based processing, then the most relevant groupware applications are typically built on high-performance database management, information retrieval, and document imaging systems.

There are many overlaps between these broad categories of products. For instance, forms are almost always used with database management systems as well as with document imaging. Furthermore, most document imaging systems also include production workflow subsystems. In fact, many workflow and document management products use database management systems to store and retrieve the objects that are used in their respective applications. The main difference between these two categories is primarily the volume, robustness of the information, and the type of application.

At the risk of oversimplification, high-volume transaction-based applications are used in corporate production based systems where there are well-organized and well-defined transactions for mission-critical data, processed in a more or less well-defined

Categorizing Groupware Applications ■ 5

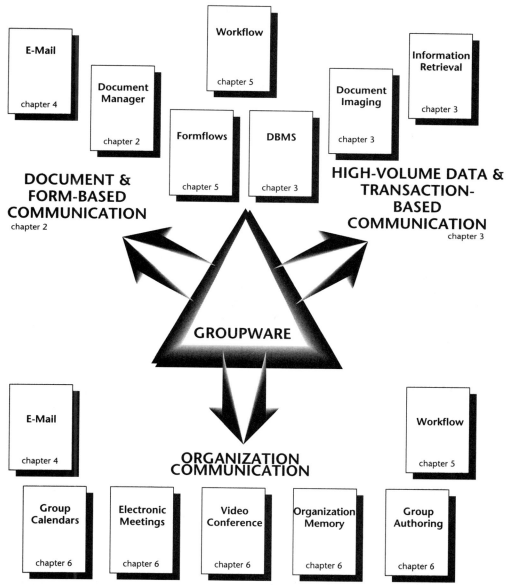

Figure 1.2 Three main categories of groupware applications.

workflow. The workflow and routing in document- and forms-based systems are developed in many cases as extensions of existing environments through "group" enabling forms and documents. E-mail, for instance, allows direct and easy communication of documents, without the need to define database schemata or business processes. Typically, workflow in this category is more ad hoc and dynamic. These categories will become clearer when the database (Chapter 3) and workflow (Chapter 5) technologies are discussed.

Organizational communications groupware: The third primary category deals with groupware applications that enhance organizational communication and collaboration. Products such as group calendaring, video conferencing, electronic meetings, and group authoring enhance the overall electronic communication in an organization. E-mail and workflow are also in this category, as are a number of emerging products that provide solutions to organization memory such as CM/1.

By and large, meetings are the predominant product category for organizing communication. Employees in an organization spend a considerable amount of time in meetings. This is especially true for managers and executives. Enhancing the communication in meetings and automating some of the tasks are therefore very important. But communication is not limited to meetings that typically take place at the same time. Organizing the messages, commitments, and the memory of an organization are also (perhaps equally important) factors which help improve the communication within an organization.

ORGANIZING HUMANS

Groupware deals not only with quantitative productivity gains but also with the enhancement of communication and collaboration among humans. This human organizational dimension is extremely important. Issues including organizational modeling, business process reengineering, and the overall infrastructure and group dynamics in an organization are aspects of the human dimension of groupware. Indeed, people form the group part of groupware. Without people to use them, all of the products and wares are meaningless.

Among the human considerations are the personal, organizational, and corporate cultures which must be taken into consideration. The tendency of humans to resist change—and especially changes that challenge well-established and well-deserved organizational hierarchies—should not be underestimated. There have been cases where technology has been abandoned because it created too many ripples in an organizational structure. As Douglas Engelbart commented about the oN-Line System project of the Augmentation Research Center (ARC) at the Stanford Research Institute (SRI) International, "The resistance to change, which we soon realized was an essential part of introducing new technologies into established organizational settings, and the psychological and organizational tensions created by that resistance were apparent in ourselves."

No other technology challenges an established hierarchical organizational structure more than radical reengineering programs based on groupware. Even the aforementioned client/server technologies pose some threat to more established mainframe-based MIS departments since client/server often empowers the individual PC users. Groupware presents several implications that threaten the inertia of a corporation. These implications may be most significant for upper management. A correct and efficient implementation of groupware implies empowered employees who can communicate between themselves, create options, make decisions, and assume roles that were traditionally reserved for upper managers. Perhaps the position most affected by groupware in the corporation is the one on top, since not only does the CEO need to ensure that employees are empowered but must also implement the policies to downsize and adopt groupware solutions that are successful. As Davidow and Malone (1993) point out in the *Virtual Corporation:*

> This will be a crucial moment for the CEO. After enforcing an apparent loss of authority and control at every step down the corporate hierarchy, can he or she make the same sacrifice? As the penultimate manager in the firm, the CEO almost by definition has the most to lose and will be the most zealous about not losing it . . . they can no longer solely lead the charge into battle but rather must devote themselves to developing the campaign strategy, leaving battlefield tactics to the smaller fighting units at the front . . . It is the job of the CEO to set the corporate vision, the corporate ethos, and to judiciously and sparingly use his or her power at right pressure points to cause change almost invisibly.

There will be uphill battles and challenges at both organizational and personal levels in organizations that are reengineering themselves. Sweeping business process and organizational reengineering means using groupware and downsized client/server technologies as the tools and enabling technologies to bring about fundamental change. Adopting the principles of the downsized corporation tends not only to flatten the organizational structure but also changes how information flows through, and decisions are made within, the corporation.

Figure 1.3(a) depicts a naive and simplified view of a traditional organizational structure where commands and information flows down from the top. Figure 1.3(b) in contrast, shows a revitalized and reengineered flattened organization structure. Here, the small individual teams are empowered to make decisions, to do several jobs at once, and to be responsible for the overall improvement of productivity, quality, and reduced cost of conducting business.

GROUPWARE: EVOLUTION OR REVOLUTION?

Computers and computing environments are recognized to be excellent tools for automating tasks that involve routine calculations and repetitive tasks. In discussions concerning "right" brain versus "left" brain, it is usually assumed that computers are

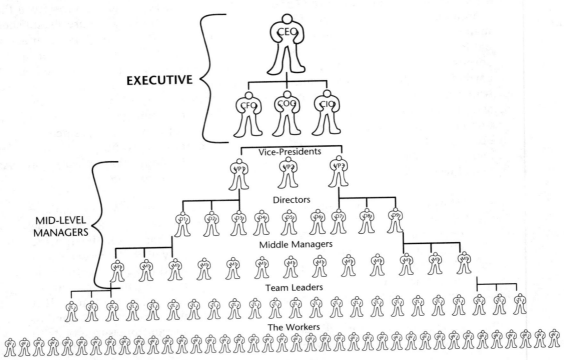

Figure 1.3(a) A traditional hierarchical corporate organization.

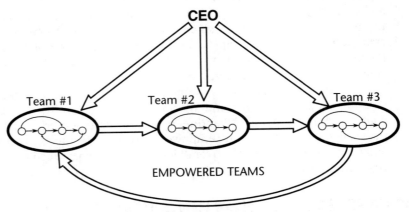

Figure 1.3(b) A "flattened" organization with empowered small teams.

excellent left brainers: They perform calculations at enormous speeds. Supercomputers can perform in excess of a billion multiplications a second!

Even with recent advances in neural networked pattern recognition technologies, however, it is difficult to write a simple program that can categorize cats and dogs. While there have been many exciting advances in the general area of pattern recognition—optical character recognition, recognizing forms, recognizing handwriting, and so on—these advances have been mostly incremental and not of the order of the magnitude of the advances that we have achieved in raw arithmetic calculation speeds. The reason is that pattern recognition is difficult to program. When it comes to the management of complex human interaction and—perhaps a bit far-fetched—organizational intelligence, the complexities escalate exponentially.

First-generation Groupware

Information technology provides the means to communicate digital information, to display information in multimedia graphical user interface environments, to organize structured and unstructured information, and to search vast warehouses of information. These are all very important enabling technologies for collaborative computing. The first-generation collaborative computing programs—or groupware—are systems that use the networking, storage, graphical display (visualization), and information organization capabilities of existing environments and extend them with capabilities for collaborative computing. The goal of these systems is to promote better communication, capture more directly various processes in an organization, and to improve the overall productivity of teams or groups working through internetworked workstations.

It must be emphasized that these, the first generation of groupware products are primarily evolutionary applications which extend the capabilities of various system components and applications. These components and applications include most of the basic technologies that enable easy access and management of information through distributed information technologies. This book concentrates primarily on these first-generation groupware systems. A key aspect of these evolutionary products is that, although they provide many wonderful capabilities pregnant with promise, the overall productivity or performance gains are not in the realm of orders of magnitude. This statement is, of course, a gross generalization. It is, nevertheless, an important point to bear in mind when discussing and considering the various groupware products. For example, it would be unwise to expect an order of magnitude productivity gain and radical improvements in time to market product cycles simply by adopting a group calendaring system for the organization. This is not to deny the utility of group calendaring systems nor to deny their potential to improve overall team performance (whatever that means).

Any groupware product, when applied correctly, can provide incremental gains in single or double digit percentage points. This statement assumes a knowledge of what to measure and how to measure it. The caveat in this statement, "when applied correctly," is the motivation of this book. Only an understanding of the scope, the genre, and the underlying concepts of groupware systems can support their correct application. Groupware systems tend to be too interrelated and interdependent to permit for haphazard, casual, and serendipitous implementation.

Despite the promises of the purveyors of groupware products, the simple purchase and adoption of any one product or system will have negligible effects. Indeed, even if that single product may function well in isolation, it may impede the later adoption of a more comprehensive and appropriate groupware strategy. With groupware, the best advice is to think about it first before you act. How long and how hard you should think depends on the size and complexity of the organization being reengineered. This advice, to look before you leap into any particular system or strategy, is not, however, encouragement to hesitate. We are fundamentally convinced that groupware systems are the way of the future. Those who get on board sooner will have a clear competitive advantage only if they get on the right train. Only you can determine where exactly you want to go; we can, however, share some ideas about what is going where and how fast these ideas might get there.

Second-generation Groupware

We must mention that like any other technology there are potentially more revolutionary groupware products and systems. Systems could potentially incorporate artificial intelligence capabilities into groupware in order to support group consciousness. Another potential aspect of intelligence that could be introduced to groupware products is the ability to learn. When these "entities" are programmed to learn, they can assist collaborative workers through active agents. "Agents" are programs that observe the user and provide useful hints or suggestions to improve work.

Whereas first-generation groupware products provide structures to collect, maintain, and upgrade organizational memory, these second-generation groupware products have the potential to learn from the knowledge of the organizational memory in a corporation. Intelligence, after all, deals primarily with the agent being conscious of its own existence. Next-generation groupware systems also have the potential of participating and making proactive suggestions as intelligent agents. These and other possible extensions of first-generation groupware products have the potential of rendering intelligent groupware systems which could dramatically increase the automation and productivity of moving and processing information within organizations.

We mention these more revolutionary "sci-fi" sounding technologies to emphasize the following points:

(a) Groupware technologies are, in many cases, in their infancy. The potential, therefore, of advances, research, and progress in this area of computer science is tremendous. Second-generation groupware technologies will employ and extend the advances in other areas of computer science including artificial intelligence, pattern recognition, multimedia, networking, graphical and other user interfaces, computer-human interaction, and object-orientation, to name a few. With the (sometimes revolutionary) advances in these technologies the potential of orders of magnitude productivity gains can be realized. There are active research projects in these areas, and the knowledge base of successful and failed applications of first-generation groupware products and systems will help accelerate and direct these next-generation groupware technologies.

(b) This book concentrates on first-generation groupware systems and products. The technologies discussed are readily available in a host of products with various degrees of complexity and robustness. Although there are many product types whose technologies are at different stages of evolution, the versions of groupware products that implement the concepts in this book range from first revisions to very mature and stable products. In the Appendix of this book is a list of names and addresses of all the companies that publish groupware products implementing concepts discussed in this book.

(c) There are, however, very real opportunities to bring about substantial improvements in productivity, quality, and cost reduction with these first-generation products. As stated, the first step is not the "blind" adoption of a technology by hopping onto the first buzzword bandwagon. Rather, success is found in the careful design and analysis of the target organization infrastructure, followed by an astute and informed mapping of the right technology to bring about the desired change. This reengineering is therefore a three-step process: first, a matter of careful analysis and planning, followed by the identification of available technologies and relevant features, and finally, the careful (and "culturally sensitive") adoption of the technology for the reengineered infrastructure.

The rest of this chapter is organized as follows: "Groupware: An Evolving Technology" discusses the infancy of the technology and its potential for growth. "LAN and WAN: Backbone for Groupware" shows how local area networks and wide area networks are the backbones—the skeletons—of groupware systems. "Groupware and Computer-supported Cooperative Work" explains groupware as computer supported cooperative work (CSCW). Because groupware products are used not only to enhance but potentially reengineer businesses, "Groupware and Business Process Reengineering" discusses the role of groupware in business process reengineering. "A Brief History of Groupware" provides a brief background of groupware, especially the context of the evolution of a number of technologies that are associated with groupware. "Object Representation and Collaboration" represents the "space" of groupware products and systems along the orthogonal axes of object representation models and collaboration models. "Collaborative Work" shows the impact of groupware on individuals, small teams, and larger enterprises. "Information Overload" explains how groupware products can be used to alleviate the information glut of a corporation. "Organization Memory" presents how groupware can be used to enhance the corporate memory (e.g., how decisions were made) in an organization. "Time and Place Interactions" discusses the now conventional taxonomy of groupware along the axes of time (synchronous versus asynchronous) and place (same place versus different places). "The Challenges and Problems of Groupware" explains the challenges and problems that individuals or corporations may encounter when adopting a groupware solution. Finally, there is a summary of the chapter.

GROUPWARE: AN EVOLVING TECHNOLOGY

When applied correctly, groupware products and information technologies that improve the overall organization and movement of information can provide substantial benefits to its users. But, as mentioned earlier, these technologies are in their infancy, and by their very nature, although the advantages and gains could be substantial, they are, in most cases, not dramatic. More specifically, consider the curves in Figure 1.4, which shows a hypothetical diagram illustrating the evolution of the technology and its potential. The X-axis indicates the level of groupware functionality as well as the efficiency in adopting the groupware functionality; the Y-axis indicates the performance gains. These curves are, of course, hypothetical, designed to explain the potential difference between first-generation groupware products and the potential of exponential (or more) improvements through a more thorough adoption of groupware.

The slope of the straight line as well as the slopes of the various points of the exponential curve are difficult to quantify. For example, the incremental functions analyzed and integrated for the implementation of groupware as extensions of e-mail in an organization could be summarized as follows:

1. Simple exchange of text messages.
2. Messages with attachments or enclosures.
3. Mail priorities and notification.
4. Ability to file messages in the e-mail system.
5. Multimedia exchange in the e-mail system.
6. Forms processing and sign-off through the e-mail system.

Further, the incremental adoption of the technology itself could have a lexicographic order—with increased understanding of business processes and efficiency in adapting to the technology. Here is an example of the adoption of e-mail technology in an organization:

1. Ad hoc use of e-mail to exchange messages between employees.
2. Process structure to use e-mail as the main mechanism for document exchange and management.
3. Integrate multimedia exchange to enrich information exchange.
4. Analyze and create forms and sign-off processes for organization tasks.

Blueprint for Adopting Groupware

While there are many examples of the incremental adoption of a particular technology, there are also a number of points that should be kept in mind when adopting groupware technologies. These are enumerated next.

Groupware: An Evolving Technology ■ 13

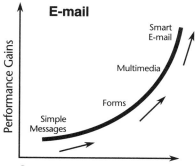

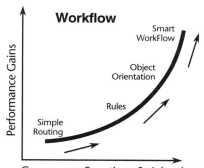

Figure 1.4 Potential performance gains through groupware.

Enhancement Technology

Groupware is, by and large, a set of technologies that enhance overall the exchange, organization, and processing of information in an organization. Groupware enhances the communication and interaction between workers; groupware also enhances organization memory. In other words, groupware doesn't solve any particular problem through information technology; groupware systems, by and large (although there could be exceptions), facilitate and enhance. The implication of this perspective is that it is usually more difficult to justify the adoption of a groupware technology than for other technologies which might directly support or solve some specific problem. Another implication is that the expectations of a groupware system and the benefits it might bring to an organization need to be realistic.

Design First

Like any other technology, the key to the success of any groupware product or strategy lies in the assessment, analysis, and design done *before* implementation. This has already been mentioned, but the importance of this point cannot be overemphasized. There are too many horror stories of failed experiments with groupware—including the most basic of groupware products such as simple e-mail. Other groupware technologies that have not delivered on the promise under certain circumstances include group calendaring, electronic meetings, and workflow. The fact of the matter is that any groupware technology (any technology for that matter) can fail if not adopted properly. Groupware, which involves the most complex area of human interaction, is especially vulnerable to failure. For example, managers have been known to remove an installed e-mail system because it provided direct access between their subordinates and their managers. In other words, the "flattening" effect of groupware on the organization could have a "threatening" effect on the mid-level managers.

As another example, some employees might find the adoption of a group calendaring system burdensome, intrusive, and impractical for their particular situation and might resist the adoption of the technology in the corporation. There are many examples of such "failures," following the impetuous rush to adopt groupware technology in a corporation. All too often the executive who shoots from the hip ends up hitting his or her own foot. It is vital to realize that, since fundamentally irrational human interactions are involved, the adoption and usage of groupware, more than any other technology, must undergo rigorous assessment, careful design and implementation.

Groupware: Here, There, Everywhere

Groupware technologies are more prevalent than most people imagine. Any product that can be used to share information concurrently, share resources, communicate among users, search large shared information warehouses, execute transactions involving many users, and so on can be called groupware. E-mail, therefore, is groupware, as are full-content retrieval systems, document management systems, and database management systems.

Some people might resist such a general definition and the identification of any product or system that involves multiple users as groupware. However, if you consider the definition of groupware as "computer aids that are designed for use of collaborative work groups" (Johansen, 1988), you can see that many more products that allow for the collaborative execution and sharing of information over local and wide area networks can be characterized as "groupware."

Although this book concentrates on the more recent technologies that have been explicitly characterized as groupware—workflow, group calendaring, advanced e-mail, electronic meetings—it also stresses the fact that groupware is a more general term which encompasses many systems providing various levels of support for collaborative computing.

While some aspects of groupware are still in their infancy, especially those dealing with organizational memory, business process reengineering, and team interaction/dynamics, the potential of groupware technologies to incorporate more breakthroughs is remarkable. As illustrated in Figure 1.1, groupware is based on many existing technologies; therefore, advances and new implementations in these technologies will enhance the capabilities of groupware products. Furthermore the lessons learned with early groupware will bring the next generation of groupware products closer to the potential performance gains promised by the exponential curves of Figure 1.4.

It would be unfair to lump all technologies that could be characterized as groupware along with those that possess these and other characteristics described in this book. For instance, document imaging systems have been very successfully adopted in the industry, and the document imaging market, both hardware and software, is growing steadily. In fact, workflow technologies have their roots in document imaging systems. Nevertheless, despite their maturity, it is important to remember that document imaging systems initially were largely digital implementations of paper-based document processing and filing systems. This is not to deny the innovative solutions, dramatic performance gains, and creative solutions through document imaging that have been achieved. The many success stories and the steady increase in products, membership, and attendance at Association of Imaging and Information Management (AIIM) events testify to this fact.

We must be careful since it is relatively easy to justify an imaging system in terms of dollars and cents. For example, it can easily be shown that if archived information is to be maintained, the rental cost of offices or physical warehouses could be substantially reduced if information is digitized and stored in optical storage subsystems rather than kept in paper form. In other words, individual components of imaging systems can be justified quantitatively. Among the components of imaging systems whose advantage is readily apparent, avoiding the cost of space for storing archived information is number one. The savings in space rental, however, is not the only advantage of an imaging system, nor the most far-reaching.

LAN AND WAN: BACKBONE FOR GROUPWARE

In the early days, computers were little more than large calculators. The 1950s and early 1960s saw the widespread use of mainframes, which were expensive systems that let multiple users share scarce resources such as CPU, disk space, printers, card readers, and so on. Users interacted either directly through electronic mail or indirectly through sharing, for instance, the same database. The concept of sharing was not much of an issue since all the "users" were actually timesharing the same system anyway. Some progress in sharing across computing systems was made when the Internet and its utility programs were introduced to help send and receive messages and files across networks through gateways.

What might surprise many people, however, is that the machine category that caused, and continues to drive, the groupware phenomena is the desktop microcomputer. Available in quantity since the early 1980s, both the Apple Macintosh and the IBM PC have become, through their internetworked versions, the backbone of groupware computing. The irony is, of course, that PCs and Macs and other "personal" workstations were developed to democratize and distribute compute power; but for individual desktop machines to be used for collaborative work, they must be internetworked.

Large System Groupware

The term groupware also applies to mainframe or minicomputer-based systems. In fact, a number of groupware technologies such as electronic mail and information sharing systems originally started on mainframe and mini systems. One of the fundamental assumptions in this book, however, is that because of the tremendous cost/performance advantages of internetworked PC-based systems over mainframe computer systems, the continuing downsizing trend of industry implies that most groupware products will actually be used on internetworked PCs.

Downsizing here means migrating mainframe-based environments and applications to internetworked PCs and servers. Client/server is an extremely important paradigm for downsized computing. Most groupware products employ one or more servers and operate in client/server architectures.

To better understand the sheer volume and impact of such downsized internetworked client/server architectures, consider the fact that there are now close to 100,000,000 PCs and it is estimated that more than 50 percent of these are networked. In fact, through the availability of very fast modems and affordability of on-line services, eventually all personal computers are expected to be networked and interconnected.

Local and Wide Area Networks

Over the past 20 years, local area networks (LANs), after modest beginnings, have emerged as the single most important backbone for corporate computing. Fortune 1000 companies have started to replace archaic mainframe-based systems with internetworked LANs. A LAN is basically a group of computers and workstations, connected through cabling and covering a limited geographical area. The workstations can communicate with servers or the nodes and with each other. Local area networks include cabling systems to connect the various workstations on the network, network interface cards, and a network operating system to control the access to various network resources as well as for communication between the workstations. LANs can be internetworked through routers, bridges, gateways, and other internetworking devices. Transmission speed within a LAN (depending on the devices used), can range from 10 Mbps (mega bits per second) (Ethernet) to 100 Mbps (fast Ethernet or fiber optic).

In contrast to local area networks, wide area networks cover larger geographic areas, and can span city blocks, entire cities, even continents. There are many different hardware/software components and technologies involved in constructing wide area networks. Some of the internetworking technologies used in high bandwidth transmission include T1 with multichannel transmission rates of about 1.544 Mbps; T2, which is about four times faster than T1; and T3, which is about 28 times faster than T1; microwave links; X.25 links; and others.

Figure 1.5 illustrates a typical "network" for a corporation, including departments where multiple servers are connected into a local area network; modems and fast-leased lines are used to internetwork the LANS.

Recent technologies such as ATM (Asynchronous Transfer Mode) are starting to narrow the huge differences between LAN and WAN technologies such as devices, connectivity, and requirements. By contrast to the more traditional X.25 packet switching technologies, ATM uses cell switching technology which is much less complex than X.25 and still allows for very high transfer rates. Different implementations of ATM have different transfer rates. For example, with satellite transmission, ATM can achieve transfer rates of the order of 45 Mbps; not very high but still better than Ethernet's 10 Mbps local area network rates. With the proper cabling and gateway, however, ATM can easily achieve transfer rates of 600 Mbps and above. As economies of scale make ATM networks more affordable, information superhighways connecting LANs and WANs at very high speeds become a reality.

What high bandwidth communications channels mean for groupware is that, since groupware entails users working in groups and requires both synchronous and asynchronous communications, the high-speed networks over long distances will enable both connectivity and transmission of large data sets (such as multimedia information) over wide as well as local area networks. This means technologies such as coauthoring, videoconferencing, multimedia e-mail, and workflow over WANs become easier to implement and accessible for larger numbers of users. The net result is that geography becomes increasingly transparent; a co-worker across the continent becomes as accessible as the worker in the next cubicle.

GROUPWARE AND COMPUTER-SUPPORTED COOPERATIVE WORK

Groupware is often considered synonymous with computer-supported cooperative work (CSCW). Indeed, the literature of CSCW, the sessions covered in CSCW conferences, and books on CSCW all cover topics that are within the domain of groupware. One attempt to clarify CSCW and groupware defines CSCW as "computer-assisted coordinated activity such as communication and problem-solving carried out by a group of collaborating individuals. Groupware is the multiuser software supporting CSCW." (Baecker, 1993) Although this definition is fine, the only term in CSCW that could mislead (or have a wrong connotation) is "work." Of course, most groupware is

18 ■ Introduction

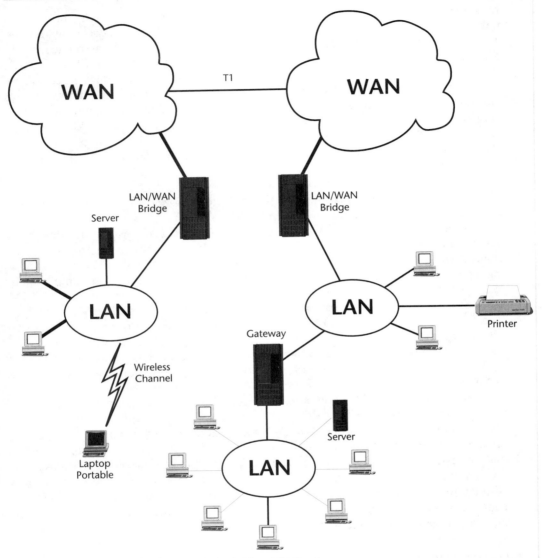

Figure 1.5 An example of an internetworked architecture.

used to carry out work; whether sending a message about a resume, arranging a meeting, collaboratively writing a business proposal, or approving a loan. The vast majority of groupware deals with work in one form or another. However, there is another dimension in groupware that is equally important. Groupware also encourages and enhances communication. These enhancements might be indirectly relevant to delivering specific "products" or "work."

Defining CSCW

An original contributor to CSCW defines it as:

> ... Computer-supported cooperative work has emerged as an identifiable research field focused on the role of the computer in group work. The questions being asked relate to all aspects of how large and small groups can collaborate using computer technology: How should people plan to work together to take advantage of this powerful medium? What kinds of software should be developed? How will group work be defined and redefined to tap the potential of people and technology? The answer will come from research across a range of disciplines including computer science, artificial intelligence, psychology, sociology, organizational theory, and anthropology. CSCW is the rubric of this interdisciplinary research. (Greif, 1988; p. 5)

Other technologies and disciplines could also be involved. The key point is that CSCW attempts to integrate research in cooperative working and organizational theory not only from a computer technology perspective but also from the perspective of the other disciplines mentioned.

The Human Dimension of CSCW

In explaining CSCW as groupware, there is a much more subtle yet important dimension to groupware that does not directly relate to work, although it could be argued that it does so indirectly and that hence this point is superfluous. This dimension is the team-building and communication enhancement support provided by some groupware systems. It is, in fact, this latter dimension that is sometimes so implicit in the technology that it gets overlooked. It is also this characteristic that is the least understood since it deals with the human psyche and the way humans interact. The benefits of a system that helps to "flatten" an organization's hierarchy in terms of communication, collaboration, team spirit, and reinforce human interactions are very hard to measure.

Some would argue that groupware, if improperly used, could have a negative effect on an organization. For instance, an insecure mid-level manager might become upset and jealous of the employees he or she supervises if they get easy access to his or her supervisor. The amount of effort exerted by a manager to protect "his or her" turf and to sabotage this openness is not beneficial for any company. Not all corporations are ready to move quickly to incorporate such novel and avant-guard social infrastructures, which are more consistent with a reengineered modern and downsized corporate structure and culture.

Groupware is the technology that encourages not only carrying out work on very specific tasks but also the collaboration and communication between team members. It could be argued that the ultimate goal of this collaboration or coordination is to carry out work; however, it is naive to assume that all human interaction in the workplace must be for a purpose. Better communication, an open and pleasant collaborative work atmosphere are goals in themselves. The benefits of productivity should be recognized as such side effects. Since people spend most of their hours during the day in their workspaces—and the future of telecommuting promises more of the same—the more communicative, collaborative, and pleasant this workspace is, the better. The workspace environment that lives within computers and within which people increasingly find themselves is, in itself, a tool that can be used to achieve individual and collaborative purposes. And like any tool, it must fit comfortably within our grasp.

Once again take the simplest and most widely used groupware function: e-mail. E-mail can be viewed as a very fast and efficient medium for transferring messages. E-mail systems are, therefore, instrumental in accomplishing collaborative work. There is, however, perhaps an even more important advantage to e-mail, which is often taken for granted. E-mail can provide a soft interrupt in human interactions compared to the hard interrupt of the telephone, which requires immediate response. It could be argued that voice messages have characteristics similar to e-mail in terms of soft interrupts, but there is a clear difference between the peremptory demands of a jangling telephone and the casual flagging of incoming e-messages.

E-mail encourages communication between staff members at different levels of an organization. As we said earlier this could cause some problems with insecure mid-level managers stuck in yesterday's management paradigm. It nevertheless allows a high-level executive to communicate very easily with all the employees in a corporation and solicit feedback from everyone. How can accessibility or openness be measured? Can the psychological and sociological implications of flatter, more democratic social models always be measured in terms of how they help carry out work directly or indirectly (such as, through encouraging people and raising overall morale)? Perhaps the only valid measurement of the subtle changes in commitment, loyalty, as well as the alignment of personal goals and identity with those of the group is in terms of the ineffable quality of work life. Few can deny, though, the positive and sometimes dramatic impact that morale can bring to any group endeavor.

If groupware implements CSCW, then it must be noted that work refers not only to specific tasks with specific goals but also the atmosphere of informal collaboration as well as human-human interactions and relationships. The research and literature of CSCW testifies to the fact that a lot of work is concentrated on this exciting aspect of collaboration that is difficult to define and quantify.

GROUPWARE AND BUSINESS PROCESS REENGINEERING

There is an intimate relationship between groupware and business process reengineering. Basically, groupware systems are enabling technologies for implementing the reengineered business process. Reengineering in the context of business implies that the existing processes and organizations that are used to run a business are challenged and replaced by qualitatively more efficient processes and organizations. The improvement in productivity and revenue is therefore achieved by throwing out some well-established principles and adopting more efficient and flexible principles for the new competitive market reality.

A key characteristic of this changing world is customization and the flexibility to respond quickly to ever-changing demand. Amplifying this trend is the emergence of many industrial nations as well as the increasing competition from developing nations. Competition will be fierce, even in those domains in which some nations, including America, thought that they owned. Therefore, the change that is needed to restructure and reengineer an organization is primarily a matter of survival. Those who do not adopt changes quickly, those who do not respond to customization fast enough, those who do not publish and produce high-quality products at increasingly shorter development cycles simply will not survive.

Reengineering

Reengineering and downsizing are not goals in themselves. Ultimately the goal is to make a corporation, a team, or an organization successful. Reengineering should be used to enhance the possibility of success and not be regarded as an end in itself. Reengineering must be implemented with sensitivity to the corporate culture, the people involved in the organization, and the corporation's sales and market restrictions. Hammer and Champy (1993) summarized several of the characteristics of reengineered business processes, and they are included here, in the remainder of this section.

Combining Several Jobs into One

Rather than having a job consist of several components with tasks broken into the smallest units and workers allocated per unit, in a reengineered business process, workers are considered to be more knowledgeable and able to handle more than one task or responsibility. Reskilling the workers rather than deskilling assembly line labor usually results in shorter turnaround time and greater efficiency.

Groupware technology can play a crucial enabling role when combining several jobs into one. The increased communication with and greater availability of other coworkers to help make decisions is one factor that helps to make this aspect of reengineering work. But perhaps a more important point is the availability of information or knowledge bases held in the structured organizational memory of the corporation. As jobs become less mundane and more involved, information technology, in general, and groupware, in particular, will play an increasingly crucial role in enabling workers to carry out their more involved responsibilities.

Empowered Workers Make Decisions

Possibly the most important characteristic of the restructured organization is the empowering of workers to make decisions. Among the many advantages to this "upside-down" approach are faster processing and higher-quality decisions, as well as increased morale and motivation of workers. The increased availability of information and accessibility of other workers along with the enabling groupware technologies can support the decision-making process and enhance the overall performance of workers.

Reduced Checks and Controls

Since workers in reengineered processes are empowered to make decisions, the checks and controls are often postponed. The result is that decisions are made faster while the overall overhead of controls is reduced; yet there is control. The difference is that the control is made later.

Groupware systems can provide many advantages for reducing the overhead of checks and controls. Even if a corporation chooses to retain many checks and controls, some groupware systems allow most of these controls to be automated through digital signatures, thereby reducing the time it takes for either checking or approval processing. The entire workflow of checks and controls can also be automated and processed more efficiently.

Empowered Workers, Empowered Managers

In a reengineered organization, both managers and employees are empowered. This means, among other things, that they can make decisions on their own without slogging through multiple levels of organizational hierarchy to get approval. For example, a salesperson in the field can be empowered to decide on the spot and inform supervisors afterwards. Or, a particular department might be empowered to spend a certain amount of its budget at its discretion, without going through either lengthy approval processes or following some Byzantine purchasing or other department policy.

Among the many groupware products and systems are tools and enabling technologies for business process reengineering. But as Hammer and Champy (1993) warn, "Modern, state-of-the-art information technology is part of any reengineering effort, an essential enabler . . . since it permits companies to reengineer business processes. But, to paraphrase what is often said about money and government, merely throwing computers at an existing business problem does not cause it to be reengineered. In fact, to misuse technology can block reengineering altogether by reinforcing old ways of thinking and old behavior patterns."

The quote can be paraphrased to say that throwing groupware at an existing business problem does not mean that the reengineering will succeed. As pointed out, the misuse of groupware could cause the failure of a reengineering attempt and justify a return to older methods—which of course could be devastating.

However, there is a flip side to the relationship between groupware products and business process reengineering. As mentioned earlier, groupware products are enabling technologies whose correct application can enhance the chances of success of a well-designed and well-executed business process. But groupware tools, also as mentioned earlier, have a "flattening" effect on organizations. After all, computer-supported cooperative work enhances cooperation and collaboration between workers; the level and quality of communication is also enriched. More important, the amount of information available to users is increased, and the quality of the information is also improved. All this means that the workers will be more knowledgeable, they will be communicating with their peers more efficiently, they will be collaborating more effectively, and the accessibility of upper management will be enhanced.

History teaches that a well-informed populace will make better decisions. In democracies, when the level of education and knowledge of the citizenry is improved, the result is a better voter turnout and resolution of various propositions. An informed and discriminating electorate becomes more selective in the officials it elects. In dictatorial regimes it is often the intellectuals and their followers who start dissident movements and foment revolution. This was witnessed very vividly during the recent breakup of the former Soviet Union. In many former Soviet bloc and east European countries, the heads of the governments were intellectuals: poets, playwrights, historians, and scientists.

How does this apply to groupware? Although as already noted, groupware products and systems are primarily enabling technologies and tools, they encourage communication and the diffusion of information. The increased dispersion of knowledge and information throughout an organization can produce some rather dramatic side effects. Consequently, although these technologies are typically adopted for the purpose of business process reengineering starting at the top and working down the organization, an inevitable and necessary result is that workers become more informed, empowered, and encouraged to be more creative.

Informed workers who communicate and collaborate with each other will tend to "take possession" of their jobs, to commit, to take more responsibility, to have greater pride of work, to make suggestions, raise concerns, and to ultimately influence change (that is, reengineer) from the bottom up. As workers become more empowered and involved, the grass roots creativity begins to effect at first small, then eventually profound, changes in the organization from the ground up.

A BRIEF HISTORY OF GROUPWARE

Groupware is a large, encompassing term, and several disciplines and fields in information technologies could be considered to be ancestors of modern groupware systems. Many "parents" have made fundamental contributions to the evolution of groupware products.

But although the technologies underlying groupware have different evolutionary paths, the term itself has its own history. According to Johansen, the term groupware started to appear in early 1980s.

> Cal Pave of the Harvard Business School used the term at about that time [early 1980s], as did Peter and Trudy Johnson-Lenz, who work over an electronic information network called EIES... There were probably other early users of the groupware term and, as usual, it is very difficult to determine who really coined it" (Johansen, 1988; p. 11).

The concept of groupware has appeared and evolved in a number of technologies. One of the simplest definitions of groupware is that it is any computing technology that helps groups work better collaboratively over digital media.

The roots of groupware also can be traced to client/server computing, which remains at the foundation of most groupware systems today: Electronic mail systems, often identified as the first successful groupware application; computer-human interaction systems such as the graphical user interface environments that enhance present multimedia information exchange over networks; and hypertext or hypermedia, which provide an associative model of information. The history of groupware can also be traced to the computer-supported collaborative research work that took place in the early 1980s.

The most important technologies that have influenced groupware systems are illustrated in Figure 1.1. Groupware deals with information technologies, and there are just too many fields that impact on it, making it difficult to easily characterize or categorize. The figure is therefore not comprehensive; it leaves out certain technologies for the purposes of clarity and not because supporting technologies are unimportant.

Client/Server Foundation

Groupware technologies and applications are possible primarily within shared environments. In tracing the history and evolution of groupware, the evolution of client/server architectures must be included. Figure 1.6 shows this evolution from environments involving "dumb" terminals to distributed databases involving internetworked LANs. Each LAN can contain one or more servers which could be file servers, database servers, messaging servers, or other peripheral servers such as optical disk servers, printer servers, fax servers, or scanner servers. It is the servers that allow the various clients on the network to share information and resources.

In the 1960s, almost all computers were mainframes and the interaction with computers was through either input/output devices such as card readers and printers or dumb terminals. In the 1970s, minicomputers were introduced but interaction still remained through dumb terminals.

File Servers

In the early 1980s, soon after the introduction of the personal computer, file servers on local area networks enabled the sharing of files and resources such as printers. Figure 1.7 illustrates a file server and its functionalities on a LAN. File servers allow the concurrent sharing of files and physical I/O blocks. With file servers most applications execute on the client workstations. One of the most popular file servers and network operating systems is Novell's NetWare.

Database Servers

The late 1980s and early 1990s saw the emergence of database servers such as the SQL Server from Microsoft and Oracle's OS/2 Server. Figure 1.8 illustrates the functionalities provided by a database server. In contrast to the file server, the main database engine functionality executes on the database server. This functionality could include integrity, security, concurrency control, and query optimization. For robustness, functionality is

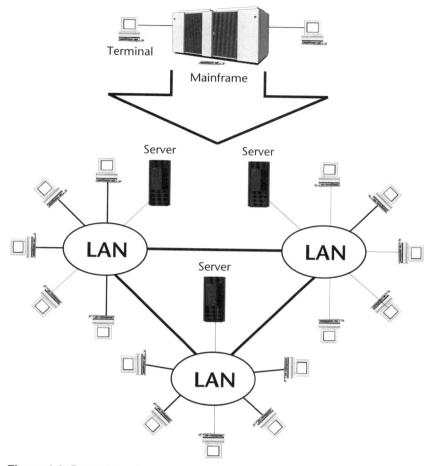

Figure 1.6 Downsizing from mainframe to internetworked LANs.

partitioned between clients and servers: client software concentrates on the front-end components and server software encapsulates all the database engine functionality.

In the early stages, these were single database servers with no way to execute transactions that involved multiple servers and multiple databases. Next came distributed databases. The earlier distributed databases allowed the execution of transactions spanning various databases and servers involving DBMSs from the same vendor. These are sometimes called homogeneous distributed databases.

The next step was to support distributed databases involving DBMSs from various vendors supporting various database models (relational and object-oriented); in other words, heterogeneous distributed databases. Replication is another technology that is used to share databases across various local and wide area networks. Distributed databases and replication are discussed in greater detail in Chapter 3.

26 ■ Introduction

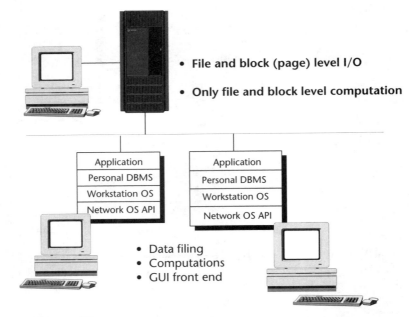

Figure 1.7 File server.

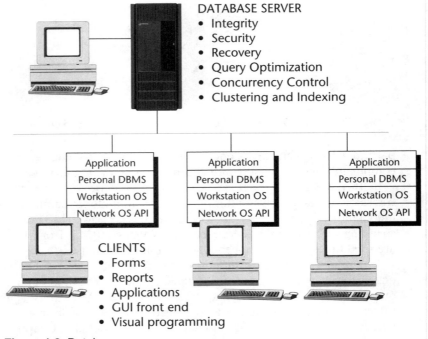

Figure 1.8 Database server.

From Sharing Files to E-mail

Besides sharing resources such as printers and files, the most popular application of local area networks to date and in the foreseeable future is electronic mail.

In the early days of mainframe-based systems, or local area networks with a single server, the sharing happened primarily within a department. Therefore, the e-mail system was used primarily to announce meetings, remind deliverables, ask questions, request help, and so on for projects and tasks within the department. In corporations with geographically distributed centers or departments, it was not uncommon in those days to find different departments using different LAN operating systems and e-mail packages.

As internetworking became possible with bridges and gateways between local area networks, it became necessary to allow for the exchange of messages between these heterogeneous systems and to allow for the interconnection and exchange of messages between different e-mail packages on different platforms. Thus, one of the most important developments in the evolution of e-mail systems was the evolution of interoperable e-mail systems provided by different vendors and having different functionalities. Through message exchange interconnection standards such as MHS (Message Handling Service) from Novell and the X.400 standard, it became possible to exchange messages and to have interoperability between different e-mail systems.

Another trend in e-mail systems has been the incorporation of advanced features. Perhaps the most important of these is the provision of enclosures or attachments, allowing users to send not only text messages but to include application documents (spreadsheets, word processor files, presentations, and so on) along with their e-mail messages. E-mail with attachments allows users to send documents and objects to one another and thus carry out collaborative work processing.

Another important enhancement of e-mail is the addition of "workflow" capabilities, including the ability to create and route forms within the e-mail package, notifications, and multistep routing. Other advanced features becoming commonplace in next-generation e-mail systems include rules for filtering and routing e-mail messages.

In the Beginning There Was Text . . . and Then There Was Hypertext

Although it might at first seem strange to trace the history of groupware to hypertext, the relationship becomes apparent when you consider the structure of hypertext. Hypertext is a tool for building and using associative structures. A normal document is linear, and is read as a serial stream from beginning to end. In contrast, reading hypertext is open-ended; it is possible to jump from idea to idea depending on interests or need.

The nearest thing to a hypertext document with which most people are familiar is a thesaurus, because it has no single beginning or end. Each time the thesaurus is consulted, it is entered at a different location based on the word used to initiate the search. Hypertext can be thought of as an enriched thesaurus where, instead of links between words, links between documents and text fragments are available.

Hypermedia extends the notion of hypertext by allowing the nodes of a hypertext network to be any multimedia data type. Thus, a node in a hypermedia document can be an image, a video clip, a voice annotation, or an animation. These nodes can also have hyperlinks to other multimedia nodes. Figure 1.9 illustrates a hypermedia document.

Memex

Bush (1945) first described the concept of hypertext, although he did not use the term hypertext. He described a machine, which he referred to as a memex, that could be used to browse and make notes in a voluminous on-line text and graphics system. Engelbart

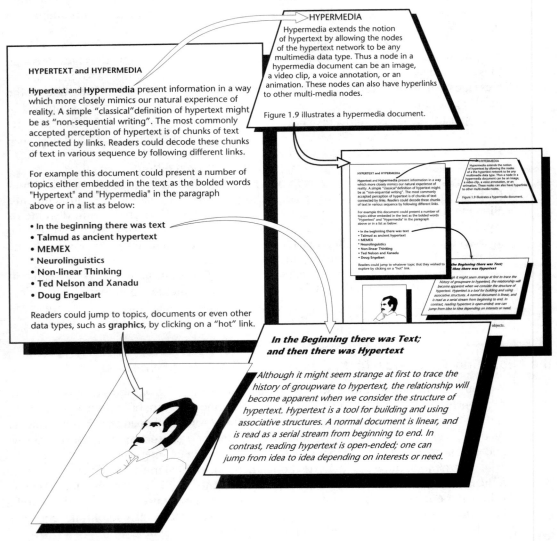

Figure 1.9 Hypermedia links between objects.

(1963) was influenced by the memex idea while working at the Stanford Research Institute. These ideas eventually resulted in a system called NLS (oN Line System) described by Engelbart (1968). NLS was a set of experimental tools designed to meet the needs of a research group by allowing the researchers to place every document pertaining to the research into a common store, and allowing the researchers to conduct all of their work and intercommunicate via their consoles.

NLS has since evolved into a hypertext system known as Augment, and Engelbart continues to advocate the development of systems that augment human capabilities (Engelbart and Hooper, 1988). Engelbart and his team at SRI laid the foundation of some of what has since become to be known as collaborative computing or groupware.

Nelson's (1965) version of the hypertext concept was more expansive and ambitious in some senses than that of Engelbart, emphasizing the creation of a unified literary environment on a global scale. It was Nelson who actually coined the term hypertext. The Xanadu project got its name from the "magic place of literary memory" referred to in the poem "Kubla Khan" by Samuel Taylor Coleridge. The long-term goal of the Xanadu project was to place all of the world's literary resources on-line and to use hypertext to link them in a way that facilitates their use.

Another equally visionary aspect of the Xanadu project was to tag this accumulated knowledge base down to a byte level for purposes of incorporation into subsequent works. Creative works would be tagged in this manner in order to apportion on a pro rata basis and to credit authors automatically and electronically for the use of their intellectual property, thus providing an elegant if grand solution to the continuing problem of intellectual property within the realm of electronic publishing.

Since the middle of the 1980s, there has been an explosion in interest in hypertext, along with the development of a large number of hypertext systems. Although these systems are based on the same general notion of associative structuring of text, graphics, and so on, they differ radically in terms of implementation. From the very beginning, hypertext/hypermedia with the ability to create hypermedia documents by linking nodes or pieces of information from different authors together with a rich collection of link types was strongly associated with the notion of collaborative work. An ideal hypermedia document has nodes and links that span a variety of authors and physical network nodes, as well as a variety of media.

Computer-supported Cooperative Work

As noted earlier in the chapter, a term often considered synonymous with groupware is computer-supported cooperative work. The first workshop on CSCW took place in 1984 and was sponsored by Digital Equipment Corporation. The main organizers were Irene Greif from MIT and Paul Cashman of DEC. Another meeting took place in December 1986, sponsored by MCC. Since the mid-1980s, regular meetings and conferences have taken place both in Europe and the U.S., and the term CSCW has become mainstream in research.

CSCW as a synonym for groupware is acceptable, with the following caveat: Interpersonal association for its own sake is a very important aspect of groupware which needs to be captured in this new emerging lexicon of computers and collaboration. The term "work" might be misleading since an integral component of collaboration deals with better communication and the general diffusion of information. A groupware system might therefore improve, for instance, organizational memory without solving or participating in any particular work process. This caveat shrinks to nothing, however, if the notion of work is extended to include social intercourse and intellectual communion as inherently productive human activities.

If, as part of the so-called "information age," the perception of information shifts from something that is contained within physical environments into something that, at least in the context of group activities, becomes the shared environment, the virtual space within which we operate as a group, each of us could share a variety of such virtual spaces with the various groups in which we associate. In terms of group functions, which tend to be communications and other information transactions, these shared information spaces are more relevant and real than individual physical circumstances.

Group Decision Support Systems

Groupware (as well as CSCW) is rooted in group decision support systems (GDSS). The roots of GDSS can be traced to information systems in business management schools and, as its name suggested, to decision support systems (DSS). According to Johansen (1988), some of the original ideas in DSS can be traced to Keen and Scott Morton who suggested using computers to help managers make decisions.

The GDSS approach is to extend DSS so that a group rather than an individual manager makes a decision. GDSS, therefore, has its roots in business management, DSS concepts, and some earlier research work in decision-making within a group, such as the SMU Decision Room (Gray et al., 1981). To help a group of people make decisions, GDSS groupware incorporates tools to help electronic brainstorming, the organization and consolidation of issues and options, and formulating group decisions and voting. GDSS systems often achieve this through systems that support same-time/same-place, face-to-face meetings. GDSS is one of the product categories (in fact, *the* most important, mentioned in the SameTime-SamePlace quadrant of the taxonomy of groupware systems).

There is ongoing research in this important field of GDSS and the impact of the technology on strategic decision-making, issue documentation, decision evaluation, formulation of policies, and so on. Some of the results of the (relatively earlier research) are summarized in Kramer and King (1988), and Nunamaker (1989).

OBJECT REPRESENTATION AND COLLABORATION

Groupware and collaboration have little meaning in isolation. We need to collaborate. But what is the purpose of collaboration? Teamwork is essential. But what are the subjects and models of business processing that the team is using? These fundamental questions must be answered if workgroup computing is to succeed. As the preceding historic review suggests, tools and products for collaborative work have been around for some time.

The two domains of Information Model and Representation and Collaboration and Communication illustrated in Figure 1.10 capture some of these environmental aspects. Although for particular cases and products, one of these dimensions may be emphasized at the cost of the other, truly successful groupware systems must advance along both dimensions.

The Vertical Dimension

The components of the vertical dimension are the objects of collaboration: the information around which users collaborate, such as application files, forms, multimedia data, tables, and so on. Collaboration does not happen in a vacuum: Workers collaborate on specific objects to accomplish specific goals. The fundamental characteristics and features of objects progress along this dimension. First of all there is a continuum of complexity and richness in the information from various applications: word processors, spreadsheets, presentation files, and so on. There is, for example, a big difference between a flat file of rows and a complex spreadsheet with several levels of nesting. To complicate this issue, earlier applications tended to be monolithic applications which either performed a single function or incorporated multiple functions in the same application. Recent interoperability trends revolve around container/compound/component application models, wherein an application can interoperate and provide a suf-

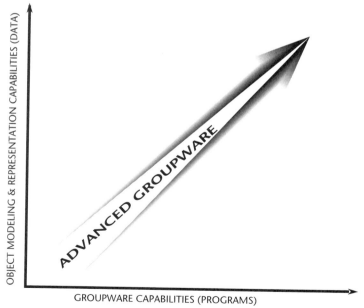

Figure 1.10 Groupware systems functionality in terms of groupware capabilities versus object representation capabilities.

ficiently common interface so that it can be either embedded into other applications or accept other applications embedding parts of themselves into it. This is the goal of emerging standards such as OLE 2 and OpenDoc.

With these multiapplication interoperability platforms, the user conceptualizes documents as containers that contain parts from various applications. The parts can be implemented by different vendors, and the user can introduce a variety of hot links between the parts, such that whenever a part is updated, all of the other linked parts are also updated. Compound document models constructed from different parts, which themselves could contain other parts thereby forming hierarchies, are still less general and therefore less powerful than true hypermedia document models. The differences between hypermedia and compound document models is discussed in greater detail in Chapter 2. Figure 1.11(a) illustrates this continuum of more advanced application models.

Advanced Database Models

At a more basic level there is a range of richness and complexity in database models. The simplest database model is a flat file of records, with no semantic relationship between various files. Some early database models, such as network and hierarchical

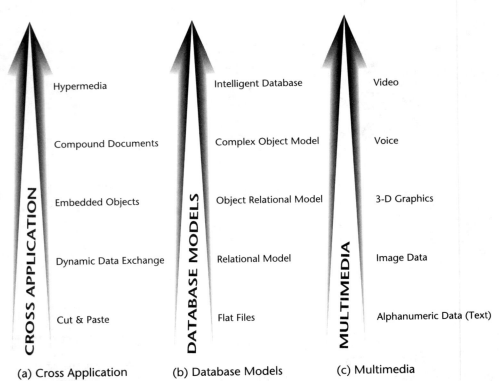

Figure 1.11 Object models and representation capabilities.

models, introduced some structure. Unfortunately, the way these databases were structured physically depended on the conceptual model. This resulted in numerous inefficiencies and maintainability problems. These models also lacked solid theoretical foundations and hence failed to evolve.

Relational databases were a step forward. Through a simple, yet elegant and powerful model, they laid the foundation of what is known today as relational (or plain) database technology. In the world of client/server architectures, relational DBMSs are almost synonymous with client/server computing (although, as explained later, this is perhaps an unfortunate misconception).

The next evolutionary step in the database object modeling arena is the incorporation of object orientation and functionality from other areas of computer science into relational models. Object relational databases incorporate object-oriented features into an existing relational database management system. Object-oriented database are "purer," in the sense that they build on a complex object model from the ground up rather than extending the relational model. Other concepts integrated into database technology include information retrieval and artificial intelligence. Figure 1.11(b) illustrates the increasingly advanced database models.

Multimedia

It is possible to lump multimedia into the information model for the simple reason that it is, in fact, a part of it. However, multimedia is discussed separately since the richness of the information, the characteristics of multimedia types, and the impact of multimedia are special. Earlier computing environments were primarily alphanumeric. Even today, applications that manipulate only alphanumeric data are quite common (such as banking). The times, however, are fast changing. We are rapidly passing out of the alphanumeric era into the sense-rich future which transcends linguistic borders. Even credit cards today carry the picture of the card's owner. Multimedia is revolutionizing human-computer interaction and providing much richer information exchange capabilities by incorporating voice, graphics, images, and video into the user's environment. Multimedia is having a dramatic impact not only in presentation and entertainment systems, but, more important, in computer-human interaction and human-human interaction.

Multimedia capabilities, especially when coupled with hyperlink features (hypermedia) more naturally map to human cognitive processes. This means not only that the messages will "read" easier and quicker, deliver a higher density of context and nuance information, and penetrate with more emotional impact, but will also tend to transcend cultural and linguistic boundaries. It might be premature to claim hypermedia as the terra lingua that will bridge the Babel of language that divides the world, but the penetration of American culture into the world at large borne on electronic and film media seems to support this view. Some of the multimedia data types are illustrated in Figure 1.11(c).

The Horizontal Dimension

The components of the horizontal dimension of the Object Representation versus Collaboration model are discussed next.

Client/Server Architectures

Although client/server architectures and components are an integral part of any groupware system, certain characteristics of client/server models provide better environments for cooperative computing. Early client/server systems were file servers that allowed for the sharing of files and other resources (such as printers) on a network. Database servers allowed for sharing database records, transaction processing, and more structured information sharing by multiple users.

As client/server architectures evolve, a trend is developing toward sharing and concurrent access across multiple file and database servers in distributed internetworked environments. These are illustrated in Figure 1.12(a). Client/servers, however, are not limited to files and databases. There are many services that can be made available across a network. Some, such as messaging services, are used by groupware products to route information; others, such as workflow servers, may be specific to groupware.

Check-out/Check-in Document Management/Library Model

Another component of the level of collaboration and sharing is the check-out/check-in model. This is closely associated with the client/database server models, and often database servers are used as the underlying technologies for products providing concurrent document or object control through check-out/check-in. Figure 1.12(b) illustrates one extreme where there is completely uncontrolled access to objects. A check-out/check-in model controls the access to objects by various users who have read/write privileges on objects. Ideally, when an object gets updated and checked in, a new version gets created. Ability to create versions by multiple users and perhaps merge these versions and have alternatives of objects are even more advanced features.

Routing Models

The simplest routing systems store and forward e-mail text messages. This component basically traces the evolution of e-mail, including e-mail with attachments, multimedia elements, and the advanced features. More advanced e-mail features include forms processing and routing, notifications for received mail and/or reply, rules in e-mail, filing, and multistep routing, which brings us to workflow. Figure 1.12(c) shows the increasingly more advanced routing and e-mail capabilities.

Workflow

The simplest workflow models are routing models for propagating information between nodes representing users or groups. For light workflow this dimension in collaborative computing picks up where rule-based e-mail system leaves off. Light workflow includes routing from node to node either explicitly or through rules. In addition to routing capabilities that can keep track of the status of a "case"—who has processed it and how much time it has spent in each node—workflow can incorporate more advanced features such as rules, conditional branching, notification, and project management capabilities. Workflow ranges from the simplest—administrative—through ad-hoc, to production—the most complex. Figure 1.12(d) illustrates some additional workflow features and functionality.

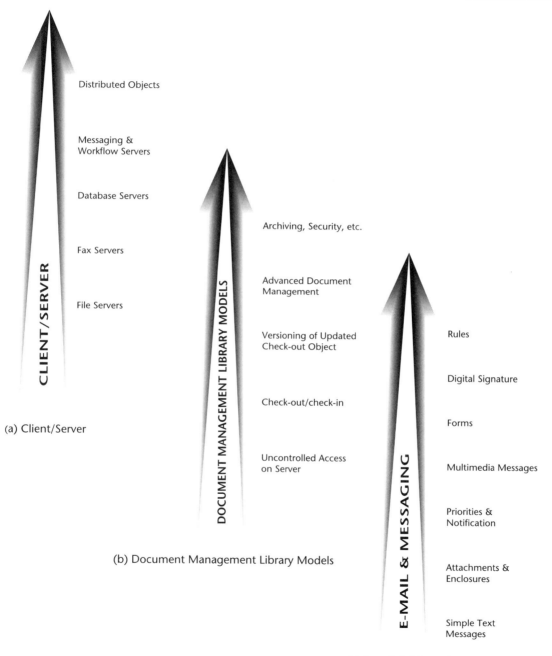

Figure 1.12 Groupware capabilities.

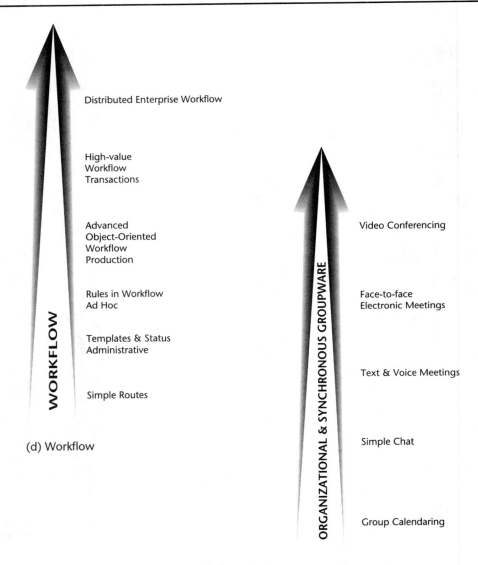

Figure 1.12 (*Continued*)

Team and Organizational Communications

Most of the systems in this component are for synchronous communication. In some sense, electronic mail systems and the other technologies such as database, check-out/check-in document management, and even workflow can be facilitators of organizational communication and memory. However, there are a number of products that provide synchronous communication and collaboration primitives. For example, a number of tools help the facilitator or leader of face-to-face meetings. Other products enable long distance coauthoring of documents through shared spaces: document conferencing, whiteboards, and synchronous multiuser editors. Desktop video conferencing allows users to communicate through their workstations via video interfaces. Augmented with powerful multimedia authoring tools, video conferencing with authoring abilities allows users in different geographically distributed locations to interact and conduct meetings—while recording the meeting itself, as well as the agenda items, suggestions, and other materials presented in the meeting. Figure 1.12(e) illustrates the increasingly advanced features along this dimension.

COLLABORATIVE WORK

Collaboration is necessary in order to increase productivity and solve specific business problems. Computing environments conducive to collaborative work provide several key advantages that help the individual worker, the small team, and the enterprise. The electronic solution must provide tangible benefits to each of these domains of collaboration and empower the individual to carry out his or her work efficiently and creatively.

The Individual

The previous section showed objects used in the user environment. Advanced object-oriented environments as well as developments in component object computing empower users to construct customized systems for their particular needs from existing components.

Computer environments are providing personal information management systems to individual users. Typical applications used in home or corporate office by individuals include:

- *Word processing:* A traditional PC application for writing letters and memos.
- *Personal Spreadsheets and Databases:* Combined spreadsheets, word processors, and personal databases constitute about 90 percent of personal computer applications.
- *Authoring and Presentation:* Systems that allow the user to prepare either production, marketing, sales, or development material for presentation, which could then be displayed by overhead projectors.
- *Calendaring and Personal Notification:* Systems for keeping track of appointments, schedules, and deliverables on laptop, palmtop, or personal computers. These types of applications are common in personal information managers. Alarms notify the users when a particular appointment or deliverable is due.
- *Project Planning:* System for planning personal projects, personal goals, and personal deliverables. This is especially valuable if the individual is involved in an overall larger project or contract.

- *Tax preparation and financial applications.*
- *Faxing and modems for interchanging information with other individuals and/or corporations:* Fax and electronic interchange are fast becoming as fundamental a requirement for conducting business as the telephone.

The key point in listing these applications (there are many more) for individuals is that information systems can organize, assist, archive, and generally improve the overall performance of individual users. Many groupware products and applications are basically the same applications that have been extended for teams and enterprises.

One approach to understanding groupware is to recognize its components as applications and information systems for individuals that have been extended for team and collaborative work.

The Small Team

The electronic problems and solutions for the small team can be seen as a superset of the problems and solutions for an individual worker. Of course, the goals and scope are different since there are the added dimensions of sharing, collaboration, and security.

We make a distinction between small teams and large enterprises because there are many differences between teams solving problems or delivering products in a small, local office or department, and a team that consists of many members, distributed around the world, attempting to come up with, say, a corporate policy. Even with smaller teams there are differences between groupware products that support informal "brainstorming" among team members and those that implement a well-defined corporate process.

Some of the groupware products that extend the capabilities of individual product categories to render them useful for small teams include:

- *Corporate database access:* Even small teams need to access commonly shared databases which capture information about the target business, personnel information, and mission-critical information. In downsized corporations, this information is stored in client/server applications where the server contains relational databases and the clients execute GUI front ends to these databases.
- *E-mail and workflow systems:* The documents that are created by users can be either routed through e-mail; or, the *cases* created can be handled through workflow systems. Here again, users are creating, editing, annotating, and otherwise manipulating documents. The e-mail and workflow systems are providing various sharing and work management capabilities.
- *Document management systems:* A document can be a word processor file or a spreadsheet. When a small team cooperates on a document, the document management system software provides concurrency control, and versioning primitives help coordinate and control the updates of the document. Privileges and security control can also be useful for document management.

- *Group calendaring:* Small teams (5–10 people) often need to organize ad hoc meetings. A group calendaring system can provide a simple and powerful mechanism for arranging and keeping track of meetings between members and groups of a small team.

- *Group coauthoring:* In same-time coauthoring systems, shared "whiteboards," screens, or documents allow multiple users to work on a document, a design, or a proposal concurrently. Coauthoring tools also allow participants to work on the same document at different times. Document management systems can, for example, provide coauthoring capabilities if used correctly.

- *Group meetings:* Since face-to-face meetings are ideal for small teams, groupware systems that support meeting facilitation can be very useful. The participants in a group meeting can be located at the same place or different places. For the latter, depending upon the underlying technology or system being used, the information interchange can involve text, audio, and video.

The key point is that almost all groupware products target the small team. These teams can consist of two to several dozens of participants. These various categories of groupware products provide several productivity enhancements to teams collaborating on projects with specific deliverables. They also enhance the communication and collaboration among the members of the team.

The Enterprise

There are, of course, many levels or types of "groups" separating a small team and a geographically distributed enterprise. The problems of a large enterprise are characteristically different from those of smaller teams or even departments.

An enterprise here means a large organization, with several hundred employees or more spread across various geographically distributed sites. In fact, even if the entire organization is on the same campus, as is the case in several large corporations and many universities, there remain some major problems with respect to collaboration and groupware that are characteristic of a large enterprise.

In terms of groupware products, there are some clear benefits for communication and collaboration in large organizations. But the benefits are primarily in the realms of electronic communication. Again, e-mail is perhaps the most successful application of groupware. Just as services such as the Internet provide to the general public various forums and discussion groups (newsgroups), large corporations also can also take advantage of bulletin boards and topics databases to carry on interactions within its own sphere. In addition to storing various types of electronic documents and corporate information, large organizations will use corporate database management systems.

However, in terms of communicating information, propagating corporate policies, and overall accessibility of corporate "memory," the applications of groupware in large enterprises involving very large numbers of employees will be rather limited. Just as it gets more difficult to make decisions and hold extensive discussions in large groups, the application of groupware also becomes more difficult and, in fact, often unnecessary when large numbers of employees are involved.

INFORMATION OVERLOAD

There are a variety of problems being solved (or attempted) through groupware applications and products. One important problem facing individuals, teams, and enterprises is information overload. Figure 1.13 depicts the sources of the information that constantly "bombard" both individuals and teams in organizations. These information sources include:

Electronic mail messages

Electronic documents

Departmental databases (stored on LAN servers)

Paper documents

Application files: word processor files, spreadsheets, etc.

Faxes

Voice mail

Scanned images

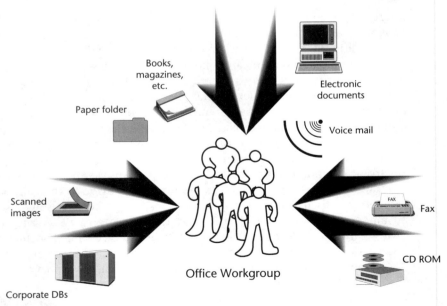

Figure 1.13 Information overload.

Corporate databases (stored in a mainframe)

Resource information stored on CD-ROMs

Books, articles, resources stored on paper

Multimedia information: video, TV news, etc.

A number of observations can be made about this information "backlog":

- A large quantity of information is involved.
- The information comes from many sources.
- The different information types are heterogeneous: text, graphics, video, image, voice, etc.
- Information originates from heterogeneous sources: electronic documents, voice mail, paper, etc.
- At a very "global" level, information is either in paper form, analog audio, analog video, or electronic form. Electronic information can take the form of database tables, alphanumeric data, word processor data, spreadsheets, images, or digitized voice data.
- The assumption that all information will be computerized in the future is unrealistic. Paper documents will continue to play a role in the office environment.

These diverse and heterogeneous information types need to be organized, accessed collaboratively, and properly disseminated and communicated within an organization. Some groupware applications attempt to do just that. More important, as information accumulates and overloads an organization, and it is not dealt with properly, that organization may develop "amnesia," either forgetting about information that was previously available, or how business processes are handled. Organizational memory is an extremely important issue for groupware, and it is discussed briefly in the next section.

ORGANIZATION MEMORY

Just as human beings can develop amnesia and forget past experiences, organizations and corporations can also experience loss of memory. This amnesia or failure in organization memory can affect not only the documents that comprise the various memos, minutes of meetings, and procedure standards in an organization but also the history and rationale behind these documents. In many cases, the latter is more serious than the loss of documentation on corporate procedure and process.

Most organizations have documents, many documents. Many organizations also maintain archives of electronic or paper interchanges as well as minutes of meetings. Unfortunately, unless the organization has a very simple structure, it is difficult (if possible at all) to extract that knowledge, experience, and the reasoning manifest in these documents. In some cases, organizations maintain convictions and carry out business plans which might be the lifeblood of the organization without understanding the reasons that played a crucial role in forming those convictions. The reasons, the logic, and the history behind the actual documents may, in fact, be the very character of the organization. To lose the sense of this gestalt is to lose the sense of corporate identity; it is a loss of culture.

Ideally, there should be a mechanism that clearly identifies the history, reasoning, and chain of thought behind every decision, process, procedure, standard, technical strategy, and business strategy in a corporation. An intelligently organized associative information memory is necessary for the corporation, which tracks not only the documents that are the "leaves," the consequences, or conclusions of the intelligent organization, but also the "chain of reasoning," the experience and knowledge base that are the "roots" supporting and producing these documents.

Most groupware systems can help to maintain organizational memory. Even the simplest groupware system such as e-mail can keep track of all the messages that either pertain to a discussion or a person or a group. This is illustrated in Figure 1.14. More advanced rule-based e-mail systems can automatically file messages in appropriate folders or containers.

Other groupware products can also enhance organization memory. For example, a database management system or a document management system provides an environment in which users can concurrently share databases and documents respectively. If historic databases and versioning of documents are supported, users could access not only the current states of databases or documents, but previous versions of databases and documents as well. Versioning with regard to organization memory is illustrated in Figure 1.15.

Another source of organization memory is the status of workflow, which can maintain a variety of information about who sent the workflow messages and documents, who received them, who approved forms and documents involved in workflow, what is the state of the workflow, and more.

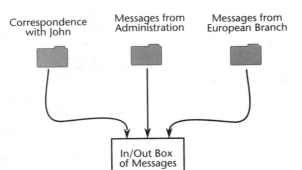

Figure 1.14 Filing of messages.

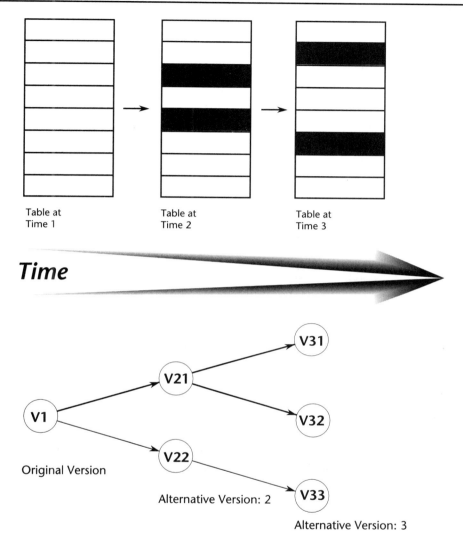

Figure 1.15 Maintaining versions and alternatives of "objects" (tables, documents, etc.) enhances organization memory.

Organizational memory is seen, therefore, as not only a recording of but also a knowledge base of all the association and reasoning of an organization's accumulated knowledge, procedures, and processes. An organization, like individuals, learns and grows. It is extremely important that the memory of the organization and its "intelligence" or knowledge be maintained and easily accessible from any point within the organization.

TIME AND PLACE INTERACTIONS

A common way to explain different types of groupware systems is to place them in the framework of two dimensions: place and time. This is usually illustrated through a graphic such as Figure 1.16.

Groupware systems can be characterized as systems that support cooperative meetings or work in the following four ways:

1. Synchronous and coincident: same time/same place.
2. Synchronous and displaced: same time/different places.
3. Asynchronous and coincident: different times/same place.
4. Asynchronous and displaced: different times/different places.

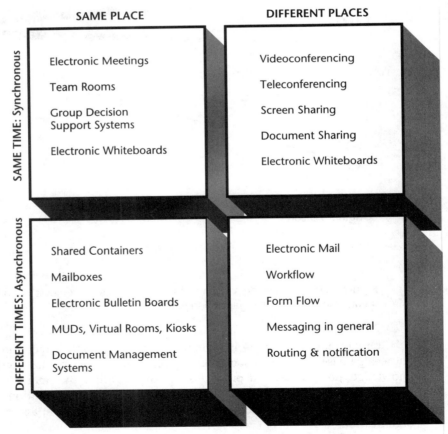

Figure 1.16 The conventional time/space categories of workflow.

The current state of modern communications technologies has placed a premium on the second category: same time/different places. For time-critical assignments, groupware products that fall under this category of quadrant are currently the most promising.

At the other end of the spectrum, at least for most business purposes with time-critical needs, the least important would be the third category, different times/same place. In other words, in the current work atmosphere, the compression of space is considered more valuable than the compression of time, perhaps because the traversal of space usually translates into time. Typically, the rationale behind conferencing systems that span distance is the simple argument of cost savings from reduced travel requirements, there are other, perhaps more compelling reasons to overcome the barriers of space.

The ability to collaborate productively in real time with co-workers no matter where they might actually be on the face of the earth is tremendously exciting. By rendering geography transparent, tight schedules can be reconciled; rare and scarce knowledge, perspective, or abilities can be congregated and brought to bear on a task or problem. For example, astronomers from all points of the globe (and beyond) could electronically convene to pool their ideas and perspectives while all watch some celestial phenomenon from their respective points of view. Clearly, the reach of the group as a whole is extended over space.

Negotiating distance and geography costs time. The ability to reconcile time-critical issues at a relatively low-time cost is a clear advantage However, these considerations assume a rather restricted and literal notion of place. This tidy notion of place, or shared space, at least, could be further challenged in the virtual corporation of the future.

All four types of interactions do make sense. The next few paragraphs explain in some detail each of the four types of interactions giving concrete examples of each. To help understand these four categories of groupware products, the concept of place needs to be better qualified. There are at least two definitions of place for groupware products:

- *Place as a physical geographic location:* In most cases, this means the same physical meeting room or office. This is the most common definition of place, and it is usually what people understand when they say place—which is why same/place same/time usually means face-to-face meetings.

- *Place as a virtual or electronic location:* A more general and in fact very convenient definition of place is to view it as a location in a virtual enterprise. This could mean a certain physical address, such as the address of a computer on the Internet. It could also mean a certain electronic meeting or conference "room." For instance, the user might pay a visit to an ongoing conference and view the text or multimedia information being accessed.

Next, these categories are discussed in more detail and examples for each category are given.

Same Time/Same Place

The first category deals with face-to-face meetings and the various computer tools that can enhance generation of ideas, recording of ideas, interaction of ideas, organization memory, and overall facilitation of the meeting. For instance a group authoring system can allow participants to coedit a document at the same time. The real-time authoring provides a synchronous model of collaboration.

A synchronous group authoring system can take place either face-to-face or distributed. For the former, a room can be assigned in which participants collaborate during a meeting or for coauthoring of a document (think of a meeting as an effort to coauthor a document containing the meeting's minutes or conclusions). The groupware system helps the facilitator of the meeting—the person leading the meeting—keep the meeting interesting, cover all the agenda items, make sure all the participants are involved, help make decisions through voting, maintain anonymity—whenever anonymity is important—and so on.

Modern technology has changed and continues to change the nature of real-time face-to-face meetings. Some of the devices and meeting support concepts that are currently popular include the following:

Electronic whiteboards

PC and a projector

PC screen sharing

Team rooms

Group decision support systems

The primary characteristic of same time/same place meeting is immediacy. Another characteristic is the time expense required to negotiate distance and negotiate timetables. A consequence of this type of meeting is to lend a premium to several personal characteristics such as appearance, the ability to think on one's feet, and be at ease in public. Issues of eloquence and personal charisma may tend to dominate the session. The argument may go not to the most rational but to the most persuasive or politically potent attendee. Clearly, certain personality types tend to predominate in this environment. Whether the sociopolitical issues inherent in metacommunications should be allowed to obscure the agenda issues or whether the political expression of any coherent body is its primary responsibility at any time is a moot point. Context may well be the determinant. For example, at a political rally, or where a leadership or policy issue is at stake, the rich layers of human interaction above and below the surface of agenda issues may well be played out. In a different context, however, such as the design of a system that would benefit all by its efficiency, it may well be advisable to diminish the impact of emotion, partisan identification, and popularity and to focus on the system in a rational manner.

As mentioned, place in a virtual corporation could also be an electronic meeting room. With this characterization, the distinction between different place and same time and same time and same place becomes fuzzy. In fact, the dimension of place takes on different connotations when dealt with in the light of virtual corporations.

Same Time/Different Places

Technologies which support same time/different places interactions are becoming increasingly more affordable and finding acceptance by more corporations and individuals. As traveling becomes more difficult, and the virtual corporation—where many of its workers are telecommuting—becomes more prevalent, teleconferencing and videoconferencing also become more widespread.

Many technologies are involved in the same time/different places category. ATM and FDDI were mentioned in the section on networking and multimedia. Modern communications technologies have changed the work world. In the past we were restricted to transacting business either within severe geographical limits, or else undergo extraordinary hardship, effort, and expense to interact at any great distance. Telecommunications have shrunk the world. Perhaps it is not exactly a global village yet, but more of an extended metropolis in which we are relatively free to transact business and to perform work in collaboration at great distances. The most cogent point to be made here is that telecommunications technologies permit us to project those dimensions of ourselves that are most relevant for decision-making and information sharing. These personal dimensions can effectively and relatively economically transcend distance. The limits of our corporeal selves can be circumvented. In the current work atmosphere, the compression of space is of value, perhaps because, as noted already, the traversal of space usually translates into time. The greater the distance, the greater the time cost; negotiating distance costs time. The ability to reconcile time-critical issues at a relatively low-time cost is a clear business advantage. Some of the technologies that support same time/different places interactions include:

Telephone conference calls

Videoconferencing (one-to-one or many-to-many)

Satellite downlinks (one-to-many)

PC screen sharing

Electronic Whiteboards

When the telephone was first introduced, some people had great difficulty using it for communication. How could they talk to someone whose eyes they could not see, whose responses they could not observe, measure, and accommodate? For others, with a strong auditory personality, the telephone was not only a natural instrument, but a godsend. For the physically unprepossessing, who nonetheless had vocal charm and were glib of tongue, this device alone turned the tables. Suddenly, they were empowered. For those with lesser speaking skills, the answer to this new state of affairs was, over time, to extend the language. Tropes and constructs were added to replace what had been lost to some extent. In short, we learned to code visual, abstract, and visceral models in aural terms. We learned to paint word pictures and to communicate what we saw by describing our visions and views over the telephone. But for some strongly visual types, this is insufficient.

For some of us, all or most interactions are over the telephone. Indeed, the ability to "give good telephone" is one of the criteria for modern management. The ability to follow, to anticipate ideas from an oral stream is necessary for personal interactions. For many if not most corporate managers, the day is spent, to a very large extent on the telephone. To be successful, telephoners need to be able to communicate in various perceptual tropes. For example, the liability of not seeing the person to whom one is speaking can be compensated for with word pictures. By denying direct access to real-life visual clues, intensely personal imagery can be stimulated by strictly oral means. Similarly, the human imagination is capable of filling in a lot of the information that we need to provide context and meaning into our communications. The challenge for the next generation is how to do this with new computer technologies.

These technologies—local area networks, e-mail, the Internet, and World Wide Web—present a whole new set of limitations to surmount and new possibilities to exploit.

Different Times/Same Place

It was mentioned earlier that the notion of place goes beyond physical locale. In the virtual corporation, a place is an electronic locality—an electronic address. In concurrent document sharing, if place is where the document resides or—better still—if place is associative and indicates the information itself (where the "address" of the information is determined by its content) then same place/different times is an extremely important quadrant encompassing any discipline or area in groupware that deals with searching or accessing information in shared information warehouses (databases, on-line services, bulletin boards, and so on).

Therefore, in the electronic world, all of the following categories are examples of applications in the different times/same place quadrant:

Searchable concurrently shared databases

Document management systems

Electronic bulletin boards

Virtual meeting rooms

Perhaps the best metaphor for the fundamental bulletin board concept is the mail drop so beloved in spy movies. These interactions are usually characterized by a very low level of personal human interaction. Indeed, the personality behind the posted missive may be as anonymous as are the authors of graffiti. The communication is severely limited to the actual content and presentation of the missive.

A good example of the bulletin board concept would be a network control center. As shifts change, different "operators" in the control center need access to network and trouble ticket info and histories. This usually requires massive databases that allow access by multiple users. Think of a 24-hour factory line, say a steel mill that can turn off the furnace only at great cost, so the previous operator of a machine or workstation must leave some information for the next shift. Maintenance crews must know the past service history of a piece of machinery. Or consider nurses changing shifts. They need to know the history of all of their patients.

Increasingly, the posting of messages is the means by which there is a different shift in the same virtual place, perhaps a newsgroup, or a bulletin board. For example, humans, in their diurnal rhythms, are driven by needs such as hunger, ablutions, or sleep, and eventually leave their computers, and other players/participants take their place. This type of venue coincidence and time incongruence has its own characteristics. For one thing, this type of "meeting" permits for more reflection and would lend itself well to certain activities that focus on the shared venue, say a chessboard, and would otherwise suffer distraction from a task focus that might be caused by more direct interactions. This type of interaction focuses more severely on the task at hand. A task, which by the nature of the relationship between participants, should not be time-critical, but rather be more of an evolving process.

Typically, such a task would have limited parameters, many, if not most of which, remain relatively static between sessions. The question is, how do we communicate shifted variables or parameters within a constrained context? In a way, traditional societies have always worked in this mode, wherein each succeeding descendant continues the work of the ancestral antecedent. This quadrant is populated currently by the most popular groupware products such as multiuser databases like Lotus Notes.

Kiosk

Different times/same place is also where kiosks are used. This would include employee-centered information kiosks where employees can access their personnel records, tap into job postings and training opportunities, or view messages either from management or customers. Kiosk users can interact with some data and can certainly act upon available information as well as provide feedback to kiosk developers. Data owners collaborate, albeit in nonreal time, to improve the effectiveness of the information resource. In some companies, especially those with flex time, commission sales forces, and casual vended services, this mode may be the only place where a mobile workforce can actually connect with co-workers.

Different Times/Different Places

Shared databases and information warehouses have already been characterized as belonging to the different times/same place quadrant. The different time/different places quadrant characterizes those products and systems that deal primarily with routing of information. For example, electronic mail indicates a collaborative work processing model where information flows between different places (the mailboxes) and at different times. Interestingly, the mailbox address itself can be characterized as same place, that is, the address of the mailbox. But note the fundamental difference between a mailbox, which pertains to an individual or a group, and a shared database, which is concurrently shared by many users. Some of the technologies in this quadrant include:

    Messaging in general
    Electronic mail

Workflow

Form flow

Faxing

The different times/different places quadrant therefore characterizes those groupware and collaborative computing model that involve some sort of information transport. A form being routed between different offices is an example; messages transferred between various offices and sites for collaborative work is another.

In the electronic equivalence of these examples, however, it often becomes evident very quickly that different times/different places is more similar to different time/same place than one would imagine. More specifically, a form that is being routed in an electronic network is the same form. In fact, what is being routed is often a reference to the form that is stored in the database. Every time a worker or a manager accesses the form, he or she is actually accessing it from the same electronic location. (Otherwise there will be many copies of the form and an overwhelming copy propagation problem. This problem does and could occur with serious consequences.)

Therefore, perhaps a better characterization of the different times/different places paradigm is a routing model. Routing and notification captures the essence of different times/different places much better.

THE CHALLENGES AND PROBLEMS OF GROUPWARE

There were many predictions about the penetration and growth of the groupware markets. Although there are some exceptions, the general consensus is that groupware and workflow products are taking longer to make significant inroads in the markets. Even ardent believers and developers of workflow and groupware products believe it will be some time before workflow products are adopted in significant ways in mainline industries. Although different analysts and reviewers might disagree about its merits, one thing is sure: the marketing and market education exerted by Lotus for Lotus Notes has definitely contributed to the education of the market and its preparation. The fact that a major player such as Lotus has exerted so much energy and spent so much for Notes (some say close to $90 million) has given the industry legitimacy and validity. Groupware is coming—and in force.

But even though there are now numerous products that characterize themselves as groupware products, there are still some interesting challenges and lessons to be learned before the widespread and (perhaps even more important) the correct adoption of groupware and workflow products is achieved.

Some of the challenges of groupware are summarized in the next few paragraphs. Notice that most of the challenges are created by the human element in computer-human interaction—everything that makes human relationships difficult to understand carries over to groupware. After all, groupware attempts to enhance and improve interaction between humans through a digitized and electronic milieu. But technology, science, and social sciences have not been able to solve or enhance substantially the quality of relationships between humans. A passing glimpse at any daily newspaper clearly indicates we have a long way to go in solving our communication problems.

One trend that is a clear reality for many of us is the growing importance of the workgroup communities with which we affiliate.

Workgroup communities are groups of people who may or may not meet one another face to face, but who exchange words, ideas, and work assignments through the medium of computers and networks. In the cyberworkspace, we engage in intellectual intercourse, commercial activity, exchange knowledge, make plans, and brainstorm. We also gossip, play games, and discuss all sorts of non-work related issues. These latter activities are sometimes perceived as, and indeed may in fact be, wasteful. Some of the more technologically enlightened managers, however, recognize these activities, within limits, to be necessary for "humanizing" contacts between workers and crucial for teambuilding. To work well together in workgroup communities, we must find ways of expressing our individual identities within the constraints of available computer network technology.

Some of us already participate in workgroup communities where we interact electronically, independent of local time or location. How a few of us work together today might be the way a larger population will participate in economic activity in the future.

Telecommuters who thought they were working from home just to avoid freeway gridlock find themselves being drawn into a different way of working. Workers are catching up to the students and scientists, librarians and educators who have been pioneering the cyberspace, forming communities based on interest and viewpoint instead of geography, time, and opportunity.

Soon, we'll be able to transfer full-motion digital video from point to point or even one point to many points. We will have the capability of downloading a publication in the Library of Congress from any point on the globe to any other point in seconds. How exactly we will use these new technologies and capabilities isn't clear. What is clear is that CMC (computer mediated communication) will change us, change our culture, and change how we work together or even how we organize ourselves to best perform work. CMC is already changing how we perceive each other and the world, how we communicate and interact, much the same way that telephones, televisions, and video cameras have changed us.

Workgroup community is not just about information, but also about the instant access to ongoing relationships with our colleagues. Social norms and shared mental models for cyberworkers are only now beginning to emerge.

The technology of groupware and the evolution of workgroup communities will not solve all the social and interpersonal problems that arise due to the intricacies of human nature. It could improve them, certainly; but then again, if not applied correctly, it could create more problems—and its adoption could be abandoned or even discouraged.

Uniformity in Product

In the context of diversity of taste, approach, and preferences this problem exists for other applications such as word processors. This is unavoidable since people have their preferences, and products often have cult followers. When it comes to adopting groupware and workflow solutions, the complexity is compounded. In single-user applications it is easier to allow exceptions and use file conversion utilities. For groupware and workflow products, users have to use the same product and be willing to cooperate using the guidelines and requirements of the groupware systems. For instance, a collaborative calendaring system is useless if the workers do not use it; in fact, it can create new problems if both personal and shared calendars are maintained. The inconsistencies and the "pain" needed to keep the two copies could lead to the failure of the group calendar and scheduling systems.

Too Much Structure or Too Much Work

One serious problem that needs to be addressed is the issue of structure. If after adopting a particular solution, the tool requires too much structure and too many requirements for its implementation, it may be doomed and subsequently abandoned. There are case studies revealing how corporations abandoned groupware solutions after realizing the amount of work needed for their implementation and successful adoption. This is related to resistance to change (discussed shortly), the natural tendency of humans. Unfortunately, when dealing with enhancing interaction between humans, drawing the line between structure and relaxing that structure is not easy. Different people require different amounts of structure, making the situation even more complex. Any experienced manager knows that people require different levels of supervision and structure. For some, structure could be an impediment to their productive and creative work. For others it is absolutely necessary, as they tend to sidetrack. If a groupware product is to be used and it tends to impose structure, clearly the first group will probably resist and the overall productivity of the team will suffer.

Challenging and Flatting Organizational Infrastructures

It is interesting to note that in terms of communication and accessibility, electronic mail had a profound flattening effect on organizations, and even faced resistance by some mid-level managers for precisely this accessibility reason. Through electronic mail, the CEO or any high-level executive is only one e-mail address away from any employee. In fact, employees can very easily send their input, complaints, observations to anyone without requiring appointments or going through various organizational infrastructures. It is very difficult for mid-level managers to control this flattening accessibility. Other groupware systems such as electronic meetings and bulletin boards have the same effect.

Unfair Distribution of Tasks

If an adopted groupware solution implies that some tasks will be automated more than others—with the result being that some workers will have to work more than others—this could result in a failure of the groupware solution. Those workers who are penalized more will object and might eventually be successful in removing the groupware solution.

Lack of Support for Exceptions and Nuances in Human Interactions

This is a necessarily vague yet extremely important consideration. Groupware is not an attempt to automate factories; it is trying to enhance productivity of humans, and the complexities involved are monstrous. Human pride; the need to be appreciated, heard, understood, and feel important; to get satisfaction and the proper credit all are factors perhaps more important in enhancing productivity than all the groupware technologies and solutions put together. Take a close look at the various cliques and groups in your work environment, and you will realize that teams are made often on very subjective and "cultural" grounds rather than for judicious or rational reasons. Still, there are areas of human interaction and collaborative work where computers and computing environments can assist and, maybe even encourage better collaborative and team-work-oriented tasks.

Resistance to Change

Another extremely important and outright dangerous problem that could cause the failure of a groupware solution is resistance to change. In fact, in many cases, the justification of a groupware solution is in terms of enhancements in productivity—which are hard to justify in dollars and cents. If the groupware also challenges well-entrenched organizational hierarchies and positions, then, at worst, it will either fail or be rendered ineffective.

SUMMARY

Groupware is about people, whether in small teams, large organizations, or national enterprises, working together. Achieving success by correct implementation of groupware is not always straightforward. Organizations and decision-makers need to carefully assess their own organizational goals before adapting a groupware solution. Groupware systems are specially important in providing effective solutions to organizations that are attempting to reengineer their business processes as well as organizational infrastructures.

Groupware as a global generic technology integrates many existing technologies encompassing all the technologies involved in graphical interfaces, object orientation, routing and concurrent sharing, and more advanced pattern recognition. Various groupware products adopt one or more of the technologies in these categories. Almost all of them support graphical interfaces and networking.

There are many categories of groupware systems and there are also many taxonomies of groupware. This chapter attempted to categorize groupware products through different illustrations and dimensions. One categorization of groupware products is through the three categories of document-based communication, high-volume transaction-based communication, and organizational communication.

This chapter also explained the categorization of groupware along the two (almost) orthogonal dimensions of object representation and collaboration. There are many aspects of object representation and modeling—in application, databases, and multimedia. There are also many aspects of collaboration—in client/server architectures, document management library models, e-mail and messaging, workflow, and synchronous groupware solutions.

This chapter also discussed the more traditional approach of taxonomies groupware along the time-space continuum. The four quadrants of these orthogonal dimensions were discussed: same time/same place, same time/different places, different times/same place, and different times/different places. Some examples in each quadrant were given.

Finally, the chapter provided a brief overview of the various problems and challenges of groupware. The bottom line is that a groupware solution must be analyzed very carefully before it can be adopted successfully within a team or an organization. Humans tend to resist change and no other technology can potentially bring as much change—or rather challenge to existing organizational infrastructures—as groupware.

2

Objects of Collaboration

Working in an office ideally means working together as a team on various tasks and projects. Whether the task is to prepare a document, complete a product, purchase equipment, or exchange ideas, multiple office workers can make decisions, document, and approve processes for each task ("work") done in the office. In most cases, office workers collaborate on various objects to produce specific results. This is clearly evident in engineering tasks. For example, various engineers might participate in specifying the design of a piece of equipment. Their goal might be to produce the final "blueprint" design specifications and diagrams for manufacturing. Each component must fit together like the pieces of a jigsaw puzzle. For instance a group of engineers designing an office chair might take these steps:

1. Collaborate to identify the various components of the chair and then assign these components to various team members for design.
2. Collaborate to specify the various component interfaces to ensure that the pieces fit together.
3. Carry out their specific tasks and monitor project progress and display the current status.

Figure 2.1 shows an oversimplified example of a chair designed through a 3-D design application. Suppose the team decides to have three major component types for the chair: a seat, legs, and a back. The engineers could then work on the interfaces between the various pieces—the types of bolts and screws used to hold it together. Then each engineer could work on the details of the various components. The final design draft, together with a detailed description of each component, could then be submitted for manufacturing.

In electronic environments, the objects shared by many employees working collaboratively may be as diverse as the single-user applications used by different employees. These objects created through collaborative efforts can be either:

(a) **Simple elements:** Simple elements include a text document, a single graphics object, an image, a voice annotation, a table, a spreadsheet, a word processor file, and so on. Most applications provide some way for displaying and editing one or more of these simple element types. Some applications have their own formats for storing these simple elements, and often include formats for text, images, video, or voice. The term "simple" elements is not meant to indicate that the element is not rich in information or that it is trivial to edit or display the element. With the exception of text, the viewing and editing of these "simple" elements could be quite complex. "Simple" here means not composite or compound. This is clarified in a moment.

(b) **Single application objects:** Single application objects include word processor documents, spreadsheets, presentations, or graphics. Each of these element types has its own structure and editor (behavior). For instance, a word processor can be used

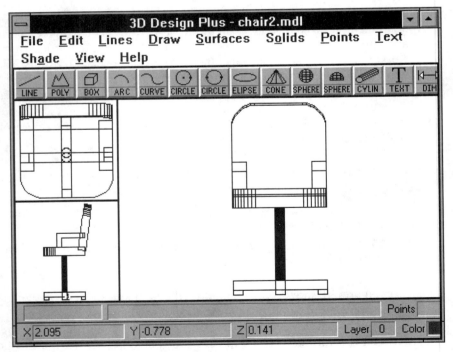

Figure 2.1 A chair designed with a 3-D tool.

to write a memo or to compose a letter; a spreadsheet can be used to prepare a budget; a presentation tool can be used to prepare a marketing pitch, and so on. A single application might include several types or elements. For instance, a word processor can be used to edit text and tables.

(c) **Compound objects:** Compound objects are aggregates of objects belonging to different applications. For example, a business plan can include text paragraphs describing the scope of the business, spreadsheets predicting the possible revenues of the business, piecharts and diagrams to describe market sectors all in the context of one "document." Compound documents and hypermedia documents are discussed in more detail later in the chapter.

It is necessary to keep these categories of applications and objects in mind in order to appreciate the extent of the diversity of the objects worked on concurrently by different workers.

DEFINING OBJECTS

An object can be expressed as an equation:

$$\text{Object} = \text{Structure} + \text{Behavior}$$

Where structure contains the data portion of the object. Typically, these are the files that the user opens and edits. For instance, the files may be text data in a word processor file, the numbers in the rows and columns of a spreadsheet, the slides of a multimedia presentation; the various elements of the desk chair design example just discussed. These are all examples of information that the application then manipulates to read and edit.

Every operating system file pertains to an application. In workstation operating systems such as Windows or System 7 on the Macintosh, when a user double-clicks on the icon of a file, the application associated with the file is launched and the file is displayed to the user in the application's window. There are, typically, two components of the structure stored in the same file. First, there are the attributes or properties of the file, such as the name of the file, who created it, when it was created, its size, and so on. Then there is the content of the file, the paragraphs and sections in a word processor document, the objects in a document containing graphics images, and so on.

Behavior corresponds to the operations that can be performed on the objects. For instance, in a word processor, a paragraph can be selected and the user can then change the font size, or other characteristics of the paragraph. Similarly, the user can create various formulae in a spreadsheet and assign them to cells. Or the user can edit a slide in a presentation and embed graphics objects. These are all examples of various operations that can be performed on different types of structure.

Every object of collaboration consists of some data captured in a representation or structure and various operations that capture the behavior (what the object does) of the objects. Everything in a collaborative computing environment can be reduced to operations on various objects. A clear understanding of objects of collaboration and a clear separation between representation and structure is very important for collaborative computing.

EDITING AND VIEWING OBJECTS

Everyone has seen impressive outputs from computer applications. These range from the simple printouts of office memos to elaborate printouts from word processors and WYSIWYG desktop publishing systems that integrate various types of fonts, images, charts, and illustrations with text. Further, multimedia authoring tools result in multimedia presentations or tutorials that incorporate text, image, audio, and video elements. CD-ROMs increasingly contain multimedia presentations and tutorials that are actually the output of multimedia authoring tools.

These examples all illustrate the ultimate output of applications which are viewed by the users who are the target audience. Typically (although not always), the application vendor can provide two utilities: one for editing an object and another for viewing. This leads to a very important issue that has particularly serious ramifications for collaborative computing: The consumption of information is different from the preparation of information. Executives who study and analyze a multimedia presentation are not interested in the particulars of the editors that were used to prepare the presentation. Similarly, managers or office workers who are asked to comment on a proposal document are interested in reading or viewing the content of the document, not in the particulars of its preparation.

There is, therefore, a clear distinction between viewing an object and editing it. An application used to edit an object is usually much more complex and involved than one used to view or present the object. On the other hand, many more workers consume information by viewing, commenting on, and generally deriving meaning from the content of an object when compared to the number of people who author, create, or design the object. Therefore, the behavior of an object can be regarded as being composed of two parts:

$$Behavior = Viewing + Editing$$

In groupware applications, viewing is often taken one step further to allow collaborative workers to either **annotate**, **comment**, or **approve** a document. Still this is different than editing the object (document) itself. Incorporation of annotation or approval often involves annotation tools to produce add-on "screens" or "films" on top of the object. Thus some users create the document or object through an editor while others comment, annotate, or approve the object (document) in a collaborative environment. These types of *workflow* will be discussed in more detail in Chapter 5.

OVERVIEW OF COMPOUND DOCUMENTS

Compound documents are those that are created from various components and applications. These applications follow certain procedural interfaces and standards supported by various compound document application interoperability standards such as OpenDoc by CILabs (sponsored by Apple, IBM, and others) or OLE 2 which is supported by Microsoft.

As illustrated in Figure 2.2, for an OpenDoc document, a compound document aggregates parts from many different applications including word processors, spreadsheets, graphics objects, audio objects, and so on. Each of these parts contained in a compound document could be authored through diverse applications. And, as long as these applications are developed within the interoperability standards, users can drag and drop or include parts from these applications to construct the compound document that contains all the relevant information for their needs. With compound documents, users need not confine themselves to monolithic applications, and can pick and choose the best (or their favorite) applications for different parts of the compound documents. Compound documents are discussed in more detail later.

Launching or In-place Editing

Compound documents consist of several parts pertaining to different types of objects or applications. There are two strategies for editing these parts:

Launching the application: This is usually what happens when, for instance, an e-mail message has an attachment or enclosure. The application associated with the object or file is launched with the file or object. For compound documents that contain many parts, the disadvantage of this strategy for the user is that the context of the current document is abandoned and another application is launched. After doing his or her

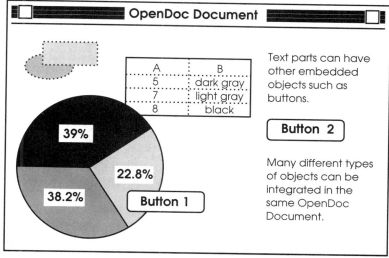

Figure 2.2 Compound document created from a variety of applications.

60 ■ Objects of Collaboration

editing, the user probably needs to close the application that was launched for that part and return to the original container document.

In-place editing or activations: An alternative to launching the application for a part in a compound document is to edit "in place," without leaving the context of the compound document. In the lingo of OpenDoc, this is called "in-place editing." In the lingo of OLE 2 this is called "in-place activation." The concept is the same, and is illustrated in Figure 2.3 for Microsoft Office in which a spreadsheet contained in a Word 6.0 document is being updated in place. Note that the toolbar buttons are those of Excel spreadsheets. Both Excel and Word are OLE 2-compliant, so the system knows how to change the buttons, menu items, and so on, depending on which part in the compound document is being edited.

STANDARDS FOR PORTABLE ELECTRONIC DOCUMENT EXCHANGE

Launchers and viewers make assumptions about the availability of application code or executables to either launch the application or viewer associated with the document or part of a document. In other words, whether editing an embedded object in place, viewing an object pertaining to an application, or launching an application, there must be an executable available (provided by the publisher of the application). This executable could be either a viewer, an executable that implements some of the applications functionality, or the full application. Therefore, it is desirable to be able to:

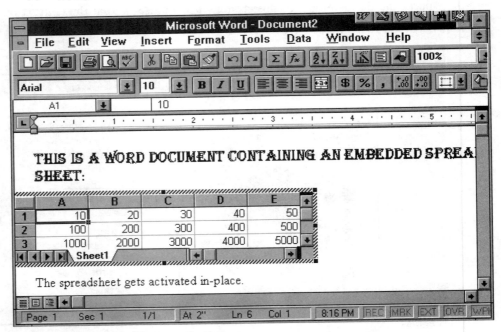

Figure 2.3 In-place editing or activation.

- Exchange documents and information between applications while retaining as much formatting and graphics as possible.
- Read and view a portable and common format while retaining all the formatting and graphics.

An alternative to launching (which requires the application to be present at the site that performs the launch) or viewing through an application specific viewer is to have common interchange formats for either the multimedia elements (such as text, graphics, audio, video, and so forth) or formatted electronic documents which allow multiple applications to view or edit the multimedia elements without losing information. There are several approaches and many types of documents that pursue this goal.

It is possible for multiple applications to read the same file format or for any one application to read the file format of another. For instance, many applications can read the file formats of very popular applications such as Microsoft Word, Excel, WordPerfect, Lotus 1-2-3, dBASE, and others. These files can be converted into the active application's format and saved. Of course, the problem is that converters and other utilities used to read the application file formats usually are available for only the most popular applications. In a sense though, these proprietary documents and file formats supported by individual corporations can become, because of their popularity, de facto "standards."

Another general approach is to write to a common and portable format which many applications can save as is and read. These standards are often supported by either U.S. or international standardization committees. There are, for example, several popular formats for imaging—TIFF, PCX, BMP—and similar standards exist for audio and video. For text documents, there are a number of formats such as RTF (Rich Text Format) from Microsoft that allow Word documents to be "read" by other applications without losing any formatting information.

Apart from these multimedia elements that appear in documents, there are standards that specify the structure of formatted electronic documents. Popular standards include Standard Generalized Markup Language (SGML) and the Electronic Document Interchange (EDI) standard. SGML is an ISO standard that is gaining popularity. There is a concerted effort on the part of the government to avoid redundancy and waste by mandating sets of document interchange standards such as CALS which is a collection of standards including SGML. SGML, a markup language, provides rules that describe the structure of documents. There are a number of products that convert popular word processor and desktop publishing formats into formats described through SGML. Actually SGML is a standard for describing markup "languages." Through SGML a DTD (Document Type Definition) can be written for specific markup standards.

One popular SGML DTD is HTML (HyperText Markup Language). HTML is the standard document description language for World Wide Web documents. An extension of HTML called HyTime adds the ability to position events in time. Many consider this feature to be crucial for multimedia.

EDI is also very important and is gaining popularity in groupware applications. It has been successfully used in business transactions, and allows trading partners to send requests and respond to each other quickly and efficiently by capturing order forms and invoices in the common EDI format. EDI is discussed in greater detain later on in this chapter.

The document interchange options are especially important for groupware applications in which documents and files must be sent from one system to another whether the systems are on the other side of the room, in other departments, across the continent or an ocean. These documents are sent, most frequently, through e-mail transport mechanisms. The recipients of these document must be able at least, to view them. Because users interchanging documents might be on different platforms and systems, if common formats are not used, then both the viewer and sender must have the same application (and often the same version of the application). Since this would, in many cases be an unrealistic requirement, document interchange formats for both structured documents and multimedia files are crucial for successful groupware applications.

COLLABORATION ON OBJECTS

In a collaborative environment there are at least four areas where communication and collaboration are used for the object types discussed in this chapter:

(a) Simple exchange of messages with attachments or enclosures: The most popular mechanism is to route a message with one or more attachments or enclosures which are application files. The recipient of the message receives a copy of the enclosed files as well as the message. Message exchange through routing is a very important mechanism for sharing information.

(b) Commenting, approving, authorizing: An alternative method of collaboration on the creation and development of an object is to comment and approve the various components or paragraphs of the object being developed, without actually modifying the object itself. In nonelectronic office environments, this can be achieved either by marking up a document, writing a comment on a design object, or using a self-adhesive note. Comments, suggestions, and approval are all communicated to the author of the object, who then becomes responsible for incorporating the necessary changes and revisions. The people who comment on or approve the object do not edit the object. This book will elucidate a number of electronic mechanisms, such as annotations, for implementing this strategy.

(c) Coauthoring: A sequence of text messages interchanged between collaborating co-workers could easily be coauthored. Something more complex, such as a design diagram, might require more sophisticated engineers who are familiar not only with the technology of the design editor but also the technology for which the objects are being designed. Therefore, the coauthoring of objects could be either general purpose—for instance, systems that allow the compilation and accumulation of messages of different types—or the coauthoring could be highly specialized, requiring skilled workers for its development. The specialization could be both in terms of content as well as authoring editors and tools used to produce the final object. Note that the collaborative environment could span local and wide area networks, which means that if coauthoring involves workers in geographically distributed sites, then all of the participating sites must have the same applications available. Typically, this means that not only must the same application be used, but also that the versions or releases used at the different sites must be compatible. Coauthoring can also be applied to document editing. Here the application involves not only editors but the groupware tools to enable concurrent yet controlled editing of the same document.

(d) Information warehouses: A less obvious but equally important area of collaboration is making information available within a small team, an organization, or even between organizations. Increasingly, most of the information stored and accessed concurrently in an organization is in electronic documents rather than structured records stored and accessed through database management systems. Both types of information, structured records and electronic documents, are important and are accessed collaboratively through a "library" model, whereby users check out an object, work on it, and check it back in, possibly creating a new version of the object. The "object" could be a word processor file, a design document, a compound document, or any other type of information. The information warehouse that contains the data can be accessed concurrently within a small team, a department, an entire corporation, or even between organizations. A good example of this is the Internet. There are a host of services and information available on the Internet, most of it free of charge. The potential of accessing this information, sharing it with others, and evolving the knowledge base of individuals, teams, and corporations is tremendous. An organization or company that allows its knowledge bases to be searched and accessed by its employees greatly enhances its organizational memory. This sharing of information and accessing information warehouses is an important type of collaboration.

OBJECT-ORIENTATION

Object-orientation and the benefits it will bring to both end users and software development in general is an oft-discussed topic that is not without confusion and controversy. For example, the September 30, 1991 issue of *Business Week* magazine had on its cover a picture of a baby happily typing on a workstation keyboard. The cover caption exhorted, "It's called object-oriented programming: a way to make computers a lot easier to use." But despite the profusion of misinformation, inflated claims, and rampant confusion about what object-orientation is or is not, the simple fact is that any computer user deals with object-orientation in some way or manner. Object-orientation is actually quite simple to define: The users' environment (the "computer") mimics the way that users deal with "real" objects in the real world.

Earlier, objects were defined as:

$$Object = Structure + Behavior$$

The structure of an object such as a word processor or spreadsheet file has both properties and structure of content. Therefore, the terms "properties" and "attributes" will be used interchangeably. For example, if the object is a file containing graphics objects, then some of the attributes or properties of the file include:

- Name of the file
- Creator of the file
- Size of the file
- Date the file was created
- Date the file was last saved

In fact, each element of the file has its own structure or set of attributes. For example, if the file contains a set of graphics objects with various shapes, then each graphic element will have the following attributes:

- Type of shape
- Location of shape
- Size of shape
- The orientation of the shape
- Relationship of shape with other objects

This illustrates that, when dealing with objects it also means dealing with the structure that reflects the state, the properties, and content of objects as well as the behavior that lets us view objects and/or edit them. Also bear in mind that everything you interact with in a computer environment is an object.

Customization

It is possible to use attributes even more effectively by allowing users to create and define their own attribute lists, thereby customizing the system to their own specific "vertical" needs. This raises the issue of custom attributes and user-defined attributes. Note that this is exactly what happens with database management systems. Implementing a corporate database requires a number of design and implementation phases. One phase or step is to identify the information model: the set of attributes or fields of all the objects involved in the application. For example, if the application is an order entry system that involves items, warehouses, and customers, then the information model should contain all of the attributes necessary to identify the following:

- Items, such as name, number, make, and so on
- Warehouses, including address, name, inventory
- Orders, including number, customer, amount, items, and so on
- Customers, including name, account number, address, and so on

An order entry system database will be created for each production company. Within a corporate groupware environment where workers share information collaboratively, there will be, in most cases, corporate databases that support that sharing. The attributes, or fields, for the different objects or object types in these databases would be customized for the specific needs of each corporation.

Often, in groupware products, there are specific application objects, messages, and other object types that are either created by or imported and managed by the groupware system. This is what is meant by "group"—enabling the application. For example, typically, a word processor file would already have the name, creator, date created, data last modified, subject, type, and so on. These are all built-in attributes. When users create an instance of one of these document types, they automatically get all of these attributes. Occasionally, however, users will want to amplify their specific business or environment with additional customized attributes. This is illustrated in Figure 2.4, which shows built-in attributes plus additional application- or corporation-specific customized attributes such that:

Object Attributes = Built-in Attributes + Custom Attributes

This form of extension or specialization is not only common within, but also characteristic of, object-oriented systems. Allowing users to customize attributes provides a

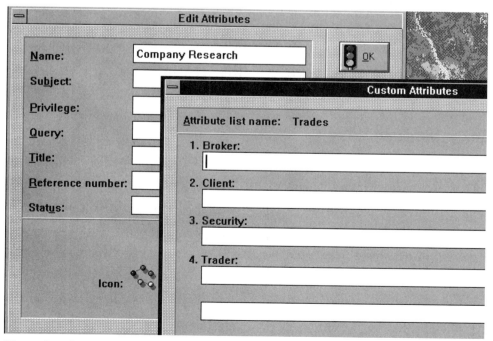

Figure 2.4 Customized attributes.

great deal of flexibility for corporations wishing to adopt groupware solutions for their enterprises. Because of the existing built-in attributes, new users can begin using these systems "out of the box." For maximum efficiency, attributes could be customized to meet the unique needs of particular organizations in terms of which and how information is organized and searched.

Suppose, for example, that the marketing department head has a spreadsheet document containing the department's budget. This spreadsheet is viewed and updated by the department head as well as various directors in the department. It is approved by the chief financial officer and the president. The spreadsheet object comes with a number of built-in attributes: name, creator, date created, and so on. For the specific needs and spreadsheet usage, the following custom attributes could be added (extended):

- Department name
- Department authorizer
- Budget period
- Budget constraints
- Sign-off list

Figure 2.5 illustrates abstractly the customization of attributes. Users can extend the system- or application-defined attributes that are built in with additional customized attributes. This extension mechanism also applies to operations or the behavior of objects. Some operations, such as opening an object and saving an object are built in. But again, as in the case of attributes, users might wish to customize and add other specific operations. Customizing behavior is discussed next.

Customizing Behavior

For certain applications it is also desirable to customize the behavior of objects. For example, if the spreadsheet package or the environment allows customization of dialogs and menu items, the modified spreadsheet could contain the specific instructions and menu items for developing and balancing budgets along the lines of some company-specific procedure. In fact, certain functionalities could even be turned off. Many of the more generic menu items that are not needed for a specific task such as developing a budget proposal could be excised, thereby streamlining the application for the specific tasks at hand. With such task-specific modifications built into the application tools, managers who develop budget proposals can focus on the task at hand. More important, the corporation could develop customized control buttons, functions, and menu items for developing budget proposals, and standardize them throughout the corporation. This amounts to customizing the behavior of objects.

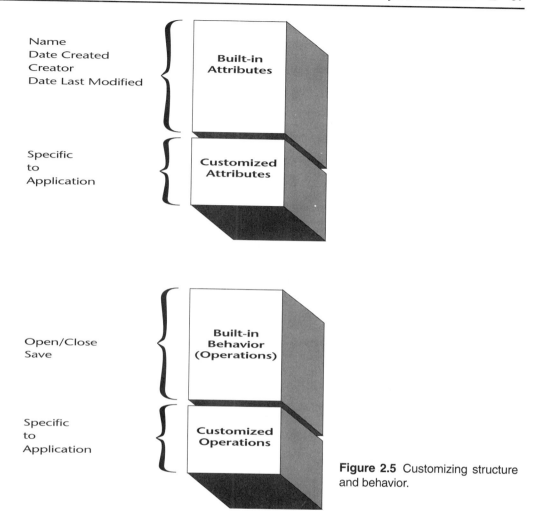

Figure 2.5 Customizing structure and behavior.

Objects and Groupware

To understand the relevance of object-orientation to the preceding discussion to groupware, consider the following:

> 1. Groupware systems manipulate simple files/elements, composite documents, and forms. Application files and container documents that contain elements from multiple applications could therefore be regarded as "groupware" objects as soon as concurrent sharing control and routing constructs are supported for these objects. In other words, groupware essentially group-enables existing applications, documents, and objects already within a user's environment. As described

in Chapter 1 and in greater detail throughout this book, various categories of groupware products can group-enable an object. These include groupware systems that are document and form-based, those that support organizational communication, and systems suitable for high-volume transaction processing.

2. Some groupware objects that are targeted specifically for collaboration include e-mail messaging, address books, workflow objects that implement processes and procedures, and so on. These groupware "application" objects also have structure and behavior.

3. The properties and content of objects can be used to enhance interactions and the organization of information within a collaborative environment. The properties of objects in a groupware system can be used to:

- Specify the characteristics of objects.
- Allow some attribute values to be generated automatically by a system to reflect the current status of an object and still retain the flexibility of users to specify other attributes, for example, the date created, date last saved, and size could be attributes whose values might be set by the system. Other attributes, such as name, subject, type, might best be set by the individual user.
- Categorize objects (for instance, grouping messages by subject) or group documents in folders by type, creator, and so on.
- Search for objects (for example, find all folders that were created before a given date). Searching is very useful for both personal information managers as well as for groupware products. Good search criteria can locate documents not only on a local area network but across entire enterprises as well.
- Filter objects (for example, display only those messages that come from the manager). Filtering can also be used to view specific subsets of messages—satisfying criteria or predicates specified by the user.

4. Customization of behavior is also important. It allows groupware application developers to customize the operations, menus, buttons and other executables for specific corporate needs.

Clearly, then, the properties of objects as well as their content are very important in the organizing, sharing, and locating of information within distributed environments that involve multiple collaborating workers.

TYPICAL APPLICATIONS

Most deliverables within the corporate environment, whether for individuals or for teams, are documents constructed using popular authoring software such as word processors, spreadsheets, and graphics packages. As previously mentioned, groupware systems often group-enable these applications and allow collaborative authoring, exchange, commenting, and authorization.

Following is a list of typical application types involving text, graphics, spreadsheet, and multimedia objects which might be used in a collaborative environment. While not complete, this list typifies the "real-world" office environments.

Word Processors

One of the most important and basic application types run on personal computers today is the word processor. These packages are used to write letters, memos, proposals, and so on. Some of the most popular word processors for personal computers include Microsoft Word, WordPerfect, and AMI PRO.

Spreadsheets

Another of the most popular applications in business is the spreadsheet. Spreadsheets organize data in rows and columns and allow the user to introduce dependencies and formulae in evaluating the cells. Spreadsheets provide a convenient tabular representation of information, mostly numeric, in a familiar format. A cell value can be linked to another spreadsheet. Thus, spreadsheet's can be organized in the form of nested hierarchical structures. Furthermore, it is possible to "link" a cell value to a formula or values in another spreadsheet.

Presentation Packages

Presentation packages are used to prepare slide presentations that involve multimedia elements. Presentation software packages such as Microsoft's PowerPoint and Asymetrix's Compel allow the user to incorporate still images, graphic shapes of different sizes, colors, and file types; voice annotations that play during slide presentations; and video. These systems require a components editor for preparing presentation sequences involving multimedia elements, as well as viewers which are runtime utilities that allow users to play back the presentations prepared by the editor.

Personal Databases

Personal database management tools allow users or small corporations to store and retrieve personal or business data (tables) through customized forms and front ends. In fact, database access front-end tools can also be used for large corporate databases, and there are some systems that can provide the same interface to both large corporate databases and personal databases. Examples of personal databases include address books, personal financial records, reference databases, and others. One consequence of the proliferation of home offices and telecommuting is that these personal databases are often used for business transactions as well as incorporating information regarding customers, sales numbers, and so on. Spreadsheet products often incorporate the type of functionality that would be expected from a personal database. Similarly, other products such as FAX software also incorporate some personal database functionality—support of address books, for instance. Key characteristics of personal databases include search capability through criteria or predicates, the ability to easily construct forms for tables, the ability to construct reports and generate reports from the tables of the database, and more. Personal databases are contrasted with corporate databases because personal database sizes and security requirements are much less involved than corporate databases. Nevertheless, in a collaborative environment the personal database can, in some cases, be shared, sent in electronic mail messages, or coedited by many workers. Unlike corporate databases where often the concurrency or sharing is done either on individual records or records satisfying certain criteria, personal databases are often flat files, and the granule of sharing and cooperation is the entire file.

Corporate Databases

Often tools that work with personal databases (such as graphical user interface forms design tools or report generating tools) also work with corporate databases. Typically, corporate databases for midsize and large corporations are managed by database servers. Corporate database management systems typically have two parts: a database server back end, which takes care of concurrent access to the database tables, and front-end tools, which allow the user to query the database and generate reports against the shared databases. The same front-end report generator, forms, or querying tools often work with both large and small databases. Corporate database access and management is discussed in greater detail in Chapter 3.

Accounting

Another type of application is the general category of accounting, tax preparation, and financial packages. Spreadsheets are often used for the accounting or financial needs of users and groups or corporations. There are, in addition, a number of "vertical" accounting packages. For instance, some tax preparation packages have tax forms already built in so that the user needs only to enter data into the form. The completed form is then printed as a standard hard copy tax form.

Forms

Forms constitute a very important data type or structure. Numerous applications can, in different contexts, handle forms. Limited forms processing ability has been incorporated into some electronic mail systems, document imaging systems, and database programming tools, to name a few. It is estimated that about one-third of all documents are some type of a form. Forms also play a very significant role in groupware systems. Often, in collaborative environments, it is forms that are routed, approved, signed off, and used as the main structure for collaboration. Often the end result of a groupware interaction is a form. Electronic mail as well as workflow packages often come with some basic form of editing capabilities. (The next section provides a more detailed discussion of forms.)

Image Editors

Image and other multimedia object editors are two fundamental types of software systems for creating and manipulating images and graphics in a multimedia workstation.

The first product category deals with editing and processing bit-mapped images. The second category deals with graphics object creation and manipulation tools.

Image editing tools are multimedia applications that enable the user to import, create, and edit bit-mapped images. These products provide the user with a computer "canvas." The user can either import an image onto the canvas or create one from scratch. These images may be either color or black and white. The image processing tool might be used to display and manipulate images at various gray scales.

Graphics Packages

Computer graphics packages allow the user to manipulate individual object elements; in other words, to describe the various attributes of the object. With graphics packages the user is provided with a canvas or space on which objects picked from a list of available object elements can be placed and used to construct a larger two- or three-dimensional compound graphics object. The objects or elements in the resulting graphics object are built from basic or elementary units or blocks, where each element has a size, shape, fill, position, orientation, and so on.

The methods, applications, and systems that are used to generate graphics range from very simple presentation packages to very advanced and sophisticated computer aided graphics packages (CAD). Other applications that also use the concept of constructing complex objects from individual elements include flow charters, organization charting products, and graphical workflow designers.

FORMS

As electronic information systems penetrate corporate and home office environments, the promise of a "paperless" office, or at least an office with better information management, becomes a potential reality. Forms are one of the most important types or structures that must be processed efficiently. Forms provide a standard way to organize information, either on paper or in an electronic form, by using an arrangement of named fields.

Unless explicitly indicated otherwise in this discussion, we use the term "form" to indicate electronic form. The electronic forms market is growing very fast. According to BIS between 1993 and 1996 large businesses can expect a 118% increase in the number of electronic forms processed each month—compared to a 4% increase in paper forms.

As stated, approximately one-third of all business documents are forms-based. There are many contexts and applications that provide support for forms. The many sources of forms include the following:

(a) In document imaging systems, forms or parts of forms are often created based on "canned" paper documents. Some systems can even "recognize" areas within the forms and automatically create the form. For example, many documents may contain the same form, and a single data entry person would then enter values for specific fields into the form for a batch of scanned images. The system would maintain both the digitized form and the editable form based on the paper form.

(b) In database management systems, graphical user interfaces and front-end tools are used to create forms through a "query" by form mechanism, display the data where the form provides an elegant front end to data records, and edit the data by entering values of fields or attributes.

(c) Forms-based packages can either act as a front end to either a flat file personal database or to create a form for single documents. Forms-based packages often have more advanced and flexible forms building capabilities than more traditional database front-end graphical tools. Forms-based packages often include graphics tools to build and display graphics elements in the form or to import images into the form. Figure 2.6 illustrates a form designed by Delrina's FormFlow form designer.

(d) There is a range of form capabilities in different groupware packages. In addition to forms for scanned images, forms in database front-end tools, and forms pack-

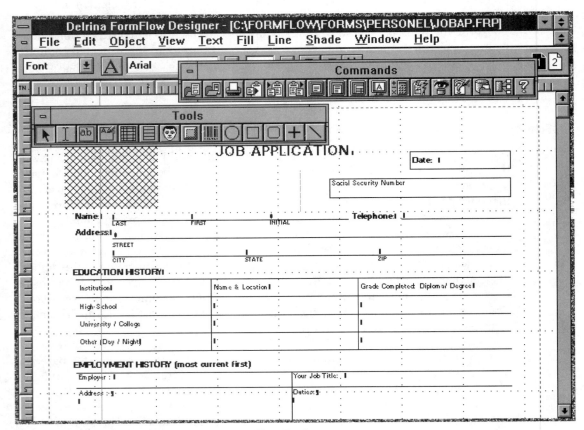

Figure 2.6 Form designed by Delrina's FormFlow Designer.

ages, a number of groupware applications also incorporate forms design and processing capabilities. These packages range from electronic mail systems to more advanced workflow systems.

Form Design Editing

For a form to be usable in any context, it must first be designed. In most cases, forms provide graphical user interface items and elements for various fields from underlying databases. Figure 2.6 shows some of the editing tool buttons in FormFlow Designer and Figure 2.7 illustrates an order form designed by ObjectVision. The form designer uses the various form designer tools to design form elements, which include:

Fields or items: Fields are the most common elements of forms. In most cases, these will be mapped to fields, column names, or attribute names of underlying databases or flat files. Example fields could include name of company, date when an order was placed, and so on. Fields can have names that can be displayed to make it easier for data entry personnel to enter values for the fields. Some form editors allow users to specify calculations for fields. In other words, instead of the value in the field being derived from val-

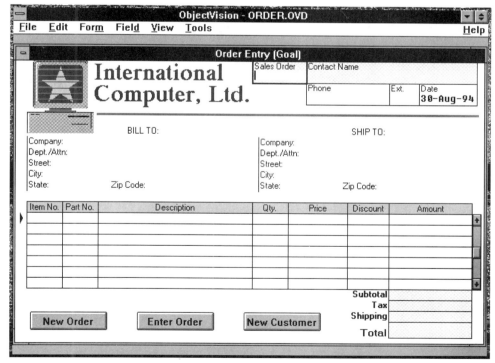

Figure 2.7 Order form designed by ObjectVision.

ues of attributes or cells in an underlying data table, the value of the field could be the result of calculated values based on a formula. The fields could be labeled, formatted, bordered, filled, and so on. There is a lot of flexibility for the forms designer in the way a field is displayed.

Buttons: Forms can also have buttons to display the next record in a database, go to another linked form, print the form, or whatever. In other words, various actions and even programs could be associated with buttons in a form. Forms used to browse records in a database could contain buttons that direct the browsing, labeled Next, Previous, First, Last. Actions that are important and common for the form are typically implemented through buttons. Some examples are illustrated in Figure 2.8.

Graphics: Most form designer tools allow the import of graphics and other multimedia objects. Note that this is different from multimedia elements that are field or attribute values from underlying databases. A form might, for example, allow the user to retrieve a memo or even a picture of a person in an image-valued field. The form designer tool could also allow the designer to import graphics logos of, say, the name of a company; or background images to enhance the presentation of form; or frames of the form incorporating graphics elements; and so on.

Tables, lists, and other collections: In addition to fields containing single values, forms can also contain sets of records presented in tabular, list, or other format chosen by the designer. Especially in database front ends, forms can draw their underlying data from multiple tables, which are often "joined" on key attributes. For instance, Figure 2.9 illus-

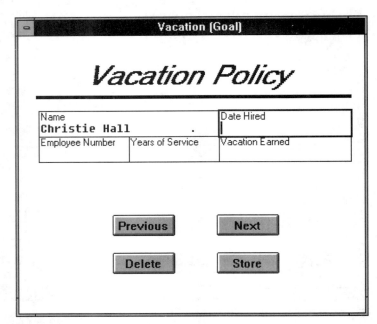

Figure 2.8 Buttons in a form.

trates a customer record and the book orders associated with the customer. A form can display both the "parent" record—in this case the customer fields—and the "children" records—in this case the orders belonging to the customer.

Once a form is designed it can be used either by itself or linked to database tables to extract the field values. A single form can be filled, printed, routed, or otherwise processed. Alternatively, a form can be used as a graphical front end to a collection of records from the same table. The table could be a base table; that is, a table that is actually stored in a database; or, it could be a view or "virtual" table constructed by combining or "joining" several base tables. The form could also provide a hierarchical view of values from underlying tables, as in the customer order example just mentioned.

Query by Forms

It is possible to incorporate querying capabilities into a forms system to retrieve records that satisfy a "sample" form. There are several mechanisms that enable database front ends to query the content of a database. Database management systems provide querying interfaces to their tables. The most popular query language is called Structured Query Language (SQL). But SQL is hard to program by end users. A number of alternative strategies have been attempted, including Query by Example (QBE), Visual SQL, and others. These alternatives still tend to be relatively complex for end users, however.

Another convenient alternative is to use the form to construct database queries. With query by forms, the user must first bring up the appropriate empty form, as illustrated in Figure 2.10. The user then specifies field values for the records to be retrieved. Suppose, for example, you were interested in retrieving customers whose name is Smith, who live in Madison, Wisconsin, and whose order was submitted after 10/10/94.

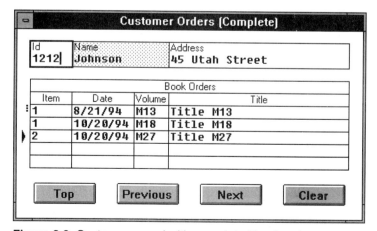

Figure 2.9 Customer record with associated book orders.

76 ■ Objects of Collaboration

Then all you have to do is fill in these values (and even use predicates such as "greater than" (>), "less than" (<), and so on. The system will retrieve all the qualifying records and display them in the same form.

Many types of complex as well as simple queries can be processed with forms. Let's say you are interested in customers who live in the midwest, have more than 25 employees, and have made no purchases within the last 6 months. Or you could specify those who have items in warehouse that retail for more than $100 and have an expiration date. All of these queries would be very easy to formulate with a query by form front end. When a user composes a query on a form, the results are also retrieved into the same form. In a sense, the forms processing system and the underlying database fill in the missing details for qualifying records. And because there will often be more than one match, these could be retrieved one by one into the form or displayed in a tabular format.

Forms in Document Imaging Systems

A great deal of effort is spent scanning forms in document imaging systems, entering data associated with the form, and then performing searches on the scanned forms. Typically, in document imaging systems, the information in a form is maintained in two formats:

- The actual image of a scanned or faxed form, as illustrated in Figure 2.11.
- The entered attribute values associated with the image of a form.

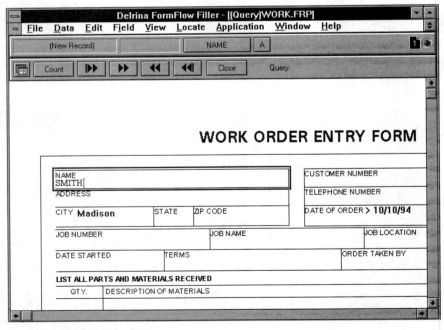

Figure 2.10 Query by form.

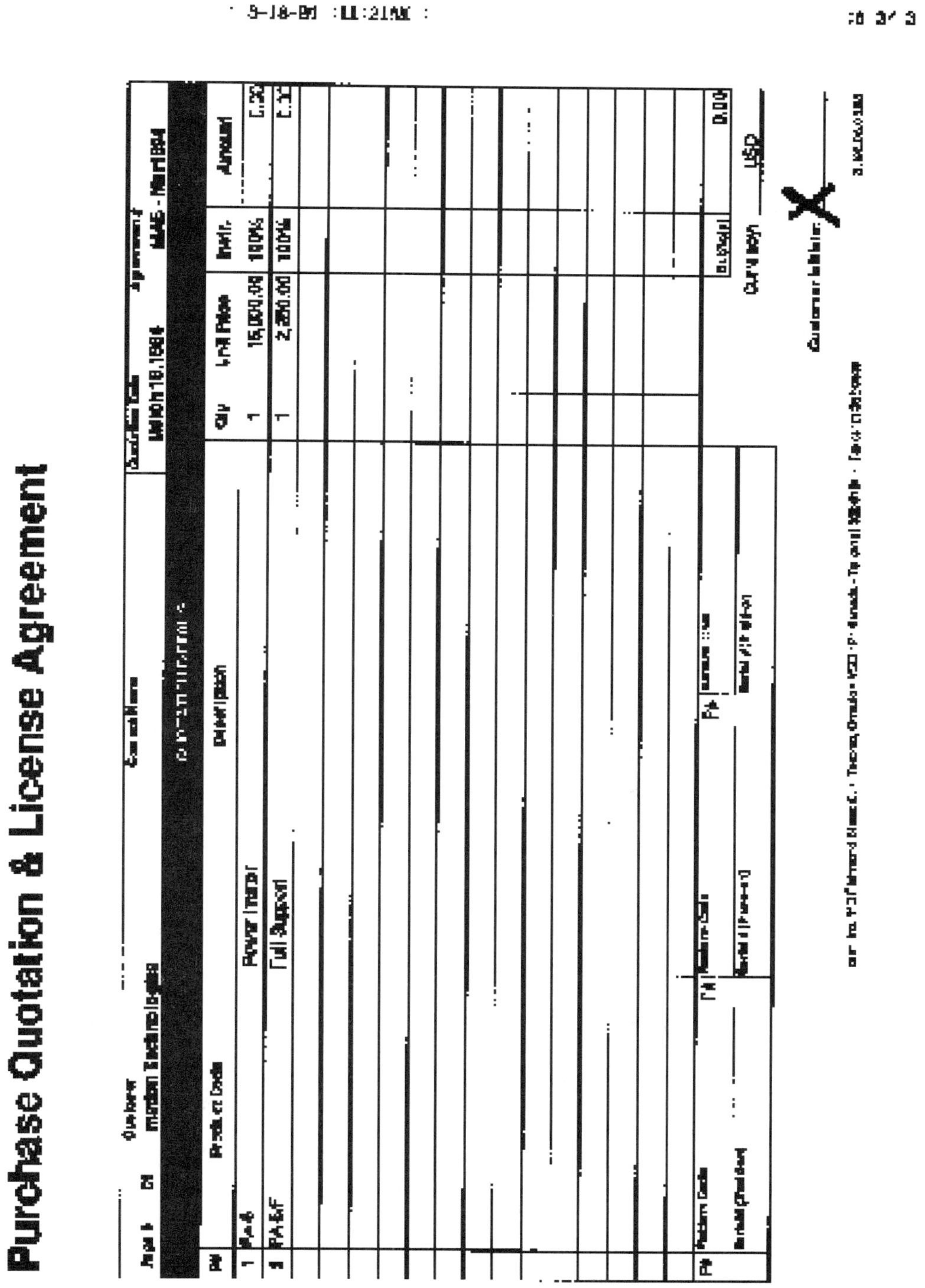

Figure 2.11 Image of a faxed form.

In document imaging terminology, this is often called indexing and identifies which attributes need to be associated with the document. The images of the forms could be either scanned images of paper forms or faxed forms. Using various recognition technologies, an image arranged as a standard form can enable the system to automate the extraction of information. Reports from the system then could be generated using forms.

Imaging systems use a database to organize stored images. This database is usually a third-party relational database package from vendors such as IBM, DEC, Oracle, Informix, Sybase, or Gupta Technologies, which is integrated into the system. The imaging system vendor may superimpose a custom interface upon the database package's native interface, thereby providing a more seamless link between the database's searching and indexing capabilities and the ability of the user to manipulate and view images.

Indexing

The technique of indexing allows a unique set of attributes to be defined and associated with a document for later search and retrieval. In manual indexing, the user is presented with an image and a blank form. The user then fills out the form with the attributes of the document, and the association of image and attributes is made by the database.

The documents may be simple and uniform, or they may range on such disparate topics so as to require the services of a skilled employee to make decisions for each image. This labor-intensive process requires a person to manually type in attributes. Some attributes, however, can be added automatically; for example, creation date and time, the name of the input station and, with fax, the originator of the document. Figure 2.12 illustrates indexing. The left-hand side is the application form's scanned image. The right-hand side contains a form whose attribute values are entered by an office worker (data entry). Even in the case of a scan station with a modest capacity, the rate of scanning clearly outstrips the speed of indexing. As a result, indexing becomes the bottleneck in an image archiving environment. Indexing can be speeded up by running many indexing stations in parallel from a single scan station.

Forms and Groupware

Much of the document and work processing in offices deals with forms. According to BIS Strategic Decisions Inc., companies with more than 500 employees use on the average 1210 different forms. Almost any business process or office procedure requires filling forms, getting approvals, and keeping audit trails in forms. It is not surprising, therefore, that groupware systems are closely integrated with forms and often incorporate some forms processing in the implementation. This section describes some ideal groupware-enabled forms capabilities which are either already incorporated or being implemented in next-generation forms systems. This discussion concentrates on those capabilities that deal with processing forms electronically in collaborative environments. A number of these features for a collaborative forms system can be summarized as follows:

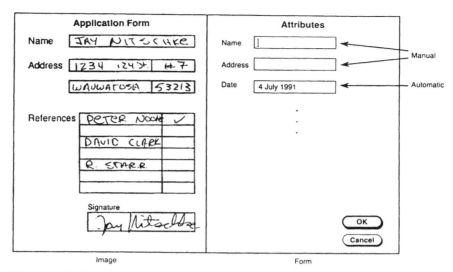

Figure 2.12 Scanned image form and indexing.

(a) Forms as front ends to databases: As mentioned in the previous sections, forms are an ideal way to view databases, either flat files or corporate databases. Database application developers design these forms for specific applications such as order entry, loan processing, airline reservations, and more. Then the forms are used either to enter data or to browse and query the database. One of the most important features of forms to groupware, therefore, is to provide a front end to databases that is easy to use and understand.

(b) Flexibility in assigning access rights for different fields or areas of a form: The notion of access rights, security, or privileges is a familiar one. The simplest example in nonelectronic offices (and still very popular) is the physical locking of documents either in cabinets or safes. Only personnel who have the key can access these documents. There is a similar electronic signature or "key" concept for electronic documents or, in this case, forms. In shared files systems and databases there is a similar notion, where users are given privileges to read (view) or edit certain files or directories (folders). Fields in forms may be edited by some, commented by others, and approved by higher-level managers. In some cases, different areas of complex forms are entered by different personnel. It is desirable, therefore, to allow various access rights or privileges to different parts of a form. Access privileges are discussed in more detail later in this chapter and in Chapter 3.

(c) Incorporating electronic signatures or approval: Forms often require authorization or approval by different people involved in processing the forms. Approval and digital signatures provide the paper form processing equivalent for electronic forms. Signatures are discussed in more detail later in the chapter.

(d) Forms and e-mail: E-mail is the most popular groupware. Processing forms through e-mail can provide efficient and inexpensive "workflow" solutions. Some E-mail systems include form design utilities and tools. Files containing forms can also be routed through e-mail—typically as attachments in messages. The resulting "form flow" solutions can solve many of the business processing requirements. When these solutions are combined with security and digital signature the design-fill-approve cycle can be automated through e-mail routing. E-mail is discussed in more detail in Chapter 4.

(e) Forms and workflow: Workflow is becoming increasingly popular, especially for either incrementally increasing quality of production or business process reengineering. Workflow routes for corporate procedures can carry cases which often includes forms. This is very similar to forms processing through e-mail, except that the tracking, security, and transaction processing can be much more complex. Workflow is discussed in greater detail in Chapter 5.

EDI

Previously, forms processing discussions have sometimes been based on a very important assumption: that the original document is in paper form. This is not always the case. But in document imaging systems the original document is converted from paper to a digital form and then processed electronically. As production, internetworking, and overall accessibility of information become digitized, much of the processing to scan and recognize characters, handwritten notes, and forms becomes unnecessary. As home users as well as businesses become interconnected through on-line services, wireless networks, and direct lines, it becomes feasible to dissipate and process information digitally between "producers" and "consumers" or "sources" and "targets" in much the same way paper information is sent and processed today.

An impressive and practical step in this direction has been the adoption of the Electronic Data Interchange (EDI) standard by many businesses, thereby allowing electronic trade, the retention of business transactions, order processing, and many other business applications. The main goal of EDI is to enhance, facilitate, and enable the transmission of business documents between computer systems of various trading partners. For instance, traditional paper flow handled either through regular mail or faxes for documents such as invoices, purchase orders, and applications could be handled through standard EDI electronic documents transmitted between various and, often heterogeneous, information systems.

EDI has its roots in the work done by the Transportation Data Coordinating Committee and the National Association of Credit Management's Credit Research Foundation which began the first phases of developing the EDI standard. The ANSI X12 standard was first published in 1983; 1989 saw the fourth release which covered 32 standards. In the following years, the number of standards exceeded 100.

To understand the use of the EDI standard, consider the form in Figure 2.13 and the corresponding representation in EDI. The overall structure of an EDI transmission is illustrated in Figure 2.14. To become usable, the incoming business documents are "translated" or mapped onto text files, application files, or formats which are used by

The SoftConnection			**INVOICE**		
1900 Deerfoot Trail,			No. 1001		
Palo Alto, CA 95012					

CHARGE TO	INVOICE DATE 12/13/94 SALES PERSON NTO
	SHIP TO
Information Technologies	Bent Elbow Studios
P.O. Box 1986	352 Bloor Street West,
Los Gatos, CA 95032	Toronto, ON M5R 2X3

YOUR ORDER NO.	CUST. REF. NO.	ORDER DATE	TERMS
P989320	66043	6/25/94	2% 10 DAYS

QUAN.	UNIT	NO.	DESCRIPTION	UNIT PRICE	TOTAL PRICE
3	Case	6900	Batteries	12.75	38.25
12	Ea	P450	Diskettes	.475	5.70
4	Ea	1640Y	Labels	.94	3.76
1	Dz	1507	Cleaner	3.40	3.40

Direct correspondence to:
Amy Mancl
(415) 812-7777

PLEASE PAY THIS AMOUNT $51.11

DATE SHIPPED 6/29/94   SHIPPED VIA Federal Express

ORIGINAL

Figure 2.13(a) Standard form with corresponding representation in EDI.

the receiving site. Similarly, when documents are sent to business partners, they are first translated or mapped onto an electronic standard form. The trading partner on the receiving end can view the document in his or her favorite format using his or her favorite application. There is no information loss, yet each partner can maintain the platforms, formats, and applications best suited for him or her.

82 ■ Objects of Collaboration

NOTES	ABCX12 FORMAT	SAMPLE INVOICE CONTENT
Interchange Control Header, ISA Segment, see X12.5	ISA*00*00000000*01*PASSWORD*01*123456789bbbb bb*987654321bbbbbb*890714*2210*U*00204*0*1*N/L	Outside Envelope
Functional Group Header, GS Segment, see X12.22	GS*IN*12345678*087654321*900509*2210*000001 *X*002020N/L	Inside Envelope
Transaction Set Header, ST Segment, see X12.22	ST*810*0001N/L	Invoice
	BIG*900713*1001*900625*P9839N/L	DATE 12/13/94 ORDER DATE 6/25/94 INVOICE # 1001 CUSTOMER ORDER # P34598
	N1*BT*INFORMATION TECHNOLOGIESN/L N3*P.O. BOX 1986N/L N4*LOS GATOS*CA*95032N/L	CHARGE TO Information Technologies P.O. Box 1986 Los Gatos, CA 95032
	N1*ST*BENT ELBOW STUDION/L N1*352 BLOOR STREET WESTN/L N1*TORONTO*ON*M5R2X3N/L	SHIP TO Bent Elbow Studios 352 Bloor Street West, Toronto, ON M5R 2X3
	N1*SE*THE SOFTCONNECTIONN/L N1*1900 DEERFOOT TRAILN/L N1*PALO ALTO*CA*95012N/L	REMIT TO The SoftConnection 1900 Deerfoot Trail, Palo Alto, CA 95012
	PER*AD*AMY MANCL*TE*415812 7777N/L	CORRESPONDENCE TO Accounting Department Amy Mancl (415)812-7777
	ITD*01*3*2**10N/L	TERMS OF SALE 2% 10 days from invoice date

		QUANTITY	UNIT	SUPPLIER CODE	DESCRIPTION	UNIT PRICE
	IT1**3**CA*12.75**VC*6900N/L	3	Cse	6900	Batteries	12.75
	IT1**12**EA*.475**VC*P450N/L	12	Ea	P450	Diskettes	.475
	IT1**4**EA*.94**VC*1640N/L	4	Ea	1640Y	Labels	.94
	IT1**1**DZ*3.4**VC*1507N/L	1	Dz	1507	Cleaner	3.40

	TDS*51111N/L	Invoice Total
	CAD*M****FEDERAL EXPRESSN/L	Via Federal Express
Hash Totals	CTT*4*20N/L	(4 Line Items, Hash Total 20)
Transaction Set Trailer	SE*21*0000001N/L	
Function Group Trailer	GE*1*0000001N/L	
Interchange Control Trailer	IEA*1*000000000008N/L	

b= Space Character   *=Data Element Separator   N/L=Segment Terminator

Figure 2.13(b) Standard form with corresponding representation in EDI.

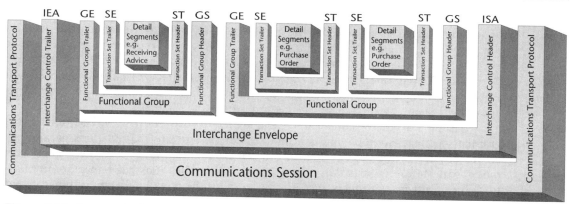

Figure 2.14 Communications session.

The approach of EDI is straightforward, yet very effective. Business information for a particular business transaction type is formatted so that the sender and receiver of the formatted information (in other words, "trading partners") have a standard way of communicating. The ANSI X12 standard takes this a step further. It addresses electronic data interchange (EDI) where an electronic form is transmitted between computer systems. EDI specifies a standard data format for forms, in terms of fields and attributes.

There is a natural synergy between EDI and groupware. In fact, the difference between business transaction processing through more traditional communications—paper or fax—and EDI is that with EDI, the information in various fields and structures comes in recognized electronic forms. When EDI is integrated with e-mail or workflow, it can automatically be filed, routed to the appropriate personnel, and hence commence a workflow for the business transaction.

COMPOUND DOCUMENTS

Related terms that are becoming increasingly popular in next-generation client/server systems are "component software," and "compound documents." Another related term or concept is the notion of an interoperability platform: the ability of objects or components belonging to different applications to interoperate, to be contained within one another, to be linked with each other, and to dynamically exchange data.

Component software is based on the notion of a component, a reusable object which can be "plugged into" other components from other vendors with relatively little effort. For example, a component might be compression or file conversion software sold by one vendor which could be plugged into word processing, graphics, and other applications from different vendors.

When components are used in content-centric documents, the resulting document containing components or parts pertaining to different applications is a compound document. Using component software in documents fundamentally changes the meaning of the term document. In the present, desktop computing realm, a document has a type which is used to choose the application that will edit, view, and print the document. With emerging component software architectures, the compound document becomes a collection of components or parts, each of which is much like a present day document. A component or a part can be relatively small such as a spell checker or a conversion utility. It can also be a part or component that is associated with a very large application such as a spreadsheet or a word processor.

A simple example is illustrated in Figure 2.15, which shows a part belonging to a graphics package, another that is a spreadsheet, and a third that contains paragraphs created by a word processor—all in the same document. The compound document model with different parts that pertain to various applications has important implications for groupware products and systems. Perhaps the most important of these is that the individual parts could actually be located on physically distributed sites in a network. Thus, the components or the parts can interoperate and be located not only in different geographical sites or nodes in a network, but also on different workstation or server operating systems.

The two leading (and in a very real sense, competing) proposals for component software and compound document interoperability are the OLE 2 (Object Embedding and Linking) standard from Microsoft and OpenDoc from CILabs (Component Integration Laboratories). A number of leading computer vendors (competitors of Microsoft) are members of CILabs. Both technologies attempt to standardize component object interoperability as well as to provide the ability to create compound documents from objects that derive from and pertain to different applications. The standardization effort involves the following:

(a) Binary representation of the objects: The binary representation of objects deals with the ability of components to be written in different languages yet retain standard interfaces such that other objects can interoperate with them. Microsoft's binary object model is based on the Component Object Model. OpenDoc's is based on IBM's System Object Model (SOM). SOM itself is an implementation (with some extensions) of the CORBA model from the Object Management Group (OMG) consortium.

(b) User interface standard: The user interface standard deals with the way a user interacts with the compound document, including all aspects of presentation, creation, interaction, menus, and integration of the parts. This is very important from the user's perspective since the interface mechanisms used to create compound documents and to have them interact is what the users will deal with directly.

(c) Storage representation standard: The storage representation standard deals with standards for storing compound document parts or components that could possibly be nested. It includes a hierarchical containment storage structure of compound documents. It also includes other issues dealing with storage such as versioning and transaction support for updates.

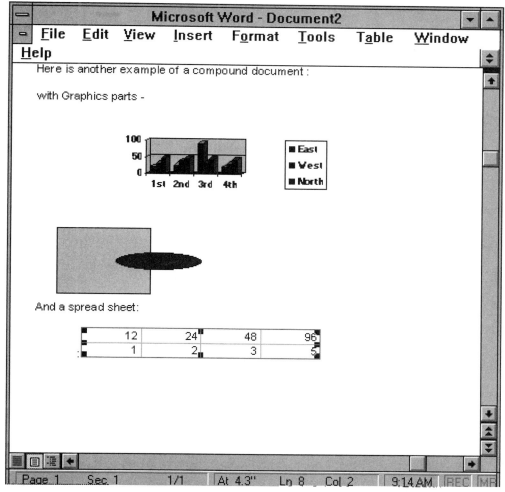

Figure 2.15 A compound document consisting of various parts from a presentation package, a spreadsheet and word processor paragraphs.

(d) Distributed and collaborative computing: This is another important aspect of compound document standards which deals with the interaction of components in a distributed collaborative environment. Some of the issues include routing compound documents or parts, concurrently sharing compound documents or parts, and distributing the parts of a compound document in an internetworked architecture.

In addition to the standards proposed by Microsoft and CILabs—which relies on IBM's SOM/DSOM (the distributed version of SOM), there are a number of other vendors such as SUN, NeXT, HP, and DEC that are also offering their implementations and standards for distributed objects. Most of these are based on the object broker specification from OMG's CORBA standard. The following sections provide a brief overview of OpenDoc and OLE 2 and demonstrate how these various categories of standards manifest themselves in each.

OpenDoc

An increasingly popular compound document model is the OpenDoc standard supported by giants such as Apple and IBM. The source code of OpenDoc is owned by an independent nonprofit corporation called Component Integration Laboratories. It is difficult to give a detailed explanation of all the concepts involved in OpenDoc. Some of the key concepts are summarized here, but users should refer to the OpenDoc manuals. A good place to start is the OpenDoc Technical Summary (Apple, 1994).

Document- or Content-based Model

As the name suggests, OpenDoc concentrates on a document-based model. The fundamental concept of a document is radically different from that of most conventional monolithic document models wherein each application vendor has its own document structure. A document in the OpenDoc (OLE 2 as well) model is a structured collection of parts. Each part is an object possibly pertaining to a different application. From this point of view, documents are more like other containers such as folders, except that there is much more structure, a richer interface model, and more enhanced representation from the end-user perspective.

One result of this shift in perspective is a significant change in how application software is written. The document is no longer viewed as a monolithic block of content, but is composed instead of many smaller blocks which make up the aggregate content of the document. Since no single application has complete control of the document, protocols must be created to keep the various cooperating pieces of code from getting in each other's way. This is a pervasive change in how applications work. Protocols covering storage management, event distribution, run-time models, and human interface management must be followed if the document is to remain editable and uncorrupted.

Parts

Parts are the boundaries in the document where one kind of content ends and another begins. Any document may have many different kinds of parts. These parts are a central notion in OpenDoc, since they provide the user with a way to predict what will happen, and how, when a change is made to a compound document.

A part can embed another part, and know little or nothing about the information contained in that embedded part. Every compound document has a top-level container part called the root part. All other parts are embedded in the root part. Parts can be embedded in parts that are themselves embedded in the root part. Every part is transitively embedded in the root part of the compound document.

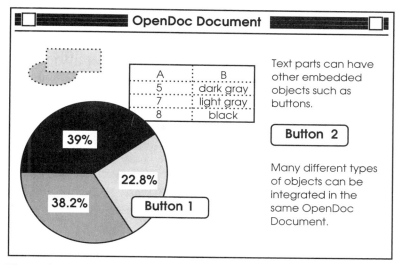

Figure 2.16 The concept of parts and how they can overlap and wrap around.

A key element of the notion of parts is that each part of a document has its own content model. But be aware that not everything in the document is a part. Notice that the rectangle and ellipsis in the upper left corner of the example document in Figure 2.16 are not parts at all, but are instead referred to as content objects. This brings up a key point: An embedded part is fundamentally distinct from the ordinary content elements like simple shapes, characters, cells, and so on. When a part boundary is reached, extra protocols must be invoked because more than one part handler is involved in providing the user with access to the information.

Part Handlers

Part handlers are the "applications" in the OpenDoc architecture. When a part is displayed or edited, a part handler is invoked to perform those tasks. Just as an application performs basic editing, display, and printing tasks for a given document, part handlers perform these functions for a part. The part handler provides the content model for the part. A part handler is responsible for the following:

- *Displaying the part (both on-screen and printed):* The part handler may be asked to display the part on a dynamic medium such as a screen or a static medium such as the printed page.
- *Editing the part:* The part handler must accept events and change the state of the part so that the user can edit and script the part.
- *Managing storage (persistent and run-time) for the part:* The part handler must be able to read the part from persistent storage into main memory, manage the

run-time storage associated with the part, and write the part back out to persistent storage. Together, a part and its handler form the equivalent of a programmatic object, in the object-oriented programming sense of the word. The part provides the state information, while the part handler provides the behavior.

Editors and Viewers

OpenDoc further breaks down the notion of part handlers into two concepts: part editors and part viewers. The difference between the two is that part viewers do not provide editing capability, but do provide full rendering and storage management. It is recommended that developers eventually create both kinds of handler for any given piece of content. The editor would be sold at an appropriate price, but the viewer could be freely distributable.

In-place Editing

In OpenDoc, users can perform in-place editing. This means that, rather than launching the application to which a part belongs and then editing the part in the application's windows, a user can stay in the same context of the compound document and edit in place.

Frames and Layout

OpenDoc provides very elegant user interface solutions for displaying compound documents with different parts. Frames are the bounded windows that contain parts. Frames can have either regular shapes, such as rectangles, or irregular shapes. The latter allows any type of part to be wrapped around or displayed in various relationships with other parts. This type of frames is often supported for monolithic applications such as graphics editors. OpenDoc brings this same functionality to compound documents containing graphs belonging to different applications.

Linking

As stated, parts can be embedded in other parts; in addition, a part can be linked. Visually, a linked part appears as an embedded part but in actuality it is embedded in a another part. The link contains a persistent reference to the actual part.

Storage

Storage is a major issue in OpenDoc. Given the presence of multipart documents, a persistent storage mechanism must be created that enables multiple part handlers to share a single document file effectively.

OpenDoc assumes that such a storage system can effectively give each part its own storage stream, and that reliable references can be made from one such stream to another. Because many pieces of code may need to access a given part, the storage system must support a robust annotation mechanism to allow information to be associated with a part without disturbing its format.

Run-time

At run-time, OpenDoc assumes that an instance of the document shell will be created for each document. This generic shell will be responsible for providing four basic structures to the part handlers. These are: the storage system, the window and its associated state, the event dispatcher, and an arbitration registry to allow negotiation about shared resources like the menu bar.

On the Macintosh, the run-time shell of a OpenDoc document will also be responsible for binding and loading part handlers for the parts that appear in the document. It is assumed that once a given part handler is loaded, any part in any document may share the part handler's executable code.

Compound Documents in Collaborative Environments

There are many aspects of collaboration for OpenDoc compound documents. There is some support of collaboration for compound documents routing, distributing objects, and concurrently sharing, each of which is described briefly here:

(a) Routing or mail-enabled OpenDoc documents: One advantage of OpenDoc is the separation of part handlers from document level functions. This places Apple and other platform vendors in an excellent position to add new features to documents without asking developers to revise their applications. OpenDoc's document shell thus provides the access to mail facilities, particularly mail sending, without developer interaction. Nevertheless, part handlers with knowledge of specialized mail or messaging systems will still be free to implement features based on those systems.

(b) Collaboration between parts through scripting: A script is a series of instructions (basically a program) that manipulates parts. Scripts are written in a scripting language such as AppleScript. OpenDoc actually has an open scripting architecture, which basically means many scripting languages (provided by operating system vendors such as Apple or Independent Software Vendors) can coexist. The collaboration between parts in OpenDoc uses scripting. Scripting creates a rich medium for coordinating the work of parts in documents, and allows users and parts to work together to perform tasks. By extending scripting to use messaging services as well as direct calls between applications, collaboration over time or space becomes available to "smart" documents as well as users. In addition, OpenDoc supports a notion of extended interfaces between parts. These interfaces extend the basic OpenDoc interoperability layer with specific added functions which developers can use to increase collaboration between parts.

(c) Concurrently sharing compound documents: Most document management systems provide some support of versioning. When users collaborate on the same document or parts of a document, various drafts and versions get created. OpenDoc enables users to create drafts of a document. When multiple users concurrently share a document, each can work on his or her own draft, which can be reconciled manually with other user's drafts at a later time. Users can look back through the drafts of the document they and others have created. Drafts are document-wide, and store only those parts of a document that have changed in each draft. As a result, it is practical for users to store several drafts of a document without prohibitive space overhead.

(d) Distributed Objects: OpenDoc relies on IBM's System Object Model (SOM) to provide a platform as well as language independent mechanism for defining objects and dispatching methods or operations on objects at run-time. For distributed objects, OpenDoc requires the Distributed System Object Model (DSOM) also from IBM. There are both similarities and differences between SOM and DSOM. The key advantage is that with DSOM the parts of compound document can be located in physically distributed workstations or servers. Complying to the DSOM implementation alleviates the software vendor (and the user) from all the various (sometimes rather complex) issues involved in handling distributed objects.

OLE 2

OLE 2 has been available since April 1993. There are now several hundred applications that make use of various capabilities offered by OLE 2. As with OpenDoc and other component-based software, with OLE 2, programmers from different companies can write objects that interact with one another in a synergistic manner—without knowing anything about the specifics of how individual objects work.

OLE automation allows one application to interact with and use the services of another application. OLE 2 uses the (perhaps most important) object-oriented concept of encapsulation, where an object satisfies a *protocol* (or provides an interface) while encapsulating or hiding its implementation. Microsoft claims:

> When coupled with the power of object-oriented programming, the standard framework of OLE 2 will spark a transformation of the software industry. This change will be as fundamental to technology as was the period of the early 1980s, which marked the beginning of the "personalization" of computing. In a similar manner, the early 1990s represents the beginning of the "componentization" of computing, and it promises to have an impact equal to that of the personal computer. Although an evolutionary step, component software represents a "quiet revolution" that will transform the way software is produced and used.

Compound Documents in OLE 2

OLE 2 also allows objects to be embedded in other objects, and one document "container" can maintain various other documents. Objects can also be embedded in other documents. As its name suggests (Object *Embedding* and *Linking*), in OLE 2, compound documents objects can be linked to either other entire compound documents or components of these documents.

Refer back to Figure 2.15, which illustrates a compound document consisting of various components from Microsoft Office (which supports OLE 2). Microsoft Office is a suite of applications that includes Word for Windows, Excel for Windows, Access, PowerPoint, and Microsoft Mail. The containing object is a Word document. The figure illustrates an Excel spreadsheet and PowerPoint image. The objects in the figure are *active* objects. They can be activated in place or be launched in their own separate windows. The figure illustrates the spreadsheet activated in place. Notice that the buttons as well as the menu items are those of Excel, but everything is still in the context of the Word document.

OLE 2 Architecture

Figure 2.17 illustrates some of the architecture components of OLE 2 (Brockschmidt, 1994). The next few paragraphs briefly discuss each of these.

Component Object Model (COM)

OLE 2 is based on COM, which provides the basic interoperability between objects that could be written in different programming languages. COM includes both an interoperability specification and an executable (called COMPOBJ.DLL).

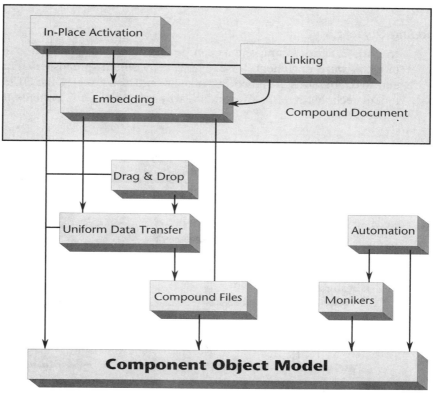

Figure 2.17 Component object model (Brockschmidt, 1994).

Objects defined with the COM specification can support one or more interfaces. The interface of an object is basically its *contract* or *protocol*. One component object (say a *client*) can ask another (say a *server*) about its supported interfaces. The server provides a handle for all the operations (functions) it supports. OLE implementations are evolving to a *location independence* solution, where the executables supporting the interface might reside on a different machine on the network, providing distributed object support.

OLE 2 Storage Model

The OLE 2 storage model is sometimes called a file system within a file. This is illustrated in Figure 2.18. Notice the hierarchical structure of the embedded object containment relationships. Notice that the structure of the storage is very similar to a directory. In fact, there are two types of nodes in the figure: storages (which correspond to directories or folders) and streams (which correspond to files). Storage objects can contain other storage objects or streams, much the same way a directory can contain other directories and files. In fact, the similarity between the structured storage of OLE 2 and an operating system directory system is more than an analogy. By all indications, it is likely that it will be adopted as the directory structure of Cairo, the next-generation object-oriented operating system from Microsoft.

Embedding Objects

In OLE 2, various components can be contained or embedded in a compound document. A word document, for example, can contain spreadsheet, graphics, voice data, and so on. In terms of embedding objects (and also linking), the OLE 2 compound document technology offers a standard way for various components to be contained in

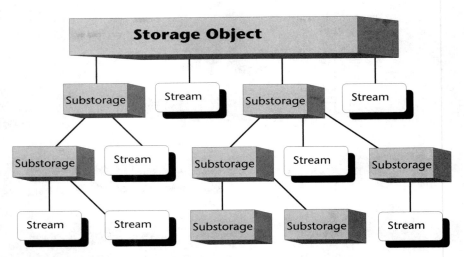

Figure 2.18 Storage object.

others and interoperate. This interaction includes editing, accessing the component object's data, and storage of the component object's stream in the hierarchical structured storage organization just discussed.

Viewing Components

In OLE 2, users can view an OLE component object even if the application that created the object is not available on their machines. Therefore, there is no need for additional software such as a component viewer to examine and/or print an OLE compound document. There is, however, an issue of the resolution of the image of the objects being viewed or printed. But viewers could still be used and associated with the component object's type on the machine of the user who is viewing the object.

This capability is available for OLE 2 users because OLE automatically stores and then uses a graphical image of objects for display and print purposes. Using OLE, users can display and print a compound document even if the applications used to create the embedded objects are not installed on their machines. These applications are only needed when users want to edit the embedded/linked objects.

In a collaborative environment users can freely route compound documents to people who may not have access to all the applications used to create the document. Other users can still display and print the documents as long as they have the container application used to create the base document (such as the word processing package or spreadsheet).

Linking and Monikers

With object linking, the container of a linked object carries the representation of the object. In fact, when the user opens a compound document with linked components he or she will not notice a difference between a linked object and an embedded object. However, in a linked object the actual data of the object is stored elsewhere (in another compound document). In earlier implementations of OLE, the linked objects were stored using absolute path names. This creates a problem if the user moves the source document of the linked object.

For this reason OLE 2 introduced monikers to handle some of the problems of absolute path names. A moniker encompasses both the location of source data and the code to *bind* to data. Binding implies linking to the source data. As long as the client compound document and the linked item or file are moved together from, say, one directory system to another, monikers (and hence OLE 2) can bind the linked data.

OLE 2 and Distributed Objects

With OLE 2, the distributed object support will be seamless. The approach for handling distribution in OLE 2 is to replace the OLE Dynamic Linked Libraries (DLLs), which are the programs in the operating system that support OLE 2, with networked DLLs. With this approach applications shipping today with OLE 2 support will require no modifications to take advantage of distributed capabilities. Also, OLE 2 provides very efficient support for handling deadlocks—objects waiting for other objects and forming a wait-for cycle which can never get resolved—both in single-user and distributed environments. Deadlocks can occur in multithreaded operating systems as well as distributed object systems.

MULTIMEDIA OBJECTS AND GROUPWARE

There is an interesting and important synergy between the emerging multimedia technologies and groupware. Groupware attempts to facilitate interactions between humans as well as between computers and humans in an organization. Multimedia technologies provide a more natural medium of interaction—namely through voice, images, and video to achieve the interaction between humans in an electronic environment.

In the early stages of electronic environments, human interactions with computers were primarily alphanumeric, and this remains a prevalent form of interaction. More recently, through quantitative incremental evolutionary changes in core hardware technologies as well as the growing sophistication of software design, the prospect of the heightened sensory engagement of multimedia has become not just more affordable but inevitable.

The realities that inexorably drive the computer industry toward multimedia are both the maturation of the personal computer as a product as well as relative market saturation for the current microcomputer paradigm. Together these realities force computer manufacturers not only to differentiate their products, but to add more perceived value and to extend the target market.

Multimedia, because it uses translingual elements such as music, motion, and image, travels well across linguistic borders and across levels of education, class, and intelligence. It is a more universal language depending less on difficult language skills than on innate human perceptual models. Multimedia is appropriate for an advertising and television literate society.

Defining Multimedia Data Types and Objects

A number of data types can be characterized as multimedia data types. These are typically the elements or building blocks of more generalized multimedia environments, platforms, or integrating tools (such as authoring tools). The basic multimedia data types can be described as follows:

Text: Although it might seem strange to mention text as the first multimedia data type, text-based information will always be integrated in any application. The forms in which text can be stored can vary greatly. Besides ASCII-based text files, text is typically stored in word processor files, spreadsheets, database fields, and as annotations on more general multimedia objects. Also, with the availability and proliferation of next-generation graphical user interfaces, the number of available text fonts has increased, allowing for special effects and imaging capabilities for text characters—color, shade, fill, and so on. Figure 2.19 illustrates some elegant text fonts available in Windows environments. Text requires the least amount of storage space. An 8.5″ × 11″ page of text consumes about 2K of storage without compression.

Audio: An increasingly popular data type being integrated into mainstream computing is audio. Currently, there are numerous audio file formats. One of the most popular is Microsoft's WAV (wave) files. Figure 2.20 illustrates the waveform of a digitized audio file. However, audio files can be quite space intensive. For instance, one second of digitized sound (depending upon the sample rate and sample size) can consume several tens of kilobytes of storage. A minute of sound can take up several megabytes. Compression can improve these storage requirements but they will still be quite large. If CD-audio quality music is stored, a 75-minute high-fidelity segment of digitized music can consume about 100 megabytes of storage. A more compact representation of sound is Musical Instrument Digital Interface (MIDI), which stores the music score that can be played either by a computer with audio capabilities or on a MIDI-compliant synthesizer. MIDI is essentially a series of compact instructions about musical events and, as such, is analogous to object-based drawing programs that define a graphic in terms of primitives and attribute parameters. In terms of resource burden, including storage requirements, bandwidth and throughput, MIDI is to digitized audio as vector graphics is to raster bitmaps. Of incidental but relevant interest, MIDI is not entirely limited to musical events but has been used to schedule, coordinate, and trigger other multimedia events.

Still images: There are great variances in the quality and amount of storage required for still images. Digitized bitmapped images are sequences of pixels which represent a region in the user's graphical monitor display. Pixels are numbers whose interpretation allows the display of a particular "dot" with different values for luminance, color, and contrast. Pixels can be as simple as 0s and 1s, indicating white or black for black-and-white still images. On the other hand, for higher-resolution color images there could be 8, 16, or 24 bits per pixel thereby allowing for the representation of millions of colors.

THIS IS THE ALGERIAN FONT

and THIS IS KNITO ....

Try Some Bragadocio

and Some Antiqua ...

Script it all and you are DONE

Figure 2.19 Various fonts in Word for Windows.

96 ■ Objects of Collaboration

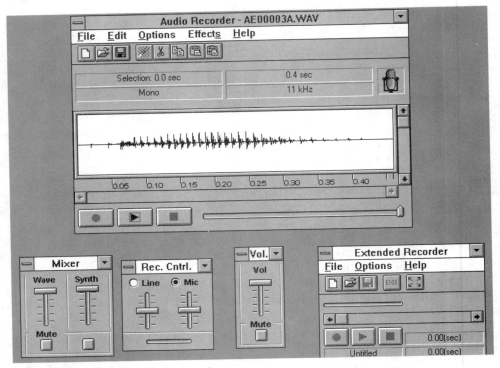

Figure 2.20 Digitized audio in wave form.

The space overhead for still images varies based on the resolution, size, complexity, and compression scheme used to store the images. File sizes for 8.5" × 11" images can vary from 10 kilobytes for simple black-and-white images (with compression) to several megabytes for complex, high-resolution color images. Figure 2.21 illustrates the Aldus PhotoStyler logo in the PhotoStyler application.

Digital video: One of the most space-intensive multimedia data types is digitized video. Video objects are stored as a sequence of frames, and depending on resolution and size, a single frame could consume more than a megabyte of storage. Also, in order to have a realistic video playback, the transmission, compression, and decompression of digitized frames requires continuous transfer rates of about 30 frames per second. There are a number of interleaved structures that incorporate timed sequencing of audio/video playback for integrating both video and audio in the same presentation. Both Microsoft's AVI format and Quicktime from Apple are popular examples of file structures that incorporate both audio and video and can synchronize their playback on a multimedia workstation. Figure 2.22 illustrates a sequence of frames from a digitized AVI video clip.

Multimedia Objects and Groupware ■ 97

Figure 2.21 Logo.

Figure 2.22 Sequence of frames from a digitized AVI videoclip.

Graphics objects: Digitized files and multimedia file structures provide a bit or byte stream stored in files. The standard file formats for text (such as ASCII files and word processor files), for images (such as PCX, TIFF, PDA, DCX), sound (such as MIDI and Waveforms), and video (such as AVI and Quicktime) have internal structures that can be manipulated by applications that recognize these structures. In addition to these byte or bit stream structures, multimedia objects can be described through basic elements such as 2-D and 3-D shapes.

These shapes can have different sizes, positions, orientation, surface, fill, and so on. Two- and three-dimensional objects generated through these design tools are usually smaller than the bit/byte stream representations. Furthermore, through design tools it is possible to manipulate the individual objects in the 2-D and 3-D composite objects. For images, bit and byte stream files are constructed through "painting." With computer graphics tools and computer aided design (CAD) packages the individual elements that comprise an object are identified with different attributes and can be selected and updated separately. The descriptions of the elements of a multimedia model are stored in 2-D and 3-D design files. Figure 2.23 illustrates various 2-D and 3-D graphics objects.

The aforementioned categories of multimedia object and data types are primarily elements of more complex multimedia objects. There are a number of tools and products that integrate and combine multimedia objects for various applications. For instance, presentation tools allow users to create multimedia presentations with various slides containing images, text, video clips, or audio annotations. Similar authoring tools allow users to develop multimedia projects that depict the timelines and flow of control between various nodes containing multimedia information. Hypermedia documents allow the representation of information through node-and-link models, thereby supporting a nonlinear organization of information with hyperlinks from one multimedia node to another.

HYPERMEDIA

A compound document that has parts and links between parts is a sort of nonlinear document or hypermedia. Compound documents can be containers with parts which could themselves be compound documents containing parts and so on. The user thus has "hyper" links from one compound document part to another. However, there are certain additional features of hypermedia that go beyond mere container models of compound or composite documents, some of which include the following:

(a) The ability to create anchors from one node to another. Thus, in addition to the embedded or linked parts concepts of compound document, with hypermedia, users can select a term in a text or an area/object in a graph and link it to another component or node.

(b) Utilities to track and facilitate navigation through a hypermedia document help to ameliorate the problem of disorientation within a nonlinear information space.

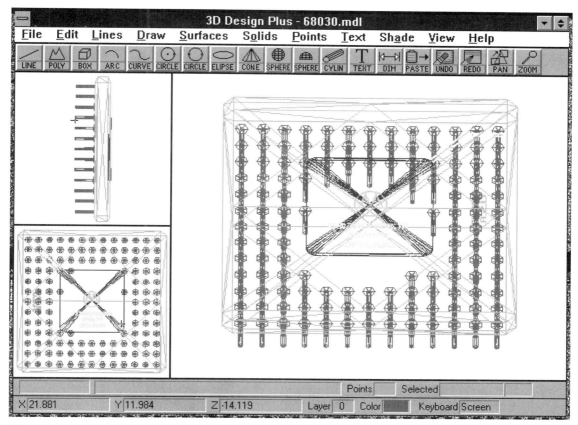

Figure 2.23 Various graphic objects in two- and three-dimensions.

In compound document systems there are rarely any tools that allow the user to browse the traversed links between the different components or parts of a compound document.

(c) Glossary and other utilities to tie concepts together and to navigate between concepts in hypermedia documents. These also allow for the creation of topical and concept indexes to associatively (versus explicitly) link various nodes in a hypermedia "document."

(d) The ability to view a document at varying levels of granularity, ranging from high-level outline to highly detailed exposition of concepts and ancillary appendices. This is very important since hypertext/hypermedia systems can be so large that it becomes desirable to have zooming capabilities at different levels of details for a document. The outline, for instance, provides an overview, a "big picture," with each item in the outline expandable to the next level of detail.

(e) Monolithic applications are often used to generate stand-alone hypermedia tutorial or documentation systems. Although most hypermedia systems allow for the incorporation of parts or nodes from different document types, many hypermedia systems also have editors and viewers for a range of media types including text, images, and sound. Hypermedia authoring systems therefore come with a host of built-in editors for these types as well as functionality to create hypermedia links between them.

Similar to compound (and in a sense, a generalization of compound documents) hypermedia document systems are very relevant in groupware environments. With groupware systems, anchors could be used to navigate to completely different nodes in a distributed environment. Conceptual links as well as the authoring of hypermedia document nodes and links could be performed cooperatively with different collaborators contributing different elements.

Ideally, hypermedia documents and systems could serve as the associative repertoire of various knowledge bases developed either in a corporation or for a particular discipline. Thus, hypermedia documents designed and implemented collaboratively and whose data could be either local or distributed can be a very useful framework for organizational memory within a corporation or discipline. The next few paragraphs present more details of hypermedia systems and expound on their relevance to groupware.

Hypermedia Documents

Hypermedia documents are built through associative structures. A normal document is linear and read from beginning to end. In contrast, the process of reading hypermedia is open-ended: Readers can jump from idea to idea, depending on inclination or interest. A popular example of hypermedia documents are the various "home" pages and related html documents on the World Wide Web. By clicking on hot links which could be highlighted text, icons, or graphics, the net surfer can jump across continents in the time it takes to make a link to the home server of the linked node and download the data linked to the hypermedia document.

A simpler paper-based example of hypermedia is a thesaurus, which has no beginning or end. Each time the thesaurus is consulted, it is entered at a different location based on the word used to initiate the search. Hypermedia can be thought of as an enriched thesaurus where, instead of links between words, links exist between documents and text fragments.

The prefix "hyper" is used a great deal in this industry. In the context of this chapter, hypertext and hypermedia refer to individual elements of a document which are linked to related information. This might be a word or picture, which when invoked (usually by a mouse click) responds with a definition, a description, or another document. Hyperlink describes any link between one document and another.

Hypermedia provides an associative way to browse through a set of documents. It complements the method of search and retrieval where the nature of a target document is specified and then a set of matches is returned. Hypermedia allows a user to find related information transparently without initiating further searches, and to form new links between documents.

Hypermedia systems are more flexible than traditional information structuring methods because they allow information in a variety of forms (media) to be attached to nodes. Thus, a node in hypermedia may consist of a sound or picture, as well as text. Nodes in hypertext (hypermedia) can include icons, anchors, and/or buttons that provide links (send messages) to other nodes.

Figure 2.24 illustrates a "node-and-link" representation of a hypermedia document with various multimedia nodes. The node types in hypermedia documents correspond to the various multimedia data types or elements as well as components or parts of applications.

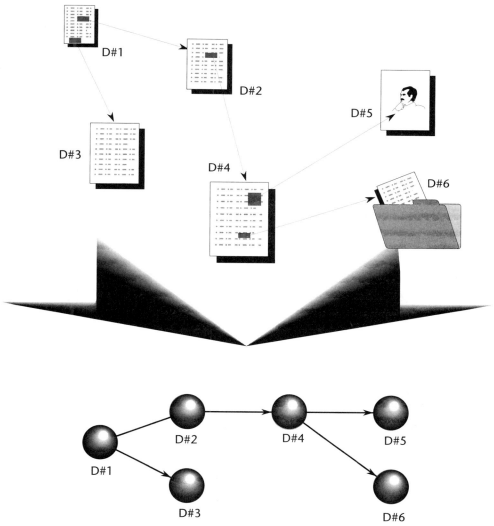

Figure 2.24 The node-and-link representation in hypermedia.

Links

Links between nodes are also objects that define the structure of the hypermedia document and provide the capability for browsing and exploring the nodes. Many different categories of links can be defined, including navigational links and links that are organizational in nature. A link can be one-directional from a source to a destination, such as a one-directional link from a multimedia document containing a voice annotation icon (the link is represented by an icon) to the voice annotation. A link can also be bidirectional between two nodes, allowing the user to treat either node as a source or a destination.

The intuitive meaning of these links can be grasped by analogy to the operation of a video camera. Links as navigational entities correspond to changing perspectives on a display in roughly the same way that the operation of a video camera changes the appearance of a visual scene. The user can simply move the camera back and forth (move to link), zoom in on a particular portion of the scene (zoom link), and then pan back out to the larger picture (pan link). Finally, while different filters can be used on a camera to highlight different aspects of the scene, hypertext provides the ability to view links in order to make them conditional on particular sets of contextual constraints.

Four types of navigational links are described as follows (Parsaye et al., 1989):

- *Move to links:* These links simply move to a related node, allowing the user to move around or navigate through the hypermedia document.

- *Zoom links:* These links expand the current node into a more detailed account of the information.

- *Pan links:* These links return to a higher-level view of the hypertext document (particularly useful in browsing facilities). Pan links are normally the inverse of zoom links, so that every zoom link has a corresponding pan link and vice versa.

- *View links:* The availability or activation of these links is conditional on the stated purposes of the user, and may also be used for security purposes. View links are hidden unless they are of interest or a user has access to them. View links provide the fundamental mechanism for customizing hypertext to the needs and interests of different users. They also help prevent hypertext from becoming unnecessarily complex and swamping users with information not relevant to their needs.

Linking Strategies

Various strategies can be used to link objects in compound hypermedia documents. Four strategies involve using relationship links, linking document regions, linking documents with actions, and using a glossary.

- *Relationship links:* Links at the document level can implement relationships between the documents. Examples of relationships include inheritance (is a), ownership (has a) and adjacency (is above, is to the right of). Adjacent links can be used to implement a spatial database, and are often used in cartography (mapping) systems. In these systems, a map is displayed on the screen, and the user can invoke hyperlinks to move to adjacent maps to the left or right, above or below.

- *Linking document regions:* A region of a document can be assigned a hyperlink. The region is defined (usually as a rectangle) by document coordinates. (This method is used in HyperCard on the Macintosh to assign actions to areas of a card. A mouse click in a particular region will run the code associated with that hyperlink. The regions are often invisible to the user.)

- *Linking documents and actions:* A document element, such as an icon or piece of text, can be linked to another document or to an action. Invoking an icon of a notepad might display a piece of text related to the original document, such as a description or a part number.

- *Glossary:* A glossary is a table of words with associated links. The link is applicable to all occurrences of the same word, or word stem, within a document. This system is used to implement a help index, or to provide a set of definitions. If a dictionary is used as the glossary for a word processor document, then any word can be queried for its definition by invoking its hyperlink.

Hypermedia and Groupware

Hypertext and hypermedia systems provide numerous advantages for developing nonlinear or nonsequential information systems. Since the outcome of a hypermedia system is a document, hypermedia processing can be described as an authoring environment. Some groupware-related characteristics of hypermedia systems can be summarized as follows:

(a) Documents on networked environments: As illustrated in Figure 2.25, the various nodes in a hypermedia or compound document can be nodes in a distributed environment. Authors and coauthors can reference information stored and maintained on geographically distributed nodes. The associative memories of individuals can be replaced by associative memories of organizations and groups.

(b) Linking concepts, parts, and text: There are so many different possibilities for linking in a hypermedia system. Linking can be done explicitly, through synonyms or through concepts. The linked components or nodes in a hypermedia document can also allow readers of documents to become authors, providing both additional notes or references to concepts in the document as well as annotations and editorials on existing nodes.

(c) Tracing knowledge or solving disorientation problems: In hypertext there is always the possibility of users getting disoriented and lost while browsing and navigating between nodes and various link traversals. This is usually known as the "disorientation" problem and can be serious in complex hypertext/hypermedia

104 ■ Objects of Collaboration

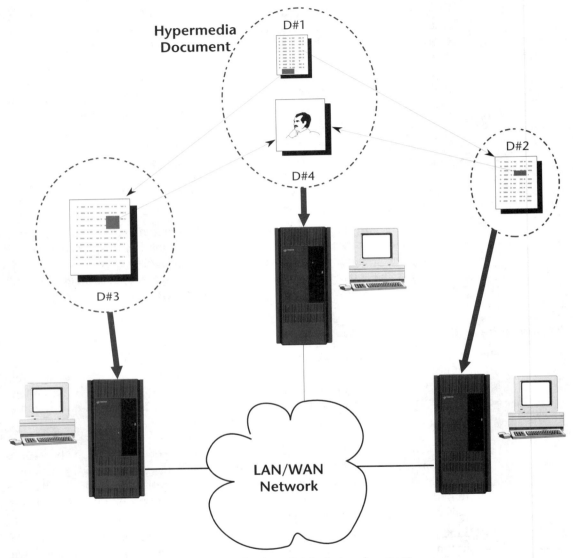

Figure 2.25 Hypermedia document mapped onto a distributed environment.

systems. Within a networked groupware environment the problem becomes more acute, since nodes can span various geographically distributed locations and multiple sites. While it is desirable to hide the details of the various node locations as much as possible, there is also the desire to know and "locate" the authors of edited nodes, either for authentication or further interactions.

(d) Iterative authoring: One of the advantages of hypermedia that is augmented with distributed collaborative computing is the ability to allow readers to also become annotators and authors. This type of more interactive, iterative, and "live" document management allows users to participate collaboratively in the development of hyperlinked documents with various authors, as well as encourage comments and annotations from different reader and authors.

CONTAINERS

Containers are very important in any groupware system. As mentioned earlier, the objects manipulated by users and groups are either simple elements—such as text, image, table, a message—or compound objects. Previous sections covered a number of object types commonly used in groupware systems. Often these objects are stored in containers or collection objects, two of which have already been discussed: compound documents and hypermedia documents. Parts and components can be contained in either compound documents or hypermedia documents. Links also can be created in compound or hypermedia documents and hence the hypermedia document is itself an aggregation or collection of other documents or parts.

There are, in addition to compound documents and hypermedia documents as containers or aggregators of information, a number of collection types that have become increasingly popular in various groupware systems. Two of the most common metaphors used in various groupware systems—cabinets and folders—are explained next.

Cabinets

Basically, an (electronic) cabinet is a collection that contains elements that are also collections. Thus, a cabinet can be a collection of drawers or a collection of folders. Electronic drawers can also be collections of folders. Figure 2.26 illustrates a cabinet. As any other object in a shared environment, cabinets have attributes, content, and security privileges. For cabinets these include the ability to read the content, create and/or delete objects from the cabinet, modify the attribute values of the cabinet, and so on.

Folders

Electronic folders are, perhaps, the most commonly used collection type in both groupware systems and personal information organizers. Many electronic mail systems, for example, use folders to organize personal mail, filed mail, sent mail, mail based on categories, and so on. Many graphical user interface environments use the folder as the main collection primitive. Figure 2.27 illustrates a folder containing both folders and documents. Similar to cabinets, folders have attributes as well as privileges associated with their attributes and content.

106 ■ Objects of Collaboration

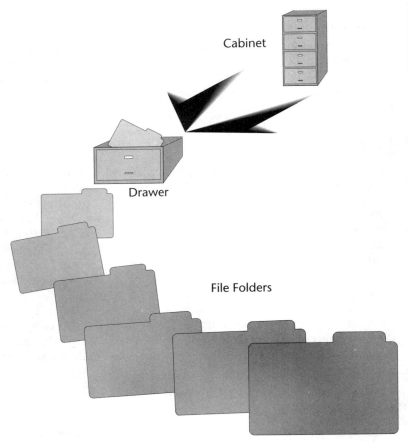

Figure 2.26 Cabinets, drawers, and folders organize information.

Other Collections in Groupware Applications

Typically, electronic cabinets and folders are used to organize and collect documents. Whether in personal information systems, electronic mail applications, shared files systems, or groupware products in general, the primary use of folder and cabinet metaphors is to collect information objects of which at least a portion is free format, as in messages and documents. Collections are also used in many other areas of groupware, some of which are listed here:

(a) Corporate Databases: An important and common application of collections is for corporate databases. Corporate database management systems contain information about accounts, personnel, sales information, budget information, and so on. Each of these is a collection and is viewed and updated usually by graphical user interface front-end applications to corporate databases. In fact, if a groupware

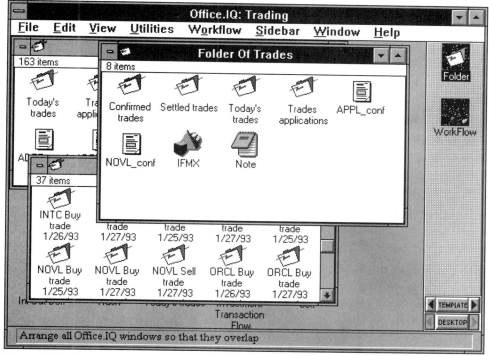

Figure 2.27 A folder with both folders and documents.

product uses a database management system to manage its objects, then these objects are also collections management by the DBMS.

(b) Address books in groupware products: Groupware applications such as e-mail or workflow products often come with some built-in capabilities to create and manage address books. These address books contain users and groups of users. Various attributes, such as name and role, could be associated with both groups or users. Groups are used to assign privileges or security, or as a unit of collaboration for coauthoring, routing, and so on.

(c) Collections to keep track of exchanges, interactions, votes, and so on: There are other collections or collection structures in groupware systems that are used specifically to maintain "traces" or "trails" of exchanges. In many groupware systems there are discussions on topics involving responses and counter-responses. Other groupware systems allow votes, either anonymous or with discussions. Still other groupware systems allow coauthors of a document to keep traces of their comments or annotations on the documents. These groupware systems often utilize additional collection structures (in addition to more generic structures such as folders) to keep track of these collections.

(d) Collections for workflow: As discussed in Chapter 5 a number of structures and collections are used to implement workflow. For the workflow templates as well as instances or activations of the templates there are various collections for storing both the structure as well as the status (tracking) of workflow. Examples include: the set of activations of a workflow, the queues for tasks on workflow nodes, the set of participants in a workflow path, and the documents used in a workflow, just to name a few.

THE MANY FACES OF SHARING

The previous sections discussed many aspects of the various objects of collaboration, including various types of objects that are used in a collaborative environment. How collections of these objects can be formed were illustrated. Both built-in attributes as well as custom attributes for organizing and searching these objects were explained. This section addresses another important concept in groupware systems that has significant implications for the overall execution and success of groupware products.

None of the objects types discussed in the previous sections exist in isolation. Objects such as documents and other types of information accessed in groupware environments reference one another. That is the whole purpose of groupware. More to the point, objects are shared and accessed concurrently by multiple users in shared environments. Therefore, the next two sections briefly explain these two aspects of sharing: referential and concurrent sharing.

Referential Sharing

When information is in paper form, and it is necessary to place the same document in multiple folders or other containers there is only one option: make copies. But maintaining copies of the same document consistently in multiple folders or containers becomes problematic. Besides the cost of the copies, which could be significant if the documents are large and complex, there must be some special business process in place to keep the copies up to date. If the copies are to be maintained consistently across geographically distributed organizations, the cost and process becomes larger.

When documents and information are in electronic form, the notion of a container, such as a drawer or a folder, holding either documents or other containers is still valid. Putting things in those containers is, however, different in a virtual space. Placing the same identical document in multiple folders or containers is perfectly feasible with electronic documents and objects. In fact, a number of workstation operating systems—UNIX, System 7, OS/2 and others—have built this capability in to the system itself. The idea is to referentially share a document or an object in general. With referential sharing, multiple container objects can be the "parent" of the same object. This is illustrated in Figure 2.28. The same document is placed in multiple folders. Also the same folder is placed in multiple folders. And because the object is identical in both folders, accessing the object through one path and, then making changes will automatically be reflected in the "reference" to the object which gets accessed from another path or through another folder or container. Referential sharing is very relevant to groupware systems where the same document must be kept up to date in various containers that span heterogeneous distributed environments within an organization.

If the underlying distributed object system is powerful enough, then from the user perspective, all users accessing the same logical object will do exactly that—access the same logical object. Of course there could be various implementation alternatives in the underlying system to achieve this, especially in distributed environments. If the bandwidth of the networking communication is high—for example, if the WANs are connected through T1 or T3 links—then physically only one copy of the object needs to be maintained. However, if the distributed network is connected through either modems or communication networks where on-line access is either slow or expensive, then other technologies such as replicated databases could be used.

Location Transparency

Ideally, the user should not even worry about the location of the objects in a network. In other words, all the information—documents, containers, and so on—in an organization should be accessed through a single "view"—the enterprise view of the organization. In distributed databases, this concept is called location transparency.

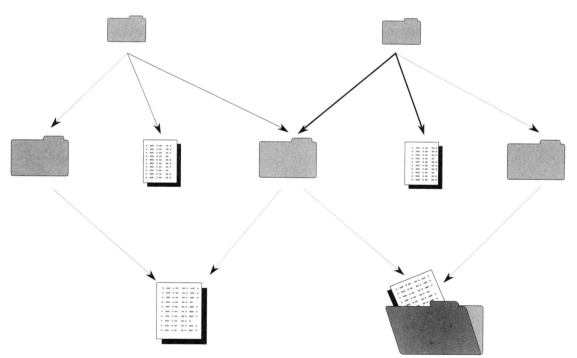

Figure 2.28 Referential sharing with folders and documents.

110 ■ Objects of Collaboration

As illustrated in Figure 2.29, all the members or users of the organization have the same view of the enterprise information warehouse. The folder at the top of the figure is viewed by all users (Helen, Sidney, and Joe), who share a common "view" of the distributed information warehouse. The enterprise information user deals with a consistent view of the enterprise data. How the objects are physically mapped onto various physical storage devices in different nodes and how consistency is maintained is immaterial to the user. There are physical implementation details and alternatives.

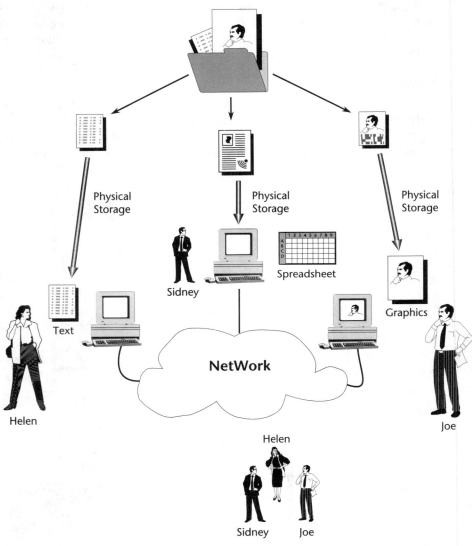

Figure 2.29 Location transparency.

Concurrent Sharing

One of the most important features in database management systems is concurrent sharing. Database management systems, including object-oriented databases, allow the same object space to be used by several people at the same time. In order to control the concurrent accesses, database management systems use various concurrency control and transaction management techniques. Concurrent sharing is extremely important in groupware systems. It provides a powerful and efficient mechanism for collaboratively accessing and sharing information.

Before explaining the benefits of concurrent sharing, consider some of the ways in which information is exchanged through one of the most popular groupware systems: e-mail. If special care is not taken to make sure that the same document or object is routed between various nodes of a network, routing documents through an e-mail package—or a messaging transport mechanism in general—could cause many problems.

Consider the scenario in Figure 2.30. Here, user 1 (Helen) sent a document to user 2 (Joe). There are now, effectively, two copies: the copy in user 1's machine and the copy in user 2's machine. Actually there is (at least) a third copy—the one in the e-mail or messaging database. When user 1 launches the application for the document in order to view it, she creates another copy on her machine. If changes are made to this document and user 2 makes changes to his copy of the document, there will be three versions of the document floating around, and potentially everyone who receives the document could have a different version. In fact, if user 1 decides to send the document one more time with additional changes, user 2 and others receiving the document could get really confused. They would need to create some mechanism to keep track of all the copies and versions. Often, users have "naming" and directory schemes. Of course, each user has his or her own scheme and strategy to keep track of document versions.

The underlying fundamental problem is that when routing—unless care is taken and the e-mail system supports it—it is copies being routed. The alternative is of course to route references and have a complementary document management checkout/check-in model to work together with the messaging system. The messaging system notifies and alerts users that they need to look at a certain document. The actual accessing and management of the document—the same document—is handled by a document management system or the underlying file server. The same object is accessed and shared concurrently by multiple users. Sometimes a system prohibits others from accessing the document if someone is already in the process of accessing that document. In other cases, users will be warned that they can only read the document since it is already checked out by someone else. The key point is that it is the same resource, whether object or document, is being accessed concurrently.

To be used effectively, a groupware database that supports concurrent sharing should include the following:

(a) Security: This is an extremely important issue. Since objects are shared concurrently, the danger of compromising strategic and critical business information becomes a crucial issue. There are several aspects to security. One deals with the

112 ■ Objects of Collaboration

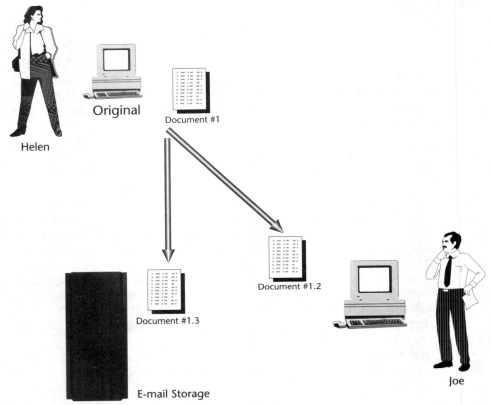

Figure 2.30 Problem of proliferation of copies of e-mail documents.

various access privileges on objects. In other words, for a given object such as a document, some users or groups may be given permission to update the document while others may be given permission only to read the document. The granule of the access privilege is also important. Perhaps the simplest and most straightforward are the access privileges granted for entire documents or, at even a coarser level, entire directories. Even network file systems implement this feature, where certain directories are visible only to a select few who have that privilege or sufficient security clearance to access the directory. The granule of the security, however, could be much smaller, perhaps to the level of objects such as cells in a spreadsheet, fields in a form, or paragraphs in a word processor file. In some cases, users are allowed to annotate a document without being able to modify the original document. Another aspect of security is encryption. The idea of electronic encryption (and it has many variations and implementation alternatives) is similar to having a lock on a door or cabinet. Only those who have the "key" can access what is inside. For electronic objects the "key," of course, is (in most cases) a password.

(b) Check-out/check-in model: Concurrently shared objects must be first "checked-out" from common areas or libraries, operated upon and then checked-in. If the process goes smoothly and the object is updated, a new version of the object is created. If anything goes wrong (either because of transaction, system, or user conflicts) the transaction can be aborted, the locks released, and any updates on the checked-out objects undone.

(c) Sign-off: Another important application in groupware, especially those that attempt to replace paper-based processes, is the ability for upper management to sign off on documents. These documents could represent, for instance, a new hire, a loan approval, a purchase approval, an expense authorization, and so on. In the paper office environment, the sign-off of the upper manager or responsible person appears as a signature on a piece of paper. In an electronic groupware system, there are many mechanisms to guarantee that the sign-off happened. Many systems attach electronic passwords to the document or sections in a document, whereas others actually show either the scanned or electronically generated signature of the manager or responsible person. In terms of concurrent sharing, the key point is that the sign-off should appear on the same concurrently shared document being "sent around" for approval. This is especially important if multiple parties need to sign off on the same document.

(d) Versioning: Access to previous states or alternate states of objects is an inherent part of many applications. Application domains that require access to the evolution of object states include engineering design applications (such as Computer Aided Design, Computer Aided Manufacturing, or Computer Aided Software Engineering), Office Automation (for document management), as well as more traditional financial or accounting applications. In these applications, the same object undergoes multiple changes or state transitions, and it is often desirable to access or investigate previous states or versions of the object. For example, consider the chapters in this book. Each chapter underwent an evolution. For some chapters, we kept various versions, which differed in organization, content, and emphasis. The final version often was an integration of different components of previous versions. We found it extremely useful to keep the previous versions and use parts of them in subsequent versions. This often happens in document management and for complex document systems. Database management systems provide all the necessary primitives such as transaction control, concurrency control, recovery, and so on to support concurrent sharing of objects in internetworked environments. Database management systems are discussed in more detail in Chapter 3.

SUMMARY

This chapter covered some of the most important applications and object types used in groupware system. The emphasis was primarily on the various groupware system documents and information types to be authored collaboratively, shared and accessed concurrently, annotated and commented on, or authorized. A recurrent theme throughout this chapter (and throughout the book for that matter) is the fact that most groupware applications group-enable existing popular applications such as word processor documents, spreadsheets, or forms.

This chapter also provided a brief overview of the concepts and advantages of object-orientation. In particular, it was explained how objects encapsulate both structure and behavior. The structure of objects is represented through object attributes as well as content. The behavior deals with those operations users can perform on objects.

Brief descriptions of most of the application types used in groupware products were also given here. Additional object types discussed in the chapter included multimedia types and forms. Special emphasis was given for explaining the importance of forms in groupware.

Increasingly, graphical user interface platforms are moving to document-centric environments. This is in contrast to the application-centric approach which has been more popular in the past decade. The transition is very subtle, and for most users the difference will not be very dramatic or significant. It is, nevertheless, a very important transition, especially for groupware. Two significant efforts are the OpenDoc standard by CILabs and OLE 2 by Microsoft, both of which were described in this chapter. With OpenDoc and OLE 2, compliance users can create compound documents that can contain parts from many different applications. The parts can interact with one another, and users can compose arbitrary part hierarchies, as long as the applications follow certain protocols. The more generalized concept of containment—hypermedia—was also covered with an emphasis on the most important differences between hypermedia and compound documents. As compound documents evolve, a number of the features contained in hypermedia systems will become incorporated into compound document environments. The chapter also discussed other container types, such as folders and cabinets.

Finally, the chapter provided a brief summary of various issues involved in the concurrent sharing of the object types discussed. These notions will be clarified and expanded in the succeeding chapters of this book.

3

Client/Server Architectures and Collaborative Computing

Groupware systems can be characterized as products that allow workers to collaborate by searching for, organizing, and sharing information. One of the foundation technologies that enables information sharing is the client/server architecture, which is the hottest recent trend in the development of advanced information systems. Client/server architectures provide a computational model. As an enabling technologies for groupware systems, client/server technologies are driven by user need for more efficient ways to share and access information.

Client/server architectures emerged in the mid-1980s, in the realm of shared files and databases, riding the wave of popularity of local area networks (LANs) as well as file and database server technologies. Today, the client/server concept is often considered a synonym for using graphical user interfaces on client nodes to access relational databases and database servers. Although this model reflects much of what is typically sold as client/server, it is nevertheless too narrow a view for such an exciting emerging market.

DEFINING CLIENT/SERVER ARCHITECTURES

Basically, a client/server architecture exists whenever a client system makes requests of a server system. Figure 3.1 presents a simple illustration of a client making requests to a server. The "system" can be a module, a process, a program, or any other entity which can, in the case of clients, make requests, or, in the case of servers, respond to requests. A client/server model is often mapped onto hardware platforms where the servers are specialized network nodes that provide services; the clients are workstations that provide the user with graphical user interfaces to access the services of the server nodes.

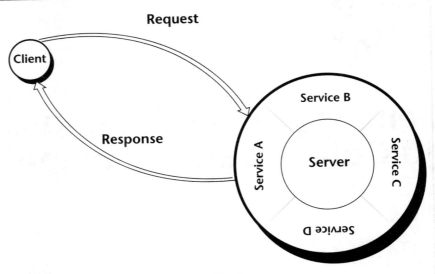

Figure 3.1 A generic client/server architecture.

A common definition of client/server is, therefore, an architecture that allows applications to access data stored on a LAN-based database server. This is illustrated in Figure 3.2 where the clients and servers reside on different physical nodes (machines). There are distinct advantages for users with those architectures where the server stores shared resources and services. The foremost advantage is that the client/server technology allows groupware applications to optimize the utilization of hardware and software resources at both the front end (the client computer application), and the back end database server (providing a centralized "repository" of shared database information). Other advantages include the parallelism that can be achieved through delegating server tasks thus freeing up the client nodes to concentrate on optimizing the user interface or interaction. Client/server architectures improve the performance of shared office data accesses in a LAN environment, and allow more users to access the same data, often using their existing PC software.

Fine-grained and Coarse-grained

The architecture illustrated in Figure 3.3 extends the client/server concept shown in Figure 3.2; it has multiple servers on a local area network, including a file server, a database server, a fax server, and a messaging server. These and other types of servers are explained in more detail in subsequent sections of the chapter. For most client/server applications and architectures, the local area network provides backbone system connectivity. As LANs find broader acceptance in business enterprises, users discover new ways to concurrently use and share data and resources. The client/server architectures where client nodes execute graphical user interface (GUI) front-end applications for accessing data or resources on server nodes are very popular and important, but represent only one model of client/server computing.

Defining Client/Server Architectures ◾ 117

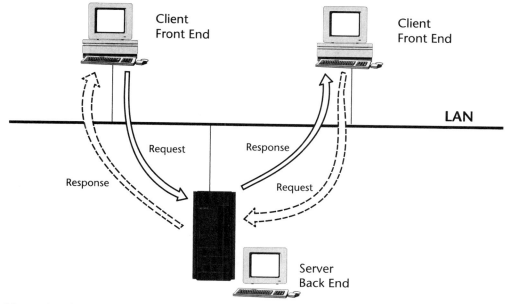

Figure 3.2 Client/server mapped onto physical nodes on a network.

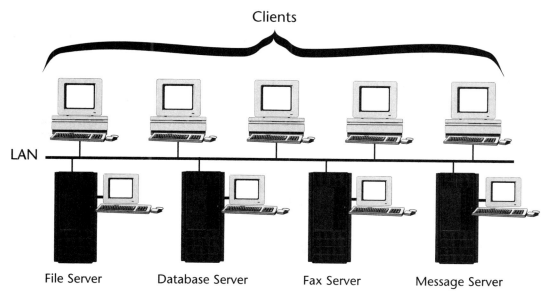

Figure 3.3 A coarse-grained client/server architecture with multiple servers.

The mapping of server and client nodes to physical hardware nodes is considered a coarse-grained client/server architecture. The server node could be a file server, a database server, or even a mainframe or supercomputer. There are many more interesting possibilities and architectures with medium- or fine-grained client/server architectures.

To repeat, client/server architectures exist whenever a client system makes requests of a server system. Nothing in this very simple definition precludes having smaller client/server systems or having both the client system and the server system on the same workstation.

Client/server computing is much more common than many people think. Every user of a word processor or a spreadsheet is using a service and, hence, a server. When you spell check a document, a spell checker server is being activated and provides the spell checking service to you or the word processor that invokes it. Similarly, calculating a formula in a spreadsheet is a service provided by the calculator "engine" embedded in the spreadsheet application. Therefore, generalizing the definition of client/server to any type of relationship between two modules or program component or objects allows for a much more consistent and flexible understanding of client/server computing.

Of course in these examples both the service and the client requesting the service are executing on the same processor. There is nothing which precludes the client and servers from executing in various "threads" or light-weight processes (light-weight processes can execute concurrently, however the resource overhead of switching between light-weight processes is much less). More importantly, both server and client workstations are witnessing the proliferation of multi-processor systems. In other words, even with smaller objects and fine-grained client/server computing, the clients and servers can be executing on different processors, or different processes, or threads.

Therefore to summarize:

(a) Clients and servers can be either large systems such as database management systems or smaller objects such as graphics elements or spell checkers.

(b) The clients and servers can execute in the same process, as different processes on the same computer, as light-weight processes on the same computer, as processes in a multi-processor system, or as different processes on different workstations or servers.

(c) Because of (b) it is possible that the same server (hardware) system or workstation can contain or execute client and server processes for different services or requests.

Object-orientation and Client/Server Architectures

Figure 3.1 illustrated two objects, one requesting services from another, and the other responding to these requests. Objects in object-oriented systems typically encapsulate or hide their implementation details, as discussed in Chapter 2. The key point is that, when objects communicate with one another, they operate as client and server. Figure

3.4 shows three objects sending messages to each other. Object 1 received message 1 and sent message 2 to object 2. In turn, object 2 sent message 3 to object 3. Object 1 could, for example, be a fax server that receives a fax (message 1) and in turn sends the fax to an optical character recognition (OCR) processor to determine the destination of the fax. The OCR could then determine the recipient and send it (as message 3) to the destination object. The fax server is requesting from the OCR process the recognition of the fax image. The fax is the client and the OCR is the server. The OCR is sending the recognized object to its destination "server."

The fundamental modus operandi of object interaction is client/server. Any object responding to a message is acting as a server. The object sending the message is the client. Of course, as Figure 3.4 illustrates, the same object can act both as a server and a client. Since anything and everything is an object in an object-oriented environment, client/server relationships range from coarse-grained to fine-grained objects. A text paragraph is an object, as is a circle in a graphic, and an entire database server.

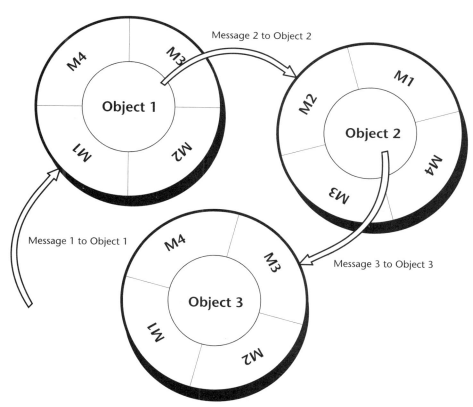

Figure 3.4 Objects send messages to each other.

Component Computing and Client/Server Architectures

Recent developments with component architectures, models, and standards are also object-oriented and, hence, primarily client/server architectures. Various standards have evolved and been implemented in the past few years which deal with component objects and interoperability between applications. Recall from Chapter 2 standards such as OpenDoc from CILabs, endorsed by Apple, IBM, WordPerfect, Novell and other large companies, and OLE 2, designed, endorsed, and implemented by Microsoft.

To elucidate the underlying client/server interaction, Figure 3.5 shows a pie chart requesting data from a spreadsheet application—essentially linking the two applications, with the spreadsheet acting (more or less) as the server providing the data.

Through compliance with interoperability standards, application components or parts can interact with and maintain various relationships with other parts. For example, an application object could be a part of another container object or linked to another object. When objects interchange information, are contained in other objects, or are linked with other objects, the underlying architecture is client/server because these objects are providing interfaces or services to other objects. Put simply, since object-oriented interaction is fundamentally client/server, the interoperability platforms such as OLE 2 and OpenDoc are essentially client/server implementations.

Of course, within OLE 2 and OpenDoc, there are several other standards and implementations as well as client/server specific architectures. For instance, the underlying technology for OpenDoc is System Object Model (SOM) from IBM. There are several such standards including: DSOM, which is the distributed version of SOM (also

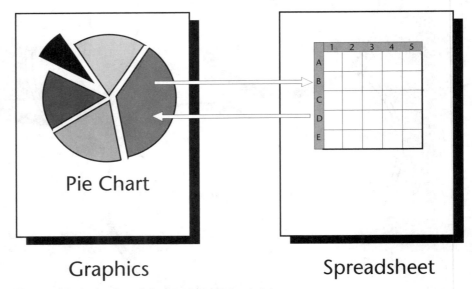

Figure 3.5 A pie chart linked to spreadsheet data.

from IBM); Distributed Object Everything (DOE) from Sun; Distributed Object Management Facility (DOMF) for Distributed Objects from NeXT; and more. Underlying many of these technologies is an important consortium called the Object Management Group (OMG).

The emergence of the OMG group and the participation of a large number of companies in its standardization effort resulted in many interesting ideas and implementations, the most notable of which was the Object Request Broker standard (OMG, 1991). The Common Object Request Broker Architecture (CORBA) allows a wide variety of "objects" to interact in a distributed environment. The architecture allows a client object to perform a request from a server object. The system is responsible for locating the object's implementation and satisfying the request. Since objects can span networks, CORBA has the potential of providing a very powerful and general distributed object management capability. A number of the enabling technologies mentioned (such as SOM) are actually implementations of CORBA.

NETWORKING

Understanding networking is very important for developing coarse-grained client/server applications. Since servers and clients are connected through networks, networking is a requirement for client/server architectures. End-users need to be "on the network" in order to concurrently share or route information.

Many issues are involved in implementing client/server groupware applications on internetworked distributed architectures, and in networking workstations and accessing services on various servers located on local and remote networks.

Network architecture should support the necessary communication bandwidth for services offered by internetworked workstations to be usable and effective. Networking here does not simply refer to local area networks, which are discussed in the following section, but also includes enterprise networking involving internetworked local area networks, wide area networks (WANs), and metropolitan area networks (MANs).

There are a number of alternatives for networking architectures. These options have serious ramifications for the overall performance of the network and therefore, by extension, the performance of the groupware applications that use the network as its communication medium. Identifying performance bottlenecks is a crucial networking issue, as the bandwidth requirements of some groupware applications are considerable. A prime example is videoconferencing.

Cabling is the physical transmission medium that connects network nodes. This is changing, however, as wireless networking is fast becoming a reality. Wireless technologies can use cellular modems, microwave, and infrared technologies. As the so-called information superhighway also becomes a force, it will consist of many different media, including TV cabling, broad-band intelligent digital networks, fiber-optic networks, ATM networks, satellite connectivity, and others.

Access has evolved beyond physically connected workstations. In all likelihood, information access over networks will happen much more frequently via "smart" telephones, personal digital assistants, interactive TVs, and other less "conventional" nodes. Again, whether for the corporate worker, individuals, or households there is the promise of access to almost unlimited quantities of information. On the shadow side, the potential also exists to create unheard of bottlenecks on the Internet and other carriers that are helping to connect this global internetworked village.

Bandwidth, response time, and throughput of applications on the network are only a few of the issues in networking. Others include security, connectivity, recovery from crashes, administration, interoperability, support of standards, and so forth. The following sections discuss a variety of issues and standards related to local and wide area networks.

Local Area Networks

The emergence of local area networks during the latter half of the 1980s brought major changes in business computing. Previously, business computing was the exclusive domain of centralized mainframe/minicomputers, presided over by expensive centralized MIS (Management Information Systems) departments. The advent of LANs, combined with phenomenal increases in PC computing power, brought about the radical decentralization of corporate information management.

Basically, a LAN is a group of computers and workstations, connected through cabling, and covering a limited geographical area. The workstations can communicate with servers or network nodes and with each other. A LAN, therefore, enables a variety of independent devices—servers and clients—to communicate with one another over a shared cabling system. The most crucial issues for local area networks include: bandwidth, or the network performance in terms of communication speeds; reliability, or the availability of the network and its ability to quickly restart in case of crashes; security, or access control for users or applications on the network; and bottlenecks, or points of congestion that affect the bandwidth and/or reliability of the network.

Both performance and the perceived response time of a network by the user are extremely important considerations. The proper choice of cabling and network architecture is crucial for the local area network to support the bandwidth requirements of the groupware application. Otherwise, the networking application could fail at considerable expense. Therefore, at least part of the success and acceptability of groupware solutions depends upon the fundamentals of the physical media.

Consider again Figure 3.3. The workstations and server are connected via a cabling system. The basic types of cables are: unshielded twisted pair, shielded twisted pair, and coaxial and fiber optic. Increasingly, wireless local area networks and communication between workstations and LANs are gaining acceptance. Some cabling and network architecture concepts are discussed further in the next sections.

A typical LAN connects from one to several hundred workstations. Through the use of bridges and gateways, LANs can be internetworked, providing access to an almost unlimited number of nodes. Each LAN can contain several nodes, providing various services to the client nodes on the network. The concept of a server is basic to the network. A server, which contains the hardware and software needed to provide services, offers a centralized and shared location for that service. The server sits at a location remote from the user, providing both multiuser and multitasking access to the shared network objects. As illustrated in Figure 3.3, servers range in functionality from generalized servers, such as file servers that provide a variety of services, to specialized and dedicated servers, such as database servers, fax servers, or messaging servers.

Cabling

To repeat, three basic varieties of (physical transmission) cables are available: twisted pair, coaxial, and fiber optic. Twisted pair and coaxial both use copper as the medium for signal transfer. Twisted pair is the oldest cabling technology, and has been used mainly for telephone connections. There are two major types of twisted pair cables, shielded and unshielded. Shielded twisted pair has a layer of insulation wrapped around the two twisted wires. Unshielded twisted pair, or normal telephone cabling, has no such insulation. The shielded cable is more resistant to interference, allowing for greater transmission speeds and distances between nodes. It is also more expensive.

Coaxial cable has long been used for cable television connections because of its ability to simultaneously handle a large number of signals, that is, different channels. Each channel runs at a different frequency and therefore doesn't interfere with the other channels. Coaxial cable consists of four different pieces. A solid metal wire forms the core of the cable and is surrounded by insulation. A tubular piece of metal screen surrounds the insulation. An outer plastic coating completes the cable. Coaxial cable supports very high bandwidths, making it an excellent choice for LANs that have a great deal of network traffic. Coaxial cable is also quite resistant to interference and can carry signals for a long distance, allowing nodes to be spread throughout an office.

In terms of bandwidths, twisted wire pair cable transmission rates are between 1 Mbps and 4 Mbps. Coaxial cable, on the other hand, can have rates of 4 Mbs, 20 Mbps, 40 Mbps and beyond.

Fiber optic cable is the most recent addition to the network cable family. It has unique characteristics, since light pulses instead of electrical signals are used to carry the data. These characteristics include immunity to electromagnetic interference, enormous bandwidth, and the ability to carry signals over very long distances. The Fiber Distributed Data Interface (FDDI) standard specifies networking bandwidths at the rate of 100 Mbps. Fiber cable consists of a core fiber enclosed in glass cladding. A protective outer coating surrounds the cladding. Light Emitting Diodes (LEDs) are used to send the signal down the optical fiber. A photodetector is used to receive the signals and convert them into a digital computer format.

Topologies

A LAN can be configured and organized in a number of ways. Network configurations range from centralized, where a single network mainframe computer performs all processing for users connected at remote sites, to fully distributed, where the processing is distributed among multiple remote sites. Typically, the LAN of the 1990s uses a distributed topology.

124 ■ **Client/Server Architectures and Collaborative Computing**

Major network topologies are grouped into the six types illustrated in Figure 3.6: star, point-to-point, multipoint, hierarchical, bus, and ring-based. The bus and ring configurations are most commonly used for LAN topologies. These six topologies are:

Star: Star is an example of a centralized architecture. The main computing site acts as the hub of the network. Each remote site gains access to the main site via a single communications line.

Point-to-point: Point-to-point networks are simple in design. A client node is attached to a single processing computer via a communication line. The client node may be used in either an on-line or a batch processing mode.

Multipoint: Multipoint networks are an extension of the point-to-point configuration. Instead of a single client node attached to the server, multiple nodes may be attached. Each node may be connected directly to the server via its own individual communications line or may be multiplexed together via a single communications line.

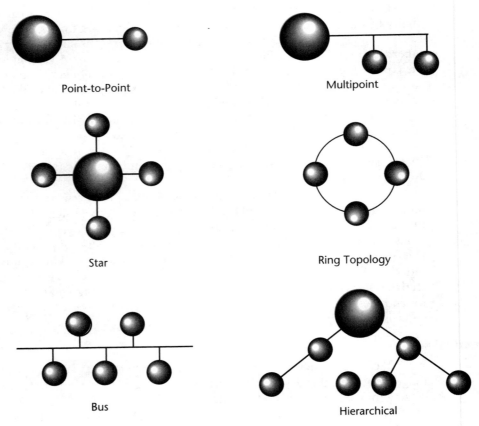

Figure 3.6 Network topologies.

Hierarchical: Hierarchical networks are an example of a fully distributed topology. Hierarchical configurations use the notion of one or more mainframes at the top of the hierarchy each of which has a midrange computer tied into it, which in turn has mini- or microcomputers tied into it. Each node has its own processing power and may access the resources of those nodes higher or lower on the hierarchy.

Bus: Bus structure topologies also are distributed architectures. The bus structure uses the concept of a central backbone communications line with arms or nodes connected off the backbone. As the signal traverses the backbone via a coaxial, fiber optic, or twisted pair cable, all nodes on the system listen to the signal to determine if it is intended for that node. This topology is flexible, allowing each node to attach to the network anywhere along the backbone. Ethernet is a fine example of bus structure topology. Ethernet networks are expected to be one of the most widely used in next-generation office environments. Platforms such as UNIX are almost exclusively based on the Ethernet topology. Ethernet is also becoming quite popular in PC-based networks with Windows or Macintosh (System 7.X) workstation operating systems. An Ethernet network cables multiple network station together so that they may communicate. The network nodes are connected at intervals to one long main cable. Ethernet speeds are typically in the 10 Mbps range, and a new technology called "fast Ethernet" is offering speeds in the range of 100 Mbps.

Ring: Ring structure topologies, also distributed in nature, use a closed loop, or ring, methodology. Each node in the ring is connected to the node on either side. The main advantage of this topology is speed of transmission, and the algorithms for avoiding and detecting data collision and garbling are simple. Ring systems typically use a token passing algorithm for resolving which packet of data goes to which node. The familiar token ring is an example of this structure. IBM's token ring is one of the most popular LAN architectures. The token ring is based on the network technology called token passing. A token on the network defines the address of a poll in a distributed polling list. Each device on the network must be polled. This polling is performed in a serial fashion around the ring. As the polling of a network device occurs, the station that has received the token has the opportunity to transmit data. The token is, in other words, the transmission security key of the network. Only the node that has received the token may transmit information on the network.

Networking Protocols and Standards

In 1977, the International Standards Organization (ISO) gathered a committee to investigate the compatibility of various pieces of network equipment. This committee lead to the development of the Open Systems Interconnection Reference Model (OSI). The OSI model defines seven layers of network functionality, whose purpose is to provide a concise network model, thereby allowing equipment from competing companies to coexist on the network. Figure 3.7 illustrates the OSI model, and the layers of OSI are described in the upcoming sections.

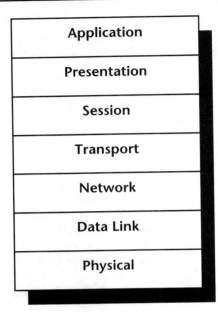

Figure 3.7 Open System Interconnection (OSI) reference model.

The Physical Link (Layer 1)

The main purpose of this layer is to transmit data through a physical medium (cables). It is responsible for moving the raw bits on the physical communication medium. The physical link layer deals with the hardware base of the network, including such items as cabling and network cards. The other six layers are implemented via software, but this layer is primarily hardware based. This layer handles the mechanical and electrical behavior of the hardware.

The Data Link (Layer 2)

Layer 2, the data link, defines the protocol for accessing and sharing the physical layer. The function of this layer is to get the data packaged and transmitted reliably from one node on the network to the next. The concept of token passing and signal collision detection belong to this layer.

The Network (Layer 3)

Layer 3, the network layer, is defined for networks that require routing mechanisms to pass packets among the nodes. This layer handles all translation of logical addresses onto physical addresses. LANs do not require this layer if they broadcast the information to all nodes on the network.

The Transport (Layer 4)

The transport layer provides the low-level connection functions for the network. This level is involved with sending and receiving packets, error detection and correction for packet transmissions, and packet flow control. The transport layer is responsible for the quality of end-to-end communication and making sure that the packets are sent successfully. If there are problems, this layer is responsible for requesting retransmission.

The Session (Layer 5)

The session layer provides for the establishment and termination of data stream connections between two or more nodes on the LAN. The main purpose of a LAN is to allow two or more nodes to connect to each other for the purpose of communication. This linking process is known as "starting a session." This layer deals with programs running on different machines and establishes the sessions between them.

The Presentation (Layer 6)

The presentation layer provides information translation services for the application layer. Reformatting and data conversion is performed at this layer. More specifically, this layer handles data unpacking, character set conversion, protocol translation, encryption, and decryption.

The Application (Layer 7)

The application layer is the highest level of OSI, and provides network services to users or client applications accessing the LAN. This protocol layer is responsible for the initiation and reliability of data transfers through its higher-level application function interfaces.

Data Transport Protocols

Data transport protocols provide a means of passing data from one network node to another. To demonstrate where these higher-level protocols fit into the network model, this chapter examines IPX, SPX, NETBIOS, APPC, and TCP/IP protocols.

Internetwork Packet Exchange

Internetwork Packet Exchange (IPX) is the underlying protocol for Novell's network software. It is a close adaptation of the Xerox Network Standard (XNS) packet protocol. IPX only supports datagram style messages (said to be "connectionless"). A datagram message is one that is never acknowledged by the receiver. This means that IPX does not guarantee the delivery of a packet, nor that packets will be delivered in any particular sequence. IPX corresponds to the network layer of the OSI model.

Sequenced Packet Exchange

The Sequenced Packet Exchange (SPX) is a session level, connection-oriented protocol. A session level protocol is a logical connection between two workstations in which delivery of a message is guaranteed. A connection must be established between two nodes before information may be exchanged. This protocol is part of the transport layer of the OSI model, one layer higher than IPX. Both IPX and SPX were developed by Novell.

Network Basic Input/Output System

Network Basic Input/Output System, more commonly referred to as NET BIOS, was originally developed by IBM for their PC-LAN product. NET BIOS supports both datagram and session level connections. NET BIOS corresponds to the network layer, the transport layer, and the session layer of the ISO model. This is a higher-level protocol than either IPX or SPX.

Advanced Program to Program Communications

Advanced Program to Program Communications, or APPC, is also a session level protocol developed by IBM. APPC provides a high-level mechanism for two programs to communicate with one another on a peer-to-peer basis. It is based on IBM's Logical Unit 6.2 or LU6.2, which provides a mechanism for creating logical connections between workstations. APPC corresponds to the session level of the OSI model.

Transmission Control Protocol/Internet Protocol

Transmission Control Protocol/Internet Protocol, or TCP/IP, was designed by the department of defense (DOD) for their ARPANET wide area network. TCP/IP is a layer of protocols, and is similar to NET BIOS and APPC in that it provides point-to-point guaranteed delivery communications between workstations. The IP is a datagram-based protocol whose functionality is similar to Novell's IPX. TCP/IP is entirely different than the OSI model; it defines its own layers and is not compatible with the OSI model.

Network Operating Systems

A Network operating system (NOS) is the software that operates the network, providing a host of services to network users. File storage and retrieval, file sharing, network administration, user and resource security, name space resolution, resource accounting, and electronic mail are all functions of the NOS. Other advanced features such as transactions and location transparency may also be part of an NOS.

An NOS should not be confused with such communications protocols as NET BIOS, as it provides functionality far beyond a particular communications protocol. An NOS can provide support for several different communications protocols. Three methodologies are currently used in the creation of network operating systems:

1. The first methodology relies on building the NOS from scratch, tailoring the NOS to the task at hand. The most popular network operating system, Novell's NetWare has taken this approach, building a NOS from scratch. NetWare has by far the largest market share for LANs and NOSes—some estimate to be as high as 70%. Instead of a general operating system with networking capabilities, Novell has designed an operating system that is specific to networking. NetWare supports DOS, OS/2, and Macintosh clients. It also supports the largest number of peripherals. And NetWare has always been the front runner when it comes to robustness. NetWare has an efficient mechanism for handling non-preemptive tasks or requests. High priority tasks for instance, run to completion although they can release resources under certain conditions to allow other tasks to go through. Another interesting feature in NetWare is the support of NetWare loadable modules (NLMs). These are basically processes executing on the file server and providing services to NetWare clients. For instance, there are NLMs for fax servers, database servers, and messaging servers to name a few. Since NetWare allows these NLMs to execute at the same level as the core operating system, NLMs tend to be very efficient services. The disadvantage is in the possibility of crashes and loss of data integrity due to ill-behaved NLMs.

2. The second methodology retrofits an existing operating system with the required functionality so that it may act as an NOS. Banyan has adopted this second methodology. The Vines operating system runs on top of the UNIX operating system, and therefore has the look and feel of UNIX. Several versions of UNIX are supported—including System V (the original platform), SCO UNIX, and others. Despite many advanced features, however, Banyan has managed to claim only 4 to 6 percent of the market share. The Vines emphasis is on enterprise-wide networking with support for a very large number of nodes, geographically dispersed servers, and telecommunications. A typical Vines installation supports 500 to 1000 nodes with a dozen or more servers. Managing such a large system can be very problematic, but Vines is very strong in the WAN area. Vines has the built-in ability to connect to host mainframe and minicomputers, a very attractive feature to the large corporate user. Banyan is attempting to differentiate itself by building its next-generation server platform based on symmetric multiprocessing, providing the ability to distribute various tasks among multiple CPUs.

3. The third method creates a separate software component which is responsible for the network functionality, and is loosely (but more closely than two) tied to an underlying existing operating system which provides the NOS layer with access to the resources of the machine. Microsoft's LAN Manager was developed following this third methodology. LAN Manager was originally built for OS/2, handling all the network requests. LAN Manager's share of the marketplace is harder to determine, due to the many OEMs that sell LAN Manager, but it is estimated at 20 percent.

Microsoft has implemented the LAN Manager on Windows NT as well. This increasingly popular server operating systems supports Windows 3.1 16-bit as well as 32-bit applications. LAN Manager offers a wide array of services from high-powered client/server features such as the SQL Server to simple resource sharing or messaging services. The other benefit is the support of the high-powered graphical user interface inherent in Windows NT which make using the various native utilities, such as Network Administration easier. Microsoft has addressed many of the past failures of LAN Manager, but LANMAN has yet to prove itself in the marketplace. A few other omissions, such as the lack of support for Macintosh workstations and the lack of server-to-server bridging, still need to be addressed. The performance tuning of LAN Manager is tedious at best, making it difficult to achieve a performance rating near Novell's NetWare.

Security and Authorization

The basic need to increase productivity by facilitating access to a growing body of information is driving the growth of local area networks. The ability of LANs to provide a growing user group with greater amounts of information with increased ease is what networking is about. But, therein lies the great paradox: One goal is to provide easy access to vital information to a large user group. The other goal is to ensure that the shared information and resources are protected and secure. Authorization defines the access rights of the users on the networks. It determines which resources a user has access to and which operations he or she may perform on those resources. Authorization and security go hand in hand.

Local area networks present a unique set of problems when it comes to security. First of all, the level of information distribution presents more avenues by which that information may be accessed. Any user sitting at a workstation can gain access to information. Unless that user's access is carefully monitored, he or she can gain unauthorized access to sensitive data. This possibility, along with the ability of remote terminals to gain dial-in access to networks, make for a difficult security situation.

Security and authorization starts with the concepts of users and passwords. The network administrator defines every new user for the system, gives the user an account, and assigns to that user the rights to various network objects. To gain access to the system, a user must log on to the system, specifying both user name and password.

There are various methods of ensuring password protection. The first is to require a password of minimum acceptable length. Another is to make sure all passwords are encrypted and are always sent across the network in encrypted form. A third way of ensuring passwords is to make all passwords unique. Finally, it is necessary to require the periodic changing of passwords.

In conventional network environment files, directories and devices can be protected by access rights. The user can be given specific privileges, such as read, write, update, delete, modify attributes, perform directory searches, execute, create, and supervisory privileges at the file level, or the directory level, or both. Files themselves may be further protected by defining attributes like read-only which prevent that file from being modified.

Some systems support a security database responsible for assigning and tracking the privileges of objects on the network. All objects, such as users and files, must be registered in the security database. The database then determines who is allowed to access which objects. Novell supports this notion by using a database called the Bindery, which binds network objects with a list of authorization rights.

All network operating systems support some form of security. Many people believe that to be sufficient; others have added third-party security software that adds security measures such as enveloping the workstation in a protective shell or encrypting all information, including filenames, on the network.

Wide Area Networks

In contrast to local area networks, wide area networks (WANs) cover larger geographic areas—city blocks, entire cities, even continents. Many different hardware/software components and new technologies are involved in constructing wide area networks. Some of the internetworking technologies used in high bandwidth transmission include T1 with multichannel transmission rates of about 1.544 Mbps; T2, which is about four times faster than T1; T3, which is about 28 times faster than T1; microwave links; X.25 links; and others. Figure 3.8 illustrates a wide area network with T1 lines connecting LANs to a WAN.

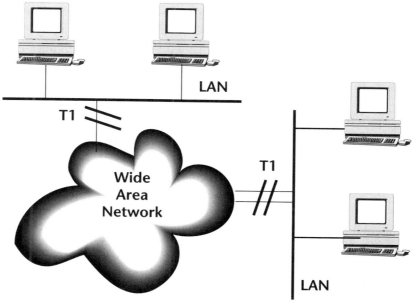

Figure 3.8 Workstations connected to wide area networks through T1 lines.

The technologies, protocols, and standards involved in constructing wide area network capabilities are quite different from those for local area networks. Designing LAN-WAN interconnects is expensive. Therefore, designers of groupware applications must be aware of the underlying technologies and options for wide area networks. One tremendous advantage of WAN is that it provides high-bandwidth communication, and the leased lines can be permanent. With emerging technologies such as ATM (discussed next) the distinction between LANs and WANs is blurring.

One alternative to these emerging—and expensive—solutions and leased line solutions is for corporations to rely on the less expensive "sometimes connected" option, which is based on regular phone lines and periodic connectivity to route messages or update replicated databases. This is the solution found in many groupware applications that use Lotus Notes.

ATM

The Asynchronous Transfer Mode, or ATM, is the latest introduction for high-speed WAN connections. ATM refers to a high-bandwidth, low-delay switching and multiplexing technology. ATM is receiving a considerable amount of attention from people in the equipment and carrier industries. The main attribute of ATM is its ability to support a wide range of voice, video, data, and imaging applications on the same public network. The key technical considerations of ATM are that it:

- Uses a cell-based protocol.
- Supports transfer rates between 10 Mbps to 1 Gbps (Giga byte per second).
- Uses either switched or permanent virtual circuits.
- Supports applications using voice, images, full-motion video, and animation.
- Is capable of providing the services to enable the information superhighway for both companies and individuals.

ATM provides a flexible framework for WAN connectivity. A generic ATM platform enables service integration using a limited number of connection types and multipurpose network interfaces. ATM is capable of supporting such services as frame-relay, circuit emulation, switched multimegabit data service (SMDS), and cell relay.

Cell relay is a key capability of ATM, and makes applications such as videoconferencing possible. A user of cell relay supplies appropriately configured cells that are destined for remote delivery. A cell consists of fixed length information units. The ability to support switched connections is another feature of cell relay. With the inclusion of signaling protocols, the user is able to specify on a per-connection, per-instance occurrence where the information should be delivered. This can occur with either point-to-point (one-to-one) or multipoint (one-to-many) destinations. The transfer of cells can take place in a bidirectional fashion (information flow in both directions).

Cell relay includes provisions for traffic management which may be individually applied to each connection. The type of control applied depends on the quality of the particular connection and the state of the network. The ability to define levels of cell loss which can be sustained for compliant cells is integral to the concept of cell relay service.

Cell relay service can be used on enterprise networks that use public communications channels, private communications channels, or a hybrid of the two. Cell relay service is designed to handle a variety of multimedia applications such as videoconferencing, animation, document imaging, CAD/CAM, groupware, multimedia e-mail, among others.

The notion of virtual circuits allows bandwidth to be allocated on an as-needed basis. ATM provides support for two types of virtual circuits, switched virtual circuits (SVC) and nonswitched permanent virtual circuits (PVC). Switched virtual circuits provide maximum flexibility in establishing dynamic connections. SVC is similar to telephone service. It allows the user to establish a data connection with anyone attached to the network. The user tells the network with which node to establish a connection. The network then supplies the user with a virtual label for the destination, which is valid for the duration of the connection. The virtual label is then included in the cell header which informs the network of the cell's destination.

PVC allows connections to be created between fixed users and/or locations. PVC is similar to the concept of a dedicated line. The user defines the intended destinations at the time a particular network service is subscribed. The user is provided with a fixed set of virtual labels which are locally significant. These virtual labels are included in the cell header.

ATM supports services that require both circuit mode transfers (characterized by a constant bit rate) and packet mode transfers (characterized by a variable bit rate). Video data typically generates a constant rate data stream (32 frames per second). Standard data transmissions, such as database queries, generate a highly variable transfer rate requirement. ATM is designed to handle both varieties of transmission in an efficient manner through the use of connection-oriented and connectionless services. Connection-oriented services are ideal for support applications such as videoconferencing and real-time multimedia. Connectionless services are ideal for supporting burst-rate LAN traffic for such applications as document imaging and groupware.

Frame Relay Service

Frame relay service is another service that should be considered in the context of supporting groupware applications. Frame relay service is a connection-oriented service operating at multiples of 64 Kbps or 1.544 Mbps. Frame relay is designed to reduce network delays and increase bandwidth utilization while trimming communications equipment costs. Increased efficiency and reduced delays are achieved by performing error correction on an end-to-end basis rather than a link-to-link basis. This makes the protocol much simpler than traditional packet switching.

Frame relay is a multiplexed service providing connectivity between network devices such as routers and between users and a public network. It is capable of supporting multiple sessions over a single physical access connection. Frame relay provides both private virtual circuits (PVC) and switched virtual circuits (SVC) as discussed, along with the concepts of ATM. The initial offerings of frame relay provided only PVCs.

The speed of frame relay makes its usefulness for multimedia networking marginal. Other drawbacks include the fact that frames are dropped during congested periods and must be retransmitted. Frame relay also suffers from a variable delay rate. Some experiments have been performed on providing videoconferencing over FRS, but the success has been limited. Nevertheless, applications that are on the lower end of bandwidth use should be able to effectively use frame relay.

Switched Multimegabit Data Service

Switched multimegabit data service (SMDS) offers a connectionless, high-speed, high-quality packet service at local area network speeds over a metropolitan or wider area network. SMDS is, by definition, a technology-independent service designed for LAN interconnection. In fact, an ATM network can provide SMDS services.

SMDS provides guaranteed delivery of variable length data packets. It requires a router specifically designed to support its protocol. Network access to SMDS is from a dedicated link, typically from a local area network to the public MAN. Initial SMDS services operate between 1.544 Mbps and 44.736 Mbps. Future plans call for SMDS to incorporate SONET (defined and discussed in the next section) and operate at 155 Mbps. Further, the high bandwidth, scalability, and packet switching makes international SMDS networks a possibility.

SMDS does not explicitly support data stream synchronization. This limitation requires applications to perform their synchronization by multiplexing the data, audio, and video streams and presenting the combined streams to the network for delivery. Since SMDS is a packet-based connectionless service there can be variations in the delay of the stream delivery. This delay is small but should still be taken into account.

SONET

The Synchronous Optical Network (SONET) was designed by Bellcore to be a standard optical interface to ease the burden of interconnecting the various types of fiber-optic transmission systems used by backbone and interoffice networks. The SONET transmission standard was developed by the ANSI and T1 committees. The initial definition included only the North American series of digital services at 1.5 Mbps and 45 Mbps. The standard was later modified to include the European service transmission rates of 2, 8, 34, and 140 Mbps. It guarantees that different vendor equipment can be hooked anywhere along the fiber cable and will be able to communicate with the rest of the network.

The basic SONET signal, operating at 51.84 Mbps, has been designated the Synchronous Transport Signal 1 (STS-1). This signal is composed of digital frames, each 125 microseconds in length. STS-1 is divided into two portions. The first is designated for transmission overhead; the second is used to carry the information to be transmitted. The portion of frame that contains the data is referred to as the Synchronous Payload

Envelope (SPE), which is capable of transporting high bandwidth data such as digital video and sound. It can also provide low-speed telephone services.

SONET consists of three layers: the section layer, the line layer, and the path layer. The section layer transports the Synchronous Transport Signal frame over the underlying optical fiber. The line layer makes use of the section layer to transport STS synchronous payload envelopes over the fiber. The path layer deals with transport issues for network services.

ISDN

The Integrated Services Digital Network (ISDN) is an attempt to provide global transport of voice, data, and video information. The International Telephone and Telegraph Consultive Committee (CCITT) defines ISDN as:

> A network in general evolving from a telephone Integrated Digital Network (IDN), that provides end-to-end digital connectivity to support a wide range of services, including voice and nonvoice services, to which users have access by a limited set of standard multipurpose user-network interfaces.

This means that ISDN, in its barest form, is a proposed set of protocols that combine circuit-switched voice services with packet-switched digital service into a fully integrated digital network. ISDN is an enhancement to the telephone local loop that allows both voice and digital computer data to be transported on the same twisted pair cable.

ISDN is a fully digital network that provides a host of standard data transport and telecommunications services. The major purpose of ISDN standards is to define how users access network services via common protocols. Indeed, ISDN was conceived for the purpose of integrating separate services into a single, logical network. Then, instead of having a cable hook-up for your TV, twisted pair for your phone, and a separate connection for your local area network, ISDN ties all of these services into a single entity, which gives you the capability to exchange data between them. For example, you could dial up a catalog company and request information on a piece of equipment. A picture of the equipment would then be transmitted to your TV screen. You could then fill out a purchase order on your computer and transmit it to the catalog company along with payment.

ISDN allows a user workstation or LAN bridges and routers to connect with one another by using digital telephone circuits. ISDN's basic rate interface (BRI) provides two 64 Kbps bearer channels (B channels) and one 16 Kbps signaling channel (D channel) that is generally referred to as the 2B+D interface. The two B channels are multiplexed inversely (traffic is split into two channels and then reassembled on the receiving end). This provides a bandwidth of up to 128 Kbps. ISDN can also be configured to allow X.25 packet data to be transferred on the D channel at 9600 bps.

Unfortunately, most telephone companies cannot currently deliver two combined 64 Kbps channels. They will instead deliver the ISDN BRI over two 56 Kbps switched circuits for a maximum effective bandwidth of 112 Kbps. Communications between telephone company exchanges can currently occur at a maximum of 56 Kbps.

ISDN also supports a higher-speed interface known as the primary rate interface (PRI). PRI consists of 23 64 Kbps B channels and one 64 Kbps signaling channel. The combination of 24 64 Kbps channels requires the use of a digital T1 circuit running at 1.544 Mbps. This limits the availability of PRI to major metropolitan areas. Hopefully, this limitation will be removed in the near future.

The configuration requirements for ISDN connectivity between two nearby LANs involve a multitude of components. First, the BRI service must be obtained for the local telephone company for each site that is to be connected, and, unfortunately, availability of ISDN service is spotty.

ISDN is far superior to standard computer modems for communications. Setup and connect time is generally 200 to 300 milliseconds when connecting within the same telephone company central office. It will take 2 to 3 seconds within the same metropolitan area and up to 10 seconds for connecting across the United States. Modems, on the other hand, can easily require 45 seconds or more to connect, making them unusable when trying to dynamically add bandwidth. Furthermore, modem transfer rates will max out at 28 Kbps (using V.FAST specs). The ISDN BRI, using compression, can easily achieve transfer rates of 400 Kbps. The digital nature of the ISDN connection also ensures better quality and performance over modems.

CLIENT/SERVER ARCHITECTURES: FILE SERVERS

The file server was the original enticement that brought about the LAN revolution. As the number of personal computers in the office grew, so too did the need to exchange information between those computers. The original primitive method of transfer, used to this day, is known as "sneaker net," which got its name from the way users typically share files. For example: Bob needs a file that is on Anne's PC, so he runs over to Anne's desk, copies the file onto a floppy disk, runs back to his desk, and loads the file.

File servers, as the name indicates, were designed to provide file services to multiple users. Through files servers users can concurrently share resources, the most prominent of which are the data and commonly used peripheral resources such as printers.

A file server can be dedicated or nondedicated. A dedicated file server takes over all the resources and cannot be used as a workstation. A nondedicated file server acts as both a file server and a workstation; it provides a less expensive LAN solution but also suffers in performance. With the falling prices of PCs, nondedicated file servers are being used less often.

The computers that house file servers have undergone significant changes in recent years. The first computers were simple PCs that were undifferentiated from the workstation. As the complexity of the network operating system and the number of users grew, the need for specialized hardware became more evident. In response to this need, companies such as Compaq make PCs designed to house powerful file servers, or "super" servers. These computers can have gigabytes of storage, contain multiple CPUs to increase the computing horsepower, and incorporate new bus architectures for improved disk performance. Other companies, like Netframe, have abandoned the PC architecture altogether and have built entirely new architectures classified as super servers. Super servers are generally based on Intel's 486, Pentium microprocessors and PowerPCs. The basic variables that must be considered when looking at super servers are bus type, bus width, microprocessor speed, caching schemes, data redundancy, and error checking.

Partitioning Functions in a Client/Server Architecture

Figure 3.9 illustrates how, in a typical file server environment, the functionality is partitioned between the file server and the clients. The file server performs the file and block or page level I/O. It typically contains and manages multiple disk volumes that are concurrently shared by the clients. It also provides primitives for controlling the concurrent access to maintain the consistency of the concurrently shared information.

Semaphores (which are data structures used for synchronizing access between concurrent client requests) are provided by the network operating system to control the concurrent activities. Logical semaphores are used to lock various logical (versus physical) objects on the network. Client software can use logical semaphores to control access to various concurrently shared resources on the network.

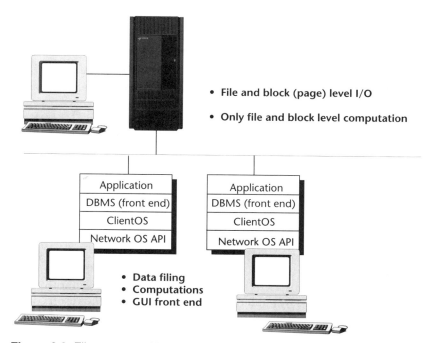

Figure 3.9 File server architecture.

File servers also support transactions. Briefly, transactions are programs executed either entirely or not at all. In the context of a file server, the transaction mechanism will guarantee that the pages of a file are consistently flushed to secondary storage. File servers deal with block or page level I/O, and the transaction mechanism is used to guarantee atomicity at the file page level. Most database management systems provide additional transaction mechanisms for DBMS objects.

File servers provide caching or buffering mechanisms to allow faster response of disk I/Os by the file server. The file server system can preload some additional data when performing reads and thus make the data available for subsequent requests. Buffering is useful because, especially for data that is accessed very frequently, the users making concurrent requests will often have their requests satisfied through the cache, without incurring disk I/Os.

The execution of the application is usually done on the client side. For instance, if three clients are attempting to execute a database management system software, then it is done on the clients' CPUs and not the server's. This is true for any application executing on client nodes. In fact, in most cases the file server appears as a disk drive or volume. Therefore, the application's data is stored on the server, whereas the executable is executed on the client (the executable's files could be stored either on a local client disk or server). As indicated earlier, there is server software that executes on the file server, but it provides file I/O, buffering, locking (through semaphores), concurrent access, backup, and authorization functionality.

An interesting trend is to have executable modules on the server side. As mentioned earlier, Novell has introduced NetWare loadable modules (NLM) which are executables on the server side. Oracle and Sybase are providing NLMs for their database server systems to execute on the file server. Several relational databases, object-oriented databases, and other services such as messaging and fax services are offered as processes or executables on file servers.

CLIENT/SERVER ARCHITECTURES: DATABASE SERVERS

With the growth of client/server computing, database servers have become an important part of the LAN environment. Database servers maintain the information base of the network, provide concurrent access to the information base, and maintain the consistency and validity of the data. Transaction control of database accesses is another key feature, although, as mentioned earlier, file servers also provide transaction and locking support at the file and I/O block level.

In the most straightforward implementation, a database server is a separate node on the network that provides an interface to client nodes. The interface, which is often in the form of a library of functions, allows client applications to submit their requests to the database server and retrieve from the server the results of their queries.

A fundamental difference between a file server architecture and a database server architecture is that with a database server, the client workstation passes a "high-level" request, in message form, to the server. This is in contrast to the block I/O and file access requests in a file server. The database server processes the request and then returns only the results. This is illustrated in Figure 3.10. The database request can be a complex query, which greatly reduces network traffic, since the code that processes the query and the data both reside at the same location.

Functions Performed on Database Server Nodes

Unlike the file server approach where all the DBMS executables are done on the client side, with the database server approach, the database management system's engine is executed on the server side. The following are some of the functions that can be performed by the database server:

(a) Integrity: The database server takes an object-oriented approach when it comes to integrity constraint. Rather than performing the integrity in the application programs that execute on the client side, the database server approach allows the debates designer to define integrity constraint with the data or as a constraint on the objects. The constraint itself, whether it is in the form of an explicit constraint (such as a range constraint, a NOT NULL constraint, or an existential constraint) or through triggers, the constraint is verified and executed on the server. It is associated with the persistent objects and its verification resides and is executed with the objects.

(b) Security: File servers have security, but at the file and directory levels. This means that various groups and users can be given or denied access to particular files and/or directories. Some directories might not be "visible" to certain users. Database servers, on the other hand, have the potential of providing security at the

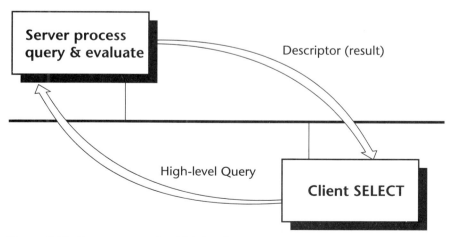

Figure 3.10 Server processing high-level query statements.

object level. Users can be granted various privileges on logical objects and collections of objects. The privilege might be read or update operations, create operations, or to execution of methods associated with persistent objects. With a file server architecture, the file server software checks and imposes the file and directory level security, executing on the file server node. With the database server architecture the software that stores and executes the database server security resides and is executed on the database server node.

(c) Recovery: Some file servers, such as Novell, have transactions support at the file I/O level and thus the file server can return to a consistent state if, for example, a client's I/O got interrupted (say the client crashed, which is quite common with PCs). Database servers and database management have much more sophisticated operations. In most database server architectures, support of recovery for logging and backing up the database is performed by the database node.

(d) Concurrency control: File servers provide very basic concurrency control mechanisms. One of the most often used techniques is to provide read or write privileges on files and/or directories for different users. With database servers, complex concurrency control algorithms can be implemented on the server side. Both optimistic and pessimistic algorithms can be supported. Furthermore, since the server recognizes the object structures, much finer granularity "object" level concurrency control can be supported. This could greatly enhance the performance of concurrently executing transactions.

(e) Method/query execution and optimization: Perhaps the most important functionality (or at least the most visible) is the execution of various queries, accesses, and update operations or methods on the client side. Object-oriented and relational database management systems that utilize a database server approach have software on the database server side which executes queries. If the query is a declarative statement expressed in SQL, then the database node might even perform query optimization to determine the most efficient access plan for executing the query. In some object-oriented and relational database servers, the system allows storing pre-compiled and optimized queries so that clients' requests need only provide parameters to get their results evaluated very quickly without incurring the overhead of compilation and optimization.

(f) Clustering and indexing: Clustering organizes objects that are frequently accessed together into "clusters" such that the I/O overhead of accessing a group of objects is minimized. Indexing also optimizes access times through maintaining index structures on the most frequently accessed attributes of collections. Both clustering and indexing are very important performance-related components of a database engine. Query optimizers often use the clustering and indexing information to analyze and find the best order of execution of queries. The database server also incorporates the storage manager module of a DBMS. The storage manager supports the clustering and indexing of persistent object collections. Clustering stores objects or records which are frequently accessed together in the same storage extent. In particular, the "children" of a compound or complex object are stored in some specified (depth-first or breadth-first) order. The software that performs the clustering executes on the database server, although clustering can be supported (and often is) with file server architectures. The same is true for indexing. With file servers, the indexing is performed on the client side, (although some file servers do provide executables on the server side). With a database server, the software to perform the indexed searches and updates executes on the server nodes.

Other functionalities and features of the DBMS executed on the database server nodes include buffer management, data verification, multimedia object management, and meta-data (schema) manager. The functions just listed demonstrate that engine features of the database management system are executed on the database server node. But a DBMS in general has other components as well. Generally, in addition to the DBMS engine there are: the application programming interface to the engine and various libraries and tools such as graphical user interface tools for application development. Figure 3.11 illustrates an architecture where all the "engine"-specific database functionality, including query processing, is performed on the server node.

Be aware that not all database servers have their functions executing on server nodes. In fact, especially in the case of object-oriented databases, some of the higher-level functions such as query processing could be executing on client workstations.

Distributed Databases

So far file servers and database servers have been discussed in the context of a single LAN with either a single file server or a database server. There can, however, be more than one file server or database server on the network. Furthermore, the LANs could be internetworked through bridges and gateways so that data stored on remote networks can be accessed from local clients. It is conceivable that users might wish to have either a combination of data on different servers or a distribution of a large database to various nodes in an internetworked architecture of LANs. Such an architecture is illustrated in Figure 3.12.

With architectures where multiple databases exist on different nodes in a LAN or on different LANs, there is a constant need to combine information from various databases. Furthermore, due to performance or locality, it is also desirable to distribute the data of large databases across various nodes and sites, hence the need for distributed databases.

With distributed databases, the client sees one logical database that can consist of many physical databases distributed across server nodes of LANS. This is illustrated in Figure 3.13.

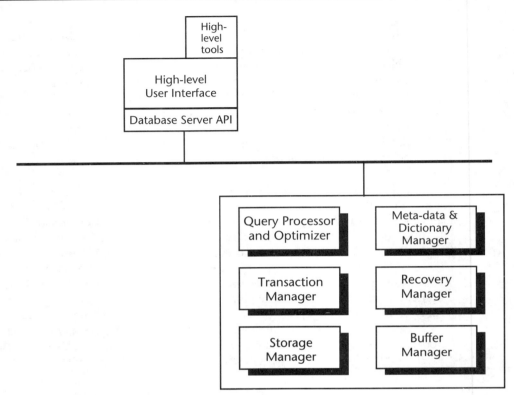

Figure 3.11 Various modules of database servers.

The discussion in this section is based on relational database technology, which is natural. The first distributed database prototypes were based on the relational model. Furthermore, it is only recently that relational DBMSs have proliferated enough so that the integration and/or distribution of database have become issues.

Approaches for Developing Distributed Databases

There are at least two approaches for developing a distributed database: a bottom-up approach, which integrates existing databases running on heterogeneous systems into a virtual, distributed database for global applications, while at the same time preserving existing applications that run against individual single-site databases; and a top-down approach, which decomposes a logically centralized database schema (against which all applications run) into fragments, and allocates those fragments to sites of a distributed system.

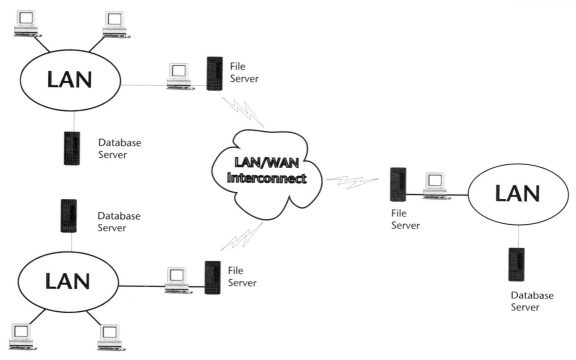

Figure 3.12 Distributed databases on internetworked LANs.

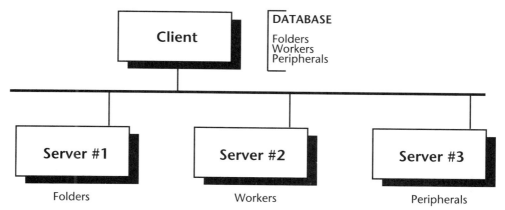

Figure 3.13 One logical database distributed across various servers.

Bottom-up Integration

The bottom-up integration approach is particularly suitable for enterprises with a decentralized organization and computation structure. The proliferation of departmental and personal databases in these enterprises is likely to have created islands of information in a heterogeneous hardware and software environment. In such a scenario, a heterogeneous distributed database can provide a virtual, integrated view of the existing databases. Because enterprises have invested tremendous amounts in their existing DBMS environments, it is important that the development of a heterogeneous distributed database preserves existing single-site applications as well as the autonomy of departments owning the existing databases.

An elegant and efficient way of integrating existing databases is through generalization. Generalization is a bottom-up approach of software construction. For instance, if one site contains all the information on salespeople and another site has all the information on developers, the two classes and their extensions could be integrated from the bottom up through generalizing them to, say, an office worker class.

Top-down Distribution

The top-down distribution approach is suitable for a homogeneous environment where uniformity can be exploited to improve performance and reliability. This approach is particularly appropriate for distributed databases developed from scratch, such as when a new database is designed for use in a distributed environment. It is also appropriate when a single-site database has grown to exceed the operating limits of its existing host database system, and it becomes desirable to reconfigure the existing single-site database into a distributed database that spans multiple homogeneous sites. Under this approach, both fragmentation transparency and replication transparency are supported. In addition, global data integrity constraints can be automatically enforced by the distributed database system, since all applications will be operating against the same global database schema.

Within the top-down design approach, the global conceptual schema of a distributed database is defined first. Integrity constraints can be specified on a schema without regard to how they would eventually be allocated to sites in the distributed database system. Next, data objects in the global schema are optionally divided into fragments. Subsequently, each object or object fragment is allocated to a site or, optionally, is replicated at multiple sites. Finally, physical database design (such as choosing the set of indices to be maintained) is performed on each allocated object or object fragment.

The most important reason for using the top-down approach to design a distributed database is to maximize the data independence in applications. With all applications working against the same global database schema, it becomes possible to alter dynamically the allocation of data to sites in the distributed system to optimize for the prevailing access pattern without incurring the high cost of application conversion. To fully exploit this flexibility, the database designer needs tools to monitor access patterns as well as to evaluate the merits of different data allocation strategies.

Characteristics of Distributed Database Systems

As discussed in Khoshafian et al., 1992a, the characteristics of a distributed database system can be measured along four dimensions:

- Autonomy
- Distribution transparency
- Heterogeneity
- Total isolation

Autonomy

Autonomy refers to the distribution of control. It represents the degree to which sites within the distributed database system may operate independently. When a distributed database is built on top of existing databases, an important measure of autonomy is whether single-site applications can continue to run.

One possibility is tight coupling among sites which presents the illusion of a single integrated database to users and applications. Each site in the distributed database system has complete knowledge of the state of the system and can control the processing of user requests that span data at multiple sites.

Distribution Transparency

Distribution transparency refers to the extent to which the distribution of data to sites (including the fragmentation and replication of logical data objects and their allocation) is shielded from users and applications. It represents the degree of freedom a database designer may have in distributing data to trade off storage cost, retrieval and update efficiency, and overheads for maintaining intersite constraints like fragment integrity and replica consistency.

Heterogeneity

Heterogeneity in distributed systems may occur in various forms, including hardware platforms, operating systems, networking protocols, and local database systems. Different hardware and operating systems may use different data representations for floating point numbers, different byte ordering for integers, and different encoding for characters. Additionally, different communication protocols may require the use of gateways, which are difficult to implement because of the differences involved. Finally, database systems may use different data models, thereby posing schema translation and query translation problems. Of course, the situation gets more complex because heterogeneity not only means integrating various relational databases, but also relational and object-oriented databases. Currently, relational database dominate, especially in business and office applications. Relational database with object-oriented features—sometimes called object-relational databases—or "purer" object-oriented databases are becoming increasingly popular and "mainstream."

Total Isolation

Another option is total isolation. Each site in the distributed database system is a stand-alone server and is unaware of the other sites. In this case, the distributed database system must be completely layered on top of the local systems, and its capabilities to coordinate and optimize activities that span multiple sites may be severely limited.

Distributed Concurrency Control

Concurrency control is necessary to ensure that multiple users do not interfere with each other. This problem is more complicated in a distributed environment than in a centralized environment. There is also one major difference: whereas intertransaction concurrency is not particularly important in a centralized system running under a single processor, it is imperative in a distributed environment if the presence of multiple processors is exploited for processing the same transaction.

Locking is widely accepted as the method of choice for synchronizing concurrent users. When transactions span multiple database servers, and when each server acquires locks on behalf of a distributed transaction in an incremental fashion, it is possible to run into distributed deadlocks that may not be detected by individual servers using local locking information.

Although some centralized database systems perform continuous deadlock detection, deadlock avoidance or periodic deadlock detection is more appropriate in a distributed environment because of the communication overhead for maintaining the locking information used to achieve continuous deadlock detection.

Distributed Transaction Management

A distributed transaction is a sequence of operations involving data from multiple sites that must be carried out as one atomic unit. Consider an organization that maintains separate department and corporate budgets. The department budget is included in the corporate budget; thus, spending for resources at the department level is also reflected at the corporate level. If a department withdraws, say, $5,000 for a purchase, it should also be withdrawn from the corporate database. The withdrawal must either happen at both databases or not at all. If only one of the databases reflects the withdrawal, there will be an inconsistency. Each withdrawal is executed as a transaction at the database site. As far as the user is concerned, the transaction is the one that updates *both* databases (which can be thought of as subtransactions).

The problem of distributed transaction management is to make sure that each transaction is executed in an atomic fashion, and that updates performed by one transaction are seen by another transaction in their entirety. If data replication is supported transparently, then mutual consistency among the replicas and continued accessibility in the presence of site failures must also be addressed.

Two-phase Commit

The problem of atomic commitment is to ensure that all participants of a distributed transaction either commit or abort. The fundamental requirements for achieving atomic commitment are as follows:

- Each participant must arrive at the same commit or abort decision.
- Each participant has veto power; unanimous consensus is required for a commit decision.
- Each participant must not reverse its decision once a unanimous decision is reached.

Rather than requiring each participant of a distributed transaction to communicate with all other participants to determine individual success/failure status, and allowing each participant to independently arrive at the same commit/abort conclusion, the conventional approach to achieving atomic commitment is to use a two-phase commit protocol. This protocol involves the use of a transaction coordinator (usually one of the transaction's participants) to collect the necessary status information from all participants of a distributed transaction. During the first phase, the coordinator requests each participant to prepare to commit the transaction. The coordinator then waits for votes from the participants. If all votes are positive, then the coordinator instructs all participants to commit; otherwise, the coordinator instructs those participants who voted yes to abort. (Those who voted no can go ahead and abort their local portion of the distributed transaction without waiting for the final decision from the coordinator.) In general, prior to casting a yes vote, a participant is free to unilaterally abort the transaction. However, once a participant sends a yes vote to the coordinator, it must wait for the final commit or abort decision from the coordinator and then terminate the transaction accordingly.

Figure 3.14 illustrates the types of messages sent during the two-phase commit protocol. When the user issues the COMMIT WORK statement, the first phase begins. The coordinator then sends PREPARE messages to the participants in parallel. Each participant that is willing to commit the transaction force writes a prepare log record before returning OK to the coordinator. The participant is then said to be in the prepared state. If a participant is not willing to commit the transaction, it force writes an abort record and returns FAILED to the coordinator. Since each participant is allowed to veto the commitment of a transaction, a participant that votes no can go ahead and abort the transaction, release its locks, and forget about the transaction.

After the coordinator has received votes from all participants, the second phase of the two-phase commit protocol begins. If all votes are positive, the coordinator force writes a commit log record, moves to the committing state, and sends COMMIT messages to the participants. Each participant, on receiving the COMMIT message, force writes a commit log record, sends an acknowledgment to the coordinator, completes commit activities for the transaction (such as releasing locks), and forgets about the transaction. If at least one vote is negative, the coordinator force writes an abort log record and sends ABORT messages only to those participants that have voted positively. Each participant, on receiving the ABORT message, force writes an abort log record, sends an acknowledgment to the coordinator, completes the abortion of the transaction, and forgets about the transaction.

The purpose of requiring participants to acknowledge both COMMIT and ABORT messages is to make sure that they are aware of the final outcome of the transaction, before the coordinator forgets about the transaction. By force writing commit and abort log records, a participant never has to ask the coordinator about the outcome of the transaction during recovery processing.

Replication and Distributed Databases

Distributed databases, where a database is partitioned into various object sets and distributed on various servers on a network and even distributed networks, is one mechanism for handling data distribution. Another increasingly popular method for providing data availability in enterprises spanning multiple servers and multiple networks is data replication.

As discussed in the previous sections, to keep a database consistent, the underlying database management systems should support distributed transaction processing. In other words, distributed database transactions that update data from multiple sites storing portions of a distributed database need to cooperate in order to execute the distributed transaction and guarantee its atomicity.

With replication, the same data or database resides in different sites managed by different database management systems. The main problem of replicated databases is the synchronization of the updates, so that, as much as possible, all replicated databases have the same state or content. One popular method to achieve this is the master/slave model, where one database is designated as the master and the other replicated databases are slaves. With this model, all updates—such as inserting a new record, modifying values of an existing record, or deleting a record—are made to the master database. Subsequently the slave databases get periodically refreshed.

CHANGE MANAGEMENT

In most corporations, changes made to a document are important, and the evolution of the document needs to be tracked. In client/server architectures, users are modifying (making changes) concurrently shared objects and user modifications need to be "managed"—probably through a versioning mechanism. One way to do this is to store the previous versions of a document as well as the newly updated version. Thus, if a document has been modified several times, the system contains a set of documents representing each release of the document.

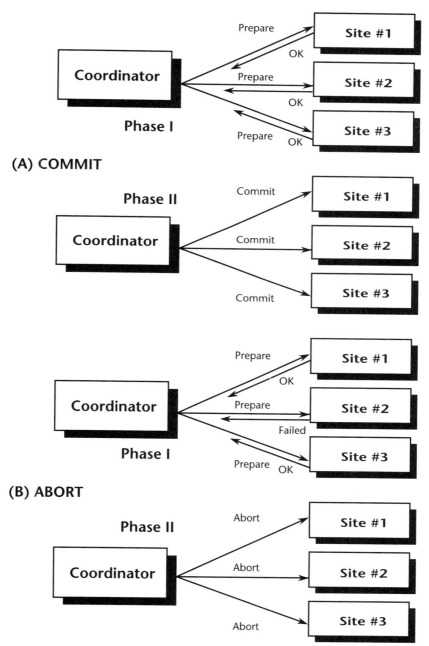

Figure 3.14 Two-phase commit protocol for distributed transactions.

Usually, the end user wants to access the most recent version of a document, and is provided that version by the system. When the user finishes updating the document, the updated document becomes the most recent version. This structure allows users to access any individual version of a document by naming a specific version as (v1, v2, v3, . . .), or by requesting a version using parameters such as the date of modification.

When several versions of a document exist in a system, the system must be able to determine the differences between two versions of a document. Version management can provide this functionality. Each document may consume large amounts of disk space, and tracking all versions of all documents can be very expensive, but several strategies can alleviate this situation. First, the system may provide a purge operation where older or selected versions of a document can be deleted. Alternately, older versions can be archived on a WORM or tape drive. Another strategy is to store the incremental changes from one version to another. When a specific version is requested, the system extracts the relevant portion of the document for that version.

If concurrent access to one document must be provided, a more sophisticated version management system is required. Up to this point, change management has been discussed with respect to documents deriving from one another linearly, as in Figure 3.15. To permit concurrent access to a document through change management, a more hierarchical change management is necessary.

In this scenario, each concurrent user creates his or her own branch of the tree. If only one user accesses a document, then only one branch is required. If another concurrent user requests a lock on a document, a new branch in the version management tree is created to track the changes made by the second user. Once several parallel branches have been created by different users, their efforts should be combined by merging the work done on the same document. This requires a mechanism for merging two separate versions of a document and recording a new version that includes all changes. During the process of merging, the software can decide how to handle changes made by the authors that do not conflict with each other. When any changes conflict, the end user should decide the result of the merge operation for that section of the document.

A hierarchical version management system provides a much richer mechanism for change management. For example, if a document provides information about a product, than information about each version of the product can be managed through a hierarchical version management system. Each version of a document may require minor changes. The change history of each version can have its own subbranch, and the end user can choose to merge the earlier changes into the most recent release of the document.

CHECK-OUT/CHECK-IN OF OBJECTS

Concurrently shared objects must first be checked out from common areas or "libraries," operated upon, and then checked in. The overall algorithm for accessing objects concurrently in client/server architectures is as follows:

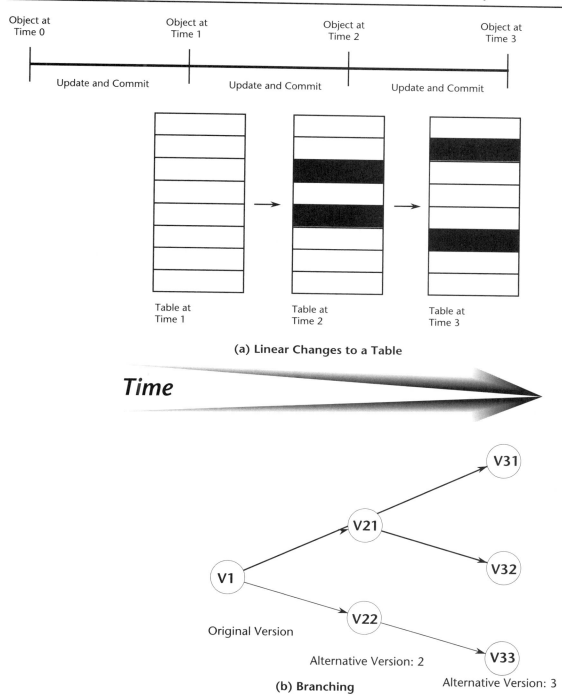

Figure 3.15 Linear historic versions versus branching.

1. Begin transaction.
2. Navigate or locate the object(s) to be manipulated.
3. Check out the objects with either read or write lock, depending on intent.
4. Manipulate the object(s), possibly updating it.
5. Check in object(s) back to common area (repository) possibly creating a new version.
6. Commit transaction.

If the process goes smoothly and the object is updated, a new version of the object is created. If anything goes wrong (either because of transaction, system, or user conflicts), the transaction can be aborted, the locks released, and any updates on the checked-out objects undone.

Figure 3.16 illustrates how the client/server architecture corresponds with an object repository and the office worker's workspace. Objects can be checked out by the following two techniques:

- Providing its unique identifier (its object number or key value).
- Providing various selection criteria.

The first strategy is obvious: The office worker simply checks out the object using a "handle." The second strategy involves performing searches and then checking out an object according to its attribute values or its relationship with other objects. For instance, documents in a folder created in WordPerfect can be checked out using the following pseudo code:

Check out Document D In Folder F1
WHERE D.Type = "WordPerfect"

Another important issue with respect to object check-out/check-in is the granule and levels of the objects. For example, when a folder is checked out, which objects have been checked out? When an office worker checks out folder F1, is he or she checking out all objects contained in F1? When a compound hypermedia document is checked out, are all the documents linked to the hypermedia document also checked out? Obviously, the process of checking out a document can imply a substantial amount of locking. Of course, in client/server architectures, the step of locking large objects reduces the concurrency and has a diverse effect on the throughput of the system. On the other hand, the process of checking in or checking out objects with a finer granule can incur a substantial overhead in locks and could even prohibit an office worker from accessing all the documents he or she needs.

Check-out/Check-in of Objects ■ 153

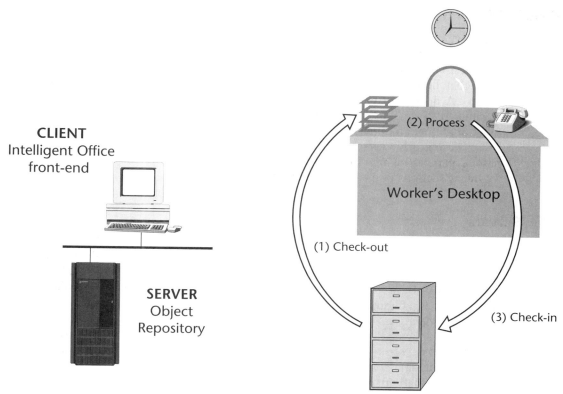

Figure 3.16 The check-out and check-in of objects from the repository.

Because an office worker has the most knowledge about what he or she needs to access, the office repository should provide the following alternatives:

(a) Given an object handle O, check out only O. Other office workers or applications cannot access or update the attributes of O and, if O contains other objects, they cannot insert or delete objects in O. However, they can access or even check out objects contained in O or reachable from O.

(b) Given an object handle O, check out O and all its immediate children. For instance, if O is a folder, this option will check out O, and all documents and/or folders immediately contained in O. The advantage here is that an office worker has access to all the objects contained in the folder, without locking the entire "universe" reachable from the folder.

(c) Check out all objects that are directly or transitively linked or reachable from the object handle. This option can be very useful for accessing self-contained hypermedia documents.

OTHER SERVERS AND SERVICES FOR COLLABORATIVE COMPUTING

Database servers and file servers are by far the most important types of servers and services for collaborative computing. Many groupware applications are actually built on top of basic file and database services. Most document imaging systems and document management systems are, for example, implemented on top of relational database servers. A document imaging system, at least on its storage side, integrates the functionality of a database server, which tracks information about documents, with the functionality of an optical file server, which stores the document images.

There are, however, a number of other server components besides file and database servers, which have become increasingly popular for collaborative computing. The following sections discuss some of these server types.

Video Servers

Recent advances in the computing power of PC workstations, compression technologies, and storage technologies have made feasible the use of video as a digital data type. Video data has, in the past, normally been stored at the local workstation on CD-ROM. This pattern of use has inhibited the development of distributed multimedia applications. There is, nonetheless, a very real need, as well as a growing demand, for shared access to video data. The same factors that impel the storage of data on network file servers and spawned the tremendous growth in client/server applications also drive the evolution of network video services: shared access, cost reduction, security, centralized management, data consistency, and redundancy.

The availability of video servers on networks becomes another enabling technology for a new breed of applications. Movies on-demand, videoconferencing, educational programming, home shopping, as well as interactive television programs such as travel documentaries, are but a few examples of future applications that would require the use of video servers.

Several technical problems limit the use of standard networks and file servers when dealing with video data types. First, video data streams can quickly saturate a conventional network topology. As few as two 150 Kb per second video streams will saturate a standard ethernet, while 8 to 10 such streams would overload a token ring.

Storage capacity has been another problem. Video requires huge amounts of disk space. A standard one-hour PLV compressed video clip requires more than 1 GB of storage. Most standard file servers have a limited amount of storage that they can address. Even a reasonably small video library would require several terabytes of storage space.

The performance of storage subsystems has generally been insufficient to meet the needs of video. Even sub 10 ms drives will become bottlenecks when attempting to pull off multiple video streams simultaneously. Generally, standard PC buses are insufficient to transfer huge amounts of video data at a continuous uninterrupted guaranteed rate.

Standard file servers cannot supply the functionality required by video. Video data must be delivered at a guaranteed continuous rate without interruption in order to avoid "jumpy" video presentation. Conventional file servers were not designed to provide continuous data stream service. Typically, file servers take advantage of the property of locality in file access by using appropriate caching mechanisms. In all cases, as the overall load against server resources increases, the response time for all users also increases. In order to prevent video glitches, a standard server must be limited to light loads, thereby defeating the ability to share video libraries by a large number of users and limiting their cost effectiveness.

New technologies such as FDDI-II and Fast Ethernet tend to remove the bottlenecks at the LAN level. Smart hubs allow a workstation to use the entire bandwidth of the medium to which it is connected. ATM, ISDN, and SMDS provide the needed technology at the LAN and WAN level. Performance-configured SCSI disk arrays combined with near-line optical jukeboxes also tend to remove the performance barrier of limited storage capacity. The remainder of this section discusses the extensions required to enable a file server to become a video server.

There are three major goals that a video server must achieve if quality video is to be satisfactorily delivered to the client.

Data Throughput

The foremost consideration is high data throughput. The nominal rate of delivery should be at least at a sustained rate of 150 Kbps. At the high end, a video server must sustain a rate of 1 to 2 Mbps, for each of the video streams supported by the server.

Data Storage

Second, the video server must support enormous volumes of information. For a video server to truly become a repository of video information, it must be able to support a multiterabyte file system. Even hundreds of gigabytes of storage is insufficient for a large number of video libraries.

Response Time

Finally, the video server must be able to provide a predictable response time. The server must be able to deliver more information to the client before the client empties the client buffer. This delivery rate must be maintained at a constant level. An empty client buffer will result in a jitter in the video sequence. The server must also be able to reject any new requests if servicing that request would cause existing video streams to jitter.

The high data throughput goal is achieved by using SCSI disk arrays which have been configured not for redundancy but for maximum performance by striping. The computer architecture must include at least a 32-bit high-performance bus. For example, on a PC, nothing less than a VL-EISA would suffice. A new high-performance SCSI is being developed called Wide-Fast SCSI. Wide-Fast SCSI provides a 32-bit performance-tuned version of SCSI which would be ideal for video servers. When Wide-Fast SCSI becomes widely available, it will be the standard for multimedia storage configurations.

Optical storage jukeboxes also could provide the needed storage capacity. Magnetic disk drives simply can't supply enough storage for a video library. Applications such as movies-on-demand will compete against the local video rental store. Movies-on-demand will therefore have to provide at least as many titles (several thousand) as the rental shop. This would place storage requirements at between 5 to 12 terabytes of video, far beyond the realm of (Direct Access Storage Devices) DASD. Furthermore, huge quantities of DASD storage are far too vulnerable to data loss. Optical storage is a very stable, archival media that is immune to head crashes. With data loss protected by optical media, the SCSI could be configured for optimal performance and not for data protection, thereby diminishing the I/O rates.

Optical jukebox technology provides near-line storage. Performance, however, is insufficient for a video server. When a video clip is requested it would first have to be preloaded to the DASD array before the stream could be sent to the client. A separate call to initialize video stream would have to be included in the video server API, but outside the time sensitive stream function calls. An optimized hierarchical storage management file system will be responsible for this staging.

The ability to maintain a predictable response time requires substantial redesign of the data file server. Predictable response time indicates that a video server must include a real-time interface for the video stream functions. The marriage of a real-time system with a file server enables a video server to provide constant data rates. The real-time logic could be implemented as a group of lightweight threads which share a common address space. These threads would perform functions such as disk I/O, listening for incoming requests, and sending and receiving network packets. Most threads could be implemented as nonpreemptive coroutines. Coroutines can suspend themselves while waiting for the arrival of a message, network packets, or the expiration of a timer. Threads that make OS level requests, such as disk I/O, that could cause the thread to be blocked, could be implemented as separate processes.

Disk I/O scheduling must be tailored to meet the real-time requirements of a video server. Disk access can be broken into cycles. Within a given cycle, all current video streams must receive their next buffer worth of video data. This cycle time dictates the maximum number of streams that could be serviced. Within a given cycle, all disk I/O requests should be scheduled to obtain the optimum I/O. One method for this is known as fully-sorted scheduling. For each cycle and for each disk, all disk blocks needed to service active streams are sorted into ascending order and processed in that fashion. If new requests arrive, and the maximum disk access capacity has not been reached, these requests could be added into the sorted schedule if those requests are beyond the current disk head position. Otherwise, these requests are sorted into a sub-cycle and processed after the full sorted cycle has been processed.

A viable video server must include admission control. The video server must reject any new request that would cause the real-time scheduler to start missing its deadlines. The video server should include real-time stream API function calls, including such functionality as load video (or initialize video stream), create video stream (start), play, record, and stop.

As mentioned earlier, video is becoming an increasingly important data type in many groupware applications. The availability of high performance video components and server, are important requirements for the successful implementation of groupware applications involving video.

Fax Servers

Fax services are increasingly becoming a popular method of transmitting information to remote sites. From simple, unintelligent fax machines requiring manual intervention to send and deliver documents, fax services have evolved to include automatic routing, workflow, and distributed access.

Fax servers are a natural extension of fax machines. Instead of requiring a fax machine to be physically present in the office, or else requiring that users must physically move themselves to a centrally located machine somewhere on the premises, a user could send or receive a fax directly from his or her workstation. Growing marketplace demand for this type of service has brought a variety of products that allow incoming or outgoing faxes to be generated from a fax server on a LAN or from a mini-mainframe centralized system.

Fax servers can be divided into two categories: LAN-based multiuser and mainframe transaction processing-based fax servers. Fax services are either application-based or part of a value-added network service.

Applications-based fax services (those that allow the user to send a fax from within a particular application) generally use the printer paradigm for faxing. This allows the user to write a memo or document and then send (print) the document to someone.

The LAN-based fax server consists of a fax board, which contains the fax modem, and possibly a graphics processor to enhance the performance of the fax process. The fax board could be placed directly in the network file server or in a dedicated workstation with specialized software which allows it to run as a fax server. Some implementations allow the fax server to run on a dedicated user workstation, but this method has performance limitations. The fax service would then be accessed through a FAX application, an application that is enabled to "FAX" (print) its documents, or through a scanner which first digitizes the paper document to be faxed.

Incoming faxes present a problem: how to route the incoming fax to the appropriate person. There is no standard for routing faxes. Printing and hand delivery is the manual solution, but this limits the usability of distributed faxing. Automated techniques include direct inward dialing (DID), dual-tone multifrequency decoding (DTMF), and optical character recognition (OCR). Using DID, the fax server converts DID routing information into a real network address and then deposits the fax into the users "in-basket." With DTMF, the sender must manually enter a network address, which is then converted from the DTMF format into the actual network address. The server then deposits the fax in the users in-basket. OCR depends on a standard fax form that contains either a network address or a user name which can be converted to a network address at a fixed location on the form. The OCR software converts the information into a usable routing address.

DTMF currently has weak international support. It requires the manual entry of routing information, manual intervention with existing equipment, and hardware modifications to the receiver. DID has the advantage of an existing standard but requires expensive DID service for the receiver, expensive hardware to operate, and has no international availability. OCR suffers from a high error rate and the dependence on everyone using a standard form. A lack of comprehensive standards is clearly hurting the functionality of multiuser fax services.

The ability to distribute a fax once it has been dropped in a user's in-basket is a feature that has just started to become available. Some sophisticated network fax packages include the concept of light-weight fax "workflow" into the fax routing capabilities. Workflow allows a fax to be sent to another user after the original receiver has finished with the fax, possibly adding some annotations. Complex rules could be established to govern how and when a fax is sent to other users. Given the popularity of faxing, fax servers will play increasingly important roles in groupware applications—especially as automatic routing and workflow integration become more mature.

Messaging Servers for E-mail Transport

Electronic messaging and e-mail is discussed in greater detail in Chapter 4. As explained there, an e-mail system consists of an e-mail front-end client component and a number of "back-end" or server e-mail services. The most important of these services are:

Transport services: Transport services typically execute either on separate (physical) server nodes or as processes on file servers or other multitasking nodes on the network. The responsibility of a transport server is to transport a message from one system to another—either on the same LAN, on different LANs internetworked through LAN-to-LAN bridges, or through LAN-to-WAN bridges.

E-Mail database servers: An E-mail database server can be thought of as an application of a database management system, containing the database of messages but also all the application programming interfaces for the e-mail client to store and access messages.

Directory services: Directory services provide services to translate user names to network addresses.

There also could be other servers or services associated with an e-mail system (such as administrative services for backup and restore). However, the three types of services just described are the most important for an e-mail back-end server.

SUMMARY

This chapter described client/server architectures and their application in collaborative computing. It explained various components, architectures, and features of local as well as wide area networks. The chapter also discussed the features of file servers and database servers. Other types of servers or services explained in the chapter include fax, video, and messaging servers.

The chapter also delved into more advanced topics such as distributed databases and various distributed database construction and concurrency control strategies. Besides database servers and the various server categories that are very important to groupware applications, this chapter also discussed a number of concepts that are features in a variety of groupware products—especially document management. These include versioning and the check-out/check-in models for manipulating objects concurrently.

4

Electronic Messaging and Mail Systems

Groupware deals with users working together as teams. Many types of groupware products support collaboration among workers and one vital requirement for collaborative work is the ability to share information and resources. Chapter 3 discussed this in the context of client/server architectures with special emphasis on the concurrent sharing of resources and information. Different file servers need to be able to search and access information efficiently. There are also other types of information servers, for example, database, video, and—the focus of this chapter—messaging servers.

The purpose of providing all of these services on networks is to give people fast and efficient access to resources. In the case of electronic messaging, the goal is to exchange and move information. In addition, users and organizations must be able to locate, organize, filter, file, and otherwise manage their shared data through a "store and forward" messaging infrastructure.

The backbone of the organization that makes this happen is the network. The networks may be simple LANs, or interconnected LANs, either within close geographic proximity or over wide area networks. Increasingly, with virtual offices, wireless networks are becoming more popular both in offices and in mobile computing. The communication options span phone lines, leased lines, ISDN, PBX, X.25—to name a few.

In many companies there is more than one LAN, and these need to be internetworked. LAN-to-LAN connectivity and LAN-to-WAN connectivity technologies and products used to be different but today these distinctions are starting to blur, especially with emerging technologies such as ATM. In general, WAN is much more complex than LAN or LAN-to-LAN connectivity. Connectivity issues for e-mail include transport and directory services within a corporation on internetworked LANs, interoperability of LANs and message interchange between heterogeneous LANs.

The increasing availability and affordability of internetworking allows for the electronic interchange of messages between computer users with varying degrees of physical proximity—between adjacent offices or across continents. One of the most elegant mechanisms provided by e-mail systems is that the same environment and products are used to interchange messages between workers in the same department, telecommuting, or on entirely different systems and in different locations.

Because people relate through a consistent interface, whether communicating with the person in the next cubicle or on the next continent, they tend to see all e-mail collaborators as a single unified group. The interaction and intellectual discourse with distant colleagues is no less immediate than with our closest neighbor. For the purpose of information-based collaborations, there is no difference in how people relate to them; therefore, within the terms of computer-mediated associations, they are identical.

THE POPULARIZATION OF E-MAIL

E-mail has been called the first successful groupware application. A special issue of *Communications Week* describing the "Rise of Networking" in the past decade identifies e-mail as the hottest technology in 1984–1994 decade:

> More than any technology since the invention of the telephone, electronic mail has changed the way business people communicate. The proliferation of interoperable e-mail systems and services has made it possible to send a message across the hall or across the world—and get a response in minutes or in hours . . .

Through the proliferation of local area networks, which are fast replacing centralized mainframe-based systems, PC-, Mac-, and UNIX-based electronic mail systems are becoming increasingly popular. However there are still a number of popular e-mail applications for mainframe based systems. One recent trend is to incorporate increasingly advanced e-mail communication between various platforms and environments. Although e-mail systems were designed to enable communication between individual users, groups of users, and special users or groups (such as administration), increasingly e-mail is also being used for communication between users and applications, and between applications.

In addition, e-mail connectivity and networking through popular systems such as the Internet present an electronic medium over which various bulletin boards, forums, and interest groups regularly and frequently communicate. Often the communication is as simple as opening an electronic "envelope" or sending a note to a destination electronically. In UNIX- and other command-based systems (such as DOS), e-mail is initiated by commands such as the following:

Mail John
Mail Marketing

These commands invoke the mail application, which then allow users to type in the message or include a file containing a document that the user would like to send, or both.

In graphical user interface (GUI) operating environments, mail typically is invoked by clicking on an e-mail application icon. Often, the e-mail application will notify the user if a new message has arrived through audio or visual alerts. Once a message is sent, the recipient of the message can choose to throw the message away, print, or store the message or reply. Users can keep on sending messages and replies to one another discussing a particular issue or topic. These message threads are self-documenting and become very useful in keeping track of the reasoning and development of topics. The messages can be organized, searched, or archived. Therefore, besides being a metaphor for posted mail, electronic mail systems provide functionality that is feasible only because of the digital nature of the media.

This observation—that e-mail is much more than an electronic replacement for mail—will be emphasized throughout this chapter in different contexts. It has serious and important implications for implementing groupware solutions.

As an example of the value e-mail adds to a simple exchange of messages consider forms processing. We discussed forms extensively in Chapter 2. E-mail applications allow the user to design and use forms in office transactions. Besides sending forms as attachments or just structured text, e-mail applications can add (although not all are capable this) several features because of the electronic nature of the interchange. The forms can appear differently depending upon the role of the viewer. Various privileges or access rights could be assigned to fields. Digital signatures and approval processes can also be integrated. Finally, the time stamps of when the form was sent, when it was received, when it was approved—are all easily recorded and accessible. The forms can be stored, searched, organized based on user defined criteria. Of course this type of processing approaches light "workflow"—and e-mail has often been used effectively for messaging based workflow.

E-mail and Organization Memory

Another advantage of e-mail is that the same message could just as easily be sent to a group as to an individual. This is accomplished much more easily than with other hard copy mail systems (such as the post office). All the recipients get their messages quickly; recipients on the same network receive their messages almost instantaneously. The message "send" affects both primary recipients and carbon copy (CC) receivers; blind carbon copies (BCC) can also be supported.

Typically, electronic mail systems involve e-mail "databases" which maintain the messages as well as message/reply histories of electronic interchanges for specific topics or subject categories. These interchanges and mail databases enhance the organizational memory within a corporation. The entire "trace," or message thread of an interchange provides a record of the evolution of a topic or issue as well as the comments of the various participants in the message trace which can be maintained and subsequently retrieved.

In fact, if the structure of a message as well as the content can be captured and maintained, and the e-mail system allows more advanced querying and report generation capabilities, then the "message" database becomes an even more effective tool for tracking the evolution of the ideas and thoughts that form the corporate culture. Such a system can greatly enhance the organization memory from which memories can be recalled from the mail database by queries on subject, participant, date, and so on. For instance, queries such as "Retrieve all responses by John no later than 4/5/94 dealing with the CIBIT exhibition subject" could be launched. Note that there could be several iterations of responses and message traces which would be relevant for such a query. Note also that, although a content retrieval mechanism could, and in some cases should, be used, this query deals with a structured database of records and responses involving users (participants), subjects, certain dates, and so on.

Various Categories of E-mail Software

There are at least four basic categories of e-mail software, each with various products and strategies. More importantly as geographically distributed enterprises attempt to communicate, various gateways and switches are used to offer conversions between messaging formats thus allowing message interchange between heterogeneous e-mail systems. The four categories of e-mail software are:

(a) Mainframe and minicomputer e-mail systems: Still widely used, there are a number of popular mainframe e-mail systems. For instance, 3270 terminals on IBM mainframes can be used to send and receive e-mail. Professional Office System (PROFS) is a popular IBM mainframe e-mail system used on 4341 and 4381 mainframes. Similarly, Digital Equipment Corporation offers the advanced ALL-IN-ONE system for its mainframes and minicomputers.

(b) LAN-based e-mail systems: There are several LAN-based e-mail systems that run on popular GUI workstations and operate on systems such as Windows or MacOS. These mail systems support a number of network operating systems including Novell NetWare, Microsoft LAN Manager, Banyan, and others. Some of the popular LAN-based e-mail systems include cc:Mail, Microsoft Mail, DaVinci e-mail, QuickMail, BeyondMail, and others. In subsequent sections we elaborate on advanced features of some of these products. Besides sharing devices such as printers and files systems to share files, e-mail is the most popular application on LANs. In small and midsize corporations or departments, LAN-based e-mail can become a very successful media for communication, topic discussion, meeting notification, exchange of forms, and so on.

(c) Internet-based e-mail: The Internet is not an e-mail system. However it provides the largest computer-to-computer wide area connectivity. Several thousand private, educational, and public organizations in hundreds of countries belong to the Internet. The Internet allows its subscribers to access on-line information sources, to interchange messages, maintain forums for user groups with common interests, and so on. The key point is that while spanning a variety of operating systems, platforms, hardware, and networks the Internet allows its subscribers to interchange e-mail using potentially entirely different e-mail packages or systems.

Many of the systems or products that support e-mail through the Internet are UNIX-based. More recently PC-based systems have also gained popularity. There are a number of companies that allow users access to Internet services through a monthly fee. These products often include intuitive graphical user interface applications for browsing the internet. Some of the features of these services are discussed in the following section.

Internet addresses are of the form:

<Name>@<Institution Host or Name>.<commercial, government or educational>

In Internet lingo, the <Name> to the left of the @ is called the "local part" or "mailbox name." The expression to the right of the @ character is the "domain." The domain specifies where the particular mailbox is located on the interconnected network. For instance, one address could be:

John@Acme.com

which indicates John's mailbox address at the Acme corporation, a commercial organization.

(d) Public communication and on-line services: Most companies purchase e-mail systems that work with their local and wide area networks and network operating systems. These e-mail systems are installed in departments and enterprises primarily for internal communication between the various staff members within the organization. Individuals working in home offices or very small companies can, however, subscribe to one of the many public e-mail services available today. It is relatively inexpensive for an individual or a small corporation to subscribe to a public communication service. By "public" we do not mean the service is free but rather that it is available and accessible to large numbers of users spanning cities, countries and continents. Resource requirements are minimal—a workstation and modem—and the potential benefits are tremendous, in terms of acquiring information, doing market research, finding and maintaining contact with colleagues, clients, customers, and other common interest associates.

Some public communications service providers are based on the Internet. Netcom, UUNET, Portal, the Well and others, offer an increasing variety of on-line services and products. Basic service usually starts with a simple dial-up account to SLIP (Serial Link Interface Protocol) and PPP (Point-to-Point-Protocol) to high-speed dedicated leased lines. The basic dial-up account typically permits the user to dial up the service provider using a modem and to remotely log onto a UNIX-based server which is connected directly onto the Internet.

SLIP and PPP accounts allow the user to dial up the service provider and become connected, for the duration of the call, directly to the Internet. Among the advantages that a SLIP and PPP connection provide is the ability to download files from source archives directly to the home office computer, and to run a variety of netcruising and browsing software directly from the home computer. For example, the phenomenally popular NCSA Mosaic browser for the World Wide Web (WWW) lets users cruise through Web servers around the world through an intuitive user friendly graphic interface by clicking on various "hot" links in html documents. An html (hyper text markup language) document is the basic hypermedia information unit for the WWW. The World Wide Web developed by the European Particle Physics Laboratory (CERN) is essentially a hypermedia publishing system that provides access to Internet information resources in a more intuitive and natural manner.

The Internet is not a product or service supported by any particular company but a TCP/IP-based network connecting thousands of networks and millions of users. As mentioned, service providers such as Netcom offer UNIX accounts to their customers and access to Internet services. Most UNIX accounts in universities and government, where the Internet began, are on the Internet. Currently, however, it is estimated that most Internet users are business accounts.

Electronic messages can be interchanged between systems through gateways with relative ease, enabling, for instance, AOL users to interchange messages with Internet users. The Internet infrastructure provides connectivity between diverse users and access to an incredibly rich set of services and information archives, which has contributed to its overwhelming success. Although there are "doomsday" prophets who predict the downfall of the Internet due to congestion from the sheer load of messages and user connectivity traffic, it is more likely that the Internet will continue to serve as the backbone of information highways connecting industry, academia, and the government/military sectors.

In addition to individuals and small companies, some of the largest customers of public electronic mail services are large companies, which use on-line services to provide up-to-date information on their products, support forums or discussion on their products, provide customer support electronically, and post demonstration or evaluation sample products as well as sales and marketing literature on the net. Customers of software and hardware products are encouraged to access these services, since companies increasingly often post upgrades through these services. Currently, there are several successful public on-line services such as America OnLine (AOL), CompuServe, eWorld, Prodigy, GEnie, EasyLink, MCI Mail, and others.

In addition to electronic mail on-line service vendors provide many diverse services including access to the Internet, on-line shopping, on-line banking, and a growing number of other innovative business services. One of the most exciting and promising aspects of these on-line services is the ability to search various databases such as encyclopedias, libraries of literary work (such as the Library of Congress database from America OnLine), and other databases for specific fields in science, medicine, humanities, and so on.

The Many Purposes and Advantages of E-mail

The careful adoption, implementation, and use of e-mail can result in various benefits to an organization. E-mail serves many communication purposes: information dissemination such as meeting notices, agenda, policy statements, and meeting minutes; the exchange of ideas; reminders of project due dates; circulating documents for coauthoring; routing forms for approval; and so on.

Obviously, e-mail is general purpose and not limited to any particular niche or market sector. It is a horizontal application—everyone needs to communicate, even individuals working at home. And just as printers and cables are essential components of a local area networks, e-mail systems have become a fundamental enabling technology, which can be applied in any business or application domain.

Further, electronic mail is easy to understand. Everyone already understands how postal mail works, and e-mail is (at least) its electronic equivalent. In many situations, it replaces the need for postal mail—with much faster and less expensive transfer times.

In addition to sending letters and other formal messages, e-mail can greatly enhance communication between staff members, reduce the amount of paper traffic, and reduce the need for many face-to-face personal meetings while greatly easing the notification of required meetings. E-mail enhanced with some advanced capabilities such as intelligent filing, filtering, and support of message threads increases the productivity within an organization by improving communication.

E-mail systems are essentially asynchronous. They provide "soft" yet easily accessible "interrupts" to the recipient who can decide how to be notified (either visually or through audio feedback), how frequently they want to be notified, and even for which types of messages they want to be notified. Similarly, the sender of electronic messages can decide when to send the messages, with what priority (although messages of all priorities usually get sent with the same speed), whether they want to receive electronic acknowledgments or receipts, and so on. All these processes, both from the sender's and recipient's perspective, happen in a friendly graphical user interface environment within the context of the user. The asynchronous nature of the communication allows the recipient to respond at his or her discretion. Many people find the time permitted for reflection and consideration to be beneficial for the quality of their responses. Yet once a response has been formulated, it can be quickly delivered to its destination. Thus, e-mail provides advantages over both "hard" interrupt synchronous telephone systems as well as nonelectronic "snail mail" systems.

Speed is a tremendous advantage of e-mail. Messages can be sent across continents within minutes, several orders of magnitude faster than any conceivable physical carrier system. This combination of a soft asynchronous interrupt combined with the speed convenience are perhaps the two most important factors for the success of e-mail systems. There are, however, many other factors which are, in some cases, more important than these two. The wide availability of e-mail, connectivity through public e-mail systems, as well as the underestimated contribution of e-mail toward maintaining organizational memory are some of the advantages of a well-implemented system.

CLIENT/SERVER E-MAIL SYSTEMS IN INTERNETWORKED ARCHITECTURES

Electronic mail systems were some of the earliest applications on LANs, internetworked LANs, WANs, and client/server architectures. Of course, these environments are the backbone of collaborative computing. In order to collaborate electronically, the communication platform must be in place, both in terms of wiring and the networking operating system, as well as the software for interchanging messages between various layers of network protocols. Figure 4.1 illustrates the various components of a client/server system to support electronic message and data interchange. This is a general purpose architecture. In a collaborative environment, users will use a client application on their client nodes to send and receive messages. The architecture of e-mail systems are summarized in the following sections.

Client Application

First there is a client application running on the client nodes. This is the package that the user interacts with through various screens and dialogs. Figure 4.2 illustrates some typical screens from the front end or "user agent" of an e-mail package. This application is "informed" either through operating system messages, call-back mechanisms, or polling whenever messages arrive for the user. Typically, the user is notified by a sound or visual cue of the arrival of a message. In this manner the client e-mail application receives messages for the user from the back-end e-mail server or e-mail services. Or, as mentioned, clients can also use mail-enabled applications that allow users to send e-mail directly from an application. (This is explained in more detail later in the chapter.)

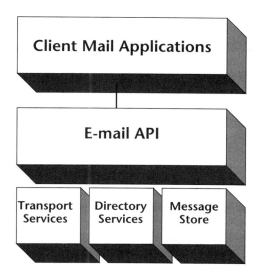

Figure 4.1 Various components on an e-mail client/server architecture.

The Server Components

There are, as illustrated in Figures 4.1 and 4.3, three basic components or modules for e-mail services, including transport services, directory services, and storage or e-mail database services. Figure 4.3 shows e-mail specific services and how they interact with other components or layers in an e-mail architecture. The mail applications and mail-enabled applications invoke cross-platform messaging application programming interfaces that encapsulate the messaging services as well as operating system specific details. Although the figure is a generalization, it nevertheless elucidates the fact that it is primarily the OS and messaging API implementations that interface with the messaging service. It is also interesting to note that next generation workstation operating systems such as Windows and MacOS are incorporating many e-mail functionalities as part of their OS. Different e-mail packages and products offer different solutions, and be aware that it is rare to find all three components sold by the same vendor. Most e-mail packages offer alternative solutions that integrate with other modules such as directory services and transport services which may be offered by network operating system vendors. The next section presents a more detailed explanation of each of these three components. Following are capsule descriptions of each component.

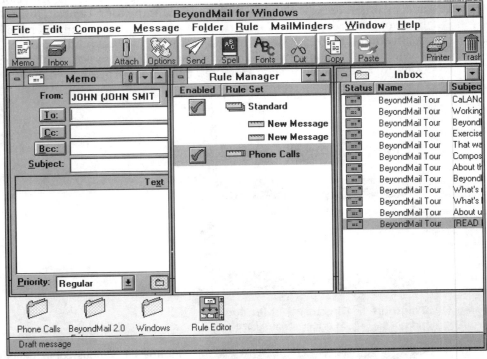

Figure 4.2(a) Screen captures from Microsoft Mail and Beyond Mail.

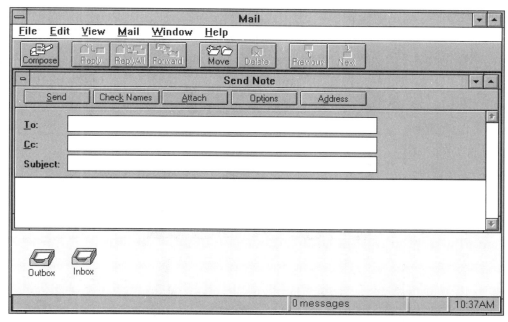

Figure 4.2(b) Screen captures from Microsoft Mail and Beyond Mail.

E-mail Transport

The transport module is responsible for actually moving messages. E-mail systems use store-and-forward communication to send messages from one workstation or PC to another. Messages may arrive out of order in disassembled packets. The store-and-forward servers reassemble, then forward the message to the final destination, usually employing routing tables. Thus a transport application reads the message header, analyzes the destination, and forwards the message using its routing table address. Messages may go through several intermediate systems; they can be stored temporarily in a site before being forwarded to each succeeding site until they reach their final destinations. The store-and-forward strategy is achieved typically by the transport components working in conjunction with the directory, mail storage, and other services on the network (especially in the source and target sites).

On a local area network where all users connect to a single server, the role of a transport service may not be crucial. If, on the other hand e-mail messages are to be sent across networks and various geographic sites, then the transport service becomes extremely important. In order to transfer messages across networks, the two prevailing connectivity standards are CCITT X.400, an industry standard, and Novell's MHS. Although an e-mail package may provide a transport service, they are usually sold separately by vendors such as Novell. E-mail packages indicate which transport services are supported.

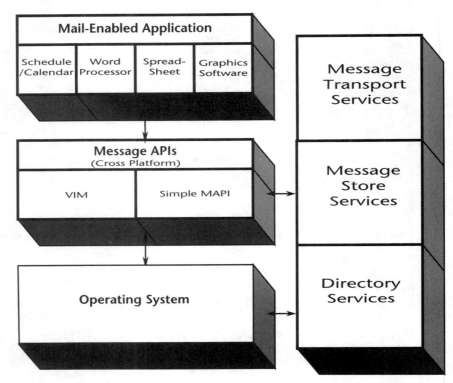

Figure 4.3 E-mail layered architecture.

Directory Services

Directory services maintain the physical locations of users who can then be addressed physically or logically. These directories can be stored either as files or as databases. Entries in the directories contain at least the names of the users as well as their locations. These services, too, may be bundled into an e-mail system or sold separately. One popular directory service is StreetTalk from Banyan. This implementation is close to the industry standard, X.500.

Another approach to directory services is to integrate them with the network operating system. In fact, in earlier LAN client/server environments the directory services and user information were decoupled from the addresses for the network and e-mail systems. Then, after installing the LAN and identifying user logins and addresses, the e-mail backend required a separate install and, in some cases, users with different identifications needed to be "reintroduced." In some systems, LAN connection and e-mail have separate login and password protection.

E-mail directory services and network directory services share the same goal: to read the network operating systems directory. For example, Novell has a very involved directory structure in its NetWare operating system. NetWare directories contain very useful information about all network users, access rights, passwords, and login IDs. An e-mail system can access and read this directory information. In most cases, all LAN users are also e-mail clients and having this information—at least as a default—is very useful.

The Message Database

This database generally contains the messages that are in the system: read messages, unread messages, message logs, information about the message originator, and attachments. More modern e-mail and messaging systems might more appropriately be called the e-mail database or the groupware database since the e-mail system might store persistent information about users, groups, messages, routing information, routing rules, and so forth.

Message database handling services typically are back-end services. The e-mail server component uses message databases to store and forward messages to individual user mailboxes, which are identified by user IDs managed by directory services. What is actually stored in an e-mail database and how it is stored varies greatly between products.

The trend in messaging systems is to present a common e-mail services interface which could be adopted by different back-end service vendors. With a uniform interface, application vendors or even in-house vendors have to deal with only a single common standard instead of supporting all the specifications of various systems. Unfortunately, there are several common messaging APIs being proposed by major back-end service vendors. The two most important of these are MAPI, which is Microsoft's standard, and VIM, which is spearheaded by Lotus.

STANDARDS AND COMMON MAIL APIs

Each vendor of a messaging system has its own implementation, resulting in many different solutions being offered to both third-party and in-house application developers for managing messaging between applications. Hence, there is a clear need for standards in both transport services and standard APIs for messaging services.

There are many advantages to having common APIs in any domain, particularly in the case of e-mail standards. For one thing, common APIs will benefit those organizations that communicate with different e-mail packages and have systems that reside on different heterogeneous workstations and are implemented on different operating systems. For both intra- and interorganization communication, the ability to easily send and receive e-mail between these systems is extremely useful.

If common APIs and standards are not supported, e-mail packages must be able to support gateways or interoperability (that is, the ability to send and perhaps even receive messages) between many heterogeneous e-mail systems. API interfaces exist to handle the message store-and-forward functionality and all address/directory functions, create messages, and access messages and attachments.

MAPI: Messaging API

MAPI, Message Application Programming Interface, is supported and implemented by Microsoft. MAPI is actually part of Microsoft's Windows Open Services Architecture (WOSA) strategy. The approach in MAPI is similar to operating system services or device approaches. It is an interface that abstracts the implementation details of the engine. MAPI specifies the API calls for messaging: send/receive messages, mailbox management, support for managing messages through filing in folders, searching for messages within folders, notification of users or applications upon arrival of messages, support of OLE, and so on. The goal is to:

- Provide common application programming interfaces (API).
- Provide common service provider interfaces (SPI).

Then, application developers only have to deal with one common interface to various services supported by a variety of service providers. MAPI provides this capability—common interface for application developers and a common interface for service providers—for messaging services. This approach also applies to other WOSA functionalities such as the standards and interfaces for databases (ODBC).

In the MAPI architecture, client applications call MAPI interface functions for messaging: to send messages, receive messages, save messages, and so on. These functions are actually handled by the service provider. The MAPI subsystem handles the calls to the service provider, which calls corresponding functions within the service provider interface, which then perform the client requests. Therefore, in order to be MAPI-compliant, service providers need to implement service-provider interface functions to perform the indicated functionality calls that get passed from the client's MAPI calls.

The MAPI software subsystem acts as a broker, coordinating the interaction of multiple clients with multiple service providers. It includes a set of MAPI dynamic-link libraries (DLLs) and the message spooler. The message spooler controls the activities of the Microsoft Windows Messaging System (WMS) which runs independently from user applications, much as the print spooler assists in the operation of the Microsoft Windows print subsystem. The MAPI spooler works closely with the message store and transport providers when sending and receiving messages. MAPI client applications do not have to monitor the message spooler; to them, the spooler appears as just another part of the MAPI system software. The overall architecture of Windows mail management is illustrated in Figure 4.4.

This means that if a back-end service such as a transport service, a message store service, or a directory/address book service supports SPI, then a MAPI-compliant windows application will be able to use the services of these and any other SPI-compliant back-end service. This is illustrated in Figure 4.5. This permits the application or in-house developer to select his or her favorite mail engine since any MAPI-compliant windows application can talk through the DLL to any MAPI-SPI compliant mail

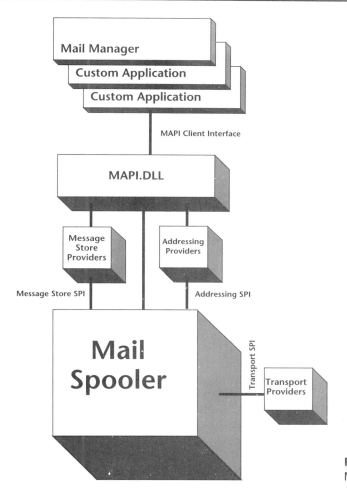

Figure 4.4 The Windows Mail Manager.

engine. Hewlett-Packard, DEC, Novell, Banyan, and AT&T have agreed to support MAPI-compliant engines.

According to Microsoft, MAPI was built to meet the needs of message-aware applications, such as a word processor application that can send as well as print the contents of the document, message-enabled applications, such as e-mail packages; and another category of applications that Microsoft calls message-based workgroup applications. (Please note that this is Microsoft's taxonomy. In other places in this chapter and elsewhere we use the terms "e-mail application" and "e-mail enabled application" to indicate e-mail front-end applications and applications that can send e-mail messages, respectively.) In Microsoft's taxonomy these applications require more extensive services from the MAPI interface—including message store, address book, and message transport functions.

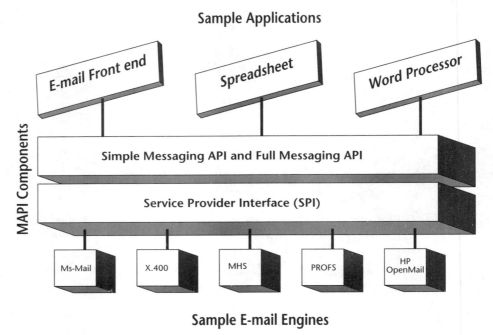

Figure 4.5 The Basic MAPI structure.

MAPI supports these three categories of client applications through functionality provided by the subsets of the MAPI interface known as Common Messaging Calls (CMC), Simple MAPI, and Extended MAPI. Developers can use either CMC calls or Simple MAPI calls to implement simple messaging applications.

CMC

CMC consists of about 10 high-level functions for messaging. In addition to being an API that is independent of service providers (hence developers have to deal with one common interface), CMC is a multiplatform interface. It was developed in conjunction with the X.400 API Association (XAPIA) standards organization, and it is supported on Microsoft Windows, MS-DOS, OS/2, Macintosh, and UNIX platforms. Because CMC is supported on several different platforms, an application written to the CMC standard can be ported to other platforms. In contrast, MAPI is a Windows-only standard.

Simple MAPI

Simple MAPI has functionality similar to CMC but is supported only on Windows. Like CMC, it also makes it easy for application developers to incorporate messaging functionality in their applications. Applications using Simple MAPI to send messages can include attachments or have OLE links to other applications. As with CMC, Simple

MAPI takes advantage of the MAPI subsystem to maintain independence from the underlying messaging system and network.

As just stated, Simple MAPI and CMC provide similar basic messaging functionality for applications. So how do you decide which is the right API to use? Because CMC offers most of the functionality of Simple MAPI and provides the additional benefit of cross-platform support, most developers should and probably would choose CMC.

Extended MAPI

But where the application depends heavily on messaging, it is probably a better idea to use Extended MAPI. Extended MAPI is a set of object-oriented functions that enable you to build advanced messaging capabilities into your application. Extended MAPI enables applications to manage the generation and handling of complex messages, large numbers of received messages, message storage, and complex addressing information. Applications that can benefit from Extended MAPI functionality include workflow, message management, unattended message filtering, and agent-based retrieval applications.

Extended MAPI provides the following functionality not available in either CMC or Simple MAPI:

- Ability to customize messages and message formats using properties.
- Ability to develop custom features for address books.
- Ability to search the folder hierarchy for specified information using search-results folders.
- Access to arbitrary properties in messages and recipients.
- Access to multiple message stores.
- Access to the folder hierarchy.
- Event notification.
- MAPI memory management capabilities.

Extended MAPI also supports advanced messaging features such as custom and smart forms. With custom forms, for example, an organization can replace the standard send-and-receive form for any given e-mail application with the organization's own time sheet or calendar containing predefined fields of information.

Smart forms take this ability another step further, enabling you to link the information entered into such fields with other applications. To extend the preceding example, a smart form could automatically extract the custom form's timesheet entries and send them to a host-based payroll program.

Extended MAPI also enables clients to access and manipulate the address book, the message store, profiles, and other standard MAPI service providers. For example, an Extended MAPI client can add names to an address book or delete a message from the message store.

VIM: Vendor Independent Messaging

VIM was spearheaded by Lotus and supported by many other corporations including Novell, IBM, Borland, and Apple. (VIM's predecessor is OMI (Object Messaging Interface), which was also spearheaded primarily by Lotus.) VIM is basically a standard API specification for messaging. Look at Figure 4.6, and note that both e-mail applications and mail-enabled applications can use the VIM interface. Different vendors providing messaging implementation can support the VIM API and provide VIM implementations. Through VIM's single interface application developers do not need to be compliant with any specific messaging vendor's programming interface.

Functions of the VIM Interface

The VIM interface is very complete in supporting messaging functionality.

Through the VIM interface, applications can compose and send messages containing text, file attachments, and multimedia elements such as images. The main categories of functions in VIM can be summarized as follows:

Note part: The note part corresponds to the message text in e-mail messages. It includes simple text note parts, but VIM also allows support for rich text note parts, PCX format for fax, color bitmap images, graphics files such as Metafiles in Windows and PICT files on the Macintosh, as well as sound and video note types.

Attachments: The VIM interface allows applications to include file attachments for one or more files by specifying the location (the path) of these files. There is also more advanced support for attachments through a stream format defined by VIM.

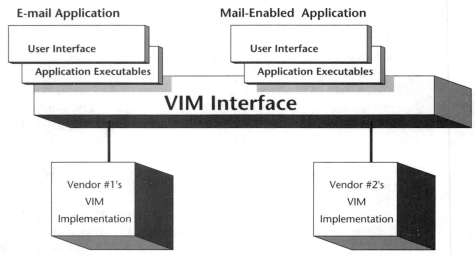

Figure 4.6 E-mail and mail-enabled application using VIM.

Application items: VIM also allows applications to define their own item types. Both sender and receiver (which in many cases would be the same application) must understand these user-defined structures.

Message containers: VIM implementations have message containers (or messaging "databases") which store the messages. Users or applications that have been authenticated can access the messages in the containers. More than one user or application can gain access to the same message container.

Receiving messages: Messages can be received by users, groups, and applications. The VIM specification allows messages to be received either by address or by name. Address specification is the conventional mailbox or in-box address of the receiver. The name specification uses VIM's support of a unique name or identifier. Names or identifiers have address book type (such as cc:Mail or Notes), address book name, and value (which contains unique entity) fields.

Address books: Address books are also supported in VIM. They are used to contain directories of e-mail users. Through the VIM interface, applications can create address books, delete address books, and add/delete entries in address books. Each entry in an address book has a unique name, a type, and a set of properties or attributes.

Transport Standards

Transport services constitute the third component of an e-mail server. The transport module is responsible for the actual movement of the messages. As noted earlier, on a local area network where all the users are connected to a single server, the role of a transport service is not that crucial, but if e-mail messages are to be sent across networks and to various geographic sites, it becomes extremely important.

One trend is for network operating system vendors such as Novell, Microsoft, IBM, and Apple to support at least the transport mechanism on the file server. All these companies offer their own solutions for transport services. These transport services may be installed either with the operating system or separately. They can (and in most cases do) have their own server component. In other words, it is possible to have a transport service that runs as a server, in which case, the e-mail system communicates with the transport service to move its messages from one system to another.

NetWare Global MHS

Message Handling Service (MHS) was originally implemented by Action technologies and is fast becoming a very important standard in the industry. More recently Novell extended it to the NetWare Global MHS message exchange protocol. There are several components to MHS. First, it specifies a message structure called Standard Message Format (SMF). Novell supports both the MHS 1.5 structure called SMF-70 as well as the new NetWare Global MHS structure SMF-71. Novell users can also run an MHS server which actually is the transport service for SMF messages. The MHS server can run on a separate server or as a NetWare Loadable Module (NLM) on a Novell File

Server. The MHS implementation allows an MHS-compliant application to "drop" an SMF message into a specific location, either its mail center or directory. MHS manages the physical flow of messages between users and applications. On networks, the transport system can transfer messages from one system to another and from one application's message directory to another.

The SMF message structure consists of the envelope, message header, and message body. The envelope is used by transport servers to send messages between applications and users—both local and remote. Some of the fields in the envelope include:

Delivery fields—Delivered-to, Date-delivered, etc. to indicate the address and date the message was delivered.

Attachment fields—Attachment, Attachment-name, Attachment-type, etc. the name and description of attachments.

Message Transfer Agent Specifications—The options can specify return of contents, receipt notification, nonreceipt notification, nondelivery notification, etc.

There are many other envelope fields but these are some of the important ones. The message header structure is similar to SMTP and X.400 specifications and contains fields such as:

From: indicating originator Importance or Priority of the message

Date: the date message was created

Date-received: the date the message was received

To or Original-to: indicating receiver

Copies-to and BCC: indicating the list of addresses receiving copies and blind carbon copies

Keywords: used to classify the message

These fields are used by the applications—e-mail or mail-enabled—sending and receiving the messages (and not the transport agents). If the message is addressed to a user on the same MHS server, then the MHS server simply copies the message file to that mailbox. Typically, there is a transfer of a message file from one MHS mailbox, which basically is a file in a directory dedicated to an application/user, to the e-mail or mail-enabled application's mailbox; the message is thus processed or transferred. If the address is for a remote system or mail center, then MHS moves the message to an outbound queue before sending it to its remote destination. In this remote processing step, messages in the queue are first sorted by destination, and then a connection is established for each remote destination; finally, the messages are transferred to the in-box of an MHS server on the remote site.

More specifically the message delivery in MHS follows these steps for sending a message:

1. A message is created and placed in the directory: mhs/mail/snd.
2. The MHS server checks periodically the directory mhs/mail/snd.
3. For every message in the directory processing the envelope it decides if the addressed user is local or remote. If the destination is local it moves the message into the user's inbox queue.

$$\text{mhs/mail/users/john/mhs}$$

assuming the user's name is john.
If the destination is remote it is moved to the outbound directory

$$\text{mhs/mail/queues}$$

The transport agent checks this queue, sends the message to remote site and puts it in the mhs/mail/snd directory of the remote destination site.

X.400

The X.400 is a messaging standard that can very efficiently provide interoperability between various e-mail systems. It is the common standard of the International Standards Organization (ISO) and the International Telegraph and Telephone Consultive Committee (CCITT) for Message Handling.

In addition to normal text, X.400 messages can contain other formats such as fax messages or even voice recordings. The X.400 standard describes the components and protocols for a Message Handling System (MHS). The X.400 MHS components include the following:

Message User Agent (MUA)—this is the highest level interface between users and other components of the e-mail. MUAs are the client application operating in graphical user interface environments. MUA interacts with other messaging components MS and MTA using X.400 protocols.

Message Store (MS)—this component provides users mailbox message storage. MUA and MTA interface with the MS using X.400 protocols. MTA delivers messages to message stores; MUA retrieves the messages and displays them to the user. Thus often MS is layered between MS and MTA.

Message Transfer Agent (MTA)—MTA is responsible for transporting messages— in cooperation with other MTA, and using the MTS backbone. MTAs also handle the distribution list to forward the messages to the various target receivers.

Message Transfer System (MTS)—this is the backbone of an MHS. It handles the distributed transfer of messages using ports. Ports can be submission, delivery, or administration. Ports can also be both symmetrical or asymmetrical. With symmetrical ports services can be provided and consumed. Asymmetrical ports are either providers or consumers. MTS systems can consist of many message transfer agents (MTAs) whose objects have ports to transfer messages to other MTA objects.

X.400 addresses have often been characterized as being difficult to use (compared, for instance with Internet addressing). There are four types of addresses in X.400. Mnemonic Originator/Recipient is widely used and provides somewhat easy to use parameters for addressing. Terminal O/R and Postal O/R support terminal and postal addresses respectively. Numeric O/R identifies users through a sequence of numbers. Some of the fields or parameters in X.400 Mnemonic addressing include the Country (C), Surname (S), Given name (G), Organization (O), and a number of parameters for domains.

For domains, X.400 specifies a public and a private service. Public domains are administered by national or governmental postal and telecommunication agencies. A domain in X.400 is called the administration management domain (ADMD). Each public domain registers many private domains, which are called private management domains (PRMD). Private domains can include governmental, educational, and private companies.

Other fields in the X.400 standard specify the organization of the recipient and possibly organization unit or suborganization, and of course the first name and family name of the receiver.

Internet and Simple Mail Transport Protocol (SMTP)

The Internet is an extremely successful implementation of internetworking and information exchange across very heterogeneous environments and networks. By some estimates the membership on the Internet is growing by about 1,000,000 a month. The Internet includes many networks such as the NFSNet and numerous commercial, educational, and government institutions. In addition to e-mail and messaging support, the Internet provides large numbers of newsgroups, bulletin boards, forums, as well as search and file transfer facilities.

The protocol for interchanging messages on the Internet is called Simple Mail Transfer Protocol (SMTP). More recent implementations of SMTP include the Domain Name Service addressing scheme. Messages on the Internet (and in all e-mail systems for that matter) have a:

<Header> <Message Body>

Here is an example of an Internet message:

From: John Smith <Johns@physics.berkeley.edu>
To: Mark Johnson <mark@acme.com>
Cc: bonny@wdc.gov
Subject: New proposal—version 2
Date: Sat, 9 Jan 94 15:13:38 +0100

Dear Mark,
I have questions about your proposal. Can you please send me copies of your references?
John

The header lists information about the sender, the recipients, the posting date, the subject of the message, and so on. The syntax for a mail address therefore is:

mailbox@subdom-n. . . . subdom-2.subdom-1.top-level-domain

For example:

john@netcom.com

indicates that the user's login name is John, and the domain—which is the name of the host in this example—is netcom, a commercial organization.

The top-level domains in Internet addressing may be an organization or a country. Examples of organizations as top-level-domains include COM for commercial corporations, EDU for educational institutions such as universities, GOV for US government, and so on. Examples of country domains include UK for United Kingdom and US for the United States.

Transport services that are SMTP compliant provide Inter Process Communication Environments (IPCE). IPCEs may cover one or more networks. Mail applications or e-mail enabled applications use or are clients of interprocess commununication. When an e-mail is to be delivered, a transmission channel is established between sender and receiver, once the communication is established the sender delivers the message through the SMTP MAIL command. When the receiver responds with OK, the sender follows it with an RCPT command—indicating a recipient of the message. If this is OK, the actual data of the message is sent through the DATA command. If everything is successful the sender issues a QUIT command.

For the message structure, the original RFC 822 standard specifies fields for originator (From); addresses of the receivers; carbon copy receivers, and blind carbon copy receivers (to, cc, and bcc respectively); date of the message: subject of the message; the ID of the original message; that the current message is a reply (In Reply To) and so on.

For handling the recent requirements of more complex messages—including multi-media elements—the Multipurpose Internet Mail Extension (MIME) was developed as an RFC 1341 standard. MIME was created by Nathaniel Borenstein of Bellcore. MIME allows for multiple parts to be contained in a message. Each part has a self-describing header that identifies the type of the part and the way the part is encoded. Seven part types are supported by MIME including text, multipart, application, message, audio, and video. For movies MIME supports the Motion Picture Experts Group (MPEG) standard. For still images it supports the popular (especially on the Internet) Graphic Image Format (GIF). For audio MIME supports ISDN encoded voice or music.

INTERCONNECTING E-MAIL SYSTEMS

There are many situations where interconnecting e-mail systems and communication (exchanging messages) between e-mail systems is extremely important. X.400 is one important approach to interconnect various e-mail systems and services. However, although e-mail vendors are starting to adhere to the X.400 standards, there is still a very important need to interconnect various e-mail systems.

One popular way to guarantee interoperability and interchange of messages between various e-mail systems and products is through gateways to different e-mail standards and products. Gateways on computer networks connect two heterogeneous networks by performing conversions between the protocols of the network so that information can be exchanged between the networks. Similarly, a gateway between two e-mail systems allows users of these systems to exchange messages between their heterogeneous systems.

Generally, different e-mail systems, supported on different platforms and by different vendors, use different protocols and cannot communicate or interchange messages; for instance an SMTP compliant message format needs to be converted to another format (such as X.400). Gateways provide bidirectional conversion and communication between two different e-mail systems. This works for situations where only a few different e-mail systems are involved with a gateway between each pair of disparate e-mail systems.

A better solutions for larger enterprises is message exchange through switches. Switches (also called multi-gateway switches) provide connections between many different e-mail systems. Some of the functions supported by switches include e-mail protocol conversion, directory synchronization, address translation, and document conversions. Often to send an e-mail from one e-mail system to another switches make two translations (unlike gateways which make only one). An intermediate format is used when a message is sent from one e-mail system to another. Thus there is a translation from the source to the intermediate format and then again from the intermediate format to the destination.

ADDRESS BOOKS FOR USERS AND GROUPS

As mentioned earlier, e-mail systems require a list identifying users and their mailboxes. Chapter 2 identified and briefly discussed the various categories of objects in groupware systems. One of these categories was users and groups or address books. Groups and users are particularly important in e-mail. The information on the set of users of the e-mail package is often called the address book. Some e-mail systems have both public address books, containing names and e-mail addresses of all the available users who can be picked when preparing and forwarding a message, as well as private address books, which are subsets of the public address book, created and maintained by individual users. Here the terms "address book" and "group" are used interchangeably. Implementation techniques for storing the content of mailboxes include operating system directory structures and databases, and in either case, the e-mail system maintains entries in the form:

$$\text{<UserID>:}\{\text{<Set of Messages Received>}\}$$
$$\{\text{<Set of OutGoing Messages>}\}$$
$$\{\text{<Set of Filed Messages>}\}$$

The first set allows the system to display all the messages that are in the user's mailbox every time the user logs in to the e-mail system. The other set allows users to either keep a log of all the messages they have sent or to retract messages that they sent through the e-mail front end but which were not actually read by the recipients or sent by the e-mail's message transport mechanism. The third set allows the user to file messages in different categories in the context of the e-mail system.

User and group attributes that are useful in electronic messaging, networking, and groupware systems, include:

Name

Company name

Social security or employee number

Office number

Office address

Fax number

Home phone number

Home address

Rather than being simple lists of the form:

<identifier, electronic address, name>

the directories used in networks and electronic mail systems can contain much more elaborate types of information. Of course, the richer this information is, the less desirable it is to replicate it. Replication (for example, in networking directories and separate e-mail address books), is laborious and can easily lead to inconsistencies and conflicts.

As e-mail systems become more advanced, and as users demand more functionality, one extension is to allow users to define their own attributes and types for address book entries. This is an object-oriented approach to address books. The system provides basic address book attributes, but also allows users to add more attributes that meet their specific needs. The address books then become specialized databases for storing information about people and companies. Like any other shared object, address books can also have levels of security which allow some users to update them and others to only read or use them. Some users might be prohibited from seeing certain address books (for example, strategic contacts or addresses of board members).

No matter how many attributes are included in a system-defined address book, specific users will always require additional attributes specific to their custom address books. Of course, memo fields may be used for this purpose. Memo fields basically are unstructured text fields which can, theoretically, be very large. If the system provides memo fields, users can incorporate additional information for their address book entries in these memo fields. Nevertheless, it is desirable to have the flexibility to allow users to define additional fields and "specialize" the system-defined address book structures. If this feature is combined with a simple yet powerful querying mechanism, extensible databases of address books customized with different number of fields and privileges for each user are possible.

E-mail systems also allow either the administrator of the mail system or the user to create groups. Similar to the network operating system's management issue—where usually only the system administrator can create groups—e-mail systems also enable the e-mail administrator to create groups. More advanced e-mail systems, where the group membership is customized to the needs of the user, also let individual users create groups to forward their messages.

Although creation of groups or address books by users can result in duplication and increase the overall overhead of the system, it is nevertheless convenient for the users to be able to add and delete members to the groups who need to receive particular types of messages.

It is also highly desirable for address books and groups to be as synchronized with network directories as possible. Otherwise, for example, a user who is introduced in the network's marketing group or address book must also be introduced in the corresponding marketing group or address book of the e-mail system. Everything must be synchronized twice if two separate systems of directories (address books) are maintained for both individuals and groups.

User-defined fields or attributes and security can be extended further to create "intelligent" groups or address books. The concept is to create groups or address books where the membership is based on various user-specified criteria and user or address book entry attributes. For example, one simple predicate might be: Send the message to all users who live in the greater Los Angeles area.

This criteria is straightforward. The intelligent e-mail system could support more advanced querying and query result composition. Other predicates or criteria that can be used to send messages include attributes such as roles, titles, education, or skill.

In a virtual reengineered corporation that relies heavily on the efficiency of its empowered employees and where small teams and task forces are created very dynamically, it is vital to have flexible mechanisms for information exchange. The ability to create intelligent groups and to send messages based on the attributes and roles of the users is one such mechanism.

DIRECTORY SERVICES

In its simplest form, electronic mail and messaging systems provide high-speed information exchange between computer users who are connected through (either LAN or WAN) a network. The users may be in close proximity, for example in adjacent offices or cubicles, or they may be in different buildings within the same corporation, across the street from one another, in different states, in different countries, or even on different continents. The ability of the electronic mail system to transcend all these physical boundaries through one uniform mechanism makes it an excellent information exchange tool.

However, these systems are not without problems. Some internetworking and e-mail systems require the sender to remember the full e-mail address of the recipient, which as shown here in this Internet address may be very lengthy:

<Name>@<Institution Name>.<commercial, government or educational>

Other e-mail systems have similar structures. And it is up to the sender to maintain a list of all the e-mail addresses he or she uses. Fortunately, there are some utilities to help with this. When electronic messages are exchanged within the same corporation, the corporation may have an account with one of the commercial internetworking services and use it as its main interdepartmental e-mail mechanism. Preferable, however is a higher-level corporate infrastructure that lets employees in the same corporation communicate simply by using the name of the person. The user of the electronic mail or electronic message interchange then doesn't have to be concerned with people changing their logins (and hence e-mail addresses), or moving. This is sometimes achieved through a directory backbone—discussed below.

The ability to send e-mail using just names is very desirable in LAN and WAN e-mail systems installed within a corporation. And this approach is not restricted to a single multidepartment corporation. It can be used with shared messaging systems as well.

Sometimes, of course, more than one person could have the same name. But an intelligent and friendly system would enable the sender to restrict and reduce the possibilities of "collisions" by allowing other logical attribute values such as: John Smith, 30, blue eyes, graduate of CalTech, and so on.

Systems that achieve name-to-address bindings are called directory services. Directory services are used in network operating systems to identify users and their locations (network addresses for e-mail and other purposes). Usually, the entries in the directories consist of a few attributes such as the login ID of the user, the name of the user, and information pertaining to the user's location, systems, and other system information. In either a local or distributed environment, maintaining large directories and keeping them consistent across distributed wide area networks can be problematic. This is especially true in large distributed systems with many users and branches.

A distributed system which maintains directories across independently operating sites provides network and electronic message administrators with some formidable challenges. One important issue is the variety of network operating systems and e-mail packages at the different sites. Even networks and servers within the same physical or geographical proximity often include a variety of e-mail packages. One department might, for example, choose cc:Mail while another might choose Microsoft Mail. You will remember that we mentioned earlier the use of switches and gateways to interchange messages between disparate e-mail systems.

Another approach to solve the problem of interoperability and synchronization of directories is through a backbone infrastructure. Backbones also provide multiple gateway services and a more robust, integrated solution with common directory support. X.400 is perhaps the most widely used backbone standard. X.400 with X.500 directory systems provides efficient directory and transport mechanisms between heterogeneous e-mail systems. Commercial products from Novell, ISOCOR, Nexor, and others provide solid backbone solutions with an X.500 common directory structure.

X.500

The X.500 standard is the directory service standard from CCITT. It is more than just a directory standard for e-mail; it can also be used to manage information about computers, networks, and users in distributed computing environments. The goal of X.500 is to provide directory services through a directory information base (DIB). The technology is similar to distributed databases and often a commercial distributed database system is used to implement X.500 distributed directories.

The standard directory information base provides the "yellow" pages for binding names of resources and people to addresses. X.500 attempts to achieve this by providing the yellow page look-up translation of names into network addresses. X.500 is being adopted now for e-mail and other services.

Through X.500 it is possible for any person or resource listed to be accessed worldwide. As more companies support and implement X.500-compliant directory services and provide solutions for interconnecting directories, the day may come when users will be able to query their X.500-compliant e-mail system public directories about users on different networks.

Several X.400 vendors are developing directory exchange products designed to comply with the X.500 standard. The North American Directory Forum (NADF) which has members such as AT&T, Bell Atlantic, IBM, MCI Communications, Pacific Bell, and the U.S. Postal Service to name a few, is attempting to provide a directory interconnection solution. When the directories of these companies are interconnected, it will enable the sharing of directory information not only between the members of the forum but their trading partners as well.

MAIL-ENABLED APPLICATIONS

As e-mail front-end and application programming standards become more accepted, the trend is for the proliferation of mail-enabled applications. Typically, mail-enabled applications treat e-mail either as a separate option or as a printer driver and allow the user to send the document to a target receiver list without leaving the application. In other words, the user could, while using an application such as a word processor or spreadsheet, select e-mail as an option.

This option could be either an explicit menu item or the user could select it as a printer driver, thereby "printing" to an e-mail server. When the e-mail option has been selected, the application then allows the user to select a receiver. For instance, a mail-enabled application under Windows can have a Send option under the File menu, similar to the Print option under the File pull-down menu. Just as print dialogs allow users to choose or even set up the printing options (landscape versus portrait, resolution, or particular printer) a Send menu item will allow the user to select between different users and groups as the target receivers of the application. The user will be able to mail either selected pages or the entire document, again very similar to printing options. When the selected person receives the message, the mail-enabled application will be launched and its content will be the document that was mailed by the user through the mail-enabled application.

Mail-enabling an application is very convenient for the user. The user does not need to leave the application and then invoke the e-mail application and explicitly include the application file as an attachment or enclosure. The document can be sent directly from within the application, an operation as easy as printing.

Mail-enabled applications can be taken one step further by allowing applications to exchange document parts through e-mail transport protocols. Although fast digital exchange over wide area networks is becoming less expensive, over long distances, continuous on-line access is still much more costly than the store-and-forward strategy used by mail transport protocols. Furthermore, in terms of availability, ease of install, and accessibility, mail transport is very common and popular. There are tens of millions (estimated about 40 million in 1995) of users of e-mail systems, and most of them have access to transport protocols.

In many applications today, as discussed in Chapter 2, compound documents are composed of different parts pertaining to different applications. One efficient way of interchanging information between documents is to have store-and-forward linking between the parts through an e-mail transport. This enables applications to communicate and to provide a client/server interchange of information using e-mail transport. The operation of such applications makes information exchange much more transparent.

Assume, for example, that the finance department in a corporation would like to disseminate its sales figures among the executives who may reside in geographically distributed nodes. The classical e-mail approach is to send the documents to everyone in a mail message. An alternative would be to link, say, a budget document or application with the more recent sales spreadsheet and have the applications communicate through the e-mail transport. The "smart" sales spreadsheet will then know how to communicate with all the applications that are linked to it and send updates to these applications. The net effect is that the next time the executives look at their budgets, they will see the new sales figures automatically updated. In fact, the executives do not need to interface with the e-mail system at all. If all the applications are thus linked, then the end user concentrates on the documents and tasks at hand. By automating the update functions, a great deal of the person-to-person message traffic using the e-mail transports will be replaced by interapplication information exchange. Of course as Wide Area and LAN-to-LAN connectivity becomes more available and affordable, distributed object connectivity and interoperability will become more pervasive. However, the transport and directory problems of e-mail systems will still be issues that need to be addressed in distributed object systems.

MESSAGE CONTENT AND STRUCTURE

Each message type (as an object) has a number of characteristic attributes that reflect the format of the message, and operations that reflect what can be done with the message, or how the message/messaging system can be manipulated. Figure 4.7 illustrates the following attributes of a message class:

(a) Sender: In most cases, messages are sent by one person and this person is identified in the header of the message sent.

(b) Date sent: E-mail messages usually identify the date when the message was sent. Ideally, the date will indicate both the sender's local time as well as the receiver's

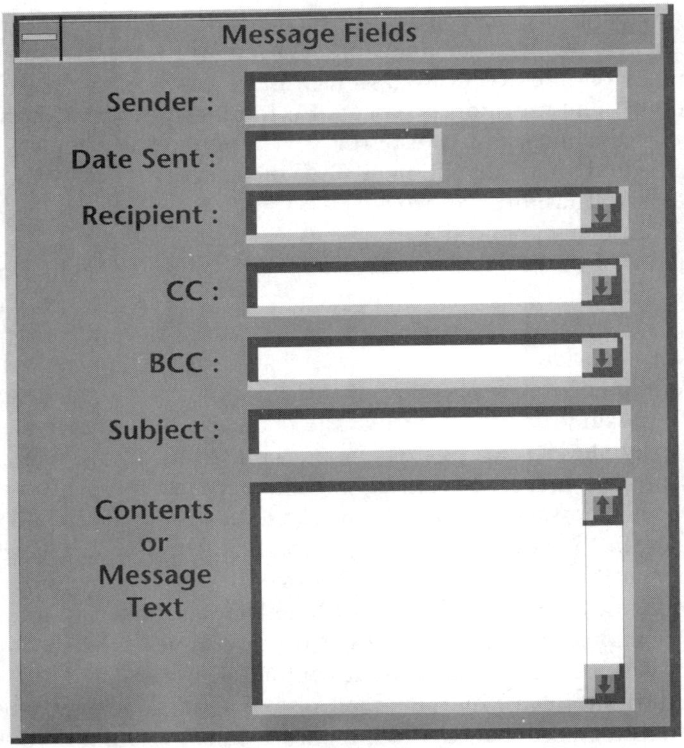

Figure 4.7 The various fields in a message.

local time. In most cases, only the sender's local time is indicated (with a possible indication of the time zone). Another alternative is to express the date sent with respect to a standard time such as GMT.

(c) Receivers: Whenever an electronic mail message is sent, the sender must identify the primary recipients of the message. These are the users or groups who are intended as the main target recipients of the message. Optionally, the sender can identify carbon copy receivers and blind carbon copy receivers. These are described next.

(d) Carbon copy (cc) receivers: The recipients in this list are FYI (for your information) receivers. The concept is identical to CC in regular (paper) mail or letters. The names of the CC as well as main recipients of the message appear in the message for all recipients.

(e) Blind carbon copy (BCC): The difference between a CC and a BCC is that the other recipients of the message will not see the names of those who received a blind carbon copy.

(f) Subject: This field indicates the subject of the message. It is an important field, as it identifies the purpose of the message. If the message is a response to an earlier message, some e-mail systems indicate this visually. Sometimes the levels of the responses (the response to a response) are also indicated.

(g) Message text: The message text is typically a note. It is the most commonly used component. In most cases, the text editor used to create this component is not very sophisticated. It may have very simple text editing capabilities or enable text editing enhanced with formatting, font, size, paragraph, spell checking, and other capabilities. In general, if the content involves a considerable amount of formatting, it will be created in a word processor and sent as an attachment.

(h) Attachments: Attachments are files or folders that are enclosed in the message. In most cases attachments (also called enclosures) are application files such as word processor files or spreadsheets.

In older messaging systems, e-mail delivered simple text messages, and exchanging simple text messages remains (and will for the foreseeable future) a very popular mechanism for exchanging information and performing collaborative work. More recent e-mail packages permit enclosures or attachments within messages. This is illustrated in Figure 4.8 for various categories of attachments such as word processors, spreadsheets, and graphics. The figure shows a prototype of a message containing attachments. In a real message the attachments would probably include icons representing files of specific application types. Therefore, the e-mail has two components:

- The text components developed using the built-in e-mail text editor: If users are just sending text messages to one another, this would suffice and they do not need any other application.

- Attachments or enclosures: These are the files of applications in the user's environment. Examples of application files include word processor files, spreadsheets, images, presentation files, and so forth.

Since the attachment to an electronic mail message may be an application file (such as a spreadsheet or a word processor file) or a hypermedia document, the recipient of the message should somehow have the ability to read or view the message. Usually, application program files are read only by the same system that created them. Some systems can import different file formats (for example, WordPerfect files in Microsoft Word). When an attachment of a particular application is received, and if the system that created the application is available on the recipient's desktop, then the application can be launched to view or even edit the attachment.

If the application is not available on the recipient's workstation, an alternative is for the mail system to provide viewers with various types of attachments. Viewers allow the receiver to look at the attachment, without actually launching an application (which can actually edit the attachment).

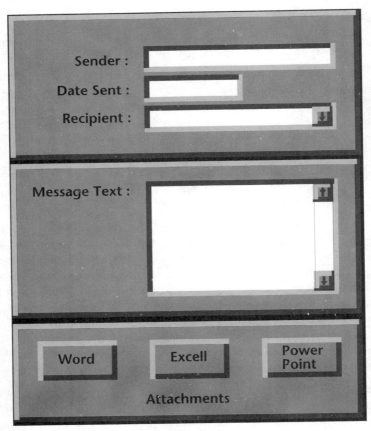

Figure 4.8 Message with attachments.

THE PROBLEM OF COPIES

In collaborative environments with intense exchange of documents and files, unless users are scrupulously careful, they can easily create a backlog of copies, all derived from the same document. The e-mail attachment and enclosure capabilities can easily result in an inundation of documents whose relationship and management will be left to the user to sort out. Capabilities including the ability to control access to the same document and to create various versions, as well as to provide locking or check-out/check-in mechanisms on documents are all typically provided by a document management system, as discussed this in Chapter 3.

Enclosures and attachments are a nice mechanism for enriching a simple text message. But if enclosures are used to collaborate in the development and evolution of a document by several coauthors, then a document management system is a much wiser choice of tool.

Document management systems, can also benefit from the various notification and forwarding primitives provided by e-mail systems. Another convenient mechanism provided by e-mail systems is the capability for referential sharing whereby users can send references to the same document or application file, such that when the application file is launched all users are looking at the same copy.

FOLDERS AND CABINETS FOR ORGANIZING MESSAGES

As explained in Chapter 2, folders and other collection objects are used in many groupware products for different functions. This is also true for electronic mail systems. Most modern e-mail systems provide a folder and sometimes a cabinet model and objects to organize mail messages. Actually, folders can be used to organize both incoming and outgoing messages.

Organizing Messages by Users

Figure 4.9 illustrates the organization of e-mail messages by different categories. For instance, the user can create a folder called "Messages from My Boss," and every time a message from the boss is received it is placed or filed into this folder. The user can thus keep track of all the important messages and at the same time better organize them.

Why not just make a copy of the message and its enclosures? Why is it necessary to keep track of the messages and have the e-mail system provide various primitives (folders, cabinets, and other utilities) to organize the messages? There are a number of reasons why it is preferable to file and organize messages (possibly with enclosures) within the e-mail system instead of making copies of the message texts in, say, word processor files and also making copies of the message enclosures within the user's file system, primarily:

- The routing information is maintained. In addition to the text of the message, there is much useful information about the message itself which is maintained by the e-mail system as attributes or structure fields. This information includes the originator, the date it was sent, the date it was received, the address list, and so on. It is true that many e-mail systems can save all this information in a text file; however, when it is in the e-mail system these "fields" are maintained in structures that can be used to sort, organize, generate reports, search, and so on. Thus, not only the message information is maintained but its structure as well.

- Messages in the e-mail system can be replied to, forwarded, and otherwise manipulated. For instance, the user might decide to reply to a message from the boss which has been kept in the system (filed it in the e-mail system) at a much later date.

Filing Messages

The preceding paragraphs described some of the advantages of keeping messages in the e-mail system. From the end-user perspective (although many e-mail users might not be aware of this) there are actually two types of "databases": messages that are kept in the concurrently shared e-mail database and the filed messages. The filed messages are usually kept in the user's workstation. In fact, the very act of "filing" usually moves the message from the shared e-mail database to the user's "private" filing area (which most of the time is stored on the user's workstation).

Whenever a user receives an e-mail message, it is placed in the "view" of all received messages which have not yet been removed from the message window. Note that both read and unread messages are in this list. In other words, the shared e-mail database stored on the e-mail server contains many messages which are read by the recipients (in most cases, most of its storage is allocated to this category).

An e-mail database where all messages are stored and maintained could, even for smaller companies, easily become extremely large and unmanageable. Every message that is somewhat "active"—in other words, that appears in the message (but not filed) list of a user—is maintained in the database. The messages in the shared e-mail

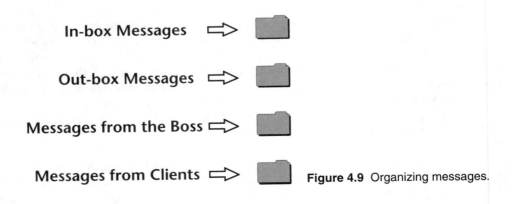

Figure 4.9 Organizing messages.

databases need to be "cleaned" up by deletion. The deletion or filing of these messages, completely under the user's control as to where they should be filed, reduces the storage overhead of the e-mail databases. Usually, when a user files a message, it is moved from the e-mail databases to the user's own private database. Therefore, filing is a more efficient method of sharing storage resources without sacrificing any e-mail functions.

The filing of e-mail messages through organizers such as folders or cabinets therefore provides organizational advantages by allowing users to store the messages in various categories that facilitate subsequent searches and accesses. At the same time, since messages are typically filed on the user's own workstation or storage areas, filing also helps to better manage the storage of the shared e-mail databases.

SMART E-MAIL AND ADVANCED ELECTRONIC MESSAGING

A number of useful and advanced concepts are being incorporated into the next-generation implementation of electronic mail systems. Here is a sampling of a few of the advanced concepts incorporated in next-generation electronic mail systems:

(a) Allow the identification of addresses by their attributes, roles, or relationships. For instance, messages can be forwarded to office workers based on interests, expertise, background, reports to relationships, and relationships with others.

(b) Support rule support for filtering messages and for taking actions when certain types of messages arrive. For instance, workers can specify through declarative rules which messages they would like to see, how messages based on content should be forwarded to different users, and where (in which folders) messages should be filed.

(c) Support full-blown multimedia information exchange with multimedia content and/or attachments. Besides text (the "native" and basic data format of all e-mail systems), next-generation e-mail systems are beginning to incorporate other multimedia types such as voice annotation, messages containing video clips, and so forth.

(d) Support a rich collection of message types and forms. The system might allow users to customize the forms for their needs.

(e) Support notification and receipt of messages. In other words, allow users to be notified if a message is read and, sometimes, if the message is not read within a certain period of time.

(f) Provide various forms of security, especially digital signatures. Security is very important if mission-critical documents are being handled.

These are few of the advanced e-mail concepts being integrated in next-generation e-mail systems. The following paragraphs elaborate on these advanced, so-called smart, e-mail applications.

Filters and Rules

Most e-mail packages today support some filtering and sorting of user messages on various message specific fields. Examples include:

- *Sorting on sender:* Sorts a collection of mail messages on the sender of the messages.
- *Sorting on date received:* Another popular sorting criteria for messages is to sort from most recent to least recent.
- *Sorting on priority:* If the e-mail system supports priorities, another possibility is to sort messages on priority, in most cases from highest to lowest.
- *Sorting on subject:* Another possibility, although less popular, is to sort on the subject of the e-mail.

This type of (almost trivial) "organization" helps the user locate important messages more efficiently. Sorting can be extended with more "advanced" types of filters. For instance, the user might be interested in:

- Only messages from John Smith.
- Only messages sent during 5/4/94.
- Only messages that contain attachments.
- Only messages sent by anyone in the marketing group.

Filters, in fact, could be constructed by combining predicates in predicate expressions on various fields of messages. Predicates are conditions on fields that are either true or false. For example:

Sender IS John

This is a simple predicate expression. Predicates can be combined through AND/OR binary predicates. The unary predicate NOT can also be used. For instance, here is a more complex predicate expression:

Message Subject Contains "Production" AND ("Problems" OR "Observation")

Some "smart" e-mail packages have incorporated predicate expressions into rules that not only can filter messages but perform specific types of actions such as filing, alerting the user, and so on. In general, a rule is of the form:

```
IF
<Predicate Expression>
THEN
<Action List>
```

In some systems, such as Beyond Mail, a rule can be activated for certain event types such as the arrival of a message. Strictly speaking, this is not necessary and conceptually it is part of the <Predicate Expression>. It is just another condition to "activate" the rule and execute the <Action List>. With events, a rule becomes an event following the If—then rule:

WHEN <Event>
IF
<Predicate Expression>
THEN
<Action List>

Here are some examples of rules, assuming the action is the arrival of a message in an in-box:

IF Message Subject Is "Monday Funnies"
THEN Delete Message

IF Message Subject Contains "Marketing"
THEN Move Message Into Marketing Account Folder

IF Message Is From Jim Boss AND Priority is High THEN
Alert Me Immediately

Using rules to specify certain criteria, office workers can forward messages to other workers and/or groups. Both messages that originated with the office worker or messages that have arrived in the worker's mailbox can be forwarded. In either case, messages can be selected for forwarding according to their subject, date, length, etc., as well as the name of the sender and characteristics of the recipient. The following are some sample rules for forwarding messages:

IF Message Subject Is "Auto Insurance"
THEN Forward Message to Legal Department Handling Auto Insurance

IF Message Sender Is a Customer
AND Customer Is Delayed In Payment
THEN Forward Message TO Finance

IF I Am Out
THEN Forward Message to My Assistant

The last example illustrates a "While I am Out" rule. The user can specify many different options with "While I am Out." For instance, if the user does not have e-mail access but can be reached by fax, then he or she can have the highest priority e-mails faxed to him/her.

In an e-mail package that supports rules, the e-mail system will have a set of built-in fields that can be used in predicates, and actions that can be used to file, forward, etc. messages. The fields can also depend on the forms supported by the system.

Beyond Mail

One interesting mail system that provides rule-based capabilities is Beyond Mail from Banyan Systems Incorporated. Beyond Mail supports both MHS and Banyan Vines. It provides all the conventional e-mail capabilities such as sending and receiving messages, support for attachments, and all other features (CC, BCC, etc.) expected from a state-of-the-art e-mail package.

In addition, Beyond Mail uses the folder paradigm for filing user's messages and standard folders such as in-box, out-box, for sent messages, for draft messages, and so on.

There are other powerful e-mail concepts integrated in Beyond Mail, but what sets it ahead of the crowd and what it has come to characterize is its support of rules. Figure 4.10 illustrates a window where a user can easily create a rule. As indicated, there are fields that can be filled in to indicate when an event happens, if certain conditions are satisfied, then certain actions will take place. This When-If-Then mechanism is filled in by the user to apply rules to various messaging situations. An example is shown here:

When—a New message arrives
If—Message is from my manager
    AND Message Subject is URGENT
Then—Alert me through an animation
    AND move the message in my Urgent Messages folder

Multimedia and E-mail

There are many possible integrations of multimedia and e-mail. Of course, since most modern e-mail packages accept any type of application file, multimedia files can be included in e-mail as attachments or enclosures. As with other attachments, the recipient of the message must be able to launch the appropriate application which can interpret and display the file or attachment type. If these applications or viewers are not available at the receiver's workstation, then the attachment cannot be viewed or played. There are many solutions for this problem, such as including a viewer in the message, creating a more standard file type that can be interpreted by many applications, and so on.

There is, however, a much more elegant option for integrating multimedia within the e-mail system. This solution allows authors of messages to create and include multimedia elements into their messages directly and to send them to recipients who can easily access, play back, or display these elements. With this option, multimedia types such as voice annotation, images, or video clips can be included in a multimedia message. The goal is to make the creation and playback (or display) of the multimedia element as easy and transparent as text.

In the Andrews Message Systems (AMS) (Borenstein and Thyberg, 1992), multimedia objects and formatted text are integrated in the messages. Most e-mail messages

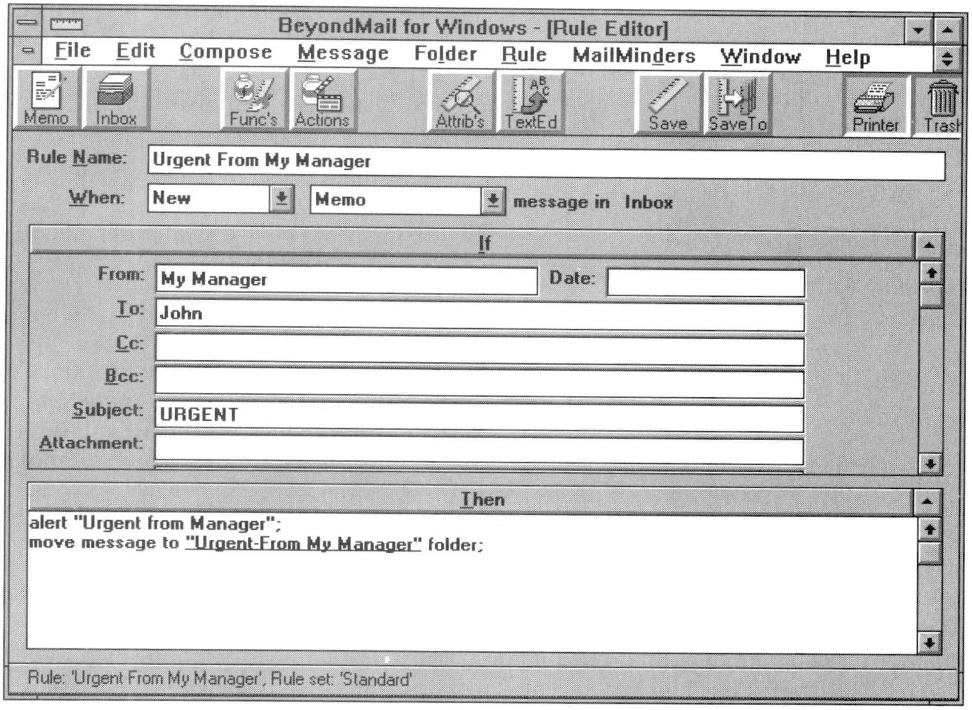

Figure 4.10 A rule in BeyondMail.

contain text, but provide little support of formatting. With AMS and other multimedia-enabled e-mail systems, multimedia data types can be used easily in the messages. The multimedia element may be a picture of the person sending the message, a voice annotation, messages with text formatted in various fonts, and so on.

Increasingly, many e-mail systems allow users to import and include graphics objects, such as images, into their messages. The key is the ease with which users can incorporate such multimedia elements into their messages. While this can be done by attaching or enclosing a document with multimedia elements, from the user's perspective, being able to include multimedia elements (images, voice, video, and text formatting) as easily as simple text messages has many advantages.

With the anticipated proliferation of interoperability platforms such as OpenDoc and OLE 2, there will be more multimedia elements "embedded" into messages in next-generation e-mail systems.

Document Annotations

When evaluations, suggestions, and approvals of documents are solicited by the document authors, they are often indicated by means of annotations on the document. With paper documents, there are many types of annotations available, including highlights, red-pen annotations, posted notes, and so on.

The notion of annotations also applies to digital documents. In fact, in a very real sense, since digital information is so amorphous, digital documents have a more flexible and extensible set of annotations. Figure 4.11 illustrates various annotation types used in Office.IQ. These types of annotations are used extensively not only in e-mail and workflow systems but in document imaging systems as well. Many document imaging systems also provide workflow functionality. Annotations can be applied to:

(a) Image documents: These documents could be faxes, scanned images of paper documents, or screen captures of electronic documents.

(b) Embedded documents of any type: The document source could, in fact, be any type of document: a word processor file, a spreadsheet, presentation graphics, which could be viewed by the system performing the annotation. Composite document models such as OLE 2 and OpenDoc are ideal for such implementations, where the user has the option of either incorporating an annotation film on top of a document or editing the document itself. And a proper implementation of security would allow some users to perform only the former annotations on a document while others would be able to author or modify the actual document.

It is therefore desirable to somehow integrate annotation funtionality with e-mail. Support of annotations could be part of the e-mail application. Alternatively a third party application could be invoked to handle the annotations. In either case since commenting, highlighting, and authorization are such common activities for processing exchanged documents, their integration with e-mail can greatly enhance electronic work processes.

Message Types

Just as multimedia elements can be supported either through attachments or through built-in (built into the e-mail system) editors and tools, the same could be said for forms and other message types. Chapter 2 discussed the importance of forms in groupware systems. Many modern e-mail systems allow users to create simple forms, but be aware that there are different approaches to the integration of message types and forms with e-mail.

(a) Mail-enabled forms package: This approach implements mail-enabling within a sophisticated and advanced forms package. The forms cannot only be created and filled by means of these packages but they can be routed as well. The routing of the forms usually incorporates an e-mail transport mechanism.

(b) Form editor within an e-mail system: Another approach is to allow e-mail users to create and route simple forms within the e-mail application. Forms created by e-mail packages are, typically, much simpler and cannot be used as complex production forms. Nevertheless, a simple form is, in many cases, all that is needed.

Figure 4.11 Office.IQ compound document with annotation.

Notification and Receipts

Conceptually, an e-mail system that has a powerful extendible rule-based system (as discussed earlier) could enable a user to specify rules that specify the sender of a message be notified if certain conditions are met. The criteria for notification can be either predefined and built into an e-mail system, defined through rules, or implemented in some combination of both rules and predefined actions:

- *Notification that message is delivered (receipt):* This approach is similar to receipt notifications in regular mail (especially certified mail), which confirm that the addressee has indeed received the mail. Obviously, the receipt of a mail message is no guarantee that the message is read, it is a confirmation to the sender that the message has not been lost.

- *Notification that message is read (receipt—message read):* A stronger type of notification is to inform the sender that not only has the message been delivered, but that the receiver has actually read the message. Actually, the notification only indicates that the message has been opened. The only real confirmation that a message has been read is for the recipient to reply.

- *Notification when message is not read after a certain amount of time:* Many mail systems on a LAN provide a mail log capability to inform the sender that a sent message has or has not been read by all the recipients of the message. If this feature is supported by the e-mail system, then the sender can check the log for the messages that were sent. However, a user can be explicitly notified if a particular recipient did not read the message after a certain amount of time by setting a notification alarm. The sender could set the time of the alarm and the type of notification (sound, dialog, a message, etc.) if allowed by the smart e-mail system. This type of notification is also useful when e-mail is sent between various sites, perhaps through intermediate gateways.

E-mail Security

As connectivity and e-mail proliferates within corporations, the issues of security become more pressing. As downsized environments and client/server architectures continue to replace centralized mainframe systems, information systems managers often justifiably raise the important issue of security. If mission-critical data is to be stored in the internetworked client/server systems, and connectivity (through e-mail or otherwise) to the outside world is also provided, then the vital information must be secured both internally and externally from hackers, crackers, and other external "intruders."

An e-mail system can provide many different types of security, including confidentiality, data origin authentication, connectionless integrity, and digital signatures. The following sections explain briefly each of these security services.

Cryptography

The base technology used to provide security services is cryptography. Cryptoalgorithms are used in various phases and components of e-mail security services. In general terms, encrypted data is transformed by means of a key: Key1. As illustrated in Figure 4.12, plaintext (readable text) is encrypted through a key and the output, ciphertext, is sent to the recipient. The recipient then must provide another key, Key2, to decrypt the ciphertext into plaintext. With the correct Key2, the ciphertext yields the original plaintext sent by the sender.

There are two predominant techniques of decryption technology.

- *Symmetric cryptoalgorithms:* Symmetric cryptoalgorithms use the same key to encrypt and decrypt the plaintext. Symmetric cryptoalgorithms mean that Key1 = Key2.
- *Asymmetric cryptoalgorithms:* The two keys, Key1 and Key2, are different. Usually, the first key, Key1, is a private key, and the second key, Key2, is public. The plaintext encrypted by the private key of a user can be decrypted with the public key of the same user. Asymmetric cryptoalgorithms are used for the digital signatures discussed next.

It is important to note that the application of encryption to various components of an e-mail message may vary. Furthermore, encryption can be applied to an entire message, to just the body of the message, to attachments, to various fields in the header of a message, to a digest of the message, and so on. Security services for e-mail might use different cryptographic algorithms for different purposes. The overall architecture is shown in Figure 4.13. The user submits a message that first gets filtered by the security service using encryption keys and various cryptoalgorithms, and the resulting encrypted message is delivered to the mail transport services. At the recipient's site, the security service uses the decryption key and cryptoalgorithms to generate and deliver the message to the receiver.

Confidentiality, Authentication, and Integrity

Other e-mail security features that may be provided by a security service include:

- *Confidentiality:* This ensures that the content of the message has not been compromised. Confidentially services attempt to protect messages from wiretapping, accidental or malicious misdelivery, and from tampering while it is sitting either in author's mailbox or in the e-mail database.

- *Origin authentication:* This service allows the recipient to protect the identity of the sender or originator of the message. In e-mail systems, it is possible to forge the identity of the sender. Origin authentication services attempt to protect the system against such forgeries.

- *Message integrity:* This service attempts to assure that the sent message is not altered before it is received. This is different from confidentiality, which attempts to guarantee that no one has wiretapped or read the message. Message integrity attempts to protect the content of the message against modifications. Integrity is sometimes called connectionless service when no ordering is assumed among the received messages.

E-mail security is becoming increasingly important because of the vast proliferation of, and growing dependency on, e-mail. If e-mail is to be used in legal contracts, for example, the authenticity of the originator, confidentiality, and the integrity of the mes-

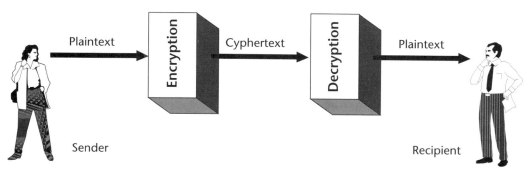

Figure 4.12 Cryptoalgorithm example.

sage are imperative. Many industry analysts consider this to be *the* critical issue that impedes the massive proliferation of business over the networks.

Digital Signatures

Another important security mechanism is digital signatures. For instance, if a form is to be approved by a senior manager, it is necessary to ensure that the approval is done by the appropriate manager in much the same way that purchase requisitions, hiring approval, project approval, or quality assurance approvals are often guaranteed by signatures on forms.

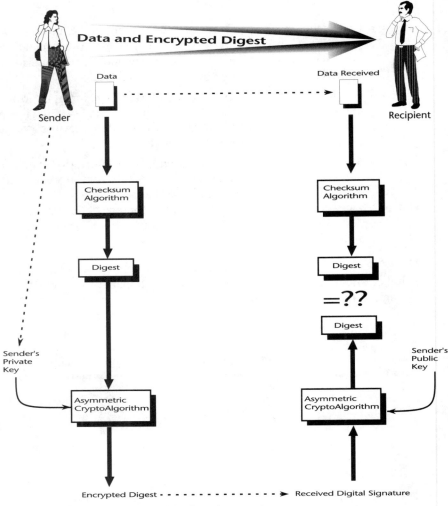

Figure 4.13 Privacy enhanced mail environment.

Most of the implementations of digital signatures use public key cryptography. This section briefly describes Apple's DigiSign implementation of digital signature.

As illustrated in Figure 4.13, a checksum of the data is created. This is called the data digest. This could be a hash value of the data with a very small probability that two data sets or plaintexts could have the same hash value. In Apple's implementation, the data digest is a 16-byte value.

The digest is encrypted using a private key from the signer. Only the digest is encrypted; the original data is not. Once the digest has been encrypted, it, as well as the public key of the user, are appended to the message before sending the data. At the recipient site the same algorithm is used to create the digest, say D1, of the message. Then the public key, D2, is used to extract the digest from the encrypted digest (ED). If D1 is equal to D2 then the signature is verified. Otherwise the message is regarded as having been tampered with and compromised.

This mechanism does not encrypt the original data or message, which means that if the data has been modified or tampered with, it cannot tell who and in what way that data has been modified. It can only indicate that the message has been tampered with in some way during transit from its source to its destination.

E-mail Workflow Support

If the various components of advanced e-mail systems are supported by an intelligent e-mail product, usually it is sufficient to support the workflow requirements in many organizations, especially for ad hoc and administrative workflow, as discussed in the Chapter 5 in great detail. Assume an e-mail system incorporates the following:

- Support of annotations
- Support of notifications
- Support of digital signature
- Support of message threads

Notification can be supported either through rules or predefined notification primitives. With just these four features, many "light" workflow features could be implemented and supported through the e-mail system itself. For example: Suppose you are preparing a training brochure. The author of the brochure sends the proposal to the editor, who must approve it and send it to the publications department. The publications staff checks if the editor has signed off and then forwards it for actual production. The production process may involve a number of iterations between the author and editor, whereby the editor incorporates annotations into the document and sends it back to the author. After a number of iterations, the editor approves the document and signs off on it. The signature is actually a digital signature, and the publications department checks the validity of the signature and commences to produce the brochure through an external publication production agency.

Straightforward workflow such as this example covers many, if not most, situations in an organization. The integrated abilities in the e-mail system could greatly improve the overall processing of such work.

Although certain important features are missing in such rudimentary workflow solutions, using a smart e-mail system with these capabilities to implement workflow could, nevertheless, be an important step toward the adoption of more advanced workflow systems. In fact, in many cases, properly used advanced e-mail systems would be more than sufficient to handle most of the workflow needs in many organizations.

TOPICS AND MESSAGE THREADS

There are two basic mechanisms for interaction and communication between members of a group using a messaging-based system:

- *Routing:* Most of the discussion in this chapter dealt with routing—a user sends a message and there is a reply. Most e-mail systems provide some support for threading or keeping track of the replies to the replies and so on. There is usually some visual way to identify and indicate both the original message and the reply.
- *Forums and bulletin boards:* An alternative mechanism that has been supported for many years in public as well as in private e-mail systems is the notion of a forum or bulletin board. Rather than routing messages, the messages are posted on bulletin boards.

Various user groups or topics of discussion can be created ahead of time as a means of focusing and organizing interaction and discussion. In most cases, users subscribe to the public forum, bulletin board, or user group and follow the discussion. The user decides when to drop into the ongoing discussion. Users can participate in a variety of ways. They can pose questions to the forum or topic. They can respond to a question or reply to a reply. Or, perhaps most commonly, they can participate passively simply by monitoring those discussion threads that attract their interest. Anyone can access and participate (provided they have the ability to subscribe).

Bulletin board may be public or supported by a certain company, agency, or interest group. Forums may also be public or supported by a particular company or group. The notion is the same. As long as users can access the bulletin board or forum, they can either respond to questions, share knowledge, pose questions, or merely witness.

These bulletin boards and forums have been used very successfully and are quite popular. They will continue to be integral points of interest along the information superhighway. For instance, on the Internet there are literally tens of thousands on NewsNet user groups. Topics range from very technical subjects such as object-oriented databases to the humanities, to religion, or to more prurient interests. Almost any conceivable topic has a newsgroup. As a relatively unfettered expression of human creativity, newsgroups and topics mirror the whole spectrum of human aspiration and experience: from the sacred to the profane, the practical to the frivolous, the profound to the silly. Any user of the Internet can subscribe to any number of these newsgroups.

Forums are also popular. Companies such as Novell and Microsoft have forums on CompuServe. Clients and other interested parties can use these forums to pose technical questions and receive support from the technical staff of these companies. The "knowledge base" or database of answers provided by the company supporting the forum is useful for many subscribers. Typically, these databases or "knowledge bases" are called FAQs, Frequently Asked Questions.

Bulletin boards and forums are usually "public," which is not to imply that it is easy to create a newsgroup or a forum. Given the overhead on the Internet, there are certain "cultures" and reasons that determine when a newsgroup needs to be created. Often, a major interest group spawns off other more specialized newsgroups.

The same concept has been applied more recently to corporate and internal mail systems. A number of products, such as Lotus Notes and Collabra Share offer similar capabilities for managing message threads and topics databases within the corporation. These systems are often integrated with e-mail systems. E-mail based on routing and topics databases can coexist.

The notion of message threads (the reply of a reply of a reply equals dialog) is also used in messaging or routing-based e-mail. But the concept of a topics database is different. In particular, it has the following features:

(a) In most cases, the messages are not routed. It is at the discretion of the user to access the messages stored in a particular topics database.

(b) Users employ point-and-click GUIs to start a topic, pose a question, make an observation, or provide a repository for some important documents.

(c) The systems that support topics databases for discussion among various participants usually allow for a graphical display of the message response hierarchy. This is illustrated in Figure 4.14. If a participant is responding to a response of a response, then, his or her response will be indented accordingly.

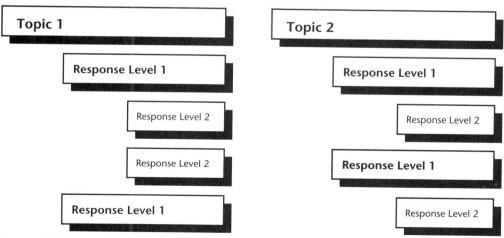

Figure 4.14 Organization of topics databases.

Corporate e-mail systems such as cc:Mail also support internal bulletin boards. The key advantage of this next-generation of groupware systems such as Notes and Collabra is the ease and elegance by which such topics databases are created, managed, searched, and displayed.

SUMMARY

This chapter discussed the main features of messaging and e-mail systems. E-mail is considered by many to be the most successful groupware application category. It is definitely the most popular and continues to grow.

The main components of e-mail systems were covered here. In addition to discussing the front-end graphical user interfaces for e-mail systems and mail-enabled applications, the various back-end components of e-mail and messaging implementations were described.

Messaging databases and directory services were discussed. The chapter also presented overviews of some of the emerging messaging transport standards such as MHS, messaging API standards such as MAP and VIM, and directory services standards such as X.500.

Finally, the chapter presented some of the emerging "smart" mail features being incorporated into next-generation e-mail and messaging products. These advanced e-mail features include rules, multimedia, and digital signatures.

5

Workflow: Computer-supported Collaborative Work Processing

In groupware technologies, workflow systems constitute some of the most powerful environments that enable collaborative computations to automate work processes. A better and more complete description of these systems would be *computer-supported collaborative work processing* (CSCWP). The approach is to have systems that assist, automate, or control the processing of work. Workflow products can play pivotal enabling roles for the successful implementation of reengineered business processes or incremental quality improvement gains in business transactions.

It is unfortunate that some earlier literature on groupware has presented it as a computation and automation domain, which is different than workflow. As pointed out by a number of experts, "At a first glance, workflow systems and groupware applications appear antithetical to one another. Workflow systems seek to automate formal policies and procedures enabling the reengineering of basic business processes. Groupware applications seek to facilitate informal group interactions by enhancing communications, coordination, and collaboration of task teams" (Bock, 1992).

From its early days, workflow had been identified with document imaging systems, and its applications had very clear and sometimes rigid prescribed steps of information and task flow. Groupware, on the other hand, has typically been identified with either collaborative meeting systems or systems that help maintain the organizational memory or assist in scheduling formal and informal meetings.

Electronic meetings, video-conferencing, and collaborative authoring are some of the most commonly used examples of groupware. Next-generation e-mail systems that store and maintain the topics and conversations that were carried electronically and provide elegant messaging databases with various querying and viewing capabilities are other examples.

There are other groupware systems or categories of groupware products that encourage and assist with more formal interactions between team members. Shared calendaring or scheduling systems are such products. These systems mean that different team members can share their calendars on a network and schedule meetings through a database of calendars—indicating if there are conflicts for a proposed meeting, making a proposal and reserving a slot, or accepting a proposed meeting time.

The "looser" definition of groupware as any system that assists collaborative work indicates that workflow is really just another type of groupware. However, we do caution the reader that the confusion between workflow and groupware will persist for some time. Depending upon the particular perspective of the author, a product category such as group calendaring can be characterized as groupware or workflow. It is one of the primary goals of this book to elucidate some of the concepts (certainly the most important ones) underlying the terms "groupware" and "workflow."

Groupware systems can be separated into two very broad categories:

- *Informal and creative interactions to encourage group communication:* Some groupware tools provide support for workers who need to cooperate in order to accomplish their tasks. These are usually casual and improvised group interactions. Electronic mail systems falls in this category, as does any document management tool. Informal interactions do not mean there are no goals or deliverables. The implication is the lack of rigid structures and requirements in accomplishing the task or deliverables.

- *Products and systems that have strict structures, policies, and procedures:* These enhance the communication and delivery procedures by making sure all intermediate steps are accomplished and all constraints are satisfied.

These are two very broad categories, and different groupware products will encourage different levels of ad hoc or creative interaction and structure. In fact, users will have different perceptions and evaluations of the same tools. Furthermore, the amount of structure will be left to the implementor or the team using the tool.

Workflow systems connote the framework for automating and enhancing the flow of work or task activities between workers and processes:

> It is, simply put, the automation of the processes that we use every day to run our business. A workflow application automates the sequence of actions, activities, or tasks used to run the process, including tracking of the status of each instance of the process, as well as tools for managing the process itself. (Marshak, 1994)

Workflow does not have to be structured. Its primary function is to facilitate the fulfillment of projects and deliverables by a team. Here is another definition that captures some of the elements of workflow:

Workflow software is the tool that empowers individuals, and groups in both structured and unstructured environments to automatically manage a series of recurrent or nonrecurrent events in a way that achieves the business objectives of the company. (Palermo and McCreedy, 1992)

The key points in this definition is the phrase "*tools that empower individuals*" to manage business activities and events. An important part of this management is collaboration and coordination between workers.

Workflow automation is the structure that is applied to the movement of information in order to improve the results of a business process. Workflow automation software actively manages the coordination of activities among people in general business processes. (Burns, 1994)

This aspect of coordination is extremely important. It goes beyond just communicating information through electronic media. It also involves individuals in an organization working on a project to accomplish a goal or to implement a prescribed business process.

Whatever the definition or understanding of workflow, there is general agreement that workflow technology (and groupware in general) *enhances productivity*. The most rudimentary definition includes the aspects of better service and turnaround for the customer. Whether what is being produced are goods, services, or information, the goal is to accelerate the production in the collaborative work environment and accelerate the production. Some would see (and there is validity in this perception) that workflow attempts to incrementally improve on existing inefficiencies. Others would view workflow as the tool by which to bring about business process reengineering. As noted in Chapter 1, "Reengineering is the fundamental rethinking and radical redesign of business processes to achieve dramatic improvement in critical contemporary measures of performance such as cost, quality, services and speed" (Hammer and Champy, 1993).

Whether used primarily as a tool to enhance existing infrastructures or as a tool to implement business process reengineering remember that workflow means *tools*. In other words, workflow technology and workflow products do not have inherent solutions to solve business process problems. Some workflow systems are computer-aided engineering tools, others are based on specific theories adopted by the product's architects and solutions based on these theories, still others are more neutral object-oriented environments not necessarily based on a particular model or theory. The key point is that the product itself (the workflow software or the tool), even if it does present a certain theory, does not contain the solution in itself.

This is very important. Like any other technology or software system, there must be a *design* step. The design step is a major strategic business evaluation of the processes in the organization, the culture within the organization, and the adoption of the proper technology to bring about the change or improvement. This might sound like a common sense or obvious observation. But like any other new technology, often the emphasis is on the technology versus the proper integration of that technology in the organization.

GIGO is an acronym for "garbage-in-garbage-out": It is used frequently in the context of software programming. Most programs accept input, process it, and produce output. The connotation is that if the input is garbage, the program will process garbage, and the output will therefore be garbage. The point is that the adoption of workflow should be preceded by extensive analysis, design, and evaluation, and all aspects of the organization should be taken into consideration.

In workflow or computer supported collaborative work processing the *work* or *work processing* is central. There is a much more direct connotation for carrying out a specific task or deliverable than the looser, ad hoc, or informal environment of a groupware system that encourages, for instance, team coordination and a group spirit, thus helping work processing indirectly.

It should be emphasized that like other groupware systems such as electronic meetings or smart e-mail, a workflow system can also have indirect or incidental benefits in encouraging collaboration. However, especially for production systems, workflow implies specific goals, tasks, and deliverables. Examples of such goals include:

- Hiring an employee for a specific position.
- Processing a loan.
- Processing a purchase requisition.
- Conducting market research for trading.
- Preparing a business plan.
- Quality assurance and control in a production plant.
- Conducting research and trade in financial applications.

A workflow system as a CSCWP application typically has the following characteristics:

(a) Computer-supported: This is the most obvious characteristic but it can be quite complex if it implies that all the participants must carry out their tasks through a computerized environment. For small teams or collaborative workers in the same department, this is straightforward since most likely everyone is on the same local area network and the environment is more or less homogeneous. However, in large distributed enterprises where each site has autonomy in deciding the type of systems and platforms they use, computer support for tasks involving multiple sites could be quite difficult. The heterogeneity can be due to the client platform (which is perhaps the most serious), the server platform, the database management system, the massaging transport protocol, the network operating system, the server operating systems, the various software systems that are needed to implement the workflow product, and so on. A computer-supported environment that involves a great deal of heterogeneity in an enterprise can become quite complex to manage and integrate. Some recent solutions in groupware have attempted to provide enterprise-wide platforms. These products allow users share and exchange information in distributed heterogeneous environments. Versions of the product execute at all participating sites and handle all aspects of distributed computation. Lotus Notes is an example of such a product.

(b) Collaborative: Workflow systems are distinct from personal information managers which help work processing for individuals. It is conceivable that a workflow system also provides help to an individual—such as through desktop metaphors, search and organization capabilities, and so on. However, to be a collaborative work processing system, the workflow product must support groups and collaboration. Depending upon the connectivity and the internetworked architecture over which the workflow systems is operating, the groups and individuals involved can be either "local" users—users in close physical proximity—or "remote" users—users who may be in different buildings, cities, states, countries, or continents. The collaboration capabilities of the workflow system must specify the scope of collaboration. Workflow products often support cases, forms, tracking, approval, and decision trees. All these functions involve collaboration by workers with different roles to accomplish a particular task. As described in (a), the workflow system must also specify the types of transport layers and platforms it supports. This is extremely important since some of the people who must be involved in the collaborative computing environment might not be on the platforms supported by the workflow system.

(c) Support work processing: The workflow system must have specific targets, goals, and deliverables. It is possible to distinguish between workflow systems that provide overall enhancements in the processing of work without specific goals or deliverables and those that help carry out specific goals and targets or deliverables. For systems that enhance the overall productivity and the collaborative environment in a corporation, many groupware systems can be categorized as workflow. In the industry, however, workflow systems are typically characterized as those that assist in achieving specific business goals. A corporation's business processes and procedures reflect its "culture," organizational infrastructure, responsibilities, and tasks carried out by different departments and individuals in a corporation. Workflow systems help carry out these processes and procedures. In most cases, a process activated for a particular goal has resources allocated to it, schedule requirements, cost estimates, performance goals, sign-off procedures, to name a few. Workflow systems can assist in processing these steps.

WORKFLOW IN DOCUMENT IMAGING

Workflow systems have their roots and initial implementations in document imaging, through companies such as FileNet, Wang, ViewStar, Keyfile, Bull, Sigma, Laser Data, and others. The reason workflow has been associated with document imaging systems is obvious: The main application of document imaging is the replacement of paper-intensive business processes through digitized documents. These documents are the scanned images of paper documents. Once the information is digitized and indexed, the main business process takes over.

Ninety-five percent of information is still in paper form. Of the remaining 5 percent, only 1 percent is on-line. The other 4 percent represents archived information (either on tapes, microfiche, or optical disks). With document imaging applications (which constitute specialized multimedia applications) there is the potential of reducing the amount of paper documents and replacing them with images and other forms (audio or video) of multimedia information. In most document imaging systems, large amounts of paper documents are scanned, indexed, in some cases OCRed, and stored for retrieval. Users can then search these documents based on keywords, annotate them, and route them in an office environment. Paper forms and forms routing performed manually can be replaced by electronic forms, with substantial gains in processing time.

Therefore, the primary purpose of these systems is to convert existing paper documents and office procedures using paper-based information into digitized documents and automated information flow. The converted paper documents appear either as images, editable forms, or free text. When they are introduced into a document imaging system, they become objects with attributes and content. For efficient retrieval and manipulation of document images, both attribute-based and content-based indexing are supported, which allows office workers to retrieve digitized documents and forms based on queries involving either attributes, keywords, or content. The images, forms, or generated text documents can either be viewed or updated by office workers. The update can be in the form of annotations on top of the image documents or through updating keywords and attribute values of the objects. Often, the processing of the images follows well-defined procedures in a corporation and it is not uncommon to find workflow systems incorporated in document imaging solutions. These systems thus attempt to replace established nonelectronic procedures and processes that are paper-based with electronic document processing.

Figure 5.1 illustrates some of the basic elements of a document imaging system primarily from a functional perspective. Images are entered into the system at a scan station. (If a large number of documents on paper or microfilm already exist, they may be scanned and indexed by an outside bureau. The scan station is then used for new incoming documents.) The nature of the scan station is dictated by the volume of paper that passes through the station and the size of the documents. The speed of scanning is dictated by the the document feed, the response of the light-sensitive device that converts a visual image into electronic form, and the power of the hardware used to subsequently process the electronic data. Processing often includes intensity adjustment, compression or dithering, and the generation of a file header. The following describes scan station types:

- A low-end scan station might be composed of a flat-bed scanner capable of one or two pages per minute, on-screen review of the resultant image, and rudimentary processing such as intensity adjustment and software compression. Indexing, clipping, rotation and rescanning would all be done at this station.

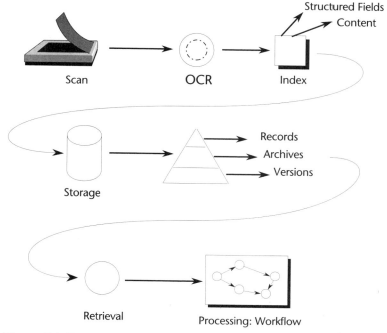

Figure 5.1 Basic elements in a document imaging system.

- A medium range scan station is capable of 10 to 20 pages per minute. A document feeder moves documents from a hopper using rubber wheels to take the documents one at a time. Compression and manipulation of the data are accomplished either as a standard function of the scanner control card, or through custom microcode on this board. Scanning is performed on batches of similar documents, and the steps of indexing and editing these documents are handled later at another station.
- A high-end scan station uses a high-speed scanner (often the size of a large photocopier and with similar functionality). To scan a large volume of paper, the document feed may employ a vacuum pump to hold each document as it travels through the scanner. The system may have the capability to scan double-sided images. The scan station may not have a screen, or it might use a low-resolution screen to show status and present options to the user. Indexing is performed at a separate station. This type of scan station is often located in a mailroom (remote from the rest of the system) so that documents can be entered at their point of arrival.

The next step after scanning is the "indexing" of the document attributes and content. If all the images being scanned pertain to a specific predefined form or have well-defined attributes that can be readily extracted from the images of the scanned documents, then a form-based indexing can be used to extract the field or attribute values from the document. Form-based indexing can be either manual—which means that a data entry office worker views each image and manually enters the form's field values for that image—or automatic. For the latter, an optical character recognition system can be used to recognize the text for either the entire document or zones. OCR can also be used to recognize forms. Through combining OCR processing with various term frequency calculation and weight evaluation techniques a document imaging system can automatically index large collections of documents. Therefore, with a combination of optical character recognition and form recognition technologies it is possible to extract the information from the digital image of a form and convert it into structured information that can then be modified, analyzed, edited, searched, and processed. Alternatively, the field values in a form can also be indexed manually. Once a digital structured form is created from the form's image, the form can subsequently be processed in various workflow scenarios.

Document imaging systems also incorporate a workflow processing system that allows office workers routing the digitized documents to achieve specific goals or tasks. Workflow systems let the user construct office processes or procedures interactively through a graphical editor or procedurally through a scripting language. Figure 5.2(a) illustrates a workflow built with Portfolio's Office.IQ graphical workflow editor. Figure 5.2(b) illustrates a workflow designed by Reach's WorkMAN. The documents that are processed through a workflow can be manipulated or updated by different workers participating in a workflow process. The workflow system can also manage queues of documents to be processed by various participants. The status of various activated workflows is also maintained by the underlying systems. For document images, users can implement various annotation tools to highlight and comment on different paragraphs or regions of a document. Figure 5.3 shows an annotated document image. In many systems, these annotation tools are also available for all information types, including word processors, spreadsheets, and presentations. Thus, just as paper documents being processed by different people in an office are commented on and annotated by participating managers or co-workers, the documents being processed in an automated information flow are subject to various electronic annotations and updates.

Through digitizing, indexing, and allowing for electronic workflow replacement of paper-based information processing, document imaging can result in financial cost benefits for a corporation. The imaging industry has understood from the very start (and perhaps more clearly than most other groupware industries) that the key to the success of the adoption and implementation of an imaging system is the cost benefit. For the imaging industry, there are some very clear quantitative benefits that can be easily shown.

TAXONOMIES OF WORKFLOW SYSTEMS

Workflow systems are a relatively new technology. As mentioned earlier, some of the earliest and most successful implementations of workflow have been in imaging sys-

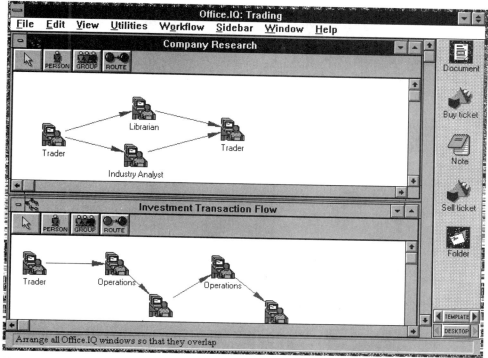

Figure 5.2(a) Workflow built with the Office.IQ graphical workflow editor.

tems. Now, however, with the proliferation of various electronic interchange mechanisms for documents, forms, spreadsheets, and other types of objects, a substantial percentage of information is generated digitally to start with. As noted earlier, the percentage of information existing in paper form is still high, and will remain so for a long time. Printer sales, which at one point were predicted to decline due to various technologies that attempted to proliferate a "paperless" environment, are showing a healthy growth. What has happened, instead, is that information generated in paper form now often exists in "soft" or digital form as well. Thus both "hard copy" and digitized versions of the same document are produced and maintained.

The new generation of workflow systems have similar goals as their imaging workflow predecessors. The starting point, assumptions, and impact are all different, however. First, earlier imaging workflow systems attempted to automate and replace existing paper-based business processes through digitized forms and workflow. Initially, there was no or little attempt to revisit the *process* itself. The conversion and replacement of paper with digitized forms and information was revolutionary enough. In fact, the problems and solutions that are used in existing document imaging systems are still very much in sync with this approach: replacing paper-based business processes with their computerized electronic counterparts.

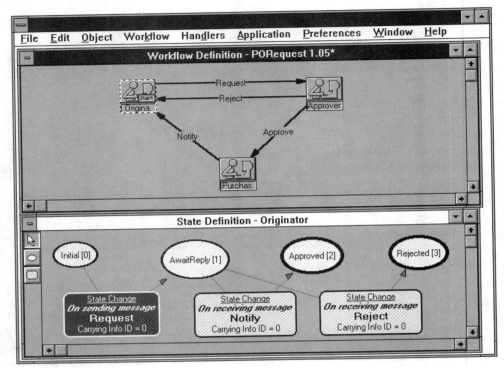

Figure 5.2(b) Workflow built with WorkMAN.

The following is a simple anecdote. All network users agree that electronic passwords provide a very safe mechanism to control network access (of course, the penetration of so-called "secure" military networks by teenage hackers would seem to contradict this). Nevertheless, this is the best method available for the vast majority of networks. A client, when told about the availability of electronic passwords in a workflow package, insisted repeatedly that what was needed was not an electronic password but the actual signature of the person performing the sign-off. This customer wanted a replication of what is "seen" on paper forms. Perhaps the notion of what sign-off means and how it can be verified in an automated, digitized networked environment should be revisited, or, more precisely, reengineered.

The next few paragraphs attempt to analyze some of the approaches used in products and other systems that characterize themselves as workflow systems. There are great variances and differences between workflow systems. There are and will continue to be various attempts to categorize products according to certain criteria. This is a rapidly evolving technology, and care must be taken before corporations attempt to reengineer their business processes. Just because a product characterizes itself as "workflow" does not necessarily mean that it is automatically suited to help a corporation reengineer or automate some of its business processes.

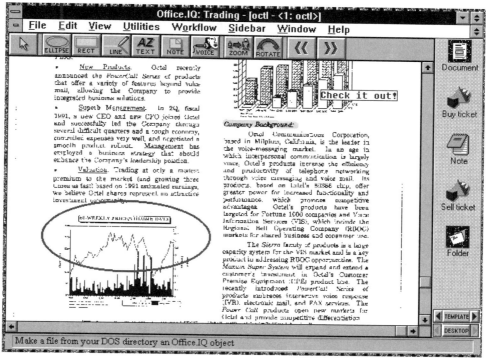

Figure 5.3 An annotated document image.

The differences (and confusion) between systems and products characterizing themselves as workflow is, of course, typical and to be expected of technologies in their infancy. The earlier association of workflow with document imaging is a mixed blessing. On the one hand, it has helped to convince the skeptics of the viability of workflow in successful business applications. On the other hand, it has set in motion certain expectations as to how workflow systems should look—to a certain extent limiting its potential application and endorsement in environments that are not so imaging-intensive.

How Much Programming Is Required?

One of the simplest way to taxonomize workflow systems is to analyze the level of programming required by the user or corporation adopting the workflow technology. At one extreme it could be said that a C compiler with some C libraries for communication, networking, and messaging is a workflow system. Since C is computationally complete—in other words, it is possible to compute in C any problem that can be solved with a computer—then any workflow system could be implemented in C. Is a C compiler a workflow system?

Although this question is ridiculous, it is surprising that, currently, a lot of products that are positioned as "workflow" are complex scripting language systems with some built-in terms which are suited for routing and workflow processing in general. In other words, some systems provide a "novel" programming language with some built-in terms that support workflow.

The other extreme is to have everything predefined or preprogrammed. Here the user is provided with a fixed set of primitives, in most cases represented as graphical user interface constructs. The user is limited to these primitives and is forced to work only with these "leggo" units to construct and implement their workflows.

Figure 5.4 illustrates the range of programming required for workflow systems. But with flexibility comes complexity. And, if the system is too flexible and a lot of programming is involved, it will also be hard to maintain. On the other hand, if the primitives in a rigid system are too restrictive, it will be difficult to implement routine office procedures and policies. As shown in the figure the most effort-intensive are those workflow solutions developed "from scratch" in a client/server architecture. This usually done by in-house corporate development before the emergence of workflow products. Workflow systems that are primarily based on routing with graphical tools are easier to implement, but they might not do the job for some. With object-orientation (discussed shortly) there is more flexibility, but the effort is still required at lower levels. When object-orientation is combined with declarative rules—which are usually easy to implement—the result is a high level of flexibility and much less complexity in development effort than a general purpose programming environment.

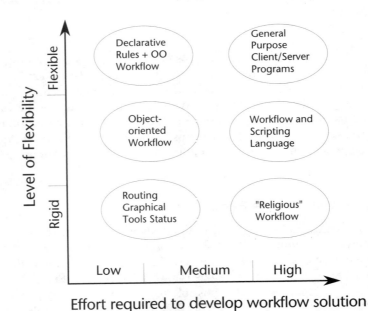

Figure 5.4 Amount of effort contrasted with flexibility for workflow solutions.

There are two main causes of "rigidity" in workflow systems:

(a) Imposing a particular theory on a workflow implementation: The demise of the mainframe and the move toward internetworked local area networks with servers sharing information across local and wide area networks have created a lot of possibilities and excitement for next-generation global enterprises. Equally interesting are the developments and advances in the field of management, organizational theory, and computer/human interaction. It is not uncommon today to find the management, cognition, or organization theory *du jour* with plenty of evidence from the real world and academia "proving" its validity. All these efforts are very useful and constructive in understanding how to best manage the future "virtual" corporations. However, since these are mostly theories, a system that imposes or even provides the software implementation of a theory must be analyzed very carefully by the customer before adopting it. Its implementation could have a profound and even devastating effect. A number of pilot trials and studies within the corporation could prove very useful. Action Technologies, for example, proposes a model based on language and human communication theories developed (or rather "evolved") by Winograd and Flores (1991). Their workflow model makes several assumptions about cognition, language, management, and organization theory. They view organizations as a "network of commitments," and believe that "managers engage in conversations during which they create, take care of, and initiate new commitments within an organization." Therefore "commitment to an action, with exclusion of other possibilities, is the common feature of the processes that precede action." Their workflow model is based upon this model: (1) opening, (2) negotiation, (3) performance or action, and (4) satisfaction or acceptance. This conversation-commitment-action model may be suitable in many situations. But to claim that it is the model that must be followed by all in every situation is a bit extreme to say the least.

(b) Limited set of primitives and closed systems: Another source of rigidity in workflow systems is a lack of flexibility for extensible components to construct workflow systems that are useful for the particular needs of an organization. If the set of primitives or the capability of the system to handle extensions are limited, the workflow system could be too rigid for an organization, and alternative strategies must be examined. The key concepts here are extensibility and openness of the system to accommodate other functions.

There is thus a trade-off. A very flexible system might require a great deal of programming—writing the code, debugging and maintaining it. The other extreme is to have more rigid systems which are difficult to extend and customize. Ideally, following an object-oriented paradigm, the workflow system should be simple to implement, flexible, and extensible.

The good news is that with reusable components, such systems are becoming a reality. The work in some of the distributed object managers such as DSOM from IBM and other interoperability standards being incorporated in operating systems such as Taligent, OpenDoc from Apple and IBM, and OLE 2 from Microsoft do provide standard and powerful mechanisms for extensibility.

As discussed in more detail later, workflow is much more than just controlling the work processing and flow. It is tightly integrated with an information model, and objects that can interoperate and share data provide a powerful foundation for future workflow systems.

Message Based and Server Based Workflow

One distinction that is often made between various workflow solutions is whether they are message or server based. Another way to put it is the distinction between "e-mail" based and "database"d workflow. In Chapter 4, we discussed how e-mail with some extensions can be used effectively as workflow. In fact there are two approaches for e-mail-based workflow:

(a) Enhanced e-mail applications: Like any other category of applications e-mail applications are becoming more sophisticated. Notifications, receipts, forms, rule-base forwarding, advanced filing, and digital signatures are being incorporated in next generation e-mail application products. These and other such features can be sufficient to support light workflow, administrative workflow, or ad-hoc workflow.

(b) Mail-enabled applications with workflow capabilities: The other approach is to incorporate "flow" capabilities into existing applications—especially those that are used most frequently in business transactions. Form applications, for instance, have been extended in a number of ways to incorporate not only mail-enabling but also workflow. For example, Delrina's Formflow allows users to send a form package, implement sequential routing of forms, packages, and track the progress of forms on a route.

With the database or server approach, the workflow system is implemented either on top of a commercial database management system or a proprietary DBMS—developed by the workflow tools vendor. The commercial DBMS option is more popular. Several document management products have taken this route. These products (especially with document imaging) incorporate workflow functionality to process documents.

One big difference between e-mail based and server based approaches is that with the latter, most of the workflow engine functionality is (or could be) executing on the server node. The client nodes handle the graphical user interface of the workflow. The server stores and manages the databases for the workflow such as the workflow definitions or templates; the tracking information of activated workflow; the documents and their attributes; the address books for users and groups; and so on. The server also handles the workflow engine. The engine is responsible for handling the workflow activations, tracking, notifications, rules, and so on. The workflow engine can interface with other transport engines to deliver the objects on a workflow's route. Here either an e-mail based or distributed database techniques can be used to allow workflow over distributed networks.

Empowering Users

Recent years have produced a lot of hype about systems and trends in downsized corporations that are attempting to empower the user. There is a consensus among analysts and trendsetters that the avant-garde corporations of the twenty-first century will be downsized energetic corporations, probably geographically distributed and whose employees are empowered with decision-making capabilities. The "flattened" organization will rely on its core of small teams to carry out the vision and goals of the business. These small teams will consist of knowledge workers with a lot of creativity and energy.

When analyzing workflow systems and their capabilities, often analysts and reviewers revert to feature lists, which really are characteristics of workers who carry out routine tasks. For example, some assume that a workflow system that automatically launches an application file that is routed to another user is in some way "superior" or "more advanced" than a system that simply routes it to a user and lets the empowered user launch the application at his or her discretion. The point is that sometimes workflow systems are criticized because they do not go far enough in automating a user's tasks. Often this "automation" amounts to treating the worker as a work processor who needs to be told what to do and set in a context for carrying out his or her precise task. The approach is the equivalent of an assembly line blue collar worker in an office environment.

Regarding the average worker as "dumb" or "computer illiterate" is the exact opposite depiction of creative, intelligent, educated, knowledge workers who will become (and are already becoming) the backbone of the downsized reengineered corporations.

Introducing such features in a workflow system that launch an application and "beep" to tell the worker to carry out a task (versus having the file, for instance, appear in the user's in/out box and tell the user what to do in a message) are not necessary to say the least. They could even be distracting and even damage creativity. In considering a workflow package, the profile of the target user is extremely important.

As discussed more in the next section, intelligent workflow systems should be thought of as assistants to the worker. The creative, exception handling capability and task processing capability of the user or worker should be enhanced by the workflow system. If the user, for example, is performing a task and he or she forgets to include some electronic documents (such as references or a credit check) the workflow system would ideally remind the worker of the oversight. The worker then can make the decision to include the missing documents.

In an ideal workflow implementation, the involvement of the knowledge worker should be at those key points that require creativity, intelligence, and knowledge. Consider Figure 5.5, which gives a diagram of a workflow system. The figure illustrates:

- Parallel routing: After the start node there are two "parallel" routes involved in the workflow.

- Condition routing: At a condition node a decision is made to either fax or proceed with the next worker.

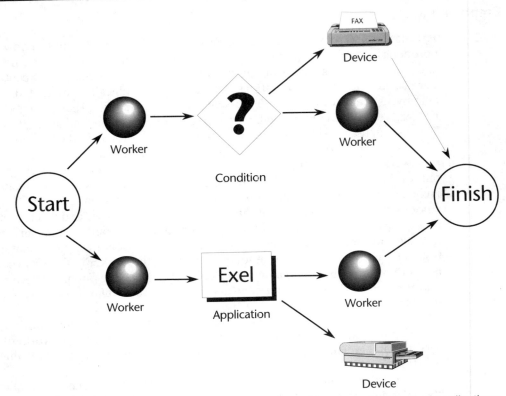

Figure 5.5 Sample workflow with workers, conditions, branches, devices, and applications.

- Devices such as printers and fax machines are also involved in the workflow.
- Applications are also involved in the workflow: They can be launched upon executing the workflow node, and the application itself could perform some actions (including routing).

As illustrated, some of these tasks, such as faxing could be handled by devices. Other tasks, such as routing, making decisions at condition nodes, and actions at application nodes could also be automated. After reducing the flow graph to decision-making nontrivial tasks involving knowledge workers, the workflow system's responsibility would be to carry out all the mundane tasks (faxing, routing to the correct person, accumulating objects to perform the routing, routing based on content, and so on) and isolate those points that need creativity, work processing, and involvement of knowledge workers. The key point is that workflow should empower the worker—encouraging creativity. The intelligence in assisting the worker accomplish his/her goals is often an essential requirement of successful workflow implementations.

Types of Workflow Technology

In the past few years, a number of reports characterize and taxonomize workflow products as having three types. There are subtle differences between these taxonomies. Be aware, however, that, in general, workflow products and systems are extremely hard to taxonomize, and attaching a label to a workflow package such as "ad hoc," "production," "administrative," or "knowledge-based" can be confusing. The concepts are not well-defined or scientific, and they rely on many generalities and imprecise terms. The science of workflow technologies, although it has a solid foundation in document imaging, is still in its infancy. The fact that it also incorporates management and organizational theory and computer/human interaction models complicates its scope and understanding.

With this in mind, here are brief descriptions of the three types of workflow systems: transaction- or production-based, ad hoc, and administrative.

Transaction or Production Workflow

With transaction or production workflow systems, there is typically a very involved policy or procedure described and imposed by a corporation. The processes are usually complex. Generally the corporation in question has evolved these various processes and procedures over time. They are at the very heart of the business of the corporation. These business processes provide a level of risk for the corporation. The tasks carried out by production or workflow systems are followed day by day with very little change; they are frequently recurring transactions. These procedures and processes usually involve various departments within the organization, and a structure has been created to enforce and implement them.

With transaction or production workflow the corporation has a financial exposure and needs an audit trail of all the activities at each step of the process that must be maintained. This is important because a lot of the work is carried out by clerical workers (although in a reengineered corporation, the clerical tasks must be made more challenging and replaced with tasks more typical of knowledge workers). However, transactions also involve business experts, and higher-level interventions are necessary for special cases.

Examples of production or transaction procedures include loan processing, insurance underwriting, and claims processing. As these examples illustrate, corporations conducting these businesses are reliant on following these procedures for their income. This financial exposure means that much care must be taken to ensure all details of the process or procedure are in place. For example, a mistake in the credit check for a loan application could result in considerable exposure for a mortgage company.

Another characteristic of this type of workflow processing is that most of the document imaging applications that incorporate workflow typically involve high volume and high value production. Massive amounts of paper documents will be scanned, its data will be entered into forms, and then processed. Depending on the application and its scope, often optical character recognition is used to perform some of the extraction of attributes or field values from the scanned images of the paper forms. This too could involve human intervention since OCR systems are not 100 percent accurate. Once the

224 ■ Workflow: Computer-supported Collaborative Work Processing

data or form entry is performed, the next step is to actually start using the form through routing it according to a prescribed business process.

As a typical example of a production system involving both document imaging and workflow, consider the loan application process in Figure 5.6. There are many steps involved in such a process. Remember, the process is at the heart of the business of the mortgage firm or the bank approving the loan. It is very important that the workflow system implementing the process is able to handle (or at least identify when manual intervention is necessary) all the steps and types of activity involved in loan processing. There are numerous forms, approvals, and steps to be followed with specific sign-off by personnel who have the appropriate authorization. The figure illustrates the use of imaging peripherals (scanner, faxing, storage, etc.) and how it integrates with the overall procedure of loan processing.

Ad Hoc Workflow

There are many tasks and activities in corporations that are more project oriented and do not use extensive processes and procedures. Whereas production-based workflow systems deal with day-to-day tasks that have more or less well-defined steps, ad hoc

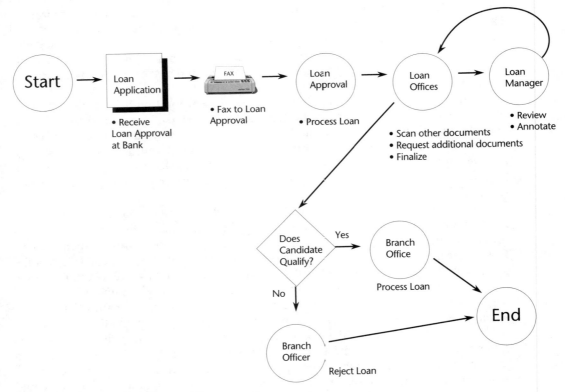

Figure 5.6 Loan application workflow example.

workflow applications have goals and deliverables whose steps and the dynamics between users are more difficult to define in detail and to any degree of predictability.

Examples of ad hoc workflow include the activities that are applied to define a new product, market an existing product, hire a new person, and so on. In carrying out the workflow for such projects, there are deadlines and deliverables but the individual responsibilities could dynamically change. Ad hoc tends to involve more creative and usually higher-level knowledge workers. Sometimes, these tasks are performed without the help of workflow systems.

The usual tools used to carry out these tasks include spreadsheets and word processors. If multiple workers and/or departments are involved, e-mail may be used to forward the documents being processed as enclosures. However, e-mail and single-user applications such as spreadsheets and word processors do not provide a mechanism for tracking the overall project.

The applications of ad hoc projects usually do not require elaborate project management systems, and these systems (such as Microsoft Project or MacProject) are probably overkill. However, even though ad hoc workflow systems are not used for production and mission-critical business processes and procedures, some project management capabilities for scheduling and delivery of completed tasks is desirable.

Therefore, ad hoc workflow systems attempt to provide some sort of control for making sure the various tasks and responsibilities of the participants are delivered on time, and that the deliverables are acceptable.

Another requirement of ad hoc workflow applications is the need to communicate constantly. This is, after all, the very nature of "ad hoc." With more structured production workflow, the task and information flow follows well-defined "routes" and "rules" with little or no change in each iteration. For example, loan applications follow the same process for approval. Contrast this with writing an engineering design document, where roles and responsibilities change dynamically and there is a steady need to interact and communicate intermediate results for approval, recommendation, and so on.

Administrative Workflow

The third type of workflow is administrative workflow. Based primarily on e-mail systems and extensions of conventional e-mail capabilities, this type of workflow handles routine "administrative" tasks. Most systems that deal with routing of forms may be characterized as administrative workflow. Other examples of administrative workflow include expense approvals, purchase requisitions, travel requests, vacation requests, and so on.

As mentioned in Chapter 4, more advanced e-mail systems have started to incorporate additional form processing capabilities including:

- *Creation of simple forms:* Capturing the attributes necessary for processing administrative functions such as all the information necessary for a purchase requisition. Of course an e-mail system can always route a form as an attachment. The creation of the form here means it is done through the e-mail package itself, versus a third-party package. Note that with the increased popularity of component based architectures and interoperability platforms such as OLE 2 and OpenDoc, applications are being pushed to include specialized functions versus "one-in-all" products.

- *Routing of forms:* Once the forms are filled, they can be routed through the e-mail system. If the e-mail or workflow system is advanced enough, it will provide field-level security or locking in the document or form. This means that only those who have the appropriate security or privilege status can update certain fields or portions of the document or form.

- *Iteration of form completion:* E-mail systems are not very efficient in handling concurrently shared objects (see Chapter 3 for a more detailed discussion on concurrent sharing). A form for any of the applications of administrative workflow might need to go through several iterations. If the process is handled electronically, it probably is preferable that the approval personnel and the worker who has submitted a request are operating on the same object versus copies of objects.

- *Deadlines, notification, alarms, and other workflow features:* For administrative workflow (as well as other workflow types), it is also desirable to have control over deadlines, including notification when a request is late, alarms to remind people to perform tasks involved in workflow, and so on.

This type of routine, less complex and low-risk processes are being satisfied by next-generation e-mail systems or workflow systems that have an e-mail backbone. However, when e-mail is "enriched" by workflow capabilities such as encryption, notification, and tracking, it may become unduly complex. Also, its application will be limited to either administrative or ad hoc workflow applications. For financially critical applications, more secure and stable production workflow systems must be used.

ASSISTING WORK PROCESSING

To repeat, workflow systems assist, automate, or control the processing of work. These three aspects of workflow systems are extremely important. In the various taxonomies of workflow systems the emphasis is usually on one or another of the features that characterizes the workflow product. Some workflow systems provide just assistance to work processing; others provide very powerful automation primitives; others handle complex scripting languages and environments; others provide detailed language and implementation primitives to control the work process. Some workflow systems, for instance, not only send or route a document to a user, but also launch the application and indicate to the recipient the task that needs to be done.

It is necessary to determine the level of automation required or desired for a particular corporation or organization before adopting one workflow (or groupware) solution over another. At one extreme are systems that attempt to "automate" every action and activity of the worker, or more to the point, to "control" and "enforce." These systems are tailored to clerical workers who handle very routine and repetitive tasks, such as data entry, forms processing, typing letters, checking calculations, and so on. The system has encapsulated these policies and procedures to assist the worker to avoid mistakes. In the taxonomies presented in the previous section, this more or less represents workflow systems that range from very detailed and involved production systems to less formal and constrained ad hoc workflow for managing projects.

Figure 5.7 illustrates an "abstract" data flow involving devices, personnel, tasks, scheduling, and so on. In identifying the benefits of a workflow system for a corporation, data flow diagrams for business processes, corporate procedures, department projects, and corporate projects must first be designed in order to have a good understanding of the problem domain before proceeding.

To determine the benefits of a workflow solution or type of workflow product to use for a particular application follow these steps:

1. *Before specifying and designing data and control flow diagrams, draw an information model of the problem domain.* The information model describes the structure of the various objects involved in the procedures, processes, and projects of the corporation. In particular, the information model can be used to describe the various attributes of the forms, structure of the documents, and the types of the collections (folders, cabinets, etc.).

2. *Next, design and construct a model of the various departments, roles, groups, and empowered workers.* (In some systems, this step may be considered part of the information model. But for this discussion, information model means documents, forms, and groupings of these.) It is important to identify the participants of the workflow because, usually, tasks, sign-off, and security are assigned to users. Therefore, the second step in the design of a workflow is the identification of the workers, their attributes, their roles, and so on. Ideally, the various security levels of the objects should also be specified.

3. *Perform an analysis of the actual work or data flow of the objects.* Using object-oriented analysis and design tools to identify the dynamic relationships of objects is valuable for this step. Object-oriented analysis examines a requirement specification and a problem domain from the perspective of classes and objects. Object-oriented design provides the detail design for an implementation using class diagrams, object diagrams, process diagrams, data flow diagrams, and so on.

4. Once a detailed design of the problem is done the next step is to *evaluate various alternative implementation strategies—especially those involving workflow products*. It is at this step and only after completing steps 1–3 that an organization can determine whether a workflow solution or product can satisfy their design requirements.

CONTROLLING WORKFLOW

Workflow systems attempt to automate and facilitate the *flow of work* in an organization in order to accomplish business goals. Although there are many forms and varia-

228 ■ Workflow: Computer-supported Collaborative Work Processing

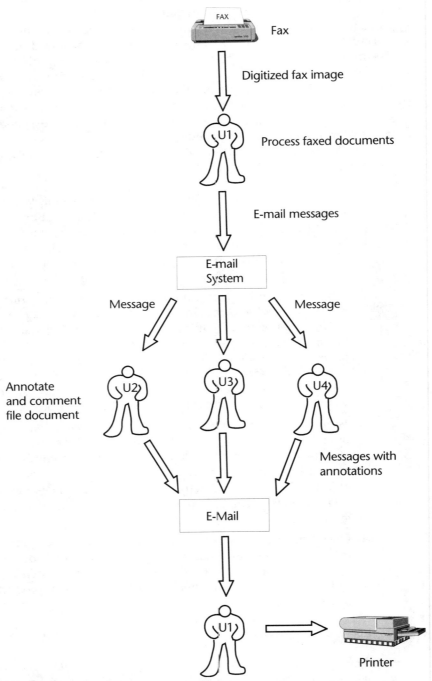

Figure 5.7 A "data flow" diagram for processing a faxed document.

tions in workflow products, there are four main elements common to most workflow systems:

- *Objective:* This refers to the workflow in place to accomplish an objective. Workflow systems typically allow the definition of the start and accomplishment (finish) of the objective. The objective could be a single deliverable—such as a document—or multiple deliverables.

- *Participants or participating nodes:* This can represent workers, processes, devices, etc. For work to flow, there must be *senders* and *receivers* or *sources* and *sinks*. The semantics and flexibility for the participants or participating nodes supported in a workflow system are up to the particular system. There are two aspects of the participants in a workflow: First is the *type* of the participant. This type could be a person, a group of people, a device, a process, or anything else that can carry out a task. The action being performed in a participating node of a workflow may be carried out by one or more users who have a particular role associated with them, which could be a title or a responsibility. The second aspect deals with the particular action involved. For instance, a user with the title/role "human resources administrator" may have to carry out particular tasks, approve a particular enclosed document, process a form, and so on. Devices and even scripts can facilitate the workflow as steps. A device probably will carry out the "task" it is designed for. For a printer, it is printing a document; for a scanner, it is scanning batches of paper; and so on.

- *Flow or linking participants:* The third component is the linking or the flow of information, documents, and instructions between the participants of a workflow. There are many types of flow control that can be supported or implemented by a workflow system. The simplest is routing a document or container. The flow process in a workflow can also entail *branching* or decision points where the next step of the workflow is taken depending on a status, availability of users with particular roles, and other conditions. The flow of tasks and documents can also involve *queues*, where a number of workers may be participating in the processing of jobs in a work queue. The sources and targets of links and flow controls between nodes of a workflow can be users, applications, workflow scripts, and devices.

- *The documents and forms being processed:* In workflow there is almost always the *case data*, which represents the information being processed to get the job done. There are as many variations of case data as there are data types. Forms are quite common in processing cases. Often, various sections of the forms need to be processed or approved by different participants in the workflow. Another common data type in cases are application files such as word processor files, spreadsheets, and so on. Images and other multimedia types are also common. Often, workflow systems (especially when images are supported) provide *annotation* tools to annotate images and pages of application data. Case data can be stored in different types of containers. For instance, compound documents may be thought of as *containers* of parts from different applications.

MORE THAN FLOW

In most of the literature on workflow the emphasis is on *work* and *information* flow between users, between users and applications (or executables in general), and between applications. Often, there has been too much emphasis on the *flow* component of workflow and not enough emphasis on the *work* that needs to be done to enhance the success of workflow applications.

Some workflow systems easily model the work processes in terms of nodes and links as discussed in the previous sections. Other workflow systems have the notion of *steps*. The terminology adopted by the Workflow Management Coalition (WMC) standardization committee includes:

Activity: A piece of work done by an application, a user, a step, a script, a node.

Process definition: When the activities are linked in a network, the result is the definition of a process that incorporates the schematic of the workflow, including the links that connect the activities. The Workflow Management Coalition (WMC) defines the activities within a process definition as an *activity network*.

Process instance: These are the activations and instances of a process (or process definition). In a workflow system, process instances are named, activated, and tracked.

If the goal is to *process* work—to have deliverables, to achieve certain goals, to complete tasks—then *flow* is only one broad category of processing work. The embellishment on CSCW (Computer-Supported Cooperative Work) for workflow—CSCWP (Computer-Supported Collaborative Work Processing) is not accidental. As mentioned earlier, groupware can *enhance* cooperative work, but it goes beyond that. For some groupware products, the accomplishment of cooperative work *in particular circumstances* is an indirect outcome. For instance, if the groupware product enhances the overall morale of the company and empowers users because they have a mechanism enabling them to communicate better and vent their frustrations or encouragement, then the effect on accomplishing work is not direct. It *will* have an effect, but not in the context of accomplishing a particular goal or deliverable. That is the essence of CSCWP—to process work. But to say that flow is the only category to get work done cooperatively is a bit narrow.

It is surprising how much work can be done cooperatively without the workflow capabilities common in today's products. In fact, when evaluating workflow products, it is advisable to see if the workflow system is flexible enough to allow the corporation or the team to accomplish their work processing goals through different mechanisms—flow-based as well as other models.

The following are a few examples of how cooperative work can be done without emphasizing flow—especially as implemented in most workflow products today.

(a) Check-out/check-in client/server model: This has already been discussed a number of times. The idea is that work is accomplished through collaborative effort. The project may contain multiple documents, design specifications, source code, and so on. Collaborative workers lock and check out a version of an object in the project, process it (work on it), probably update it, and then check the object back in. The checked-in object is a new version. If all the other collaborating workers work on their parts and make sure it can be integrated, the result is cooperative work processing but with little flow. Cooperation is achieved through accessing objects in a common library and resolving possible conflicts during integration. This more or less is what happens in the development of application software, CAD, CAM, and so on.

(b) Smart container: Another method of collecting information to get work done is through smart containers. Smart containers—such as smart folders or smart compound documents—determine which objects they should contain. Often, this is specified through high-level predicate expressions or queries. The difference between a smart container and, say, a flow system where the workflow sends an object to a container is that the container itself is smart and does not depend on an external message to populate or organize itself.

(c) Hot linking with other data and applications: Interoperability standards such as OLE 2 and OpenDoc, and distributed object standards such as CORBA are becoming increasingly prevalent in collaborative work processing. With these architectures a document-centric model of information allows users to aggregate parts or components from different sources. Figure 5.8 shows a compound document where various types of objects were authored by different users. This is an oversimplified illustration. Various users can be authoring the same part or parts that belong to the same application. A compound document collects parts from different authors and serves as a medium for collaborative work; therefore, a single document can contain information from various authors. The parts of the documents can be not only on different physical nodes, but they can have different security levels. For instance, assume a group of workers is preparing a business plan. They can collaborate on the same document, with the technical architect working on the technical section, the finance director working on the numbers, the marketing director working on market predictions. This is illustrated in Figure 5.9. The security levels can be set so that each author can update his or her sections and read and annotate (through electronic highlighters and note attachments) the sections of other coauthors.

OBJECT-ORIENTED WORKFLOW

Object-orientation is a term that has numerous connotations. It has been incorporated with graphical user interfaces, software engineering, client/server computing, particular programming languages (such as Smalltalk or C++), multimedia, and more.

Groupware systems have always had an association with object-orientation. This is particularly true of workflow systems. The term *object-oriented workflow* is common.

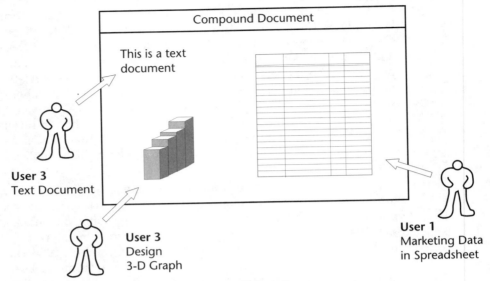

Figure 5.8 A compound document with multiple authors.

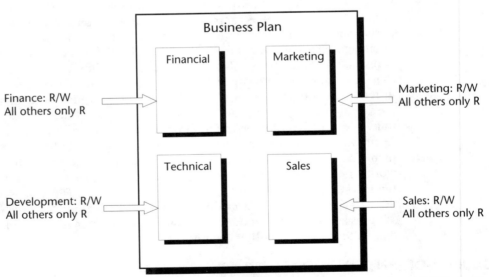

Figure 5.9 A business plan with objects that have different security privileges (R/W stands for read/write; R stands for read).

Evaluations or reviews of workflow products often include labeling the workflow product as object-oriented. So, what *does* it mean? What makes a workflow system or product object-oriented?

To answer these questions there must be a basic understanding of what is meant by object-orientation. In Chapter 2 we discussed a number of object-oriented issues. The following is a brief overview of this term for the purpose of understanding and characterizing object-oriented workflow.

Object-orientation

Chapter 2 defined objects through this equation:

$$\text{Object} = \text{Structure} + \text{Behavior}$$

where *structure* contains the data portion of the object. The structure contains the values of the fields or attributes of an object. These could be attributes of workflow templates, workflow instances, tasks in workflow, forms processed by the workflow, and so on. *Behavior* corresponds to the operations that can be performed on the objects. For instance, a user can request the list of all modifications and annotations on a document after a certain date; a manager might request the distribution of task duration by the participants in an active workflow. The behavior of objects are thus captured in the operations associated with the object.

To organize and process objects there are three fundamental concepts of object-orientation:

$$\text{Object-orientation} = \text{Abstract Data Typing} + \text{Inheritance} + \text{Object Identity}$$

Each of these concepts provides various advantages to object-oriented workflow systems as discussed in the following sections.

Abstract Data Typing

Abstract data typing models are various classes of workflow objects, where each class instance has a *protocol* (*behavior*), a set of messages to which it can respond. Thus, there are classes for workflow templates, workflow participants, workflow queues, office peripherals, folders, documents, and so on. With abstract data types there is a clear separation between the *external* interface of a data type and its *internal* implementation. The implementation of an abstract data type is *hidden*. Hence, alternative implementations can be used for the same abstract data type without changing its interface.

In most object-oriented programming languages, abstract data types are implemented through *classes*. A class is like a factory that produces *instances*, each with the same structure and behavior. A class has a name, a collection of operations for manipulating its instances, and a representation. The operations that manipulate the instances of a class are called *methods*. The state or representation of an instance is stored in *instance variables*. The methods are invoked through sending messages to the instances.

Sending messages to objects (instances) is similar to calling procedures in conventional programming languages. However, message sending is more dynamic.

Abstract data typing allows the construction of complex software systems through reusable components: the classes. Thus, through abstract data typing programming becomes modularized and extensible. Abstract data typing supports a much more natural representation of real world problems: the dominant components are the *objects* rather than the procedures. Abstract data typing allows objects of the same structure and behavior to *share* representation (instance variables) and code (methods).

Inheritance

Inheritance allows a class to inherit the behavior (operations, methods, etc.) and the representation (instance variables, attributes, etc.) from existing classes. Inheriting behavior enables *code sharing* (and hence reusability) among software modules. Inheriting representation enables *structure sharing* among data objects. The combination of these two types of inheritance provides a most powerful modeling and software development strategy.

Inheritance is achieved by *specializing* existing classes. Classes can be specialized by extending their representation (instance variables) or behavior (operations). Alternatively, classes can also be specialized through *restricting* the representation or operations of existing classes. When a class C2 inherits from class C1, then the instance variables and the methods of C2 are a superset of the instance variables and methods of C1, respectively. The subclass C2 can *override* the implementation of an inherited method or instance variable by providing an alternative definition or implementation.

Inheritance organizes the classes of workflow objects in inheritance class hierarchies. It models the hierarchies of workflow templates, office workers, peripherals, folders, and allows representation, protocol, and implementation to be inherited from superclass to subclass.

Object Identity

The third fundamental concept of object-orientation is object identity. The inheritance hierarchies organize the object-oriented code and support extensibility and code reusability. Object identity organizes the objects or instances of an application in arbitrary graph-structured object spaces.

Identity is a property of an object that distinguishes the object from all other objects in the application. In programming languages identity is realized through memory addresses. In databases identity is realized through identifier keys. User-specified names are used in both languages and databases to give unique names to objects. Each of these schemes compromises identity.

In a complete object-oriented system, each object is given an identity that will be permanently associated with the object, immaterial of the object's *structural* or *state* transitions. The identity of an object is also independent of the location or address of the object. Object identity provides the most natural modeling primitive—to have the same object be a subobject of multiple parent objects.

With object identity, objects can contain or refer to other objects. Object identity clarifies, enhances, and extends the notions of pointers in conventional programming languages, foreign keys in databases, and file names in operating systems. Using object identity, programmers can dynamically construct arbitrary graph-structured composite or complex objects, objects that are constructed from subobjects. Objects can be created and disposed of at run-time. In some cases, objects can even become persistent and be reaccessed in subsequent programs.

Object identity organizes the *instances* of workflow classes (that is, the objects) in graph-structured object spaces. It allows objects to be referentially shared: For instance, the *same* document can be referenced in multiple folders, be involved in multiple workflow cases, and so on. All the attributes of workflow objects (workflow templates, instances, queues, folders, peripherals, policies/procedures, workers) reference other objects directly, thus constructing compound object spaces. These object spaces are most natural and direct in workflow applications.

Object-oriented Features of Workflow Systems

How do these fundamental concepts of object-orientation get reflected in workflow systems? Which makes them object-oriented? Before answering, a word of caution. Just because a workflow system is *implemented* in an object-oriented language such as C++ does not necessarily make the workflow object-oriented from the *user's perspective*. If, however, the workflow systems has an *open architecture* where VAR (vertical application developers) and other corporate developers can *specialize* and *extend* the workflow system through inheriting from the C++ class library implementing the workflow engine or designer, then labeling the workflow product as object-oriented is appropriate.

These are features or characteristics that make a workflow system object-oriented:

(a) The "everything is an object" paradigm permeates the product: This means there is a uniform "object-oriented" feel to the product. Objects are created as instances of classes; they have attributes and behavior, and can references other objects; and objects—or classes—can be specialized and extended for the particular circumstance or application of the workflow. This means, for instance, that the nodes, links, and queues in a workflow are all objects with attributes, states (values of attributes), identities, and an *interface*. In addition, *tasks* are performed at each node, link, or even queues of a workflow. For nodes, these tasks correspond to the operation performed on the incoming objects of the queues: scanning paper documents, OCRing image data, forwarding incoming messages, and so on.

(b) Templates/processes as classes and instances or activations as objects: The workflow template—also called *process definition*—is itself a "class" object from which instances of workflow can be created. The workflow instances or activations are also objects (these are sometimes called *process instances*). An instance of a workflow class contains attributes indicating the type, description, initiator, and various statistics about the workflow, or rather the *process*. Figure 5.10 illustrates a workflow template for hiring a new employee. There is one workflow template for the process—similar to the notion of one *class* such as an employee class or a department class. When there is a candidate, such as John Smith, an *instance* of this class will be created. Figure 5.10 also illustrates instances of the class for John and May being interviewed. Now a class—a process definition—is like a factory. It contains the descriptions of the various instances—process instances—that it creates. It also contains descriptions of the behavior of these instances. More specifically, the number of nodes or activities, the types of nodes, the sorts of routing, even the scripting, the decision branches, and so on are all described by the class. In fact, since the workflow process definition is itself a class, there are attributes and behavior that pertain to the class or process definition itself. In other words, a process definition or a workflow template class defines:

- The overall process of instances—nodes, links, branching, etc.
- The behavior or various operations defined for the process instances: Not all workflow or object-oriented workflow systems allow this. But it is a very useful concept for a workflow to be able to define operations for particular processes. If this feature is not supported, there will be generic operations that apply to all processes. One common generic operation is the display of the status or progress of the workflow, including how much time was spent at each activity node, where the current bottleneck is, etc. However, a more flexible and more object-oriented workflow system

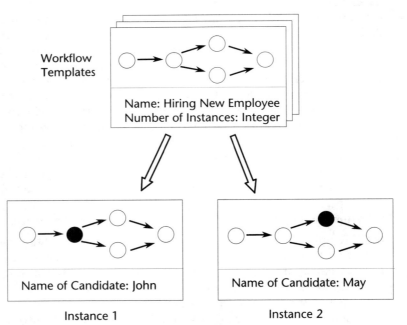

Figure 5.10 Hiring template and instances.

would allow workflow designers to create special operations for particular processes and allow the users of these workflows to invoke these operations, which are more process or application specific.

- Since the process definition is also an object, it too has states—attributes—and behavior which applies to the class object (versus the instances). When designing a process, there are attributes specific to the process itself. Some trivial ones include the name of the process, the purpose of the process, the creator of the process, and so on. These are illustrated in Figure 5.11. Note that there are attributes that apply to the instances: the name of the instance, the person or process/activity that activated it, the date it got activated, the date it got completed, and so on. Thus, there are two types of attributes: those pertaining to the process definition and those pertaining to the process instances. But more interestingly, there is also behavior associated with the process definition—especially if the process definition keeps track of all its instances. For example, there can be an operation associated with the hiring process to ask which are the hires currently in progress. Other operations can ask the process to chart the duration histograms of process instances. This is very important, and although some generic operations could be provided by the workflow system, it is better to have extensibility.

(c) Specialization or inheritance: The workflow templates can be *specialized*, and one workflow class will inherit from another workflow class. Given a workflow class, office workers can specialize and create other workflow classes which extend existing classes. For instance, given a workflow class for hiring new employees at a corporate level, a particular department can introduce additional nodes or rules to extend and specialize the departmental hiring workflow procedure. This is illustrated in Figure 5.12. Specialization is very important. It means workflow

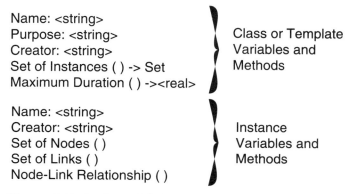

Figure 5.11 A class defining class variables/methods and instance variables/methods.

templates or processes can inherit both behavior and structure from one another—describing the behavior and structure of both workflow processes as well as process instances. As another example, a large corporation can set up a purchase requisition process. Various branches and departments can specialize. Often this specialization cannot be arbitrary and there will be restrictions. In other words, specialization for workflow must take into account various rules for restricting or setting the framework for specializing,

(d) Composite workflows, nesting, and referential sharing: As mentioned, one of the important concepts in object-orientation is object identity. Through object identity, systems can support *referential sharing of objects*. This means objects can be nested within other objects, referentially shared by multiple objects, and overall complex containment and referential "hierarchies" can be constructed. In object-oriented workflow, composite and nested objects appear in at least two contexts: the information objects—documents, forms, folders, etc.—and the workflow processes and instances.

- *Containment information objects:* As noted, workflow usually has a deliverable, which usually is a compound document, a signed-off form, or other container objects. The objects are typically composite objects. This is important since each *element*, part, or member of a composite object can be assigned to a user in the workflow. For instance assume the workflow is implementing forms routing for an approval process with the ability to input some data in the form. The various department heads or managers approving the form must be given write privileges only to the part of the

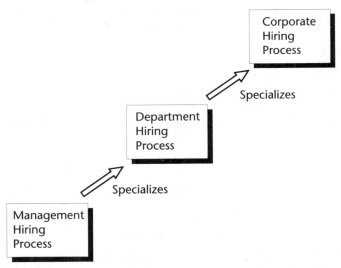

Figure 5.12 Specialization of hiring processes in an organization infrastructure.

form that needs to be written by them. They must be given only read permission on the rest. This was illustrated in Figure 5.9. Similarly, if a compound document is circulated through a workflow and different users are asked to incorporate annotations on views or images of the document, then the annotations are also objects contained in the compound document. This was illustrated in Figure 5.3. As shown, annotations are themselves objects which have position, shape, color, author, and so on. In fact, in component object models such as an OpenDoc container document, each of the parts of the document is an object. The object has its own application which defines and implements the behavior of the object. The objects can be stored in a database, distributed on a network, or stored in a file server.

- Sometimes the workflow process itself is complex and contains nested subworkflows. For instance, if a trader is attempting to buy or sell securities there are at least two work processes: the research for making the decision and the workflow for the actual trade. Even a simple workflow such as interviewing a candidate can involve other workflows such as to prepay an out-of-state travel expense. It can be contained or referenced in a larger "container" workflow. Figure 5.13 illustrates nested workflows or subworkflows. As shown, the same subworkflow can be part of more

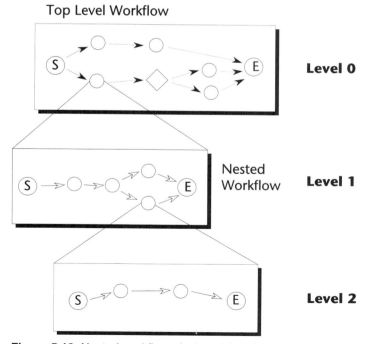

Figure 5.13 Nested workflows (subworkflows).

than one container workflow. Again, object-orientation here means to have a unique identifier for each workflow, and create referential sharing relationships and containment hierarchies for both the process definitions (workflow templates) and process instances.

WORKFLOW FEATURES AND CONCEPTS

Given the current state of workflow products, it is difficult to describe all the features available in the market today. In fact, it is even difficult to characterize which products should be considered as workflow products. The chapter later covers standardization efforts that are underway to define the scope and function of workflow products.

This section presents a number of *components* of workflow. Note that a workflow product does not have to have all these components; in fact, as described, some workflow tools are very basic yet very useful. As software becomes component-based and specialized—thanks to standards such as OLE 2 and OpenDoc—it becomes increasingly important to understand the components of a workflow system. Potentially, as these components interface, get embedded or accessed by other components, users will be able to put together workflow systems using these components as "leggo" boxes.

This trend is clearly seen in the e-mail industry where users can choose a transport mechanism (such as MHS), a directory service (such as an X.500 product), and an e-mail client tool (such as ccMail) from completely different vendors. It is conceivable that in a workflow system the user can combine from different vendors:

- A diagramming graphics tool that depicts the process.
- The routing mechanism and workflow engine.
- The storage or databases for the workflow meta-data and status information.

Graphical Workflow Definition

Many workflow products today have graphical diagramming tools to define workflows. Usually these graphics diagramming tools are bundled with the product. We already saw examples from Office.IQ and WorkMAN. Figure 5.14 shows a workflow designed graphically by FileNet's Visual WorkFlo. More specialized diagramming tools with nodes and links can also be used to depict workflows. With different sets of nodes, links, and drawing palettes, electronic-pencil products can be used to draw flowcharts of workflow processes—and hence the blueprint of reengineered business processes. Figure 5.15 illustrates such an example from Visio. There are many other such products for Windows, the Mac, or UNIX workstations. Notice that a diagramming tool just represents the *static diagram* and control flow of the workflow.

Diagramming tools can also be used to design the information model for the various classes involved in workflow. As already discussed, object-orientation can be used to model various workflow classes and objects. There are a number of tools, methodologies, and notations that can be used to perform object-oriented analysis and design.

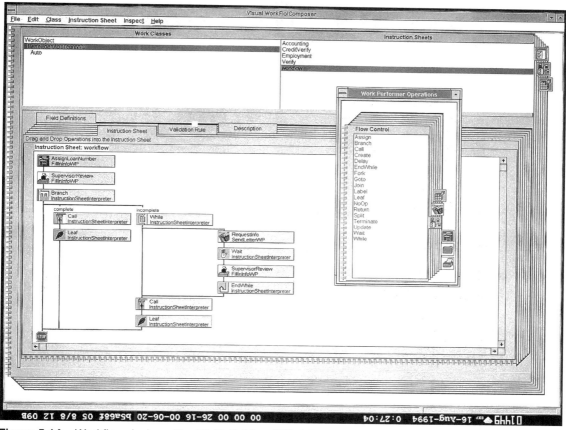

Figure 5.14 Workflow designed by FileNet's Visual WorkFlo.

These methodologies are used to model the information contained in the workflow templates, the users, the processes, as well as the behavior or methods that are associated with these object classes.

Are flowcharting tools, diagramming tools, object-oriented analysis and design tools, or entity-relationship diagramming tools workflow tools? Hardly. It is very useful for a workflow system to have easy-to-use graphics tools to represent the workflow templates. Further, if the workflow system is also an extensible object-oriented environment, it is useful to have a diagramming tool to design the information model of the various objects or classes involved in the workflow. More specifically, if there are various classes of users with attributes and operations associated with them, diagramming tools can design the classes of objects used in the workflow. However with workflow tools there are "live" and active objects associated with the nodes of the workflow. The workflow diagram is actually a program that gets activated and executed by the underlying workflow engine.

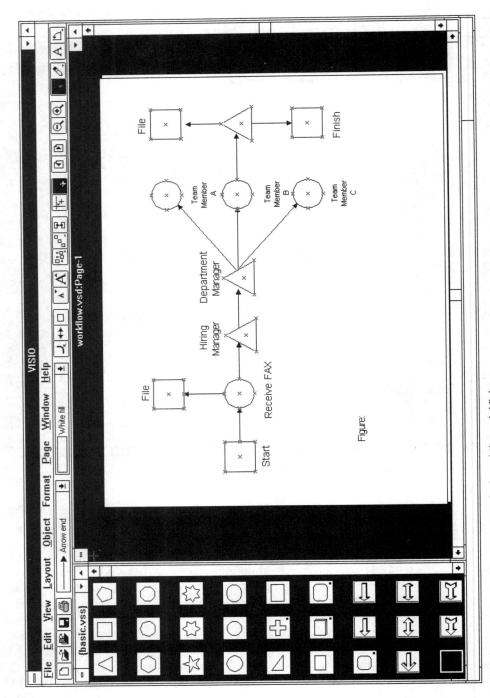

Figure 5.15 A workflow diagram designed through Visio.

Process Definition and Activation

Whether defined through a diagramming tool or a graphical front end to a workflow system, what is being defined is the *process* or workflow template. The process captures the rules and steps that need to be followed for particular business procedures and policies. Therefore, the nodes, links, workers, peripherals, actions, rules, and all other objects involved in the definition of a workflow template must be associated with the objects participating in the workflow.

Workflow templates can be thought of as classes describing the structure of their instances (the activations of the template). In the definition of a workflow template, there are two types of variables (structures) and operations (behavior):

- Those pertaining to the instances or workflow template activations: Overall, the most important component of the definition of a workflow template is the definition of the various tasks, activities, workers, roles, and connection types involved in the workflow; in other words, the structure and behavior of the instances of the workflow template. This was illustrated in Figures 5.10 and 5.11 which show the template of a hiring process with various instances (activations).

- In addition to the instance structure and operations, the workflow template can also define structure and classes pertaining to the workflow template as a whole. The number of instances in an operation is associated not with a particular instance but the aggregate of the instances as a whole, in other words, the class (that is, the workflow template). Other examples of template variables and operations include the description of the template, the creator of the template, the person who last modified the template, who has security clearance to modify the template, and so on.

Tracking, Status, and Statistics

Like any other manufacturing process there are time critical issues of workflow that need to be analyzed and evaluated. Therefore, one of the most important features for workflow is the ability to track the status and various statistics of an active workflow. The time-critical information should be automatically tallied and managed by the workflow engine as work progresses.

Figure 5.16 illustrates in tabular format various status information associated with active workflows, nodes of active workflows, and links of active workflows. This information should be available to managers, and reports based on it could be generated for better monitoring and reporting. If a particular task is taking longer than it should, the manager (or the person/process monitoring the task) can set a notification to be informed when a task has exceeded its allotted time for completion. Even after a workflow is completed, maintaining a history of the time it took to accomplish is very useful for analyzing potential bottlenecks and improving the overall quality of the process.

(a) Status of all instances of a template

Active Workflow			
Name of Active Workflow	Time Activated	Worker/Process which Activated	Expected Duration

(b) Node Status

Active Workflow			
Node #	Node Name	Tasks Done	Duration at Node

(c) Link Status

Active Workflow			
Link #	Link Name	Time Link Traversed	Objects on Link

Figure 5.16 Various tracking information for workflows.

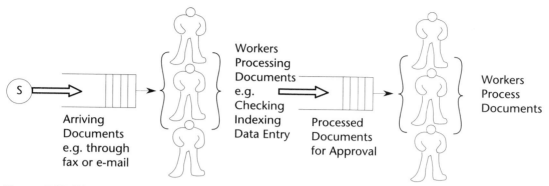

Figure 5.17 Work queues.

Work Queues

Another very useful feature in many workflow applications, especially production applications with assembly line-like processing of work, is the support of work queues. This is illustrated in Figure 5.17, where the worker has a queue of tasks that need to be processed in some order. The order could be first-in-first-out or some other order.

Queues are very useful if repetitive tasks are performed by the worker. The workflow manager can keep track of the number of tasks being processed by a user, the rate by which tasks get completed, the duration of each task, and so on. The task queues in Figure 5.17 show the possibility of having one or more workers assigned to a queue. A workflow product can have a many-to-many assignment of tasks to workers (the queue worker is many-to-one: many tasks in the queue assigned to one worker). In a sense, the queue is assigned to a group. As each worker completes a task, he or she goes to the next entry in the task queue.

Cases

Workflow systems often support—implicitly or explicitly—the notion of a *case*. Whether it is a folder containing a medical history, documentation for a legal case, or objects for the design of a particular product, cases are common in many disciplines. A case can be captured in a simple document, a form, or a folder containing documents. Typically, the person (process, or device) who activates a workflow creates a case object—for instance a folder—that gets routed to the participants in the workflow. For instance, if John applied for a loan, a case folder for John's loan application will be created. Then, various case documents such as credit references, job verifications, and asset verification, will be inserted in John's loan application case folder.

Case objects (typically folders) are associated with an active workflow. The various participants in a workflow either insert documents, edit documents or other objects (forms) for the case, annotate existing documents of the case, and so on. The case folder gets associated with the active workflow, and managers or other workers involved in the case can investigate the progress of the case both through examining the workflow status (to see which are the links or arcs that were "traversed") and the case status.

Groups and Roles

The nodes on which cases are routed can be devices, processes (including other workflows), applications, or people. Examples of devices involved in workflows include printers and fax servers. Examples of applications include spreadsheets and word processors. But the most important category is people, those who do the "work" in workflow.

The workers in the workflow can be identified as individuals or groups. In other words, the links in an interconnected workflow process can involve either individuals or entire groups. An example of the former is "John Smith"; an example of the latter is "Marketing Department."

For both individuals or groups, it is useful for the workflow system to support *roles*. A role indicates a title, function, or a label assigned to an individual or a group. In many cases, group names may be adequate to identify the role of the group. But sometimes an additional role attribute for the group is required. For instance, assume a large corporation holds a monthly staff meeting that involves processes and many details. Also assume that the responsibility for organizing the staff meeting is assigned to an alternating department (a group). Thus, although there are departments with descriptive names such as "Marketing Department," "Sales Department," and "Administration," the role of "Staff Meeting Coordinating Group" will be assumed by different groups. Workflows involving the role "SMCG" do not need to be modified each month.

Although groups are often sufficient for indicating roles of individuals, in a number of situations roles assigned explicitly as attributes of individuals are also useful or necessary. There are two mechanisms for characterizing individual workers. One is when the individual is a member of a team, department, or a group, and the relationship is many-to-many since the same worker can be in more than one team, department, or group. The object representing the individual can have the inverse of the many-to-many relationship. The insertions and deletions in groups are explicit.

The other alternative is to have a set of role attribute values that describe the roles of the user. Again, the relationship between role names and workers is many-to-many since many workers can have the same role and the same worker can have many roles. The distinction between roles and group membership is subtle, and in many cases groups are more than adequate to handle individual roles. However, as the example with groups suggests, roles are also useful since they depict assignment of responsibilities and authorities. Roles are also easy to understand. Furthermore, in many situations, there is at most one person with a given role in which case using groups is artificial. Examples of such roles include "Office Manager," "Conference Coordinator," or "Project Manager." Roles are useful in workflows. When an individual with a given role is reassigned or leaves the company, and the role is assumed by someone else, then it is not necessary to modify all the workflows that use the role.

Retraction

Retraction is a special kind of "ad hoc" modification in a process. When managers give a particular responsibility to a worker and the worker does not meet that responsibility, often the task is assigned to someone else. That is the essence of retraction. A workflow system that supports retraction allows rerouting the case object to the employee who gets assigned the task. There are several ways to achieve this. If roles are supported, the manager who is assigning the task can change the role assignment. Alternatively, the manager can retract the task and assign it to another worker explicitly.

One important issue here is the contribution of the workflow system in task assignment and retraction. A workflow system supporting retraction can help project management if it keeps track of the progress and status of various assignments, retractions, and reassignments—the duration of a task assignment, when the task was retracted, the state of the case at that time, the worker who was assigned to the retracted task, and so on. Maintaining this information and subsequently analyzing it will help the manager improve the overall performance of the processes and hence the quality of the deliverables.

Rules and Conditions

The previous chapter discussed rules in advanced e-mail systems. Rules allow messages to be routed based on certain criteria or conditions. In a workflow system that supports rules, there will be a general mechanism for defining the predicates or predicate expressions, involving states or attribute values of objects pertaining to the workflow instance. Here are some examples of predicate expressions and actions for various scenarios in workflow instances:

> If Workflow "Loan Application" at Node Hiring Manager for Approval has taken longer than 3 days AND hiring request is URGENT THEN send memo to Department manager.

> If all documents for "Pending Case" have been inserted in "case folder" and Case Supervisor has indicated "Approved" then forward folder to Administration AND file the folder AND Archive the folder AND FAX a copy of the documents.

As mentioned, rules are already incorporated in some advanced e-mail packages such as BeyondMail. However, rules in workflow systems have much more extensive applications since the set of objects and actions are more complex. Rules in workflow involve (or could involve) entire processes and many more action types.

Notification

Notification in workflow is in some sense a superset of notification in e-mail systems. Notification can be considered as a special case of rules, and it can be supported as built-in conditions and actions as in:

SEND RECEIPTS to <worker being notified>
IF Workflow has reached a certain stage;
or
SEND NOTIFICATION to <worker being notified>
IF at a certain node there is no activity.

Workflow notification can be activated as a result of:

- *Changes in object states:* This is similar to the notion of triggers in relational databases—when the state of an object changes, a notification set up in the workflow informs a worker or takes some action.
- *Timing constraints:* This includes timing constraints upon tasks, actions, communication, or links. Based on timing constraints users can be notified when a certain action has happened (such as the participants have received the current case folder) or an action has failed to happen within a certain duration (a participant failed to send a certain document for the case within a prescribed timeframe).

Although there are other conditions that may activate a notification, these are the two primary criteria for sending notification in a workflow environment. As mentioned before, notifications can be very useful in monitoring the progress of workflows.

Suspense or Rendezvous!

When information is being collected from various sources, it is often necessary to have all the documents of a case before proceeding to the next stage. For instance, when someone applies for either a position or a loan, there are various documents that need to be gathered before proceeding to the next phase. A worker (or a process) is usually given the responsibility to verify the documents that need to be present before proceeding to the next phase. Workflow systems can assist the worker by supporting the specification of all case documents that are necessary before proceeding to the next phase. The case folder, for instance, will be suspended until all the necessary documents are inserted into it. Once the system checks for this and verifies it, the case folder is either automatically routed to the next node or the worker handling the case is allowed to proceed (is allowed to forward the case folder to the next node).

Suspense can also be applied in approval processes. For instance if a certain purchase requisition needs approval from several managers or personnel in a specific order, the case folder or document can be suspended until all the managers give their approval in the prescribed order.

Rendezvous is another popular term to express the same concept as suspense. The idea is that if a case (or items/objects in a case) moves along several paths simultaneously at some point the collected information needs to come together. That's the rendezvous point—it is where all the predecessor routes need to be traversed before proceeding with the next step.

Iteration

Iteration is a special case of suspense. When several participants are working on a case or a document that needs several iterations, the "product" may have to go through several reviewers before it is finalized. It is not realistic to indicate in the workflow all the possible iterations. Nevertheless, it is highly desirable to keep track of all the iterations, the number of iterations, the time it took for each iteration, and so on, until the case is completed.

Workflow and Project Management: The Importance of Schedules and Status

Unfortunately, in this first generation of workflow products, there is little support of advanced project management functionality. In fact project management software can also be thought of as a diagramming workflow software. Project management software here means the specialized time management systems that allow the definition of tasks, duration, resources, task dependencies, and so on. Examples of project management software include TimeLine, Microsoft Project, and Mac Project.

Project management software allows managers to design Gantt charts, Pert charts and time lines of major deliverables. Resource tables and cost estimates are also supported. Project management systems do not deal with the flow of information per se, although usually there is information that flows between various resources or departments. Project management is very important to guarantee that high quality products are delivered on time. But the tracking of projects with a project management tool is static and up to the manager while workflow is dynamic. Workflow systems have several components that can track, alert, notify, route, and otherwise communicate the progress of projects. Therefore integrating advanced project management capabilities in workflow provides an ideal environment for high quality and timely completion of projects.

EXAMPLES OF WORKFLOW

This section presents several "real-life" examples of workflow. As these examples will show, applications of workflow vary from simple processing of expense reports to complex loan processing applications. In terms of the taxonomy presented earlier, the former is an example of simple administrative workflow and the latter is an example of production workflow.

The examples also will illustrate that workflow applications are by and large "horizontal." This means that administrative, human resources, and corporate procedures and policies can be implemented through workflow solutions independent of the business of the corporation. It also means that workflow technology can be applied to many different vertical applications, including financial applications—market research and trading, engineering design and production, insurance claims processing, loan applications processing, medical records processing, and new drug application processing in pharmaceutical companies.

These examples are drawn both from more generic office processes—human resources, expense reports, etc.—as well as some vertical applications of workflow.

Hiring Process

In the hiring process, the goal is to employ a person satisfying the requirements of a particular department. The following people are involved:

- *Front desk:* Receives resumes and handles the applications for employment and sends them to the proper managers.
- *Personnel:* Keeps track of all resumes. If a candidate is to be hired, personnel also takes care of checking for legal work status, history of candidate for insurance purposes, fixing the date the candidate will start, and so on.
- *Hiring manager:* Coordinates the members of her or his team to conduct the interview and evaluate the candidate. Checks references, salary requirements, etc. of the candidate.

Figure 5.18 illustrates the overall workflow for hiring a candidate including how each team, role, or participant is involved. Note that a manager in charge of a large or

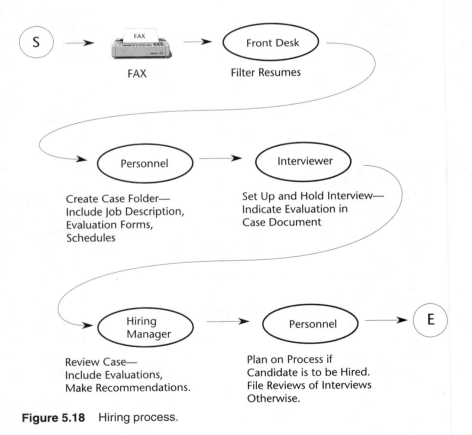

Figure 5.18 Hiring process.

even a medium-sized department can at any point check the status of candidates and take appropriate actions. The audit trail of hiring candidates is a very useful knowledge base, which, if information is recorded and managed properly, can help managers and departments find better candidates and have a faster turnaround time for hiring.

Purchase Requisitions

The second example is also very common in many organizations. A worker needs to place an order for a piece of equipment, office supplies, office furniture, software, hardware, etc. The personnel involved to complete the purchase requisition include:

- *The worker:* Fills in a purchase requisition form.
- *The worker's manager:* Approves the requisition. There is a lot of room for automation here, depending upon the particular policy and procedure for purchases in a corporation. For instance, the department or corporation can have a policy whereby a worker can go directly to the purchasing department if the order costs less than a certain amount and if the department is within its budget.

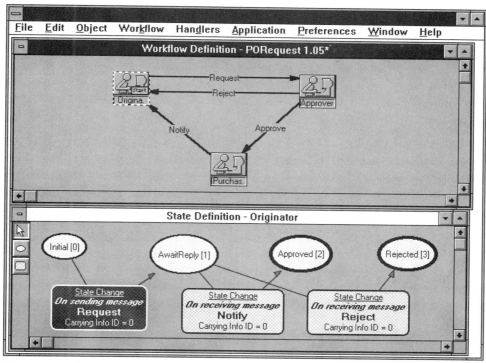

Figure 5.19 Purchasing using WorkMAN.

- *The purchasing department:* Places the order, receives the item, and sends it to the worker.

This simple workflow is illustrated in Figure 5.19. Note that an organization might not have a purchasing department, and this activity may be handled by an administration, accounting, or G&A department.

Again, a workflow tool can be very useful. A notification or alarm can be set to indicate that a purchase requisition was not satisfied within a certain period of time. Then, neither the purchasing department nor the worker needs to be constantly aware of its status—the workflow system can automatically handle it.

Trading: Research and Purchasing

This is a more "vertical" example. For securities trading there are at least two workflow components: research and trading. For the research, the workflow involves a librarian and an industry analyst. The librarian gathers on-line and other information about the corporation being considered for trading. The industry analyst makes her or his recommendations based on previous performance history, predictions, and so on. The information is sent to the trader who makes a decision to purchase.

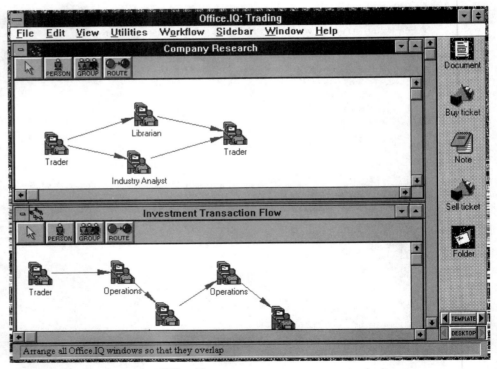

Figure 5.20 Trading using Office.IQ.

Figure 5.20 illustrates both the research and the investment transaction workflows. The form to perform the trade as well as the number of shares to be purchased is sent to operations for confirmation. Operations in turn sends the trade posting to the accounting department. Accounting sends the settlement of the trade back to operations. After processing, the settlement is forwarded to the trader.

Quality Assurance and Production

In any corporation that is involved in delivering goods or services, quality assurance and the management of quality are requirements for success. Often an entirely separate department handles the quality assurance and **certifies** a product before it goes out to sales. The process of certifying a product can be implemented through workflow. In fact, the precertification problem or bug tracking processes can also be implemented through workflow. Many phases in the production and delivery of a product can be integrated with a workflow based solution. The entire total quality management and production can be envisioned as one large workflow. There are many milestones and incremental steps between a requirement specification of a product to its certification. Some of the milestones include **alpha**, **beta**, and **final** release. For each of these milestones there are nested or subworkflows that implement the interaction between, say, the production/engineering and quality assurance departments. When, for instance, problems or defects are detected proper forms are filled and routed on a workflow route.

Besides tracking the status of various defect or bug reports, a number of quality assurance databases are maintained to log and archive the progression of fixes or enhancements. The processes can be quite complex and each category of product—and each product for that matter—has its own specific requirements for tracking, processing, and implementation in general. Workflow systems can play very important roles in the successful management of large production processes.

WORKFLOW STANDARDS

Currently there are a number of standardization efforts and common interfaces for e-mail systems. These standards mean that various e-mail product vendors, e-mail-enabled applications, and e-mail-based applications will have fewer interfaces on messaging transport and directory servers to deal with. Standards also support message exchange and interoperability between applications. And, since many workflow systems use e-mail transport services and back ends, e-mail standards help e-mail-based workflow applications as well. However, since workflow deals with business processes, standardization for workflow extends beyond interoperability through message exchange.

The Workflow Management Coalition (WMC) was formed in August 1993 to address the issue of interoperability and the ability of various workflow products to work together. More than 70 companies have joined WMC in the past two years and this number is expected to increase. By defining both the terminology as well as the application programming interfaces for a workflow standard WMC hopes "to promote the use of workflow through the establishment of standards for interoperability and connectivity among multiple workflow products, and a common set of standards for the deployment of workflow across industries."

In any real world problem that is to be solved through a workflow system the first step is the design of the business process in terms of a workflow *template*. The template that describes the process can be either graphical, in a particular workflow scripting language, or a textual representation. The standardization effort is not so much in the area of designing or defining the workflow, but with the ability of different workflow products to import and export the definition or templates created by various vendor's tools.

Once a workflow template is built, the next step is to create an *instance* of the process and activate it. If the template implements the different steps for hiring a new employee, the instances will be the interview processes for various candidates. The WFC recognizes standardization needs for *workflow enactment services*, which incorporate workflow management engines and provide the overall run-time environment for managing various active workflows. Through standardization, it is hoped that various workflow engines will be able to participate in processing a workflow instance. One of the roles of the workflow engine is to *interpret* the process templates for particular workflow activations. It is the WFC's goal that a workflow process created or defined through one tool can be exported and then activated and interpreted by a variety of workflow engines.

Another standardization goal is the ability to interchange the *information case data* between various workflow engines. If there is workflow-related meta information in case data and it is presented in a standard format, it will be available for interpretation by various products. Case data are typically associated with applications such as work processors, presentation tools, spreadsheets, imaging systems, or graphics tools. Another area of standardization effort is for workflow engines to have a common application programming interface for invoking the tools or applications for case data.

When a workflow process template instance is activated, sometimes "work" needs to be presented or requested from agents or an end user. In the simple resume tracking example, users who are interviewing a candidate might be asked to provide feedback on the interviewee's resume or their interaction with her or him. In some cases, there is a list or a queue of activities assigned to a user. The WFC is working to standardize through an application programming interface the *worklist*, which is a collection of work activities assigned to a particular node, usually an end user.

The WFC also plans for standards to store and retrieve various status and progress reports about workflow activations. This information would help to keep audit trails, identify bottlenecks, and evaluate the overall efficiency of the workflow.

WORKFLOW ARCHITECTURES

The previous sections described various concepts associated with workflows. There is great variety in workflow solutions and approaches, and in product capabilities—their underlying models, features, platforms, scalability, and so on. Standardization efforts will help, but it is not clear how widespread workflow applications will be and how often organizations with different workflow systems will feel the need to interoperate.

There are also differences in the architectures of various workflow systems, but there are several modules that appear in most. These components will be explained in the context of a client/server architecture. Not all workflow systems or products follow

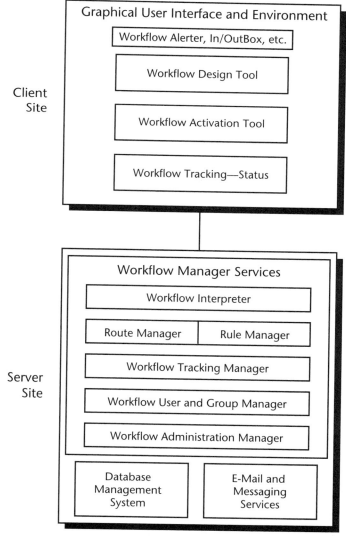

Figure 5.21 Various components of a workflow architecture.

this client/server architecture, nor are all the components presented here present in all workflow products. But these components are important modules in a coherent workflow system operating in a distributed and internetworked client/server environment.

Figure 5.21 illustrates a workflow architecture. On the client sites or nodes there are three main components for workflow:

- *Workflow design tool:* Allows for the definition of workflow templates. The design tool can be a graphical design tool. It can also be a scripting environment, including parsers, debuggers, and development environment for the fourth-generation scripting language used for workflow definition or design.

- *Workflow activation tool:* This component is responsible for "activating" the workflow templates in terms of functionality. Much of the "handshaking" between the workflow services manager (the workflow "engine") and the client side when starting a workflow, terminating a workflow, or suspending a workflow happens by this module.

- *Workflow tracking, status:* This can be integrated in the activation tool, if preferred. The workflow status management tool displays the status of various active workflows. It indicates the time taken to complete various tasks. It can be used to identify potential bottlenecks and improve the performance of workflows in future iterations. This component interacts with the workflow engine to retrieve the information about workflow status from the underlying workflow database.

These are the three main components on the client side for a workflow module. There are many subcomponents on both client and server nodes. For instance, the definition and management of users, groups and roles; the components that manage rules and dynamic decision making at run-time; and so on.

Workflows manipulate deliverables (case data) that are documents, forms, and other application objects. Often, applications are involved in the workflow so that the output of a task can be embedded automatically. The workflow products can incorporate a number of built-in tools such as text editors and forms designers. Alternatively (and this is becoming increasingly popular), either through embedded objects or linking, the case data can be stored and manipulated through third-party applications and tools (word processors, form designers, spreadsheets, and so on).

On the server side are the following components:

- *Workflow manager services:* All the workflow engine-specific functionality is combined in this large module. The actual interpretation of workflow templates, the tracking of workflow status, the maintenance of workflow users, groups, roles, and every aspect of defining and running workflows (except for the front-end graphical modules) are performed by the workflow manager services (or the workflow engine).

- *Database management services:* There are other modules (probably external to the workflow system) with which the workflow system needs to interact to get its job done. Some of these modules can be implemented and provided by the workflow vendor. Another option is to interface to other standard modules such as a DBMS (database management system). The DBMS is one of the most important modules. Increasingly, workflow systems are incorporating *concurrent sharing* capabilities, in other words, the ability for multiple users to concurrently read and/or update objects under transaction control. This is exactly what is provided by DBMSs. Therefore, using either commercial relational DBMS or object-oriented DBMS interfaces the workflow engine uses the persistence and concurrency control capabilities of the DBMS to allow workflow objects be defined, created, searched, and updated.

- *Messaging, transport, and communication services:* Besides a DBMS and especially when workflow must span multiple networks and LANs, it is becoming increasingly clear that e-mail messaging transport engines provide a relatively inexpensive platform on which to exchange workflow messages, case data, notifications, and so on. Thus, most workflow systems will incorporate both a DBMS component (either proprietary, embedded, or an interface to a commercial DBMS) and an e-mail transport services interface. The workflow manager can interface and use other interfaces of the e-mail as well. In fact, e-mail systems also have "databases" that store messages. The workflow system can theoretically use these to manage its objects. Another service provided by e-mail is address books. Here again, the workflow system can use the e-mail's directory services and avoid, for instance, replication of directories. Another category of services is provided by network operating systems. Here also there are a number of services that can be used by workflow engines including file storage, directory services, and various application servers.

SUMMARY

Workflow systems are becoming increasingly popular in a host of applications. Workflow attempts to capture the information "manufacturing" processes in an organization. This is the first generation of workflow products. But if processes and procedures within corporations are analyzed carefully the potential for productivity enhancements through workflow solutions is real.

Workflow organizes processes in corporations through various nodes representing people, devices, applications, or other processes. And links—representing the routing of documents, requests, instructions, and commands. There are many different approaches for designing workflows including scripting languages and graphical design tools. Workflow systems are sometimes very flexible, and allow the workflow system to use or implement any model of communication, collaboration, and work processing. At the other extreme are workflow systems based on a particular model, theory, or "religion" of human interaction, corporate organization, and work processing. Users of these systems must carefully analyze their situation to ensure that it indeed matches that of the model incorporated in the workflow product they are considering.

The chapter discussed three types of workflow: ad hoc, administrative, and production. Various workflow solutions pertain to one or another of these types; some support all three types. This is important, especially if all three types exist in the same corporation. Currently, however, most workflow products favor one or the other.

This chapter also discussed some of the basic workflow concepts including graphical tools, status, work queues, rules, case, groups, roles, retraction, iteration, and project management issues. It also discussed some recent trends in attempting to standardize workflow systems that would allow interoperability between various workflow products.

The chapter concluded with a description and overview of workflow architectures in client/server environments, elucidating the various client and server components that can be expected from a next-generation workflow system.

6

Electronic Meetings (EMs)

The fundamental concept of groupware is collaboration between workers. Whether the interpersonal interaction is one of the many thousands of casual business transactions that constitute day-to-day life in the business world, or a high-intensity relationship that comes with coauthorship, groupware systems are being designed to support and enhance how we work together. But collaborative support systems are in a state of hyperevolutionary flux, so this chapter attempts to present basic principles and general considerations.

This chapter builds on the discussions of the previous chapters to concentrate on a crucial aspect of groupware, namely electronically enhanced meetings and collaborations. Two themes dominate the earlier chapters. The first is a concentration on asynchronous groupware systems where interaction between collaborating workers occurs at different times. These relationships tend to be cooler, less intimate, and immediate than interactions that take place at the same time, and they tend to revolve more around the content of the communications and less on personal issues. The second theme is a focus on basic and evolutionary groupware products. While difficult to quantify or categorize neatly, in terms of market penetration and popularity at least, the technologies of client/server architectures, e-mail, and workflow (in decreasing order of popularity or importance) more or less comprise "evolutionary" groupware systems.

This chapter deals with another important category of groupware products: electronic meetings (EMs). It is tempting to categorize electronic meetings as either same-time/same place or same time/different places systems. Either category is fine since most electronic meetings are usually synchronous. We will, however, also discuss "distributed meetings" which occur over a period of time. In this chapter we describe the characteristics and features of EM software in general as well as popular utilities for schedule meetings—both electronic and face to face, called group calendaring systems.

BASIC PRINCIPLES

To understand the future it is useful to review the past. Therefore, to better appreciate the basis of computer-supported collaborative work consider some of the seminal ideas of computer pioneers Douglas Englbart and Harvey Lehtman. Englbart is credited by many with inventing the mouse concept as well as bit mapped graphic displays, full screen editing, hypertext, computergraphics, multimedia, virtual reality and computer supported cooperative work systems.

> To some extent, the personal computer was a reaction to the overloaded and frustrating timesharing systems of the day. In emphasizing the power of the individual, the personal computer revolution turned its back on those tools that led to the empowering of both colocated and distributed work groups collaborating simultaneously and over time on knowledge work. Computer-supported cooperative work (CSCW) deals with the study and development of systems that encourage organizational collaboration. Most groupware products fall under this classification. CSCW projects can be classified into three categories: tools for augmenting collaboration and problem-solving within a group geographically colocated in real time (e.g. CoLab at Xerox Palo Alto Research Center); real-time tools for collaboration among people who are geographically distributed; and tools for asynchronous collaboration among teams distributed geographically.

The last of Engelbart's groupware categories encompasses e-mail (Chapter 3), shared databases (Chapter 4) and, in general, the rest of the book other than this chapter. The first two categories, synchronous meetings and collaborations, both local and remote, are the focus of this chapter.

Although specific products are optimized for specific activities, for the purpose of this discussion, the differences between meetings, collaborations and coauthorship may be considered primarily a matter of degree. Most meetings are held for the purposes of making decisions and planning, but planning a task list is not far from preparing a report or producing a piece of real work.

THE REALITY OF WORK

People are gregarious; they need to share information and collaborate. To be sure, individuals have unique points of view, but there can be no doubt that more can be accomplished when people work together than apart. Conferencing groupware is one way that technology helps people get together and get things done.

We thought that success is creating tools for collaborative knowledge work was essential to the necessary evolution of work groups in increasingly knowledge-rich societies and to increasing organizational effectiveness. Until the recent growing interest in CSCW, most developers limited their analyses to technical issues and ignored the social and organizational implications of the introduction of their tools; such considerations were, however, key to our work.

There is growing recognition that some of the barriers to acceptance of fully integrated systems for augmenting groups of knowledge workers may be more social, not solely technical. The availability of rapidly evolving new technologies implies the need for concomitant evolution in the ways in which work is done in local and geographically distributed groups—Doug Engelbart ("Working Together, *BYTE,* December 1988).

It would be a grave mistake to think that groupware is only about computer technology. Machines cannot replace human interaction but can speed and enhance the processes that ordinarily take place within the context of a meeting, thereby liberating time for more crucial discussion of issues and building consensus. Ideally, these efficiencies and enhancements lead toward a higher-quality of output resulting from more streamlined and efficient meetings.

Technology is not just about electronic gizmos and things that go beep when the wrong key is pressed. The hardware and the software that animates the hardware are only two of a broad range of technologies available. Technology is about technique. An important technology is that set of techniques and behaviors that these other technologies have been designed to support: business practice.

What makes this technology important is that it is the core practice to which other technologies must conform and support.

It is crucial to understand this technology of business practice before attempting to introduce any system or software tool. New ways of working as a group must be considered. The old organization paradigms and models used to assemble a motor car may be inappropriate for the assembly of an information structure or a knowledge-based enterprise.

Working Definitions

There are many definitions of collaboration. For purposes of developing a theoretical understanding of the collaborative process, for pragmatic real-world purposes collaboration can be defined as "people or organizations working toward a common purpose. Collaborations may be between one or more people, or groups."

Because much of the new technology obscures what is normally thought of as meetings, for the purpose of this discussion, meetings are defined as occasions for collaborations to take place. Meetings may, under this loose definition, occur at the same time (synchronous) or at different times (asynchronous), in the same place (co-incident) or at widely dispersed locations. The inherent characteristics of each form of meeting support different activities and may involve different types of personalities.

Each technology supports specific forms of communications and human interaction. For example, the telephone is a device that clearly favors the quick thinker who is also articulate and glib; people who have the vocabulary, timing, and delivery enabling them to effortlessly communicate with word pictures, pitch, and nuance.

And technology hasn't stopped evolving; it continues to grow swallowing up ancillary technologies like telephone and cable television. New combinations of older technologies are combining to form new capabilities, which only add to the arsenal of tools available. For example, e-fax is coming. And the more tools available the more important it is to understand the fundamental concepts that determine their choice and govern their use.

BUILDING A COLLABORATIVE SYSTEM

Certain basic elements are necessary for any system designed to support collaboration in a community of knowledge workers. First of all, there must be an ongoing collaborative dialog. Without exchange of information, there can be no concentration of effort. Collaborative dialog must take place on different levels. There must, for example, be communication about purpose. Everyone must understand what it is that must be accomplished, at least at some level. A subset of this evolutionary form of communication is the *why* of the *what* that is proposed. A subset of common motivation is the issue of group identity and the relationship of individual roles and identities within the context of the group.

Clearly, these issues are often taken for granted by many workers, and therefore need no explicit discussion, but in a functional group, they undergo continual if transparent, renegotiation. This form of collaborative dialog includes most of the necessary political, sociological, and interpersonal communications needs of a group. Decision support tools and videoconferencing are two technologies which support this communications requirement.

Another level of collaborative dialog is simply logistic: how to synchronize activities. Who can expect what from whom and when. The simplest and most easily accepted form of groupware such as calendaring and scheduling software supports this form of ongoing dialog.

Yet another form of collaborative dialog has to do with the substance of the collaboration. With information enterprises, at least, this form of dialog is analogous to the meshed gears that coordinate the various machines that make up the assembly line. Tools discussed later in this chapter such as document conferencing tools and decision support tools address this form of required dialog. Tools for the composition of messages and for subsequent review, cross referencing, modification, transmission, storage, indexing, and full-text retrieval are therefore vital to any CSCW system.

Document development and production tools are also necessary for collaborative effort, including tools for composing, studying, and modifying document drafts and for high-quality photo composition.

Others include:

- Tools for submission authentication and comments, administrative support for editors, sequential delivery and tracking for approvals chains, and automatic "ticklers" for those who fail to respond to RFCs.
- A backlinking facility for handling superceded documents.
- Tools to catalogue and index internally generated items such as bibliographies, clippings, etc.
- A "superdocument" for coordinating the handling of very large and complex bodies of documentation and associated external references, often called a "community handbook."

The term community handbook needs further explanation: It can be defined as a uniform, complete, consistent, up-to-date integration of the special knowledge representing the current status of the community. Such a handbook would include the principles, working hypotheses, practices, glossaries of special terms, standards, goals, goal status, techniques, observations, and more of an active community, whether scientific, business, or otherwise.

Such specialized information sets would require some form of consistant dissemination. One of the fundamental characteristics of information, especially in information enterprises, is that its value increases commensurate with the scale of distribution. The more that it is distributed, the more valuable it becomes to everyone. Another characteristic of information as a commodity is that it is a wasting asset. Therefore, it is imperative that some mechanism be developed for the dissemination of group and activity relevant information. One of the ways of meeting the special training needs of a community of collaborating knowledge workers is to develop and use computer-based instructional tools.

SYNCHRONOUS LOCAL MEETINGS AND COLLABORATIONS

Typically, in the evolution of technology there is initial resistance to anything new. The first technologies to be widely accepted are usually those that mimic the known and the familiar. Groupware is in its infancy, and its most successful products are those based on familiar paradigms and processes. One such paradigm is time management.

Time Management and Scheduling

One of the areas of least resistance to penetration of the business sector by workgroup support tools is scheduling. The concepts are familiar yet the benefits are tangible. Humans are social beings, naturally inclined to coordinate individual activities and purposes with those of others to achieve some common purpose. The ability to do so is a principal distinguishing characteristic of the human race.

A meta activity necessary for cooperative activity is some form of synchronization. Whether an orchestra, a football squad, or an engineering design task group, there must be a means of organizing personal tasks and activities, and synchronizing individual actions with those of our partners in purpose.

A common frustration often expressed about working in groups within the corporate setting has been the scheduling of meetings. The minor irritation of playing "telephone tag" can degenerate into confrontations and power struggles. Then there's the embarrassment of double-booked (or not booked at all) rooms or equipment.

According to one study, the cost per person of attending a single group meeting is around $50. If you regularly attend a weekly status meeting with your team, the cost of your attendance would be $2,500 per year. Multiply this by every other team member. To make this significant investment worthwhile, you need to maximize member participation while minimizing the cost of the logistics.

Today, the trend is away from isolated host resident time management tools to LAN-based enterprise-wide calendar connectivity catalysts. The most familiar version of scheduling software is the personal time manager. The screens and windows of most scheduling software is designed to mimic traditional devices; for example, the electronic calendars look very much like paper calendars—some even include not only a scene, say a sunrise over the Grand Tetons, but animate the scene.

Scheduling tools can be divided into two categories, personal or group-oriented, although it may be difficult at times to differentiate because of the expanding and overlapping feature sets. The differences have more to do with the inherent design focus than with how the products actually work.

Personal Information Managers (PIMs)

Personal information managers are programs that organize your appointments, scheduled events, notes, and to-do lists. Personal management tools include the calendar, to-do list, alarms, "tickler" files, personal information managers (PIMs) and contact managers. Figure 6.1 shows a sample Appointments screen.

Perhaps the most critical aspect of PIMs is the interface. The commands, menus, buttons, and other graphical devices should feel natural and comfortable. If the interface does not present a clear and simple logic, then it is less likely to be used, rendering it pointless.

Contact managers are similar to PIMs except that they tend to be specialized and deal more with calls and letters that you make and receive in the course of conducting your business.

Harvey Mackay, author of the best-selling *Swim with the Sharks without Being Eaten Alive*, preaches that the ability to track people in both your personal as well as your business life is vital to success. One personal management product, from Cognitech Corp., called Sharkware, includes an audio training tape that guides users through 66 items to know about a contact and 22 questions to prepare for when searching for a job.

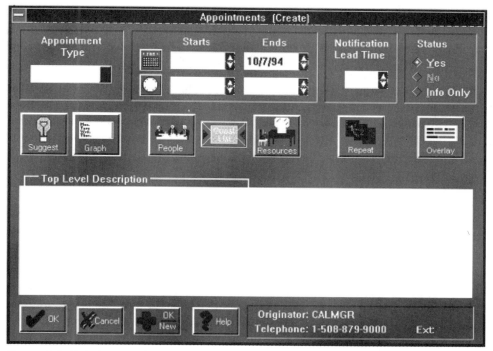

Figure 6.1 Entering appointments into a PIM calendar.

The size of contact lists varies between products. The ability to drag and drop entries to or from a contact list to a calendar, a telephone book, or a mailing list is a convenience that becomes more appreciated the *less* you notice it.

The ability to annotate and document contacts is useful for a personal organizer. This feature becomes increasingly valuable when it is available across a workgroup. Another useful feature is automatic dialing. Many PIMs not only store telephone numbers but can dial a telephone automatically. A call timer is another bell and whistle that is appreciated and used by people such as a traveling sales rep who makes a lot of calls.

Alarms that remind the user of meetings, appointments, or scheduled tasks range from utilitarian to fancy. A scheduled time and date might be marked by a Looney Tunes animation clip played from the hard drive; or, a specified program or file might automatically open along with the reminder. You can have Porky Pig remind you (courtesy of a sound board) to do your quarterly returns; you can also have your accounting program show you a specified updated report. Also useful, and becoming increasingly available, is the ability to send alarms or even short messages to a pager.

Appointment calendar schedules may be presented in a variety of views including text, time-line, or Gantt charts. Figure 6.2 shows a Select Time screen for appointments. Calendar views can be by the week, month, or year. Another feature becoming accepted is the ability to share calendars. This is one of the features that raises personal information managers into the realm of groupware. The benefits of interlinking time management tools within and across a group substantially increases the value of already valuable tools.

Printing support might include the ability to print reports, cards, letters, envelopes, and labels. An associated feature is the ability to download schedules and calendar information from the home computer or a portable to the office computer or network. One of the problems, however, of PIMs is the problem of keeping files in sync between several computers.

Some PIMs go beyond managing contacts, appointments, and telephone numbers. One utility can manage objects, which can be people, activities, projects, or documents. Each of these objects can be annotated or "tagged" with relevant pieces of information such as name, address, telephone number, start or end times, task lists, status, or whatever. This information can then be sorted, grouped, and linked to other pieces of information.

Indeed, some PIMs aspire to rival the Windows Program Manager in launching other applications or opening documents. To-do lists can be organized by priority or category. For example, items can be organized by group items and personal items.

Another useful desktop accessory is the notepad. Many notepads mimic post-it notes, and appear whenever the applet is opened and disappear when it is closed. Electronic post-it notes are a powerful feature for adding special comments and information ticklers.

Many PIMs allow for the easy movement of information from one function group to another. For example, you can drag a name or other piece of information from a telephone directory to some other part of the program.

Group Schedulers

The value of calendars and scheduling increases with scope. A growing number of products permit time management for groups as well as individuals. Group schedulers may be resource specific. For example, a scheduler that manages human resources would be called a project management application. A scheduler that is used to coordi-

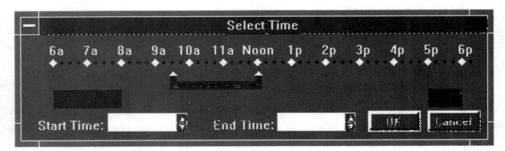

Figure 6.2 Selecting the time and duration of an appointment.

nate tasks is called a workflow manager. Basically, however, schedulers work in the same way. Many products support the scheduling of resources in the same way as people. Resources such as meeting rooms, audio visual equipment such as overhead projectors, VCRs, or videoconfering roll-abouts are each assigned calendars of their own as if they were workers. The calendars for these resources can be polled for availability along with prospective human attendees.

A project manager scheduler is used to coordinate resources—primarily people—for the completion of a specific project such as the construction of a building or development of a product.

A workflow manager scheduler is used to automate the scheduling of an individual task through a systematic process such as the processing of a loan application or an insurance claim.

A contact manager scheduler is used to coordinate information about clients or professional contacts. Typically, a contact manager will have some sort of "tickler" or "nudger" alarm function as a reminder of some scheduled event such as a fax, a mailing, or a client call.

A document manager scheduler is used to track a document from creation to completion through storage to retrieval.

Enterprise-wide Group Scheduling

There are several architectural models upon which enterprise group scheduling may be implemented: client/server, store-and-forward, peer-to-peer, shared file, and host-based applications. Currently, the two most popular architectures are client/server and store-and-forward.

The model of greatest interest here is the client/server model. Two elements that essentially define the client/server model are bifurcated application specific logic (that is, divided into at least two discrete processes: client process and server process), and a real-time communication link between the processes. Usually, the client process and the server process each run on separate machines.

This model, because of the centralization of calendar data, supports some of the more advanced features such as common time availability. The store-and-forward model requires the duplication of data sets and all of the concomitant problems with redundancy, data integrity, propogation delay, and resource inefficiency. The speed of communication possible with the client/server model is a very clear advantage.

The store-and-forward model uses semaphores or messages to communicate either between different parts of the same application or between different users. These messages are not necessarily delivered in real time, but may be stored at intermediate points called "post offices" and forwarded at periodic intervals to the next network node until it reaches its destination.

Because of the problems just mentioned, with respect to common time availability, the time span available for scheduling is limited. Because of the necessary duplication of individual schedule data and the resulting storage costs, the time window within which group events may be scheduled is curtailed.

268 ■ Electronic Meetings

The nonreal-time nature of store-and-forward can give rise to more scheduling conflicts, requiring further resolution. On the other hand, since the inherent nature of e-mail is store-and-forward, the opportunity exists to build a system with one basic mechanism and one integrated interface that serves both purposes.

Advanced Scheduling Features

One of the most indispensible features of schedulers is the ability to archive. Past appointments can be archived and later searched. You might, in anticipation of a scheduled meeting for example, wish to review notes made from a previous meeting with a client.

Another feature, multiple views, allows users to display their calendars by day, week, month, or even the entire year at a glance. These views may be printed out in various formats which may include current to-do lists, deadlines, and critical path milestones.

Calendars that are based on a local area network permit a great deal of flexibility with scheduling groups, meetings, and assigning tasks. Tasks may be assigned and schedules set either by a manager/coordinator or by negotiation within a group.

One of the time savers provided by LAN-based schedulers is the use of a Free Time Search capability to identify common time availability within the target group (see Figure 6.3). For example, if you want to call a meeting of a small team to review a document plan, a number of scheduling software products will allow you to search all of the calendars for the members of the designated group to find the first available common time slot that meets the required criteria. Criteria may be simply that all the members are available, but it may also include the availability of necessary resources such as a meeting room or slide projector.

When a suitable time has been found, the person calling the meeting, will use the LAN-based software to enter a tentative time into all members' calendars (see Figure

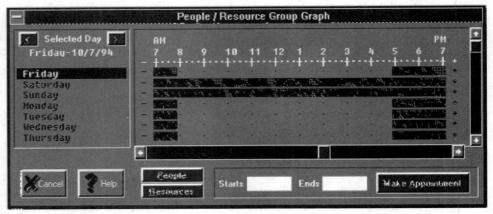

Figure 6.3 People/Resource Group Graph showing common time availability.

6.4). Often, the software will also follow-up with an e-mail to all of the participants reminding them of the proposed meeting including time, place, participants, assigned priority, and agenda. (Meeting Maker from On Technology, supports the distribution of an agenda up to 16 pages in length.) Each of the team members has the ability to either confirm acceptance of the proposed meeting time, to decline, or to propose an alternate time. Subsequent negotiation may take place via e-mail with all interested parties being carbon copied.

A growing number of schedulers have the ability to import and export schedules from and to other vendors; some are able to download schedule information from portable palmtop computers. In this way schedules and appointments that were entered at the home office or on the road may be imported and integrated with local area network server-based schedulers.

Security and Access Privileges

Security may be provided by a couple of different methods or a combination. Password protection restricts who can log into a user account, and access privileges may be defined on a user-by-user basis.

There are two sides to access privileges: your access and access you grant to others, and the access that you have been granted to other's schedules. Personal privacy is maintained by restricting access to an individual's calendar or to-do list to only a lim-

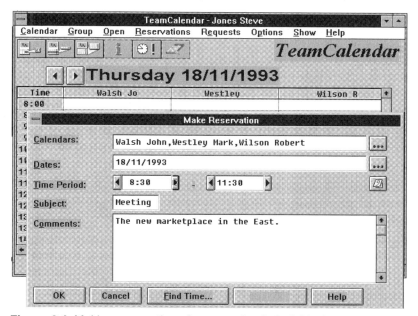

Figure 6.4 Making reservations for a meeting in individual group member calendars across a network.

ited public view. Then, unless you have been granted privileges by the owner of the calendar, you would be able to see only those blocks of time that were occupied and those that were not. These blocks of time would not be visible across the network otherwise.

A higher level of privilege may also be granted. You may designate a proxy enabling someone to see and to schedule your calendar on your behalf. You could, for example, grant your co-chair read and write access to your personal calendar, or let a colleague stand in for you when on vacation, sick, or out of town.

Lists and Notes

Scheduled events are entered into an event list along with various specifics, such as a description of the event with a text annotation, a category from some predefined range of activities, a date, start and stop times, viewing privileges, definition of the group, as well as the room or equipment needed. E-mail requiring confirmation of receipt may also be generated automatically from this event database.

Events can be sorted by user-defined categories such as appointments, meetings, or even birthdays. Meetings can be subcategorized as either regular, holiday, or critical.

Another common type of list is the to-do list in which tasks may be assigned, either for yourself or for one or more other colleagues, in a to-do list window. Each task may be assigned a priority, a date that it will appear on either your or someone else's calendar, and a deadline date. Tasks may also be defined as repeating, which means they will appear on the designated calendars at the specified intervals. For example, the preparation of a monthly progress report may be assigned to each of your project team leaders. An electronic notepad can be used to write notes and reminders for yourself.

Notifiers and Alarms

Notification of scheduled events and task assignments may be sent out automatically to team members. These events and tasks may be accepted and confirmed or rejected. Confirmation will automatically update either the calendar or the to-do list or both.

Alarms may be arranged to remind yourself of events. The alarm may be some visual cue that pops up on your screen or it may be audible. A snooze interval can also be set. Some schedulers support Windows WinBeep, allowing alarms to be sent to pagers. Other group scheduling products even provide time zone support and adjust automatically for differences in time zones for widely dispersed groups.

Group scheduling is practical, however, only if everyone in a workgroup is able to and committed to using it. For workgroups in heterogeneous computing environments, the ability to communicate and exchange schedules across platforms is only one requirement. Equally important for mixed-platform workgroups is the use of standard protocols. Additionally, a consistant interface across platforms and ease of use can greatly increase the chances of integrating group scheduling into regular team activities.

A very useful feature, as just noted, which provides a great deal of flexibility, is the ability to designate proxies. With this feature you could, for example, grant your assistant access to your calendar while you are on a trip or on vacation or just otherwise occupied. The proxy feature has a lot of potential for tightly coupled collaborations.

Increasingly, personal and group schedulers support most popular day-timer formats in printout and screen display. The recognition factor of a well-accepted business tool can help overcome the inevitable initial resistance to new technologies.

Another increasingly popular feature is the ability to work off-line with schedules. This means that you can take your calendar with you along with your portable computer, say on a flight, and schedule events when not connected to the server. When you reconnect to the server, the scheduler will automatically send out meeting proposals and update the network calendars.

SCHEDULING A MEETING

Because of the relative high penetration and ease of acceptance for scheduling software, especially group scheduling applications, there is a convergence of feature sets, and the differences between most schedulers is a function of the price; obviously, the higher the cost, the larger the feature set. More features does not mean necessarily better, however.

To better understand how a group scheduler is used in the real world, here's an example that calls together a work team using a generic group scheduler. Follow these steps:

1. Identify who you plan to invite to your proposed meeting. They may be designated either as required or optional.

2. Set the agenda and fill in agenda details. Most of the group schedulers allow you to query the availability of resources and reserve a meeting room and necessary equipment such as an overhead projector or a whiteboard.

3. Select a time. Time slots for your meeting can be selected either manually or using an automatic time-picking feature. To select manually, you would typically click on a button and drag in the calendar window to select a time slot. To help you find a time that is mutually acceptable, a composite of the schedules of involved staff is displayed. When a time has been selected, usually some indicator such as an icon is displayed alongside each attendee name. An automatic time-picking feature locates the earliest time slot available for all.

4. Send a meeting notification message to each guest. You can also send CC or BCC messages to other workgroup members for information purposes.

When your prospective guests receive your meeting proposal, they can indicate whether they will attend by clicking on a Yes or No button, or choose to postpone a decision until later. Meetings that have been scheduled will appear in both the daily and monthly calendar windows.

Details of any meeting can easily be displayed on the screen by double-clicking on an event title. Most group calendaring applications can also serve as personal calendar programs. Other group members won't be able to see what you're doing or planning to do but they can see if you're busy during a proposed meeting time. A small check mark in a square indicates whether a calendar event is personal or group-oriented.

Ease of use is critical to the success of any software tool. For calendaring and scheduling software, one of the most critical features is the ability to navigate easily and intuitively throughout the views. Navigation tools must allow you to move quickly among dates in both the month and day calendar windows. Clicking on arrow to move forward and backward in time is an increasingly common and logical interface. One set of buttons can move in increments of months, another set in years, and a button that moves you home to the current date is indispensable. The daily calendar window can display a schedule in either single-day or a five-day business week format.

Workgroup System Integration

Some group calendaring applications provide access to other groupware system functions such as electronic messaging or shared databases. For example, your calendar could open a window to serve as both an e-mail in-box as well as a means of tracking meeting proposals that have been sent and received.

Such message windows can contain folders for storing different categories of e-mail and meeting messages. For example, separate folders can be created for active messages (new meeting proposals; notices of changed, rescheduled, or canceled meetings; and responses to proposals), meeting refusals, to-do proposals sent by other users, and CC messages and CC to-do items.

To-do items can be personal or assigned to others, and can be prioritized to one of seven levels. Reminders can be set both for yourself and for others. You can use the to-do list window to view items and create new ones.

SCHEDULING SUMMARY

Because of the familiarity of these group coordination and personal management support tools, LAN-based scheduling tools are finding market acceptance within the corporate community. Scheduling groupware is friendly, familiar, intuitive, and easy to learn and use.

One of the major impediments to collaborative support systems within large companies has been a determined rear-guard action by insecure middle managers who view groupware in general as a threat to their power and authority.

By empowering everyone in an enterprise to schedule a meeting, regardless of where they are on the network or corporate ladder is a revolutionary step toward the virtual corporation.

SYNCHRONOUS LOCAL MEETINGS

The fundamental issue about meetings is venue, both in terms of place and time. With meetings, there must be shared environment, but defining exactly what constitutes a shared environment is vague and in a state of flux. How much and what type of information is necessary before there is a sense of a shared space varies with the situation and the sophistication of those involved.

For example, resolving some complex interpersonal issues may require a good deal more bandwidth to support the subtle nuances of expression that most humans need to achieve a sense of experiencing the other person. On the other hand, many rudimentary transactions may be and are performed daily that require little, if any, personal expression. It may be argued, that removing the personal elements from many business interactions is beneficial and tends to streamline the process. For example, how much human interaction do people truly wish to engage in with either a bank teller or a telephone operator? Many people prefer the efficiency of the ATM to the bland pleasantries of the trained teller.

Meeting Categories

Meetings were characterized in Chapter 1 as having four possibilities of human interaction in terms of time and place. To reiterate briefly, the four categories of meetings are:

Same time, same place

Same time, different places

Different times, same place

Different times, different places

In a broad sense, tools such as videoconferencing and meeting room support tend to amplify the more political and interpersonal interactions within a group. More personality neutral forms of communication, such as bulletin board forums or e-mail tend to restrict the group focus to the ideas being expressed. These systems do so more by default than by design. They simply lack the bandwidth to provide either immediacy, real-time interaction, or the sensory-rich information channel required for nuanced human dialog. Despite these restrictions, or in part because of them, there are many people who prefer to communicate and interact with their colleagues at the distance afforded by these personality neutral means.

Synchronous and Colocal Meetings

Synchronous and colocated meetings (that is, same time/same place) are the central focus of this chapter. Modern technology has changed and continues to change the nature of real-time face-to-face meetings. Some of the devices and meeting support concepts that are currently popular include the following:

- Electronic copyboards
- PC and a projector
- Team rooms
- Group decision support systems

Much work has been done at the University of Arizona in developing tools to support a variety of meeting functions. Special meeting rooms are beginning to spring up around the country that have been equipped with high-end systems to support agenda creation, idea processing tools that elicit ideas, and decision support tools. One such system from the pioneering Ventana Corporation is called GroupSystems. It supports not only real-time meetings but can also be used for distributed situations. Real-time meetings may be one-to-one, one-to-many (a presentation), or many-to-many.

The primary characteristic of this type of meeting is immediacy. Another characteristic is the time expense required to negotiate distance, and to negotiate timetables. A consequence of this type of meeting is to lend a premium to several personal characteristics such as appearance, the ability to think on one's feet, and ease in public. Issues of eloquence and personal charisma may tend to dominate the session. The argument may go not to the most rational but to the most persuasive or politically potent. Clearly, certain personality types will predominate in this environment.

Whether the sociopolitical issues inherent in meta communications should be allowed to obscure agenda issues or whether the political expression of any coherent body is its primary responsibility is a moot point. Context may well be the determinant. For example, at a political rally, or where a leadership or policy issue is at stake, then the rich layers of human interaction above and below the surface may be played out. In a different context, however, such as during the design of a system that would benefit all by its efficiency, it may be wise to diminish the impact of emotion, partisan identification, and popularity and focus instead on the system in a rational manner. It could be argued that the practice of sending these latter issues for study offline to a committee of specialists serves just such a distancing purpose.

Computer-enabled Meeting Rooms

Computer-enabled meeting rooms for hire are proliferating. Among the most well-known is the Decision and Planning Laboratory (DPL), a prototype electronic meeting room at the University of Arizona's College of Business and Public Administration.

The DPL demonstrates how high-technology conference rooms can provide major productivity and time-saving benefits. The DPL, also known as the Arizona Room, consists of 24 workstations, a pair of rear-screen projectors, an electronic copyboard, a video copy stand, a podium (consisting of two workstations, video displays, and switches for sound, video, and lighting systems), and facilitating software.

Proprietary software consists of five functional groups:

- Brainstorming
- Issue analysis
- Prioritizing
- Policy formation
- Stakeholder identification

IBM has established 18 DPL rooms and reports a person-hour savings in excess of 50 percent, with a 92 percent decrease in team project times. Similar rooms are expected to be adopted incrementally.

Electronic Meeting Support Systems

There is a broad range of meeting support software. Some group conferencing software is used to support real-time meetings; other applications let groups and organizations create and hold meetings where the participants can join according to their own time. Other of the more expensive alternatives provide decision support tools that permit agenda creation, rating systems, voting support, as well as meeting reports.

A great deal of research has been done (Doyle and Strauss, 1976) that shows that not only do meetings consume a large part of the typical working day but that many, if not most, people consider them to be largely a waste of time. Efforts have been made to better justify the cost of meetings by introducing a variety of improvements, as discussed in the following sections.

Group Support Systems (GSS)

Group support systems are popularly called groupware. Together, they describe a set of team-oriented computing and communications tools that support a range of group tasks, from brainstorming to decision-making.

Research shows marked improvements in efficiency and results from meetings that have been supported by GSS. For example, Grohowski (1990) reports that IBM has documented over 56 percent time savings in a sampling of more than 900 meetings. Post (1992) reports a 71 percent reduction in actual time spent in meetings during a project at Boeing. In this study, GSS provided labor cost savings and increased group performance, resulting in a 91 percent decrease in overall flowtime—the actual duration of the project.

The remarkable successes of GSS are, however, balanced by failures. The most striking lesson to be drawn from the studies of implementations of groupware is that success hinges primarily on the facilitator. How GSS is introduced, adapted, and applied is more important than the groupware being utilized.

The big question is: How do you facilitate a workgroup using GSS, specifically, to plan, coordinate, and direct workgroup activities? While some aspects of the facilitation can be off-loaded onto the group support systems themselves, such as activity structuring, scheduling, and voting support, groupware is fundamentally a tool that must be used with understanding and sensitivity.

The fundamental motivation for this book is to provide some consideration of issues and principles that are fundamental to all groupware, and an appreciation that while one GSS tool may be appropriate for one situation it may not be for another. GSS in and of itself cannot address issues such as meeting design. The most crucial element in the successful adoption of any GSS strategy is effective human facilitation.

Meeting facilitation is a process that must be carried out before, during, and after the actual event. The process is composed of a series of activities or a set of functions. The functions might be carried out either by the meeting leader, a specialist, or the members of the group themselves. Generally, one person is designated as the formal primary facilitator. Other participants might be designated as secondary facilitators. Some companies try to rotate the responsibilities within the workgroup under the theory that by taking turns playing all roles, a greater appreciation of other functions is fostered, along with a sense of project "ownership," which leads to increased morale and productivity.

The role of meeting facilitator is not new. What is new is the careful consideration of what makes a good facilitator, the dissection of the anatomy of a meeting, and the examination of group processes. The next section covers some of the more useful conceptual models and frameworks.

Group Decision Support Systems Groupware (GDSS)

The roots of GDSS can be traced to information systems in business management schools and, as its name suggests, in DSS (Decision Support Systems). Some of the original ideas in DSS can be traced to Keen and Scott Morton who suggested using computers to help managers make decisions, management judgments, and enhance the overall decision-making process for managers.

The group decision support system approach extends DSS so that a group (versus an individual manager) makes a decision. To help a group of people make decisions, GDSS groupware incorporates tools to facilitate electronic brainstorming, organize issues, vote, and help formulate decisions by the group. In many cases, GDSS systems achieve this through systems that support same time/same place face-to-face meetings. Recall that GDSS was one of the product categories (in fact, the most important) mentioned in the same time/same place quadrant of the taxnomy of groupware systems.

Research is ongoing in this important field of GDSS, and its impact on the technologies of strategic decision-making, issue documentation, decision evaluation, formulation of policies, is being tracked.

Meetings are a critical component of business conducted within and between organizations. One model is called the "goal directed meeting" model. This model is an outcome-focused framework which describes a meeting as a basic change process that transforms a problem (present state) into a desired result (outcome state). This is accomplished by a series of actions involving available resources, people, and technology.

The agenda (defined as a series of action steps) can be described in terms of four core information processing activities: generation, organization, evaluation, and communication. For example, in order to solve a defined problem, a group might be required to, first, generate information; organize the information into alternative courses of action; evaluate the alternative courses of action; and, finally, communicate the decisions. By considering these generic activities, an agenda can be built. This model is also useful for categorizing and classifying GSS tools in terms of their relevant activities.

SYNCHRONOUS AND REMOTE MEETINGS

Synchronous and geographically displaced (same time/different place) meetings are considered by many to be the most important form of meeting today. Modern communications technologies have changed the work world. In the past, restrictions were imposed by geographical limits. Telecommunications have shrunk the world. Perhaps it is not yet a global village, but more of an extended metropolis, yet it is possible now to transact business and perform work in collaboration across great distances.

The technologies that enable and support this form of human interaction include:

- Teleconferencing
- Videoconferencing
- Data conferencing
- Virtual reality and cyberspace

Telecommunications technologies permit people to project those dimensions of ourselves that are most relevant for decision-making and information-sharing meeting purposes. They make it possible to transcend distances and time.

In the current work atmosphere, the compression of space is of value, perhaps because the traversal of space usually translates into time. The greater the distance, the greater the time cost. The ability to reconcile time-critical issues in a relatively short amount of time is a clear business advantage.

Technologies that support same time/different place interactions include:

- Telephone conference calls
- Videoconferencing (one-to-one or many-to-many)
- Satellite downlinks (one-to-many)
- PC screen sharing/whiteboards

Teleconferencing

How business is conducted has changed. For many people, all or most interactions are over the telephone. Indeed, as stated earlier, the ability to "give good telephone" is one of the criteria for modern management. The ability to follow and anticipate ideas from an oral stream is necessary for personal interactions. To be successful, telephoners need to be able to communicate in various perceptual tropes. For example, the liability of not seeing the person to whom one is speaking can be compensated for with word pictures. By denying direct access to real-life visual clues, intensely personal imagery must be stimulated by strictly oral means.

The human imagination is capable of filling in a lot of the information that is necessary to provide context and thereby meaning into communications. The challenge for the next generation is learning how to do this with new computer technologies. These technologies, from local area networks and e-mail to the Internet and World Wide Web present a whole new set of limitations to surmount and new possibilities to exploit.

Desktop Teleconferencing

Currently there are more than 30,000 desktop teleconferencing rooms operational, and this number is growing by about 10 thousand per year. Teleconferencing is a $3 billion industry, and is used for everything from day-to-day interactions to telemedicine, telecommuting, and teleeducation.

Electronic Virtual Meeting Rooms

The ultimate electronic meeting would allow every remote participant to have full access to every other participant and all of their data. There are things that can be done in an electronic meeting that cannot be done in a normal meeting. You can participate in a meeting from your cubicle, from a laptop, or while sipping a cocktail by the swimming pool. Anonymous meetings can be held in which the identity of the participants is not known. Meetings can be distributed over time and span time zones.

Voice Mail

Asynchronous meetings via voice mail are becoming increasingly popular in certain market sectors. Within some companies, voice mail has become the messaging medium of first choice. Considering that local area networks at Silicon Graphics of Mountain View, California support not only e-mail but v-mail (video mail) as well as a highly sophisticated graphical environment within which it is easy to call a meeting on-line that includes videoconferencing and the transmission of multimedia rich documents, this is no mean endorsement.

The factors behind the popularity of voice messaging are ease of use, instant (or near instant) gratification, and emotive expression. Most of the other media however seductive they may be, tend not to be real time in terms of preparation. Voice messaging systems today offer a mixture of the features of bulletin boards and of e-mail with the added value of the personal warmth afforded by the telephone.

Voice Mail Threads

Like bulletin boards, discussion threads—a chain of messages circulating through a distribution list—provide a workgroup with an effective and intuitively familiar and easy-to-use means by which to hold an asynchronous meeting. The message content, of course, is largely dictated by the inherent strengths and weaknesses of the medium. A linear stream of the spoken word is a poor medium for a technical report; it is, however, an ideal medium for a quick and personal comment or point of view. Voice mail is quick and easy to use; it is personal and expressive; it is immediate and urgent. It is also, however, primarily a serial stream of data that must be "read" in real-time. It is not as easy to scan for the relevant detail as is more graphic material.

Like e-mail, voice messages can be responded to, sent initially, or forwarded to a distribution list along with annotations. With a voice gateway, faxes can be received into a voice mailbox and retrieved from any touchtone telephone or other dial tone multiple frequency (DTMF) device. Most operations on the mailbox can be executed from a remote site by touch tone phone. The more sophisticated telephone systems have turned the telephone into a rudimentary terminal keypad that you can use to interrogate a database for your bank balance, movie showtimes, flight schedules, daily horoscope, or reservations.

Some ancillary benefits include that voice message meetings are self-documenting and support annotations. The more sophisticated systems have user-friendly interfaces that will prompt the user for input.

Faxmail

A new player in the groupware arena is the ubiquitous fax. Not the clunky facsimile device that spews paper in practically every office in the world, but a new and improved fax technology. Microsoft Corp. has developed a product for the nascent faxmail market. It is called Microsoft At Work and is based on a new messaging protocol that promises a direct and simple way to send messages and to exchange files over the public dial-up network. The At Work protocol is based on the ITU-T's ECM recommendation, but includes proprietary extensions. Using At Work, all communication is handled through a single-user interface, thereby blurring the distinction between e-mail, fax, and binary file transfer. In keeping with the single-interface paradigm, users can store all of their e-mail addresses and fax phone numbers in a single directory.

The future success of faxmail is not, however, assured. If it delivers on its promise, it might indeed become the next-generation fax technology. Furthermore, what made Group 3 fax so popular—ease of use, unattended operation, instant delivery, and virtually guaranteed compatibility—could make faxmail yet another messaging layer in the groupware toolbox.

While faxmail won't replace e-mail, it could extend communications to both remote users and otherwise incompatible e-mail facilities. Faxmail could become something equivalent to an ad hoc X.400 delivery service. If the expected onslaught of mobile data users ever materializes, demand might soar. And the icing on the cake would be that, with a little modification, this technology also could be pressed into the same service of groupware as e-mail or bulletin boards.

Conferencing Software Features

The two fundamental elements essential to any meeting are people and information. The purpose of any meeting is for people to transact information in some form or other. Meetings are always political in nature. How people reconcile differences, explore options, and find some common purpose invariably involves political considerations.

Developing Options

The process of developing and exploring options is one of divergence. Software can support divergence by providing an environment that encourages brainstorming. Some of these features are: anonymity that encourages off-the-wall ideas without embarrassment; open access to participation; quick display and feedback so that other participants can be stimulated by the ideas of others.

Some of the higher-end groupware meeting support systems provide voting tools for helping a group reach a consensus. Voting tools have an almost a subliminal effect of consolidating the group by representing it as a unity rather than disparate individuals. The feedback afforded by rapid tabulation, analysis, and graphic representation can provide a perspective on the decision-making process that drives the process more directly in the direction in which it was trending. The introduction of positive feedback into any system will tend to exaggerate the natural tendency of that system.

Electronic Voting

Stand-alone applications are beginning to appear that are designed to support electronic voting. One such product, eVote from Frontier Systems of Palo Alto, California attempts to redefine electronic democracy.

eVote invites member of the electronic community to propose a vote on any subject. The proposer of the vote can direct eVote to take either a "yes/no" or a "numeric" vote. Votes can be "public" like a show of hands, "private" like a secret vote, or "if-voted" where the entire community can see who has participated in the issue, but not how they voted.

Voters can change or withdraw their votes while the vote is in progress, and issues can be grouped while the vote is still in progress. For example, a grouped issue might be presented as "Choose 3 out of the following 5 items."

Frontier Systems presents eVote as a kit for performing experiments in electronic democracy in cyberspace. eVote is also available as an application programmer's interface (API) for embedding eVoting functions into other UNIX C and C++-based groupware programs. The idea is to enhance existing cyberspace discussions.

Group Systems from Ventana

Ventana Corp. under the leadership of Jay Nunamaker, an established expert in the field of group support systems, has introduced GroupSystems, a set of high-end tools for driving consensus and decision-making in both distributed meeting as well as face-to-face meetings. This technology is based on research done at the University of Arizona.

Meetings are set up with the Meeting Manager which has its own tool set. Whoever calls the meeting becomes the session leader and has more options than the other participants but may choose to grant these functionalities to the other participants. Whoever "owns" the project or meeting can set the role of and call upon each participant.

An Agenda tool prompts the leader for the name and duration of each meeting segment. The tool will then autopilot the group through the agenda, suggesting other tools that might be useful to participants.

Group process tools range from Brainstorming, wherein participants build a common base of ideas and options, to Stakeholder Identification, a template for adopting alternate points of view for issue evaluation; there are also idea consolidation tools and decision support tools, which bring the group back together.

Ease of use and technical transparency are evident in the graphical approach taken in the interface design of Group Systems. For example, ideas can be categorized by dragging them into named idea "buckets."

In the looser distributed form of meeting, information can be identified as either "new" or "old," which makes it easier for participants to drop in and out without losing the thread.

Generating ideas and brainstorming is a divergent activity where the goal is to flesh out issues in great detail. Once a breadth of ideas is achieved, the dynamic turns around and moves to a conclusion by convergence—voting and consensus seeking. Votes can quickly be tallied, displayed numerically or graphically, and analyzed. The feedback afforded by displaying the spread of the votes can help drive the group toward a consensus. In those areas where there is general consensus, agreement is accelerated. The time saved can be spent restating, reviewing, and resolving issues where there is a large standard deviation.

Information Centered Meetings

Information is the lifeblood of society. The information era, forces relationships to revolve around the information, rather than focusing on the information as an expression of a relationship. Evidence of this phenomenon is that the primary environment is now abstract, not physical. What was once a tool used to cope with physical realities has, for many people, supplanted the materiality of the world.

Some of the current technologies used for distributed meetings are limited in the amount of personal information available within the meeting space. This may be a liability in terms of supporting the interpersonal expression required for the fulfillment of the political process inherent in decision-making. But this limitation of bandwidth also has beneficial aspects.

By removing, to a large extent, issues of personality and identity, it is possible for meeting participants to focus on the other primary dimension of meetings: the information content. Indeed, if a document is to be the result of a meeting, and that document is required to present some information, then the development of that information may be better facilitated in an environment where the personalities involved in its production are shrouded by time and/or space.

Anonymity

Another benefit of intentionally constraining the availability of information about other participants is to afford anonymity. Anonymous meetings enable participants to focus on the message rather than the messenger whose identity is not known. Information that might be crucial to the resolution of an issue, which might not be as forthcoming in a public forum, may well be captured in a venue where sources are protected by personal anonymity.

The anonymity afforded by electronic meetings tend to stimulate brainstorming sessions by removing some of the inhibitions that typically restrain involvement. People can be more open and free with what they say.

MEETING TOOLS

Meeting tools follow the evolving process of a meeting. The more comprehensive meeting systems such as Ventana's GroupSystems, The Meeting Room from Eden Corp. and VisionQuest from Collaborative Technologies, usually provide a full complement of meeting support tools.

Tools for planning a meeting include scheduling and agenda creation capabilities. Agenda items can be entered manually on the spot or imported from a prior activity such as idea generation. Increasingly, tools for driving meetings to productive conclusion are finding favor in the marketplace. Process facilitation includes tools for generating ideas, and consolidating ideas. For example, the Brainwriting tool, which is a component of Visionquest from Collaborative Technologies Corp., presents participants with a box at the bottom of the screen into which ideas can be typed. Pressing Enter automatically adds the idea to a list at the top of the screen.

Unless the meeting was strictly for informational purposes, some decision or decisions must be made even if only when to hold the next meeting. Decision-making support includes tools for evaluating and ranking alternatives, and for voting. Idea evaluation may be either by some numeric ranking scheme or by dividing the ideas into predefined categories.

DISTRIBUTED MEETINGS

A distributed meeting is one that takes place over a period of time. Meeting participants may or may not be party to the "meeting" at the same time; they may check in and out. (Figure 6.5 shows a distributed meeting—a bulletin board forum.) Distributed electronic conferences can be held over e-mail, voice mail, or dedicated meeting software. Most popular technologies that support distributed meetings have been discussed in previous chapters. There are, however, a few considerations worth reviewing in terms of applying these technologies specifically to group meetings and the concept of a meeting distributed across time as well as geography.

The benefit of including people who might otherwise not be able to participate in and contribute to a meeting is not limited to traversing just time zones or conflicting schedules. There is growing evidence that the very nature of distributed meetings brings into play people who would otherwise never engage in or contribute to traditional face-to-face meetings.

As technology increasingly supports business communications and moves into more knowledge-intensive enterprises, the capture of this formerly dormant brain power becomes increasingly significant.

But, although meetings distributed over space, for example by means of telephone conferences or videoconferencing, have become accepted, the concept of a meeting that extends across time is not as familiar. The element that seems to cause the most problem is the lack of real-time interaction between personalities.

Possibly, those people who are most comfortable in social situations are those who miss the opportunity of engaging in real-time association. Others who are averse

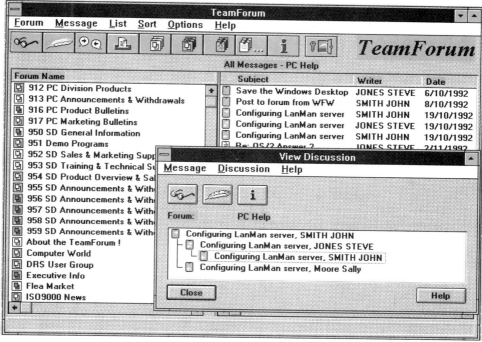

Figure 6.5 An example of "distributed meeting"—a bulletin board forum.

to direct social interaction may find the idea of a distributed meeting much less alien and more inviting.

Distributed meetings can actually be more valuable than real-time meetings because people can "sleep on" ideas before having to make a comment. In terms of content, the overall quality of thought resulting from a meeting that is distributed over time improves, even if the drama suffers.

And although a distributed meeting lacks the immediacy and intimacy of same time/same place confrontations, there are things that can be done in a distributed meeting that cannot be done in real-time face-to-face meetings. One of the remarkable characteristics of this type of meeting is the ability to include people who usually are left out of "normal" meetings. The shy, the retiring, the awkward may all find it easier to participate in proceedings without the intimidation of real-life meetings. Another characteristic unique to distributed meetings is the ability to perform last minute research and case building during the course of the meeting.

While distributed meetings are not likely to replace any of the other options for group conferencing, they certainly provide benefits by affording the opportunity to involve more people in meaningful ways into the process of meeting, whether the purpose of the meeting is to develop options or to achieve consensus.

There is ongoing debate over which meeting quadrant is most important. This is a moot point. Each quadrant has particular characteristics that make it appropriate for certain types of interaction. It is not really a question of which quadrant or mode of interaction is more powerful, but which is more *appropriate*.

In terms of potential impact for reengineering a business, at least in the short term, the most significant improvement can be made in the same time/same place quadrant. Confusion, inefficiency, and rework resulting from unclear decisions and lack of commitment resulting from in-person meetings may be one of the major barriers to getting things done. Technology, perhaps because of the deeply ingrained experiences most companies have had with this type of meeting, seems to have had minimal impact in this area. Beyond adding some flash and pizzazz to presentations, technology has made only superficial inroads on traditional face-to-face meetings.

One of the reasons for resistance to introducing support technologies into more traditional organizations has been, as noted earlier in the book, the insecurity of middle management: fear of losing control. The real cost of maintaining control, however, is the loss of low-level and front-line input, often the most productive source of productivity gains.

The particular forms of social interaction that have come to be accepted as "normal" meeting behavior is, of course, culture-specific. The constituency that makes up the workforce has changed dramatically in the most potent knowledge-based industries, with concomitant changes in political expression and interpersonal interactions within the context of business-oriented group meetings expected in the future.

The dramatic impact of technology on some of the other quadrants will also cause changes to the form of face-to-face meetings. For example, technology that can almost instantly tabulate and analyze the results of voting, as well as display the standard deviation resulting from a vote will find a place in real-time face-to-face meetings.

Technology has had the greatest impact in the different times/different places quadrant. Workflow systems are taking off. Unlike meeting support technologies, people who decide to implement workflow systems are typically not those who are impacted by them.

MEETINGS SUMMARY

In the real world, work is done by groups of people working together. Technology can help people work better together. The specific body of technologies that have been and are being designed is called, collectively, groupware.

One important category of groupware, and the main focus of this chapter, is electronic meeting support (EMS) software. Another category is time management or scheduling software. Scheduling software may be used for individual time management or, more usefully, to coordinate and manage group activities. One of the most widely accepted forms of groupware is called Enterprise Wide Group Scheduling.

Electronic meeting support systems are still in their infancy. As an immature product set that is still in a state of evolutionary flux with varying degrees of market acceptance, consideration of EMS systems must begin with an analysis of basics. While it is useful to consider meetings from the point of view of the nature of the interactions in terms of space and time, this analysis becomes bogged down with systems that overlap or span categories or involve enabling technologies from different quadrants. Still, until the market "speaks" more decisively, this academic approach can garner some useful insights.

Conferencing software features are discussed broadly. The industry is still so poorly defined with products that range all over the map that many products seem to be more a collection of random feature sets than coherent tools.

Meetings may be held for informational purposes only or for working out issues and making decisions. Usually, however, although meetings tend to emphasize either information or people issues, most meetings require both elements.

Electronically supported meetings tend to enforce better planning and waste less time. Because the agenda is integral to the e-meeting process, participants tend to stay more on topic, to develop a wider range of alternatives for consideration, involve a broader base of participation, drive decision-making, build consensus that ultimately translates into a stronger commitment to decisions that were taken, and last but not least, are self-documenting. The bottom line is that software supported tools can save time and money.

WORKING TOGETHER: COLLABORATIVE AUTHORING

New technologies for mingling data, voice, and video are changing the ways people work together. The rapid evolution of technologies and the various possible permutations and interdependencies add up to a growing range of new functionalities and unexplored potential.

Cooperation may be defined as operation without interference. No other assumptions can safely be made about the nature of the operations being performed by the respective operators, although the implication of assistance is there. Collaboration, on the other hand, implies not only a congruence of interest but a singularity of purpose. When people collaborate, the assumption is that they are moving not only in the same direction without interfering with each other, but to the same destination.

Collaboration Technology

Collaboration technology has been defined as any combination of information technologies designed to overcome the following barriers to collaboration in large-scale organizations:

- Distance
- Heterogeneity of databases and computer systems
- Coordination and global visibility of common information
- Usability

Meetings vs. Authoring

The principal difference between group meetings and collaborative authoring is a question of scale, duration, degree, and locii of activity. Typically, meetings involve more people, say a work team or a design, discussion, or study group. Authoring, at least at this point, tends to involve fewer people.

The difference in terms of duration is subtle. A coauthoring process or system usually is designed for multiple sessions, but this is not necessarily the case. Consider a distributed electronic meeting convened for the purpose of drafting some document, say a proposal, and this distinction loses its clarity.

The degree of interaction provides some differentiation. Purely informational meetings may be considered to be relatively passive and more of a presentation (one-to-many) than an active meeting (many-to-many, one-to-one). Active meetings tend to be oriented about people issues, such as making decisions, which has been defined as essentially a political act. Collaborative authorship can be considered to be more content-oriented.

In other words, meetings tend to deal more with people issues, whereas authoring sessions tend to deal more with information or content issues. The difference is of course relative, since both elements must be present for a meeting to take place.

Where the primary activity takes place is perhaps more important. Although preparation and support material may be required, the principal activity of a meeting would be expected to take place during the meeting. Collaborative authoring systems tend to support subsidiary efforts such as the integration or reconciliation of efforts which have been performed elsewhere.

The differences between tools that support meetings and tools for coauthoring are subtle and primarily a matter of degree.

Clearly there is no clear distinction.

Current work group software is still sequential (that is only one person at a time can work on a document at a time even though two or more may be viewing the work as it progresses). Since much of human interactivity is dialog this constraint may not be quite the liability that it may appear to be. In fact, as anyone who has participated in a telephone multiparty conference can attest, without some flow control and restraint in place participants are almost assured of blindly stumbling into and over each other at some point in time.

Interactive Editors

Editors may support fully coupled sessions as well as asynchronous or loosely coupled cooperation. A fully coupled session would include real-time interactive shared space such as whiteboards.

Design was one the first of the application domains studied by CSCW researchers. The earliest efforts involved research into various forms of shared drawing surfaces, such as whiteboards. Not surprisingly, since design engineers were charged with designing and engineering a design system, computer or engineering design was the focus of much of this early activity, but few design disciplines have not been radically altered by computing, and the trend continues toward more intensive computer-supported design.

More computer-supported cooperative work technology systems that address a broad range of design disciplines including graphic design, textiles, fashion, and product design are anticipated.

Essential to communication is that people transmit and receive on the same channel, at the same frequency, synchronized in time. Whether calling plays on the gridiron, or playing parts in a symphony, people need to get in step, in the same key. SMPTE time code keeps the sight and the sound synchronized in a film. Everything in nature moves in cycles, whether to the clock of the rotating earth or to the crystal that pulses CPU cycles. Even in real time, communication is a process of iteration. Someone speaks; another listens. During this phase, two people are active. While one is speaking, the other is actively watching the expression of the speaker, monitoring not only the content, but the nuance of the expression, to integrate this "new" material into an internal database of existing knowledge. Knowledge is information in context.

Electronic-supported conversations must also work in a similar to and fro manner. There are, of course, differences. The differences depend on the nature of the medium. Technology has allowed people to shift the dialog in both space and time.

Participatory Design

Currently of interest primarily in academic circles, participatory design is sometimes called the "Scandinavian approach" to system development. It advocates a high degree of worker involvement in the design of computer systems which they will eventually employ. The fundamental themes of PD are mutual reciprocal learning and design by doing. The former recommends bilateral collaboration between system designers and the workers for whom they are designing systems. The latter theme translates into creative design by empirical hands-on practice.

A crucial element to practical collaboration is some sense of shared space. While collaborators are usually chosen because of complementary abilities or skill sets there must be some sufficient overlap to provide some "common space," whether temporal or imaginary, physical or psychological.

Whiteboards

Perhaps the simplest example of a shared space is a metaphor for a physical device: the whiteboard. One of the best things about a live meeting is that everyone can see the same information at the same time. The shared whiteboard attempts to provide the same facility to participants who may scattered all around the country.

Xerox Liveboard can be considered a whiteboard on steroids. It is marketed as an electronic groupstation that allows people in dispersed locations to access and interact with shared data. It is a 486 computer running Windows with an oversized LCD display and infrared pen input. A modem is all that is required for a hookup.

One of the keys to this technology is that the marking "ink" is treated as an object that can be compressed. In this compressed form, it can be sent as tokens over ordinary telephone lines to appear on one or more other connected liveboards.

The net result of whiteboard technologies is that people in widely dispersed locations can work on what logically and effectively is the same surface. Files can be loaded into the Liveboard from the desktop, and any information added during the meeting can be saved for further use.

Brainstorming

Brainstorming is a divergent process, during which the goal is not to converge points of view and reach a consensus or to find some common ground, but to cast a net as broadly as possible to capture as wide a set of alternatives as possible. Various techniques have evolved to support this activity, usually directed at "loosening up" participants. Spontaneity, impulse, and fun are encouraged. The ambience often considered to be the most conducive for brainstorming is one of play rather than serious consideration. What may be considered an off-the-wall idea in one context may be, in the light of other information or point of view, the innovation that most neatly solves the problem.

And even if the more extreme ideas aren't directly applicable to the problem at hand, the annunciation of these ideas might be a trigger for someone else. Sometimes, otherwise unrelated ideas may combine to form the beginning of a solution.

A major problem in most business organizations, with their characteristic requirement for discipline and concerted effort, is personnel inhibition. Fear of ridicule or speaking out of place especially constrains front line-level personnel, the very people who often have the most practical, insightful and useful suggestions to make because they are involved with the day-to-day production processes.

Many traditional brainstorming techniques are based on game-playing, with an attempt to inject a sense of "fun" into the creative process and to reduce the insecurities and fears of participants. Most of these programs have met with limited success at best. Far more promising is the factor of anonymity being offered by several meeting decision support tools that give participants the safety they seem to need. Furthermore, the very process of submitting ideas anonymously to a list during a brainstorming session has the effect of priming the pump for new ideas. Trends become more apparent as the ideas that are stimulated in individual participants are fed back into the realm of the group consciousness.

Videoconferencing

Is it real or is it memorex? The question applies not only to the promise of a technology that attempts to provide the same interpersonal experience electronically as a real-life encounter, but also to the technology itself.

The roots of the word videoconferencing are found in the two Latin words: "videre" means "I see," and "conferre" means "too bring together." A popular idea is that videoconferencing creates the illusion of people sitting down in the same room at the same time. Videoconferencing is more than that. The benefit of each participant having his or her own computer or workstation at his or her fingertips with full access to networks and workgroups far outweigh the dubious benefits of sitting in close physical proximity chewing breath mints and counting flecks of dandruff. It can be argued, in fact, that physical distancing tends to focus the group dynamic toward the sharing of information content (knowledge, processing abilities, and point of view) and away from issues of personality.

Visual communications technology approximates natural modes of human communication. People respond to visual clues, and the ability to see the responses of those with whom you are communicating can provide the ability to better respond as the occasion demands. This ability is important for personality intensive situations such as pervades public relations, marketing, and advertising.

Distance education and training also benefit from two-way interactivity.

Video Telephones

Video telephones let users see as well as hear the other person. The fact that a great deal of interpersonal communication is nonverbal makes the advantages of videoconferencing obvious. The technology, however, remains expensive and immature. The actual value of videoconferencing depends heavily on individual work habits and communication needs.

Many Fortune 500 companies and some educational institutions use dedicated professional videoconferencing systems to save on travel costs. Such centers consist of a specialized computer system, video camera, audio/video compression hardware, telecommunications hardware, videoconferencing software, and input devices at each site that can cost from $20,000 to $50,000 to set up.

Fully equipped videoconferencing rooms can be rented on an hourly basis at many locations. Desktop videoconferencing is expected to grow in the 1990s through the use of improved compression tools and digital video software, but few microcomputers currently in use are powerful enough to work with videoconferencing signals or to accommodate the extra hardware required.

AT&T Bell Labs introduced the Picturephone, a digital, video-enabled telephone, at the World's Fair in Flushing Meadow, New York in 1964. The device was heavy (26 pounds), cumbersome, and delivered a small (5.25" × 4.75"), blurry (less than half NTSC resolution) images. The biggest restriction for wide market acceptance of the Picturephone was bandwidth requirement. The video signal was compressed but required digital transmission networks.

The major hurdle in videoconferencing is the sheer mass of information that must be transmitted. Early pioneering efforts at designing group conferencing systems by Nippon Electric Corporation (NEC) and British Telecom in the early '70s used analog television technology. However, digital networks generally outperform analog networks at transporting complex motion video signals, and this, therefore, is the direction most research has taken. The availability of large-scale solid state memory in the early '80s revitalized progress. Solid state memory was the means to store the massive bit streams of picture data during the processing sequence.

One of the early products to use Very Large Scale Integration (VLSI) technology was the U.S. Defense Advanced Research Projects Agency (DARPA) sponsored Widcom. Although doomed to become a footnote in the history of technology, Widcom, by consolidating a large number of circuits onto a single chip, was able to reduce the transmission bandwidth requirement to the digital equivalent of a telephone line.

CODEC

The heart of a videoconferencing system is the codec, a device used to code and decode analog video signals into a continuous stream of bits. The stream being transmitted is converted into a series of video frames by a video camera. Typically, this is an analog signal which is then fed into a codec for digitization. The codec samples the analog video signal, essentially a voltage waveform that represents (is analogous to) the intensity of light in the scene at regular time intervals, and reduces the continuously variable waveform into a series of discrete voltage levels denoted by a binary number. This bit stream of ones and zeros is compressed in some manner in the codec. Although there is a variety of compression algorithms competing for market dominance, compression is essentially a process of throwing out some of the "less necessary" bits. Debate continues to rage about how many and which bits are more or less necessary. Figure 6.6 illustrates this process.

Video Compression

Digital video is expensive in terms of bandwidth. A lot of information describing all of the pixels in each frame must be moved in a short period of time in order to be displayed in real-time. The resource expensive requirements of digital video throughout are partially realized by data compression and decompression techniques. (See Figure 6.7 for a graphical representation of this.) For real-time video displays this usually, though not always, means hardware codecs (compression/decompression devices).

Before considering the current state of compression technology, consider in a little more detail the video bandwidth problem. An uncompressed television signal that has been digitized requires a network capable of transmitting data at the rate of about 90 million bits per second (Mbps). This requirement can be cut in half by dropping the horizontal and vertical synchronization signal components required by analog television. Compare this requirement to a typical Ethernet bandwidth of 10 Mbps, or more dramatically to current high-speed modems that can transmit at the rate of a little over 28 thousand bits per second (28.8 Kbps).

Integrated Services Digital Network (ISDN) is an international specification for transmitting digital signals over existing analog telephone networks. ISDN specifies a maximum transmission speed of 128 Kbps. ISDN also provides a pair of higher-speed

Figure 6.6 Digital video compression process.

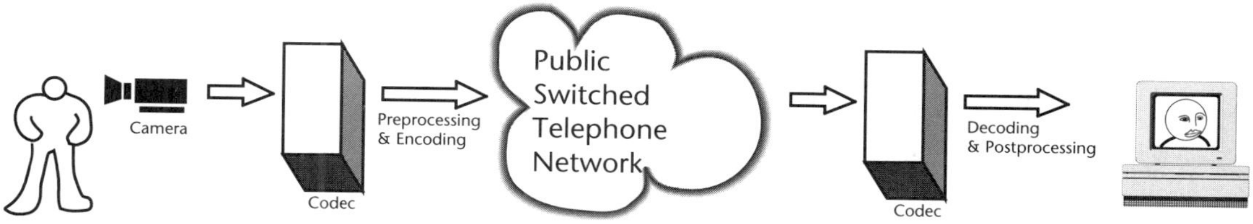

Figure 6.7 Videoconferencing compression and decompression.

interfaces: one for North America that combines the equivalent of 23 telephone lines to provide 1.472 Mbps of transmission bandwidth, and one for Europe that provides for 1.92 Mbps over 30 digitized channels.

From 1978 to 1986, compression technology progressed at a rapid pace halving the transmission bandwidth requirements every two years. A picture that required 6 Mbps in 1978 could be transmitted at a rate of 256 Kbps by 1986. By 1988, the transmission rate requirement had dropped to 112 Kbps. Forty percent of today's systems require transmission speeds between 112 Kbps and 128 Kbps. Seventy-six percent of today's systems run below 384 Kbps. Figure 6.8 shows the progression from 1978 to 1994.

The latter limit, 384 Kbps, is typically the point that divides higher-end videoconferencing systems, which are usually supported by dedicated point-to-point connections between permanent sites. Explosive growth has been experienced and is further anticipated in the sub 384 Kbps range. These lower bandwidth systems can more easily be implemented as dial-up videoconferencing systems, many of which can be used as easily as placing a telephone call.

Pulse Code Modulation

Pulse code modulation is one way of converting the continuously variable video signal into a stream of discrete values. Figure 6.9 depicts this process.

A continuously variable analog signal envelope waveform is sampled at regular time intervals. The instantaneous value of the signal at the time of sampling is assigned a number value that is the closest available approximation of the signal value at that instant in time. The goal is to reduce the waveform to a string of binary numbers. How close the digitized value is to the actual value depends on the degree or granularity or resolution of the sampling device; the finer the numeric division then the closer the fit. The digitized reproduction is always a stairstep facsimile and must be smoothed at the playback to better approximate the original waveform.

Run Length Encoding

One general compression strategy is called run length encoding (RLE) which is basically a process of representing a string or "run" of unchanged bits by a more compact formula that can be decoded at the other end and reconstituted into the original, or acceptable facsimile of, the uncompressed video image.

292 ■ Electronic Meetings

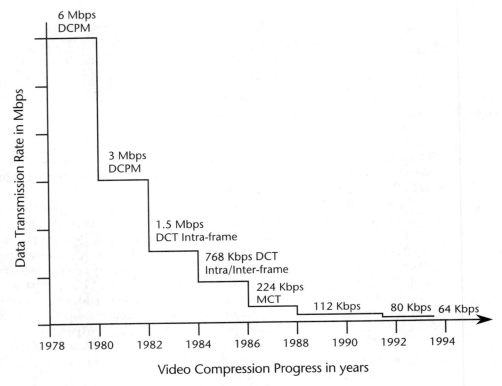

Figure 6.8 Advances in digital video compression.

Another general compression strategy is delta-based. Delta is the Greek letter used by engineers to denote incremental change. Delta-based systems rely on the fact that, in many types of video images, a great deal is static and doesn't change from frame to frame. This strategy is particularly appropriate for videoconferencing, which, as currently practiced, is for the most part of the "talking head" variety. Backgrounds are chosen so as not to distract from the "head." An additional bonus of the static head shot and neutral background is the availability of higher compression. The less things change between frames in the video image, the more the video stream can be compressed.

More sophisticated techniques such as MPEG 4 can achieve high orders of compression by throwing out whole frames relying on the information in key frames to reconstitute the discarded frames by interpolating backward and forward.

Standards

One of the major impediments to video teleconferencing has been the profusion of proprietary and incompatible standards. Among the more popular digital video codecs are: RTV, PLV, Indeo, Tru Motion, QuickTime, Video for Windows, and Captain Crunch, as well as several variations of Motion JPEG and MPEG.

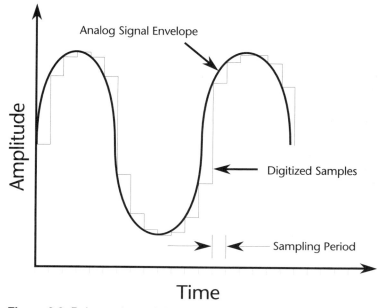
Figure 6.9 Pulse code modulation.

JPEG, the Joint Photographic Experts Group, is an International Standards Organization (ISO) scheme for encoding single images. One of the advantages of JPEG is the ability to edit to single-frame accuracy.

MPEG is a data compression/decompression standard for digital video which uses predictive techniques to interpolate frames from preceding and succeeding key frames. By taking advantage of the fact that changes between frames are usually small, MPEG can achieve higher rates (more than five times) of compression than motion JPEG, which compresses each and every frame.

MPEG is an internationally recognized standard devised by a joint ISO-IEC technical committee, the Motion Pictures Experts Group. The first official standard is called MPEG 1, also known as ISO/IEC Draft International Standard CD11172, the "coded representation of picture, audio, and multimedia/hypermedia information."

MPEG 1

MPEG is a publishing codec that addresses the integration of both motion video and synchronous audio while accommodating the random access nature of interactive multimedia.

The MPEG I standard is for a data bit stream of 1.2 Mbps with image quality comparable to VHS tape. The Standard Image File (SIG) defines a resolution of quarter-screen, 352×240 pixels at 30 frames per second (fps) of NTSC video. PAL is $352 \times 288 \times 25$ fps.

There are "full-screen" versions of MPEG I but these images are actually interpolations of the original quarter-screen data information.

MPEG II

MPEG II is a superset of the MPEG algorithm directed at the broadcast industry. MPEG II starts at a data transmission rate of 6 Mbps to 40 Mbps, sufficient for HDTV with full-screen and 704 × 480 pixel resolution in NTSC mode (704 × 576 in PAL mode) in CCIR 601 format. CCIR 601 delivers 60 interlaced fields per second like NTSC television.

MPEG II is field-based, not frame-based; it stores two interlaced images at 704 × 240 pixels; twice the resolution of MPEG I rendered at twice the speed. MPEG II also addresses the delivery of packet-switched video over Ethernet or Token Ring networks.

MPEG III

MPEG III was originally planned as a standard for the high bandwidth requirements of HDTV, but work was discontinued when it was found that MPEG II would scale up sufficiently for HDTV.

MPEG IV

MPEG IV is the planned standard for video in bandwidths below 40 Kbps, such as videoconferencing, telecommunications, and dial-up video.

Standards are already in place for digital telephone networks for data throughput rates above 64 Kbps. Recommendations H.261 for video compression, H.251 for audio compression, and H.221 for multiplexing add up to the H.321 standard for high-bit rate videoconferencing over digital switched networks.

The prospect for the lower-end, sub 64 Kbps is more complicated. The International Telecommunications Union's (ITU) Study Group 15 is committed to delivering a draft recommendation for low-bit rate videotelephones by February 1995. The mandate of Study Group 15 is to establish standards not only for stand-alone home videophones, but also for collaborative computing and multimedia terminals for workstations and personal computers, as well as for mobile radio.

Currently, an interim recommendation called H.32P is imminent, with plans to adopt MPEG IV for both video and audio compression by late 1998. H.32P is based on H.26P, an enhanced version of H.261, for video and AV.25P for audio. An important standard has been the adoption of V.34 operating up to 28.8 Kbps as its mandatory modem.

Videoconferencing has had a troubled childhood. For many years the science fiction promises of Dick Tracy-like wrist monitors with which people could maintain visual communication have been touted, oversold, and soundly rejected. If it worked, it didn't work very well. If it worked even passably, it was very expensive, requiring special equipment, special rooms, and special technicians. Even with these specialized and expensive resources, the results weren't worth writing home about, let alone sending a video message.

Product Snapshots

InPerson, from Silicon Graphics

InPerson Desktop Conferencing software has been announced by Silicon Graphics (SGI) of Mountain View, California as the most significant advance in collaboration products. InPerson is an attempt to synthesize and combine the visceral sturm und drang (sense-rich experience equals emotional impact) of real-life meetings with the convenience, speed, and ease of computer networks for sharing information. SGI means to turn your IRIX workstation monitor (SGI of course) into a window through which you can associate productively with your colleagues.

InPerson is an all software solution which, it is alleged, can turn your workstation into a communications center through which you can "call" your colleagues and, using live video and audio, interact and work with them in real-time on selected files, captured images, or text documents.

If you, as part of a design team working on a product prototype, wanted to share ideas with your colleagues, you would call up the group, bring your work up on your screen, and go. They would be able to hear you and see you through the monitor-mounted video camera; you would be able to hear them and see them.

InPerson claims to be as convenient as a multiline telephone. It is launched by clicking on a desktop telephone icon that places your calls and rings when you receive a call. You can make conference calls, put a call on hold, and both make and receive calls coming in over another line.

Unlike simple telephones, callers with similar equipment appear in a video window. If the workstation you called or received a call from does not have the video capability, then a still image of the other party appears while you talk in real-time and work on a file.

InPerson runs on the *Indigo Magic User Environment* with its slick Motif point-and-click interface. Because of the seamless integration with the operating system environment, you, the user, can distribute your whiteboard work through **MediaMail** or incorporate your work with other Indigo Magic applications such as Showcase.

To distribute files to conference participants, all you need to do is drag a file from the desktop to the InPerson Shared Shelf and the file is automatically distributed to all conference participants. InPerson Whiteboard lets conferees collectively view and annotate an imported file or captured image, which could be a video snapshot, an onscreen window, or some selected portion of the screen.

Whiteboard mark-up tools include text, freehand drawing, circles, squares, and arrowheads, and allow customized colors and line thicknesses. Any of the conference participants can cut, copy, and paste to edit objects that have been drawn on screen.

Pages can be added for large projects that require more work space with a single mouse click. Jump from page to page by clicking on the page tab. Your page location is indicated to other conferees by a personal cursor which is displayed on the tab of the page you're viewing.

The entire Whiteboard can be saved to a file for future reference when the call has been completed. The saved file documenting the collaborative group session can then be distributed to co-workers via MediaMail.

Video compression eats up more CPU cycles than does any other software-based video application. InPerson reduces CPU overhead by using an efficient MPEG delta-based algorithm for video compression which compares successive images in a video data stream, and sends only those areas of an image that change.

InPerson uses a "multicast" network transmission protocol to transmit data through existing network routers over any TCP/IP network: Ethernet, FDDI, or ATM. IRIX uses "tunneling" to bypass routers that don't support multicast routing. Required network bandwidth depends on how many participate in a conference, and their selected video frame rate and resolution. Video is adjusted automatically to avoid network congestion.

PictureTel Corporation

PictureTel Corporation of Massachusetts provides two videoconferencing systems for distance learning, telemedicine, and telemarketing. The low-cost system (less than $10,000) is aimed at a mass market of single-user desktops.

A desk-top system, called PictureTel LIVE, PCS 100 is marketed as a personal visual communications add-on for personal computers running Microsoft Windows 3.1. This system provides dial-up visual communications, screen sharing, and collaborative computing over public switched digital networks (PSDN).

The PictureTel LIVE, PCS 100 personal visual communications system provides full-color, full-motion live video and audio communications capabilities fully integrated with a screen-sharing, collaborative computing environment. PCS 100 consists of two ISA boards providing video and audio compression and switching, high-resolution Super VGA accelerated graphics, video windowing, and a BRI ISDN interface. High-resolution, full CIF video and 7 kHz, full duplex audio is supplied for communications between desktops as well as with group systems. PictureTel's version of the increasingly common videoconferencing monitor-top cameras is called the FlipCam. This rudimentary video device features manual zoom, focus, and aperture controls, as well as an innovative speaker phone/handset combination.

The PictureTel LIVE desktop system is designed for dial-up visual communications in conjunction with collaborative computing capabilities. You can make a video call to work one on one with another desktop video user or attend group meetings or classes remotely.

All PictureTel videoconferencing equipment is fully compatible with any system operating in the H.320 mode configured for either NTSC or PAL. Higher up the product line is the PictureTel System 1000.

System 1000

System 1000 is a full-featured group videoconferencing family that provides full CIF support for the TSS (formerly CCITT) H.320 videoconferencing standard. It is available in two models: Model 30 and Model 50.

Model 30 is equipped with a 20-inch monitor, FlipCam, picture-in-picture, multipoint, choice of five languages, and integrated BRI interface. Model 50 has a 27-inch monitor, pan, tilt and zoom camera, camera presets, multipoint, picture-in-picture, a cart, and integrated ISDN BRI interface. Both systems can be configured with optional V.35/RS-366, dual CSUs or RS-449 interfaces. An optional feature package for either model includes two times CIF graphics, far-end camera control, VCR audio, and 384 Kbps operation.

Cornell Video CuSeeMe

CuSeeMe is a videoconferencing program that may be the only software available for the Macintosh that supports real-time multiparty videoconferencing over the Internet. At the present time, at least in its prerelease stages, CuSeeMe is available free from Cornell University under copyright of Cornell and its collaborators.

CuSeeMe provides a one-to-one connection for videoconferencing. Within the limits of available hardware, you can establish and maintain a one-to-many, several-to-several, or several-to-many conference by using a reflector. Each CuSeeMe participant can decide to either send, to receive, or to do both. It was written for the Macintosh by Tim Dorcey with design assistance and sponsorship by Richard Cogger, who also wrote the documentation, of the Advanced Technology Group in the Network Resources division of Cornell University's Information Technology department (CIT).

CuSeeMe displays 4-bit grayscale video window at either 160 × 120 pixels or double that diameter. At present audio is not supported. It is designed to provide minimal cost conferencing. Receiving requires only a connection to the Internet and a Mac with

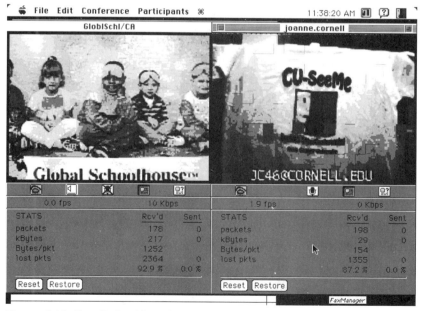

Figure 6.10 Two CuSeeMe video examples from the Global Schoolhouse.

a screen capable of displaying 16 grays. Sending requires the same plus a camera and either an AV-Mac, a SuperMac VideoSpigot board or a QuickCam plus Quicktime and SpigotVDIG extensions to the System folder.

The Connectix QuickCam is a tiny golf ball sized camera that provides low cost videoconferencing capability for the Apple Macintosh for less than $ 100(US). Cost is contained because the device feeds a serial data stream from the CCD inside the camera device into a Macintosh serial port. The image data stream is not an analog video signal, therefore no additional conversion or digitizing hardware is required. There is a great deal of interest in both CuSeeMe and the QuickCam as a means of inexpensive teleeducation or distance learning at academic institutions. Predictions abound, however, that since each participant draws an individual video feed from the reflectors, that as CuSeeMe becomes more popular, the cumulative demand for bandwidth will crash the net, especially when viewers in the United States log into reflectors in Europe.

CuSeeMe has been used to multicast events ranging from university lectures in Paris to alternative culture "happenings" in the Nevada Desert such as "The Burning Man" and from the Rolling Stones Tour to Prince Charles visiting a school in Los Angeles.

While the novelty and low cost are attractive, the resolution and frame rate is low. The value of videoconferencing is severely limited if audio is garbled, lip synchronization is lost, and gaze regard is not available because of limited resolution.

Show Me

Sun Microsystems has started from the basic assumption that all business in all cultures is conducted on a face-to-face basis. From this they extrapolated that people are essentially gregarious and simply want to talk to each other, and presumably to see each other while they talk. Show Me, available on the Sun SPARC platform, includes whiteboard and shared application functions.

Proshare

Intel has a similar desktop videoconferencing and application sharing system for the PC called ProShare. Intel's two major ideas about videoconferencing are that the PC is the platform of choice, and that most work in businesses large or small is conducted one on one.

After the Northbridge earthquake damaged several major thruways, Intel donated 18 ProShare systems to the Telecommuting Center in Los Angeles. The centers were set up to help get people off the freeways and onto the information highway. (Not a bad marketing idea either.)

Besides the videophone idea, Intel has another card up its sleeve which it calls personal conferencing. The personal conferencing strategy complements the people-centered videophone product line by focusing narrowly on the information content. Personal conferencing software allows separate users to work with the same document on each of their screens at the same time.

Traditional videoconferencing systems support eyeball-to-eyeball interactions. Data conferencing systems are optimized to share on-line information such as spreadsheets, word processing documents, presentation files, database, scanned or acquired images, and other unspecified data types.

Since much of today's business information is generated on-line and stored in digital format, some vendors of dedicated videoconferencing equipment are building data elements into their desktop systems. Unfortunately, most of these systems suffer from video compression bottlenecks and high-cost, high-speed DSP-boosted communications interfaces.

Intel has decided to hedge its bet on a big future for casual videophone by also taking up the opposite point of view. For business users it has decided to keep the user's eye on the business at hand, not the eyeball. Data conferencing doesn't waste scarce PC bandwidth on the heavy load of pumping a video data stream down a wire. A conscious choice has been made to present the conference participants with a shared space where they can work together on data files.

Existing information can be cut from a spreadsheet or other application and pasted into a common whiteboard. The contents of the whiteboard are protected; changes made in the collaborative window have no effect on the original data.

Bitmaps or objects can be pasted into the whiteboard, and because the whiteboard application is OLE-compliant, another OLE-compliant app such as a spreadsheet could provide server services to the collaborative program, which acts as the client. Embedded objects could therefore be edited in the server application, and after an update has been performed, the changes are reflected in the contents of the client whiteboard.

Another nice feature is application sharing. One of the collaborators must pick a window or file that the other can access. Both coauthors can then work on the document throughout a shared session. The remarkable thing is that both partners are working directly on the source data and not some screen representation.

Application sharing is accomplished by the data conferencing software on one machine intercepting screen drawing commands and sending them over the phone line to the receiving system, where the commands are executed in parallel with the drawing commands, which originated on the receiving machine. Sending relatively small command tokens instead of big bit maps is an efficient way to use the limited communications bandwidth. This, of course is transparent to the collaborative authors, both of whom need know only that they can both draw on the same image at the same time.

It appears that Intel is building systems that will be poised to exploit what many believe will be the next quantum leap in processing horsepower: digital signal processors (DSPs). For more discussion about the dramatic impact that these silicon devices might have on the entire issue of videoconferencing, data conferencing, and collaborative computing, refer to the section on hardware infrastructure later in this chapter.

NCSA Collage

NCSA Collage is a network scientific data analysis tool from the Software Development Group at the National Center for Supercomputing Applications. With integrated image display and analysis tools, color table editing functions, and spreadsheet display of floating-point numbers, this application can distribute data analysis and visualization functions across a network. Currently supported platforms include MacIntosh, X-Windows, and PC-compatible.

Collage can load arrays of floating point numbers for either a spreadsheet style of display or generate cartesian or polar images from the numbers. Convolution and other image processing functions can be performed on arbitrary (not necessarily rectangular) selections within images. Communications can be established with remote processes which are controlled remotely. Most significantly, in terms of group collaboration, most of these operations can be performed on any machine that is participating in a collaborative session with NCSA Collage.

One of the interesting features that NCSA Collage provides is the ability to recount dependencies between data objects of various kinds. An example of this type of association would be the relationship between a raster image and the scientific data set from which it was generated. Make a selection in a raster image, and the corresponding selection automatically appears in the spreadsheet window containing the data. The spreadsheet depends on the raster object for selection.

Whenever NCSA Collage creates objects by loading a file, or by initiating a collaborative session, an icon representing the newly created object is placed in the local browser window. The window is the tool used to create various associations. To associate two objects, click the first object and drag it over to the object that will depend on it.

Some dependencies are created automatically. For example, a raster image is automatically associated with a scientific data set if the raster image was computed from that data set. Raster images depend on scientific data sets for selections. Selections made in the data sets are also displayed in raster images and vice versa.

A raster image also depends on the color table that is used to display it. Change the colors in a color table, and any raster image dependent on that color table will also change instantaneously.

The raster image and the data set used to generate the image are codependent. Not only does the raster depend on the data set for selections, but the data set depends on the raster for selections. Selections made on raster images are reflected in the spreadsheet if an association exists.

The fundamental paradigm that frames the collaborative aspects of NCSA Collage is WYSIWIS: What You See Is What I See. This principle is not, however, followed slavishly. Collaborating scientists may still perform analysis privately; not all of the analysis done while participating in a collaborative session needs to be public.

As a participant, you might want to preview an image and perform some functions on it privately to determine how relevant it may be to the collaborative session. Each user has the option when loading an image or data set to publish immediately or wait. An image or data set that is not published immediately can be stored or processed and published later using the local browser window.

In addition to operations that can be performed collaboratively on common objects, there are some features specific to collaborative sessions: sending messages to other collaborators, sending images of portions of the screen, drawing on a whiteboard window, and sharing text editing features.

You can access a chat box from the Collaborate menu. You can transmit text entered into the chat box to other collaborators by placing the cursor on the line containing the text and depressing a single key. Transmissions can also be limited to selected text. Screen capture, whiteboard and text editor windows are located on the Tools menu which is available only during collaborative sessions.

The screen capture window is unusual. It is a floating window that is resizable and mobile so that any portion of the screen may be bound by its outline. Only the title bar and boundary of the window are visible. The content of the floating window is transparent. To transmit an image, size and position the window over the desired area and click on a button in the title bar. Whatever is visible through the window will be transmitted to your colleagues.

The white board is rudimentary. Whatever is drawn into it using the cursor as a pen is transmitted to session participants and displayed on their whiteboard.

The text editor works like any other simple text editor except that text is transmitted as it is being changed.

HARDWARE INFRASTRUCTURE

Technology is layered on top of technology. This means that the limitations of each layer of technology depends on its supporting layer. Software applications are limited by the hardware platforms and infrastructure upon which they operate.

The rapid development of hardware power is crucial for the development of groupware. Some of these are:

- Next-generation CPUs
- Digital signal processors
- Cheaper mass storage devices
- High bandwidth infrastructure

Next-generation CPUs

A new generation of CPUs, largely but not entirely RISC-based, are just now coming into play. Whereas once Intel owned most of the market, challenges by the PowerPC and others will make it into a real horse race with one assured winner: the end user. Between hardware and software is the issue of standards. One of the most interesting developments is the formulation of a computer audio I/O standard. The standard includes the definition of an electrical interface including left and right stereo channels, volume/mute signals as well as various control signals such as out-of-range signals, out-of-jack warnings, and so on.

Computer Integrated Telephone (CIT) is supported by industry giants like Intel, Dec, Hewlett-Packard, and Microsoft. The Microsoft Telephone Application Program Interface (TAPI) bridges the desktop computer and the network through the telephone.

While the current installed base of audio input-output devices is barely over 600,000, industry predictions are for 17 million by 1998, and 38 million by 2003. In all likelihood, this standard will almost instantly transform the ubiquitous touch tone telephone into a portable handheld cellular computer terminal. How a device that can jack into the proverbial data highway but still retain its innate voice capabilities might figure into collaborative work situations is open to speculation.

Cable Television

Another technology is the cable industry. Apart from carrying game shows, football games, and sitcoms, coaxial cable is capable of handling gigabytes of data. It is, by virtue of already being in place, a strong candidate for becoming at least an interim transmission medium for broad-band networks. Perhaps the most compelling argument for reorienting this medium from the distribution of analog television signals to becoming the backbone of an interactive digital data stream is that cable already wires together more than 70 percent of the United States.

There are two divergent strategies for integrating the two technologies. Computer smart servers may be put into the system either at the head end, at the distribution source, or at the tail end, on the set-top.

Smart Servers

The argument for using smart servers for interactive digital services is that handling all of the digital signal processing at the head end provides the enhanced ability to mix the interface, data, and images. The set-top converter remains a dumb terminal connected to an analog TV. The more stunning visual effects to which the television generation has become accustomed can be delivered by expensive processing equipment available to the program distributors. The client of central systems get graphics and animations of the quality of sports programming instead of the familiar computer graphic interface.

Set-top Box

A more popular solution is spurring a race to provide the "smart cable converter" or set-top box that connects to the familiar television set. Some of the major players include the Intel-Microsoft-General Instrument consortium, as well as Scientific Atlanta which is hedging all bets with three distinct systems based on three different CPUs.

The Digital Signal Processor (DSP)

One of the most signal events to impact on collaborative authoring, videoconferencing, and data conferencing is something that has not yet happened. The DSP is a force that has been held back for a long time but now appears ready to be unleashed into the microcomputing universe, with potentially revolutionary results.

A digital signal processor is a programmable processing chip that has been optimized to perform operations on signals. A DSP is essentially a microprocessor that has been souped up with A/D and D/A converters and a high-speed multiplier and, as everyone knows, multiplication is central to signal processing. While the DSP is not new (it was developed in the '70s), the definition of standards and the development of suitable programming interfaces has brought the DSP to the very edge of widespread use.

Widespread use of the DSP will (not could) dramatically boost compute power, and in the process revolutionize the PC peripheral board business. For starters, a single-card multifunction product will replace all of those dedicated modem, sound, codec, and similar add-in cards. New (RAM-based) DSP chips and multitasking software that enables a single board to take on multiple personalities means that you will simply download whichever algorithm is appropriate for communications, speech processing, sound editing, or even image/video decompression.

The Macintosh Quadra A/V, as well as other leading edge machines, is DSP loaded. Although the applications aren't there yet to take advantage of the new potential, the hardware is ready, willing, and able to plug the computer directly into a telephone socket and play voice mail, speech synthesis, or take voice input.

The DSP may very well be the boost that videoconferencing needs before it becomes compelling to the general marketplace. Mixed-media modems can bring real-time, remote, interactive data sharing to the desktop in a low-cost, easy-to-use platform. Businesses that haven't flocked to desktop multimedia could find this new breed of modem irresistible. Once mixed-media modems bring multimedia capability to the business desktop, the potential uses for the new found power will be numerous.

Multimedia Conferencing

Mixed-media conferencing is the foundation for a new generation of telecommunication applications. The much vaunted information highway is not just rhetoric. Much of the industry, including Intel, is betting that data conferencing might well be the first "killer" commercial multimedia application.

Initially, teleconferencing was little more than a souped up telephone that let one group of people in a room somewhere talk to another group of people at the other end of the phone line in a room somewhere else. The current generation of telecommunications products uses DSP technology to provide high-fidelity audio by balancing multiple microphones and signal processing to eliminate room echoes and line delays.

Videoconferencing adds a video layer onto the transmission. Distant colleagues can see each other without hassle, expense, or travel. Videoconferencing is still, however, an expensive proposition requiring significant investments in equipment and dedicated facilities with special communications lines.

Data conferencing, on the other hand, makes efficient use of transmission and CPU resources to send text, bitmapped images, graphics, spreadsheets, drawings, and other data structures over standard phone lines. Audio as a continuous data stream is, like video, intentionally left out of the data conferencing strategy as being too resource expensive.

Some data conferencing solutions finesse the resource expense of sending voice along with the data stream by using a second phone line that is dedicated to voice only. This requires the availability of another available phone line as shown in Figure 6.11. Other systems digitize the voice and ship it along with the rest of the digital data on the single wire. Still others simply leave the voice component out of the conference.

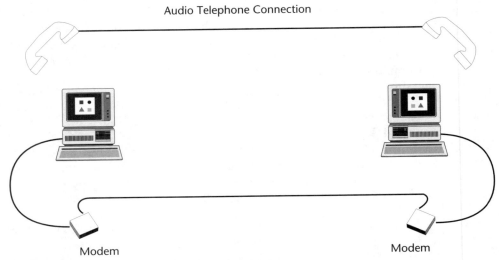

Figure 6.11 Point-to-point document sharing collaboration setup.

Voice Coding

Voice coding for real-time interactive communications over a phone line requires more processing power than today's PCs can deliver. The new breed of mixed-media modems can handle voice coding as just another element in the data management library. Speech compression is still required to limit the load.

A typical scenario for a data conferencing application would be to code the analog speech signal into a compressed digital form at the send end, mix the digital audio packets with the rest of the data stream, transmit the data, separate the data packets at the receiving end, and decode the audio back into an analog signal, all in real-time. The tightest bottleneck of this scenario is the POTS transmission bandwidth limitation.

POTS = plain old telephone system

VoiceSpan

An alternative technique for incorporating voice into personal conferencing is to use VoiceSpan technology from Bell Labs. VoiceSpan increases the capacity of existing phone lines by splitting a single line into three virtual channels: one for voice or low-quality audio, one for data, a third for control information. Using VoiceSpan, users can talk over the phone while simultaneously sending data, faxes, still images, or data from file-sharing applications.

No speech coding or compression takes place with VoiceSpan. Channel coding is based instead on a DSP mapping an analog voice signal onto a digital signal and sending the hybrid signal over a full-duplex, equalized, echo-cancelled modem using amplitude modulation onto a standard telephone (POTS) line.

Hardware Infrastructure ■ 305

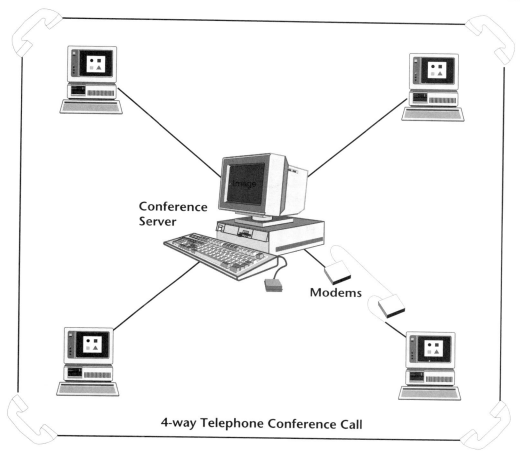

Figure 6.12 Real-time document conferencing setup with three LAN nodes and one remote node.

Another interesting approach to providing speech capability to data conferencing applications is based on Wave Guide technology. Wave Guide technology developed at Stanford University entails modeling audio events as resonating chambers. By varying parameters within software models of standing wave guides (cylinders with one open end) it is claimed that very human sounding voices can be synthesized.

Vocorders

Vocorders, otherwise known as source or parametric coders, are used to encode analog speech signals in terms of parameters which are then used to drive a speech production model based on human vocal tract shape and excitation levels. Vocorders are computationally demanding but can operate at much lower bit rates than waveform codecs.

306 ■ Electronic Meetings

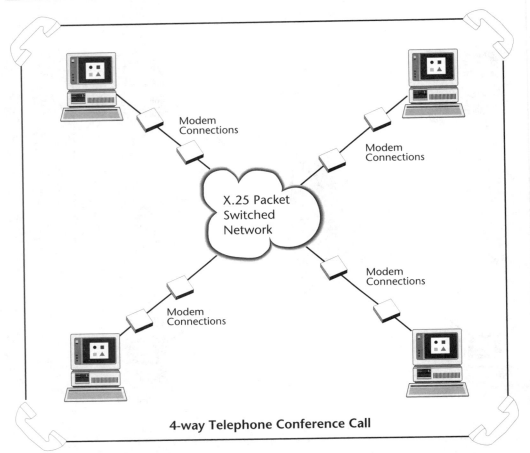

Figure 6.13 Document conferencing setup using X.25 PSN to connect to UNIX server.

The DSP Deluge

DSP vendors like Intel work with hardware manufacturers to provide tight integration with a variety of host environments. Significant developments include, along with the DSP itself, sophisticated, preemptive multitasking DSP operating systems, clean interfaces to the host hardware and software, and need-specific multimedia libraries.

AT&T, for example, has based its VCOS operating system architecture on a DSP kernel, runs an applications server on the host, and provides a separate API for each. The structure of IBM's MWAVE is similar.

The proprietary nature of DSP architectures have kept them off the desktop—until now. Under the auspices of the Interactive Multimedia Association (IMA) Digital Signal Processing Technical Working Group, a set of Windows-based standards is evolving—standards that promise to bring the DSP into the mainstream.

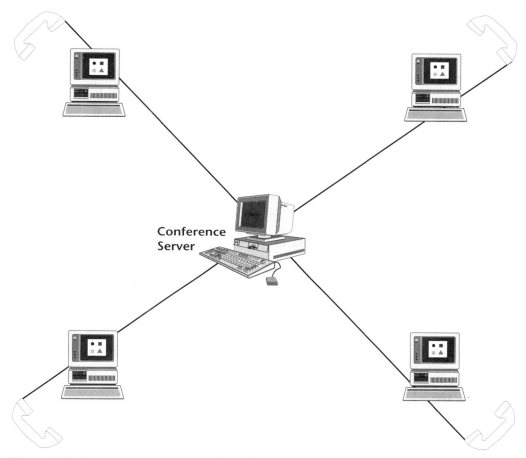

Figure 6.14 Four-person document conferencing setup connected to conference server via ISDN.

A standard DSP API is the beginning of a new era of multimedia. The evolving standards architecture revolves around the DSP resource manager, which connects any compliant DSP hardware/software engine to standard multimedia device drivers used by high-level applications.

Data conferencing applications can place a heavy load on desktop computers. Without the support of a DSP, even Pentium and PowerPC-based machines have difficulty maintaining adequate performance. Design trade-offs involving compression factor, speech quality, computational complexity, and line delay all add up to make data conferencing a multidimensional challenge for computer designers.

Hardware Summary

RAM-based general-purpose DSPs with sophisticated multitasking operating systems, algorithm libraries, and application programming interfaces are poised to revolutionize

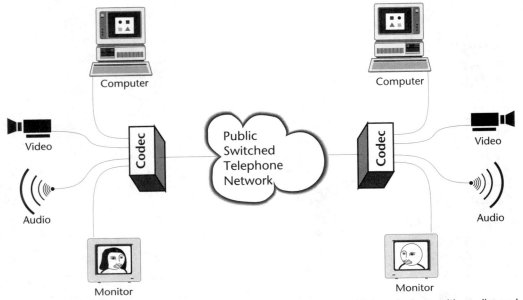

Figure 6.15 Document conferencing setup using computers multiplexed along with audio and video channels through the user port of videoconferencing CODEC by RS 232 serial connection.

the mainstream desktop. The availability of low-cost, high-performance, multipurpose DSPs capable of running several different tasks concurrently could bring multimedia onto the desktop in a big way. Tomorrow the desktop; the day after, the living room.

THE HUMAN FACTOR

Groupware is more about people than it is about computers or networks, because while technology might extend the notion of meetings and facilitate a subset of the genre, without people there would be no need for these products at all. And, in order to use and evolve the new systems for optimum use, people must:

(a) Understand its purpose.
(b) Understand how new technologies extend and enhance the range of possibilities.
(c) Devise strategies for exploiting the range of possibilities to better achieve goals.

Perhaps the single most overlooked aspect of enterprise reengineering is by far the most important: people. This is especially true with the advent of the knowledge industries. There is, of course, a crucial difference between information and knowledge. Knowledge is information within a context of understanding. It is in the area of this understanding that most of the value is added in the knowledge industries. It is this understanding that differentiates so profoundly the knowledge worker from the information processor. The information processor is still within the framework of the industrial paradigm: bolting together pieces of information instead of steering assemblies, filling out forms instead of crimping pieces of sheet metal, and so on.

In the knowledge business, workers are not mere adjuncts to the machine; they *are* the machines that process the material that moves down the line. This definition of knowledge, information requires *a* context, not *the* context. The significance is important; there is not a single knowledge or truth but a range of possible truths from which to choose. Consider some of the ramifications of this idea on industrial relations, on human relations, on personal identities, and on corporate identities.

Shared Workspace

The concept of shared workspace has captured the imagination of many researchers in academic and industrial institutions. The result has been a number of exploratory projects. It would be pointless to audit the entire spectrum of exploration, but it is fruitful to sample a few representative projects.

Generalized profiles of generic systems lose sight of one of the fundamental realities of real-world engineering: that everything is a trade-off. The gain of one characteristic is usually at the expense of another. To get a flavor for the current state of the art of shared workspace tools, this section examines the following UNIX applications:

- wb
- MultiDraw
- Mscrawl
- Xspy

wb and MultiDraw are object-oriented drawing programs. Mscrawl is a bitmap-oriented paint program. Both wb and Mscrawl have rudimentary drawing tools; MultiDraw has a versatile and rich set of drawing tools. Xspy is a program used to share a read-only copy of an X-window, thereby sharing programs that are not distributed themselves.

wb

wb, written by Van Jacobsen at Lawrence Berkley Labs in Berkeley, CA, represents the current state of the art in distributed whiteboards. It is designed to be used exactly like a whiteboard in a conventional classroom. It is limited to simple drawing features and supports no advanced drawing functionality. It does, however, support the distribution and annotation of postscript "foils" much as a lecturer would print for use on a conventional overhead projector.

There is no concept of floor control; any user can draw at any time. All wbs in the same conference will, unless they have explicitly disabled this feature, switch to the same page as the drawer.

Mscrawl

Mscrawl is a shared workspace program based on Wscrawl. The difference is in the underlying multicast protocol which is based on UDP. Whenever the user draws a line, that line segment is broadcast and displayed by all the other multicast listeners. The protocol must be reliable so that all drawing parts are transmitted and appear in the same order on each screen.

A few menus help the user to draw, air-brush, or erase lines and shapes, to type or to import various files including text, image (xwd format), or bitmap (X11 bmp), using a variety of colors, pen widths, and fonts.

MultiDraw

MultiDraw is a multiuser drawing editor based on IDraw (from the InterViews package). Currently, MultiDraw uses the ISIS toolkit distribution. ISIS provides various broadcast protocols. MultiDraw uses ordered and reliable broadcast; no messages are lost and all broadcasts are guaranteed to arrive in the same order to all participants in the group. As a single user editor (IDraw), MultiDraw is capable of making complicated drawings and has been in common use.

Xspy

Xspy is a tool for sharing an X-window across a network. The other network nodes view a read-only copy of the original window. Xspy does not require any changes to be made to the X-server.

Xspy tracks changes to the original window and periodically sends out updates on a multicast address. How often Xspy should check for changes can be specified by the sender. Xspy can be set in a dynamic mode, and adapt the update frequency according to the frequency of changes to the window.

Awareness in Shared Space

Successful collaboration requires an awareness of both individual and group activities by all participants. CSCW systems typically support this sense of awareness with active, information generation mechanisms which are separate from the shared workspace.

Awareness of the self as an individual participant and the self as a part of a group activity is critical for productive workgroup activity. Information that is inherent in the shared workspace gives users vital clues about where they and their collaborators are, thereby allowing users to move smoothly between close and loose collaboration, and to assign and coordinate work "on the fly." These types of passive awareness mechanisms promise to effectively support workgroup collaboration while avoiding the problems associated with active approaches.

Studies have shown ("Awareness and Coordination in Shared Workspaces" by Paul Dourish and Victoria Bellotti, CSCW 1992) that information sharing, awareness of both of group and individual activities, and coordination are central to successful collaborative writing. Awareness, in the context of group activities within a shared workspace can be defined as the understanding of the activities of others which provides a context for individual activities. This context can be used to ensure that individual effort is coincident to the group activity. Context is thereby used to evaluate individual actions with respect to group goals and progress.

The context within which a workgroup collaborates is formed not only by the object of collaboration, but also by the means of collaboration: how that object is produced. Context is more than the content of individual contributions; it includes the significance and relevance of that contribution to the goals and purpose of the whole group. Only when individuals are aware of the character as well as the content of how other group members work can they make sense of the group activity and modify their own contributions accordingly. The burden of providing this information to all workgroup participants is on the system.

Awareness information is required to coordinate group activities in every task domain. Although those disciplines that are most familiar are addressed here, specifically collaborative text editing, the same general processes apply to other many areas of knowledge work.

Awareness information can be provided by mechanisms that generate information actively and explicitly, in isolation from the shared work object; or it may be collected passively and distributed, and presented in the same shared workspace along with the object of collaboration. The latter strategy, which leverages the information inherent in the process of collaboration, is clearly restricted to synchronous systems where all collaborators are virtually co-present and working at the same time.

Awareness in Collaborative Writing Systems

The focus of this chapter is on synchronous real-time meetings and collaborations, therefore this is the strategy explored in terms of collaborative writing. First, three collaborative writing systems are discussed, noting especially the mechanisms they provide for sharing awareness information between collaborators.

Quilt

Quilt is an asynchronous collaborative authoring system developed at Bellcore. Quilt presents a superstructure that manages the specifically collaborative aspects of group authoring without attempting to manage all aspects of document production. Quilt doesn't know which text editors are being used. The primary thrust of Quilt is to coordinate collaborative authoring. This means ensuring that work progresses; that redundant work is minimized; that information, including the substance of the work, the management of the work, and information about the interpersonal relationships within the group, are shared.

The primary mechanism available to Quilt users is a hypermedia system that represents the document with annotations, an audit trail as well as an integrated electronic mail and conferencing system. Annotation allows users to make comments about the document material. Using audit trail recording, collaborators can review each other's activities. E-mail and conferencing allows users to communicate about work-related activities.

The degree of access to the document is controlled by the role assigned to each participant. Explicit roles define the character of a participant's activity; a colleague who is assigned the role of "reviewer" has a clearly defined and readily understood role.

Quilt takes the active approach to information sharing and coordination in asynchronous collaborative authoring. The distribution of awareness information is an explicit activity. Uncertainty about the character of others' work is reduced by the imposition of roles on all participants.

PREP

PREP is an asynchronous editor that can be used by groups to collaboratively author documents. It is most appropriate for the early stages of the writing process: brainstorming, initial text production, commenting, and revision. The structure of information in PREP is very general. "Chunks" of information can be linked together to form "drafts," and to form matrices that relate parallel information streams. This model is supported by an interface that displays information in columns presenting information streams in parallel. Relationships between parallel information streams is emphasized by a spatial layout; for example, a view might present four columns, one for the document plan structure, one for draft text, and two for annotations.

PREP also uses explicit role assignment to define areas of responsibility and to control access to the information streams. But PREP attempts to ameliorate the stifling influence of rigid role assignment by supporting a model of "communication about comments" which permits explicit annotation and structured or directed messaging to provide a means for generating awareness and coordination information. Information about the content of activities in progress is divorced from the activities themselves, but must be provided separately through some other channel.

The problem with both Quilt and PREP is that, in a natural collaboration, roles tend to be fluid and are continually renegotiated. The direct mapping from role to an edit activity may not be appropriate. For example, a reviewer may wish to edit the text being reviewed, rather than merely make annotations.

The problem with the active feedback mechanisms of these first two editors is that collaborators tend to feel restricted by their roles, and consequently in the activities they can undertake at any time.

GROVE

GROVE is a synchronous, multiuser editor used to create and edit textual outline documents (tree-structured documents that may be viewed at various levels of specificity). GROVE may be used in both face-to-face and remote collaborations.

GROVE will, for example, show other users' text entries in a window for any outline nodes also opened on the local user's screen. Each node is marked as either open, closed, or terminal (that is, without any subnodes). Document views may be public, private, or shared. Access (who can see, edit, or create a node) can be controlled at each point in the tree.

GROVE differs from Quilt and PREP in that it has no explicit notion of role. The notion of "view" differentiates the information presented to each user, thereby reducing the shared document as a common group resource for reference. GROVE, while based on a model of synchronous collaboration and external communication channels, in an effort to prevent editing conflicts and provide a mutual awareness of activities, does constrain task elements.

Mechanisms for Awareness Information

CSCW systems vary in how they provide an awareness of self and group. The brute force "informational" method requires collaborators to inform each other of their activities. Software control systems, for example, require users to maintain a "rev log" of some sort. E-mail can provide an authoring system with a channel for sharing this information.

Another common strategy is the explicit assignment of specific roles within the collaborative systems. Each role describes that individual's relationship to the shared work object and to other participants, and typically is linked to a specific set of operations. For example, in a shared authoring system, the role of author might be associated with the read, write, create, delete, and edit operations, while the role of reviewer might be limited to read and annotate.

Although the explicit assignment of roles reduces uncertainty about the actions an individual might take, and provides a greater awareness of the role of each team member, this awareness provides information only about the character of the activity, not the content. Knowing where they are with respect to their colleagues is useful for people to understand the operation of the whole but provides very little insight or information about what is to be done.

Problems with Information and Role-restrictive Approaches to Awareness

Problem #1

The user who provides the information does not benefit directly. And, as Jonathan Grudin observed in an article about the "Perils and Pitfalls" of introducing groupware (*BYTE,* December 1988):

> An application can fail if it requires that some people do additional work, especially if they are not the ones who perceive a direct benefit from using it.
>
> Groupware supports people who work in different roles, such as an author and an editor, a manager and individual contributors, or a professional and a secretary. To succeed, a groupware application must be used by all of the relevant people. But often some will benefit more than others, while others will have to do extra work.

In role restrictive situations, there is often a significant trade-off with respect to benefits. The price of heightened group awareness is the restriction of potential individual activities. A further problem for role-restrictive CSCW systems is that while explicit roles may allow for easier social organization of rationalized collaborative activity for conventional interactions and collaborations, a shifting situation may require a shifting of roles.

In informational systems for supporting awareness, the cost of supplying the information is borne by the individual in the form of additional workload while the benefits accrue to the group. In a business environment where individual reward is based on individual performance, the "wasting" of individual resources on something of scant personal benefit is not tenable. Correctly matching benefits to those who incur the costs is one of the problems cited in Grudin's analysis of the failures of collaborative systems.

Problem #2

That the individual bearing the burden doesn't benefit directly in no way guarantees that anyone else will either. Colleagues receive what the initiator of the information deems to be appropriate, and what is appropriate depends on the context of the other individual's activities. So, information provided in this way may not be sufficiently specific or relevant, or may reflect different assumptions about aspects of the joint work.

Problem #3

Information delivery is controlled by the sender, not the recipient. The sender, however, cannot predict what information will be needed and when. The information is not continually available for browsing. It might be difficult to separate the information that is relevant to any given activity from information that isn't. Thus, not only is the producer of the information burdened in the act of producing, but the recipient is restricted in the act of using the information.

Having set up the context of conventional strategies for supporting awareness of and within a group shared workspace, it is now possible to examine a less imposing method for creating a sense of "shared space": the shared feedback approach.

Shared Feedback

Shared feedback provides information about individual activities to other participants by presenting feedback on operations within the shared, rather than the private, workspace.

ShrEdit

ShrEdit is a synchronous, multiuser text editor that runs on an AppleTalk network of Macintoshes. ShrEdit was developed as a tool to explore the support of design meetings. ShrEdit allows multiple users to collaboratively edit a set of documents. Each user can have a number of shared and private windows.

Private windows contain documents that can be seen and edited only by the "owner" of that window. A private window can be used for making notes or creating text which can later be cut and pasted into a shared document.

Shared windows present a view onto a shared document. Although a document is shared, each user's view can be unique; each user's window can be sized differently, and aligned on a different part of the document.

Each user also has an edit cursor within each shared window, and more than one user can edit text concurrently although more than one edit cursor cannot exist at the same point in the document. Each user can see only his or her own edit cursor. Cursor "collisions" are indicated with an audio signal and a pop-up window.

Shared windows are locked at the level of text selection. No user can edit text selected by another user. All users' edit actions are displayed in all shared windows with a low latency.

The names of all active session participants are displayed in a control window associated with each edit window. Users can, through this control window, locate other users. ShrEdit will scroll to the current edit cursor location in the document. Users can also "track" a colleague and see that user's view (as far as possible given differences in window shape) including the position of his or her edit cursor and text selections. This view will persist until switched off. Each control window records whether participants have a selection in the associated window, are tracking someone else, or tracking you.

ShrEdit tries not to impose a structure on user activities. It is eminently egalitarian in that all participants have equal access to the shared document windows and can type at any time. Nor does ShrEdit support awareness beyond showing everyone's text as it is input, and providing rudimentary information about whether participants are editing or tracking someone. This freedom allows users to adopt very different working styles.

In a study conducted by Dourish, Bellotti, and Judy and Gary Olsen, groups of three designers (all with previous experience of working together) were observed while solving open-ended design problems using ShrEdit. To simulate remote collaboration, collaborators were separated and then linked by video and/or audio.

Designer groups could devise their own work methodologies. The researchers report being struck not only by the diversity of the design solutions, but also by the variety of work processes, which the designers later commented were compatible with the way they would normally work together.

The shared workspace focused the designers' work and discussions. Talk dominated the activity of the collaborating designers with many periods when nobody in a group was typing, while two or all three talked. Even when everyone was typing, there were frequent sporadic bursts of conversation. Subtle inflections of voice, interruptions, humor, or just grunts were also used to convey or cut off information. Not only did speech allow for the exchange of design ideas, it also helped to maintain an awareness of group member activities with a very low overhead in terms of the additional effort required.

This talk was greatly contextualized by the shared editing space. Conversation frequently referred to or implied the context of the shared documents. Often the information being generated in the shared workspace acted as a focus which curbed digression. The awareness of others' work through the shared space enabled group members to organize their individual activities and provided impetus for design contributions.

Most of the participants moved continually between concurrent, but relatively independent, work, through discussions and coordination, to very tightly focused group consideration of specific items. These movements were opportunistic and unpredictable, reflecting a sensitivity and awareness of the state of the rest of the group rather than under some direction or schedule.

Group activities varied continuously. Individuals could type, edit, read, talk, listen, or think. Individual collaborators would frequently stop typing and watch the contributions of one or both of the others. This might prompt debate and reorganization of document or individual roles. Participants were under no agenda or constraint. The various individuals would confer with whomever and whenever they desired.

The designers, aware of authorship and recognizing that the need to engage work with personal meaning requires a sense of "ownership," would tend to partition responsibility for, and rights over, different parts of the shared documents. One group, for example, adopted a convention under which each user had his or her own window, which nobody else could write in but which everyone could read.

The lack of structure imposed on the shared space by the editing tool removed work-process constraints. This freedom in conjunction with the ongoing awareness of self and each other allowed the coauthors to vary their activities dynamically and opportunistically in response to the changing state of affairs with the group and the growing document.

Although not required to do so, users often volunteered information about their activity to the group spontaneously. Letting other members of the team know what they were doing became extremely important. Little use was made of private windows. Not only would the collaborators describe what they were doing, but would explicitly ask others to look at their work.

One group assigned each participant a shared window into which, by consensus alone, only that person could type. They also assigned the group a window into which all three could type. Everyone could see everybody else's work. The status of that work, although public, was clearly the contribution of an individual and not the group.

Use of Shared Feedback in ShrEdit

ShrEdit provides some shared feedback functionality, in that it automatically represents activity within the shared space. It does so without any explicit informational and role restrictive mechanisms to facilitate collaboration. Despite the lack of such control mechanisms, users remained sufficiently aware of each other's activity to negotiate and adapt both the content and character of their own work within the context of the group activity. The lack of imposed structure inherent in the tool permitted each group to organize the activities in a flexible but coordinated manner.

The implication of this and other experiments seems to indicate that the organization of collaborative effort doesn't require either the burdensome effort and overhead of explicit, system-structured information exchanges, or the inflexible restriction of predetermined roles. The implication is that groups can organize themselves in ways that are subtle and dynamic rather than formal and static.

Awareness Summary

Awareness of self and others within a collaborative context is a critical issue for groupware systems. It is fundamental to coordination of activities and sharing of information and critical to successful collaboration.

There are a number of aspects to the role of awareness. High-level awareness of the character of a colleague's actions allows workers to structure their own activities and avoid duplication of effort. Lower-level awareness of the content of another's actions allows finer-grained work sharing and synergistic group behavior.

Shared Feedback: An Alternative Approach

An alternative approach to increasing awareness is to automate the collection and distribution of information. This automatically assembled information base can then be presented as background information within a shared space. This is the quintessential shared feedback approach: present feedback on individual activities within the shared workspace.

This approach emphasizes low overheads for both providers and recipients of awareness information. Information is available when needed as a context for individual activities. The tyranny of imposing prestructured restrictions is avoided. Although not a requirement, this approach is commonly associated with exclusively synchronous applications.

Individuals, given the opportunity to peripherally monitor and comment on the activities of their colleagues, will communicate their activities, even when working independently, and allow others to comment on their activities or to observe the consequences for their own actions. This can be achieved without increasing the workload of the individual information source. Conversely, collaborators can explicitly modify their activities in full "public" view in order to communicate information and solicit responses via the shared workspace or ancillary communication channel.

By reducing the imposition of roles, shared feedback systems provide for a more dynamic and flexible model of negotiated role assignment. These information sharing and coordination mechanisms can be available in a collaborative tool and orthogonal to the task itself. Shared feedback is more of a design philosophy which can be applied equally to a range of tools that embody particular work styles, or to a single tool that can be used in multiple ways.

Semisynchronous Systems

There is a natural correlation between synchronous collaboration and passive, workspace-based group feedback. How relevant the shared feedback strategy is to asynchronous systems depends on how strong a fundamental distinction exists between synchronous and asynchronous approaches.

Change bars are examples of document-based representations of activity. Change bars or similar representations could provide further information, such as the nature of changes and the identity of the person making the change.

Details of past activity can be held within the document and retain the advantages of passive collection and distribution. Document-based representations can be presented at various levels of specificity. Users can therefore access information as it becomes relevant. Such information could also remain fluid and change over time to reflect the progress of the group and individual activities. Information can be presented differently to collaborators, as appropriate for their various evolving involvements in the group activity. The workspace could, then, hold more than the object of group activity, and also become a persistent record of that activity.

By presenting past activity information within the shared workspace, the division between synchronous and asynchronous activities blurs. A semisynchronous system supports both synchronous and asynchronous work modes. In asynchronous use, the workspace presents past activity information, providing individual awareness of the activities of other participants integrated with the work object itself. In synchronous use, this information is presented live as it happens, providing participants with the awareness of the current activities of others.

These are not two different modes of the system, but rather two facets of a single view of awareness information. Such a system can present current information on synchronously co-present collaborators, as well as representations of past activities by other collaborators who are not synchronously present. The shared workspace thereby becomes a persistent space in which collaborators can interact, rather like a room in which one can either talk with other people who happen to be there at the time, or leave notes for those who arrive later.

Summary of Shared Space Awareness

Awareness of group activity within collaborative systems provides a context for individual activities and thereby supports group progress. Two traditional methods for promoting group awareness include an explicit and coercive approach using directed messaging, and another that uses clearly defined roles and scripted activities to convey information to the group about individual actions and plans.

A third approach is to present shared feedback and results from individual activities to the group at large through the shared workspace. This conveys a continually updating sense of the actions of individual collaborators as well as the overall progress of the group. This method has the following advantages:

- Reduces the cost to individuals of information production by collecting information passively and avoiding restrictions on activities.
- Allows participants to look for and extract the awareness information that is most relevant to them.

- Presents awareness information through the shared workspace. Users can therefore find relevant information along with the shared object, and browse awareness information and the work object concurrently.

Shared feedback can be applied in situations beyond synchronous collaborative systems through the use of persistent, semisynchronous workspaces.

THE ARCHITECTURE OF CONVERSATIONS

Organizations run on human interaction, not data. The most critical relationships in any business are not between bits or digits but between people. People work with computers to get things done. People get things done by placing orders, requesting reports, producing reports, and releasing products, not by processing data. Real work is organized as a network of interlinked actions. And actions are embodied in language. The ability to anticipate and to affect the behavior of others through language is not just an important condition of human beings but approaches the very essence of being human.

Research on the design of computer-supported cooperative work systems is increasingly being focused on human interactions and the linguistic dimension. In the conventional view, however, language is held to be a system for representing the world and for conveying thoughts and information. While useful, this perspective ignores the fundamental dimension of language as commitment, as a construction that can shape the very world in which people act.

For example, a traditional linguist would analyze the statement "The door is ajar" as the conveyance of information; a description of a particular state of affairs. But the same statement could have an altogether different interpretation. Given a context, the implied meaning of the statement may call for an action, say for example, that it's my screen door that has been left ajar and there are mosquitos outside. Or, alternatively, my arms are full of groceries and I'm coming into the house. If an action is indicated, that action—whether to close the door and keep the mosquitos out, or to kick the door open so that I can get inside—depends on the situation.

Whenever you convey information, you are embedded in a context that makes it relevant to something getting done. The actual meaning of the words only serves as a starting point for an interpretation which could lead to a sequence of interconnected actions.

Action-coordination Systems

A category of groupware called action-coordination systems applies principles of conversation management to help people track what's going on and what needs to be done. Some analysts predict that these types of systems will provide a central framework for the integrated office systems of the future.

Action-coordination systems are based on a theory of language developed by Flores and Winograd which grew out of work on "speech acts" in the philosophy of language. According to this theory, by uttering or writing sentences, you perform speech acts that will impact not only your own future actions but also the actions of those whom you address. Whereas traditional language theories consider how words convey information, speech-act theory considers how utterances connect to future possibilities and consequences.

The basic conversation for action is a transaction that starts with a request or offer made by one person to another. The exact words may be formal statements like "We hereby petition the court...." or casual utterances like "What's happening?" A conversation can be characterized as a dance, wherein particular linguistic steps move toward completion. For example, if someone requests an action from you, you can promise to comply or decline. If you promise to complete the action, then you would have to fulfill your assumed obligation and report completion or else revoke your promise. If it was you who requested an action, you have the option to either cancel your request, request a progress report, or else declare that your conditions have been fulfilled and the action has been completed.

For example, a conversation for action that was initiated by Moe requesting some action from Joe could be choreographed as a series of "dance" steps. The opening sequence could be as follows:

1. Moe asks Joe for a favor.
2. Joe can respond by either:

   a) Promising to do the favor.

   b) Declining the request (thereby terminating the transaction).

   c) Making a counter offer by suggesting an alternative action.

Each act leads to a different state, with its own possibilities for further acts by Joe and responses by Moe. For example, if Joe had decided to be a good guy and promised Moe to grant the favor, his next standard move in the conversation would be to report that the request has been fulfilled. Moe could either accept this report or express dissatisfaction with the fulfillment of the promise.

A conversation naturally moves toward a state of completion wherein no further moves are anticipated. This result can accrue from either a successful completion, or from abortive acts, such as withdrawing the original request or reneging on the promise.

The state-transition diagram applies universally regardless of topic or language, intentions or plans of the conversants because it generates the full logical range of possible speech-act sequences. This mapping of possibilities is used in action-coordination systems to organize records of what has been done and to present them to the conversants as possibilities for further action. In the general action-coordination systems proposed for the future integrated office, such a structure will form the basis for declaring and automating specific work practices for particular individuals or groups.

THE VIRTUAL CORPORATION

Reengineering and downsizing is the blueprint for the '90s and beyond. The management model for the future is away from the standing army and toward the raising of local levies for local purpose. The "virtual" of virtual corporation is derived not from the virtual reality of Gibsonian cyberspace, but from the concept of virtual memory. In the early days of computing, virtual memory described a variety of schemes for fooling the computer into thinking that it had more memory than it really possessed. A virtual corporation may appear to be a powerful entity with vast resources whereas the reality would be a judicious assemblage of numerous collaborations formed in a just-in-time, as-needed basis.

The term virtual corporation is attributed to Jan Hopland, an executive at Digital Equipment Corporation (DEC) who is responsible for plotting strategy for DEC's information technology business. His use of the term virtual corporation describes an enterprise that could marshall more resources to bear on any given situation than are currently available by collaboration, not growth or expansion. He coined the phrase while engaged in research exploring the future of management in the '90s.

"It was clear that we were entering an age in which organizations would spring up overnight and would have to form and reform relationships to survive. 'Virtual' had the technology metaphor. It was real, and it wasn't quite real," said Hopland.

As large megapolies struggle with their own inefficiencies, inertia, and bulk, desperately bouncing from one crash diet to another, their executives struggle just to get things done. Moving large corporations is like docking an ocean liner. By the time a view of an opportunity may have diffused up through the ranks and been translated into terms that the decision-makers can understand, the opportunity may have passed.

It is also characteristic of large institutional companies that the people who make the decisions have had to work their way into those positions over time. Often they continue to make decisions on the basis of the way things used to be, like generals fighting yesterday's battles.

Small companies, on the other hand, struggle to find the resources to get things done. While they are agile enough to get through the fleeting windows of opportunity, they are often too small to make much of a difference. They all too often lack either the expertise or depth to fully exploit the opportunities that the large companies may not even have noticed.

The answer to both the large and small company is the virtual corporation, a temporary network of independent companies—suppliers, vendors, customers, and rivals—linked by information technologies to form a single "virtual" corporation. They are thus able to share unique skills, costs, abilities, and markets for a common purpose.

Rather than the rigid hierarchy and political gridlock inherent to vertical integration, the virtual corporation promises a fluid and flexible collaboration that almost spontaneously forms to exploit specific opportunities.

The New Corporate Model

A virtual corporation is a temporary network of companies and independent vendors which has been quickly organized to exploit a quick-changing opportunity. The concept of a transient association permits each of the players to focus on honing and developing those areas of expertise at which they excel, without the burden and high overhead of trying to build in-house technologies, resources, skills, and knowledge of which they may have no special ability, training, or insight. When that missing element is needed for a project, it can be borrowed, rented, or shared in some partnership, alliance, or other co-prosperity arrangement.

Within the confederacy of a virtual corporation, companies can share resources and skills as well as cost and access to global or sector markets. By focusing and concentrating their resources on their special areas, each of the partners can bring to the venture only that at which they are best. At least, that's the theory.

Less Is More

One of the key ideas required for an environment that affords wide-scale virtual corporate activity is the stripping down of the constituent elements to their bare essentials. The trend to downsize and to focus on core activities appears to be moving many companies toward that elusive ideal of the lean and mean business machine.

Partnering is the way to fill in the blanks. Today, while companies are still in a period of transition between the old and the unknown new, while the infrastructure is in the process of being built, the early stages of partnering are evident in the twin trends of alliances and outsourcing. An electronic venue to serve as an informational clearinghouse for quickly locating suppliers, talent, manufacturing, and specialized services is not yet available.

Flexibility

The ability to configure a task force for the specific task at hand is one of the foremost arguments for the virtual corporation. For example, if the joint project involves selling into a new market, say Mexico, it might make more sense to involve in the partnership someone or some group with the language skills, regional familiarity, and knowledge as well as the personal network of business contacts rather than trying to "grow" your own information and skill base.

Excellence

Because the virtual corporation is formed of companies that have been stripped down to their bare essentials, the joint endeavor has the possibility of aggregating only the "core competencies" required by the effort. Because the "best" is often merely the most appropriate, by putting together consortia of specialized companies, the virtual corporation has the potential of world-class performance.

Globalism

One of the major stresses on the giant multinational corporation has been the conflict between maintaining a consistent and unified corporate culture while still operating within many different world viewpoints. On the one side of the fine line lie charges of cultural imperialism whereby the company is identified with a particular nation; on the other side is slow, and sometimes not so slow, drifting apart of geographically and culturally displaced divisions.

The concept of the virtual corporation neatly avoids either of these two pitfalls. Because the association is transient and task-focused, the relationship is essentially opportunistic and ephemeral. When the job is done, either the parties go their own ways or find another project that would involve all or some of the former collaborators. By blurring the traditional boundaries of what makes a company, sometimes to the point at which it becomes difficult to separate competitors from allies, suppliers, vendors, and customers, the jigsaw puzzle enterprise can incorporate elements from around the world.

Opportunism

The essence of the virtual corporation is opportunism. The motive for companies banding together is to exploit specific and shrinking windows of opportunity. When the need disappears, so does the glue that holds the parts together. Unlike traditional corporations, which have been designed for interdependence from the ground up, the disassembly of the virtual corporation is not a costly and traumatic layoff or merger whereby the stronger corporation swallows the weaker and spits out the redundant and undesirable parts. Alliances must be mutually beneficial and make sense within the context of a single project.

Strangely enough, the concept of the virtual corporation affords the promiscuous employee, who hops from one corporate home to another, some stability by letting small intimate workgroups to form corporate modular units that could market their services in a variety of combinations to the same corporate employers without losing ongoing collaborative relationships.

Speed

Once a team has been formed, the relative independence of the partner companies permits teams of people to work concurrently on their computer networks in real time rather than sequentially.

Technology

Not only does the fluid state of world political and social structures encourage the versatility and flexibility of the virtual corporate relationship, but the growth of information networks provides the means for the formation of and linking of sometimes distant entrepreneurial concerns.

Partnerships may be found through the window of the desktop computer node, formed electronically on-line without benefit of legal counsel or fees, and even consummated entirely on-line.

Life Goes to the Movies

Perhaps the best model for collaborative knowledge enterprises is the movie business. Most of the time, Francis Ford Coppola is a private individual. While reading scripts and scouting future projects, the corporate being that is Zoetrope Studios might be no more than a handful of people: Coppola, perhaps his wife, a personal assistant, and some other associate or two. But when a major project has started, such as Apocalypse Now!, Zoetrope Studios swells to gargantuan proportions. Thousands of people become fully immersed in a project with a budget that might rival the GNP of a small nation.

One of the most important functions in the preparation of a major film project is the casting director. Not only are actors auditioned and tested for various on-camera roles, but so is much of the off-screen talent. Specific set designers are hired because of the "look" that they can impart to a project. Camera crews are retained for the specific values that they can provide to the director's vision. Set designers are screened, down to the humble carpenter, for required skill sets. Even the caterers are carefully selected. Everything must work together.

While strong arguments are being made for the virtual corporation, and circumstances are conducive to and trending toward the transient relationships of scaled down and fast-moving corporate teams, there are obvious and real dangers.

Loss of Control

By forsaking the cost of building, developing, and bearing in-house experts and expertise, the company also abrogates a great deal of control. Companies cede control over those functions to which it entrusts its partners.

Technology Leaks

Technology is information. Once ways of doing things have been shared, it may be difficult to recapture a monopoly over proprietary techniques, methods, and technologies.

Loss of Power

One of the major impediments to technological change within corporations has been middle management. Having earned their position and authority with yesterday's tools, middle managers are often loathe to adopt techniques of which they may have scant familiarity or expertise.

Dealing with outsiders who are outside the reach of their authority requires a politesse and negotiating skills which might not be standard issue within their own corporations. The shift from command mode to consensus may be difficult for some.

The virtual corporation demands the same skills that distinguish the best venture capitalists from all of their project managers. They need to be able to build trust and relationships; to negotiate "win-win" deals; to find compatible partners who are appropriate for the project at hand; and to maintain that tricky balance between freedom and control.

Corporate chauvinism in the form of devaluing work performed by outsiders and dismissing anything that was not-invented-here are two of the stereotypes that many middle managers will have to grow out of in order to work effectively within a virtual corporation.

The traditional American virtues of self-reliance and independence sometimes manifest themselves in a macho dedication to going it alone rather than as part of a group.

The Hollow Corporation

One fear that has been voiced is that of the hollow corporation: a company that serves the interest of investment capital at the cost of native workers and local manufacturability by outsourcing jobs to low-wage countries.

The shape of the modern American corporation was largely designed in the 1920s. Pierre S. DuPont and the legendary Alfred P. Sloan developed the formal theory of decentralization as an organizing principle for giant complex corporations. This form was based on the industrial paradigm but expanded and extended to the vastness of the American and global marketplace.

It has been argued that the meta model for American corporation has its roots in the Civil War. Demobilization released many military acculturated men into a turgid economy. Part of the answer was reconstruction, but another part was the settling of the west. In terms of social organization, the centralism of the industrial plutocratic north had prevailed over the decentralized agrarian land-based aristocracy of the south. The capitalist industrial organization become the model for the reaffirmed Union.

Demobilized soldiers fled west. Some sought the independence of homesteading, gold mining, commercial activity, or the cattle business. One of the most dominant forces in developing the West was the railroad. The organization of railroad companies was based closely on the military model: strictly hierarchical with a rigidly defined class structure. The success of the railroads in opening up the country and the astonishing success of the railroad companies in building fabulous wealth for the railroad magnates inspired and defined business organization in America for a century.

Henry Ford introduced the assembly line at the turn of the century. Not only did the car help to define the nature of America, but the means of production defined the production process including the strictly delineated roles of workers within the industrial process. While Ford didn't invent the notion of the worker as an adjunct to the machine, and a subsidiary machine part at that, he realized the concept into a immensely successful commercial enterprise.

Alfred Sloan formalized the natural inclination of American business into the corporation as it has come to be known. Perhaps the acme of this paradigm was IBM. When it fit the time, IBM could do no wrong. When it lost contact with the evolution of social realities, becoming inverted unto itself, it could do no right.

So what's wrong with such a long and hallowed business tradition? Why is there suddenly a need to change the way things have been done in business for over a century? Why does what made IBM great for so long seem to be what makes it so wrong now? The answer is manifold.

The world has changed. Some parts have changed more in the last few decades than they have in the last few centuries. Whereas once the primary context for American business was the United States, the context today is global. The markets are interdependent, and while the U.S. might set the tenor for the world, there is much that is beyond control and sometimes beyond comprehension, certainly without preconceived notions and traditions.

Some of the changes in world societies are political. With alternate economies in disgrace, capitalism and democracy, while not equivalent or even interdependent, provide a theoretical and practical framework for most of the business practiced in the world. What the pillars of American business share is the value of individualism and the mechanism of pluralistic market validation.

The world, however, is not the United States. Other nations and cultures have their own histories, traditions, and points of view. That American products export best when they are malleable to local conditions is proven by the phenomenal success of the Pacific Rim tigers. How this tradition evolves remains to be seen.

Kiretsu is a Japanese term for trading alliances. Electronic kiretsu connotes the enhanced possibilities of everyday work between companies. Because of the inherent differences in cultural tradition, the virtual corporation confederacy concept, which relies so heavily on individual responsibility, creativity, and initiative, may well be America's answer to the Japanese kiretsu.

Accountability vs. Responsibility

In the traditional corporation, authority devolves from the top down. Every individual is accountable to someone. As corporations became more complex, the meshing networks of accountability and conflicting interests tended to circumscribe the options available to individual corporateers.

Virtual corporations permit much less direct control. The relations that form the virtual corporation rely far more on each partner and require far more trust. The fate of each partner depends on the other. Each partner must assume full responsibility for his or her respective part, and trust the other partner to fulfill his or her part. The virtual corporation is an exercise in codestiny.

Andy Grove, chairman of Intel Corp., still smarting from a bad experience outsourcing a Japanese partner to manufacture flash memory on Intel's behalf, calls the virtual corporation "a business buzzword that's meaningless. It's appetizing but you get nothing out of it." Other critics charge that the entire rubric of the virtual corporation is just a smoke screen to cover mass layoffs and to "hollow out" American corporations, not to mention selling some books and seminars to the gullible and trendy.

The general consensus, however, seems to be that even if the visions of the futurists are never totally realized, the trend is toward virtualized business practices. Many business managers, while too cautious to jump on any bandwagon until it costs more to stay off, seem to be able to read the writing on the wall for the old ways of doing business. Cost containment and sticking to what you know makes good business sense at any time.

And then there is the inevitable pull of technology that is sucking everyone into the future. When technology presents a better way of communicating, working together, and transacting business, *not* using the technology will cost more than reengineering a business to take advantage of the new tools.

REENGINEERING INDUSTRY

The industrial era is over. Rather than trying to breathe life into a moribund paradigm by improving methodologies inextricably bound to industrial era development principles, we should address the challenge of reinventing ourselves. A leap into the knowledge age requires a discontinuity; a fresh start and courage. The mania for reengineering and salvaging attendant cultural values maintains the industrial era focus on decomposing issues into component parts which could then be plugged into an equation for some predefined model and solved as if it were some kind of problem. This involves using the developed tools of discrete and linear process analysis.

There is a danger in adopting a focus that shifts processes and capabilities but ignores culture; resists the capability of evaluating a holistic system, and denies the capacity for expression. While this focus is supportive of corporations engaged in the daunting issue of organizational transformation, the process of shifting a viewpoint of strategic capacity from models based on mechanical predictability into models that are sufficiently flexible and fluid to respond to what is essentially a chaotic universe, it is a fundamentally unpredictable and unknowable situation.

Many organizations are taking steps toward adapting to the environment at hand. These corporate beings in transition may not always find the technologies that they need, however, because many tool designers remain tied to the existing hierarchical organization model, consciously or otherwise.

There is concern that the term reengineering may become confused with the more fundamental context shift which is now in mid process. Reengineering has been used, often euphemistically, by the major networks to describe the relative reactionary acts of desperation by small businesses floundering in the wake of the collapse of one of the giants, say IBM. These businesses were undergoing something more drastic and far from voluntary: a complete transformation—from captured suppliers of a stolid giant to an open marketplace, a situation disturbingly reminiscent of the turmoil in the former Soviet Union.

Reworking internal operations—reengineering—was clearly a secondary concern, if one at all. Yet the term reengineering was applied antiseptically to the entire process, leaving the impression, intentional or not, that in the midst of epochal shifts in business climate, an analytical approach to reworking existing business practices into a more efficient format would carry the day. Plainly this is fantasy, sort of like believing that introducing Japanese-like morning exercises would somehow vitalize a sagging assembly line.

The inability or unwillingness of the mainstream media to respond to complex issues obliterates the sense that something profound and epochal is occurring. Opportunities for making a complete break from the past do not present themselves overtly;

they will, rather, be fickle and unstable. Connecting with them will not be a matter of adopting new ideas that fit into models used to understand the way things used to be, perhaps with the vain hope that somehow the clock will reverse, letting people settle back into the familiar. Tomorrow's battles are never won with yesterday's strategies.

The critical part of this effort is that it is in full public view. By witnessing events, people become participants, willing or not, and party to and responsible for the consequences.

Creating the necessary discontinuity does not live in a briefing book or on a whiteboard. It is cultural revolution, plain and simple—a complex web of ideas that require a new language to disseminate and refine. It also requires patience to work through the process: willingness to take chances and make mistakes, and the courage to embrace and affirm the essential chaos of the process.

This notion of culture is key. Cultureware is a term that refers to the use of communications tools to engender a culture where results that are unpredictable and unrecognizable from the common perspective can be produced.

If you honestly seek real organizational transformation—with all of the attendant imponderables and unknowns—then it is absolutely necessary to lay in a communication backbone that supports the ongoing evolution of an organizational culture that takes risks and provides immediate response and rewards. Such nonintuitive and indeed tenuous approaches require intense communications to continuously reinforce the process of true team-based, whole-systems-derived organizational thinking.

Facilitation

As the year 2000 approaches, the millenial spirit is rising throughout society. From the apocalyptic vision of evangelists to the organizational experiments of Fortune 500 companies, everyone can smell a major sea change in the wind and is working feverishly to anticipate the coming era.

The paradigms of the past are exhausted. The fundamental change in the communications infrastructure and technologies present a medium for social interaction and commerce on the basis of information that has never been known on such a scale. Intense exchange of information is becoming available over distance and time on a breadth and with an ease and at a cost that will fundamentally change how people deal with each other, in business, in politics, and in personal lives. In short, the very forms of society are on the table.

Facing profound and revolutionary change makes many people deeply uncomfortable. Entrenched power groups and institutions are threatened and defensively tend to oppose or at the least to minimize the imminent changes. Even the most conservative realize that team organization working collaboratively, often at distance, is a key organizational issue of the '90s.

Although it is easy to become dazzled and distracted by the support tools for groups, which are increasingly becoming available on the open market, most experienced managers realize that the biggest challenge lies in the understanding of facilitation and group interaction within electronic environments. To better appreciate the human side of groupware, some basic ideas about the nature of meetings, group technologies, and facilitation must be introduced. To build on these ideas the next sections consider some generative conceptual models that can be used for facilitating both traditional and electronic contexts.

MUDs

MUD stands for multiple user dimensions and represents a novel approach to computer conferencing that emphasizes informal, team-building interactions among communities of users. MUDs originated in network gaming at the University of Essex, England in 1982. (Originally, the acronym stood for Multiuser Dungeons after the popular Dungeons and Dragons game.)

Today, MUDs have evolved more generally as software-based, conference-like environments which let two or more users interact simultaneously over a network. "Muddlers" as MUD dwellers are sometimes called, engage in text-based communications that are more like real-time spoken conversations than e-mail messaging. Despite the sensual paucity of the MUD experience, inveterate "muddlers" swear that they share a virtual reality that engages the imagination with a communications richness approaching intimate physical encounters.

One of the best known MUDs and a favorite hang-out is LAMBDA.MOO which is modeled loosely on the real-life home of its creator, Xerox PARC researcher Pavel Curtis. Typing LOOK BIRD while in his virtual living room will return a florid and detailed description of Pavel's cockatoo.

In a more serious vein, Curtis is launching ASTRO.MOO as an environment that supports communications among astronomers. A programming language built into ASTRO.MOO allows the participants to build props and specialized devices such as shared calculators to support their interactions.

Another interesting extension of the MUD concept is a multimedia MUD which augments the text messaging with simultaneous voice features and slow scan video. Given the resource efficiency and relatively low bandwidth demands of MUDs, the practice developing in some high-bandwidth network videoconferencing installations of turning on a video window in the labs of collaborators who may be some distance removed and leaving it on all day, may become more common.

As Paul Saffo writes in "The Future of 'Virtual' Conferencing" (*PC Computing*, January 1993):

> These virtual spaces could exist entirely in cyberspace, or be mapped onto locations in the building. The lounge could be a virtual twin of the actual lounge down the hall. People sitting in the physical lounge could interact with MUD visitors via a large-screen display, allowing meetings to be attended both physically and electronically.

Computer conferencing has drawbacks. For example, most people can't type as fast as they think; indeed, many would-be conferees don't type at all. This fact has a way of limiting their participation in on-line discussions. The primitive on-line computer conferencing of the early 1980s has been overtaken by telephone conferencing, which is giving way to primitive videoconferencing over the POTS (Plain Old Telephone Systems). Technological change comes in quantum leaps. Few analysts foresaw the mass adoption of fax technology by business. Fewer foresaw that faxes would be sent from desktop computers or from airplanes in flight.

MOO

In "The Common Place MOO: Orality and Literacy in Virtual Reality," Don Langham writes:

> In the Phaedrus, Plato has Socrates deliver what may be the earliest protest in Western history against the dehumanizing effects of "modern" technology. With the benefit of our literate perspective, it is easy to say that with his condemnation of writing, Plato establishes Socrates as the earliest Luddite. Yet, as modern critics acknowledge, writing is not without its dehumanizing qualities insofar as it encourages the isolation of the individual from community. Today, there is enthusiasm for computer-mediated communication's potential for ameliorating the divisions and isolation of print. For some rhetorical theorists, computer media promise to revitalize rhetoric by reintroducing the forgotten canons of classical rhetoric, memory, and delivery. Among composition theorists, computer-mediated communication promises to move the writer out of the isolation of print into a hypertextual network of readers and writers. Whether CMC will have the democratizing, liberating effects its enthusiasts believe remains to be seen. But from the outset, there is reason to believe that CMC may alter the nature of human interaction as fundamentally as writing and print have, perhaps producing a new way of "being" in the world.

Xanadu

Visions of the future abound as the millennium approaches. Some of the most optimistic visions center on the possibilities offered by the looming digital communications infrastructure to provide a venue for an electronic agora for the global village. One such grandiose vision is Ted Nelson's project Xanadu.

Xanadu is many things other than a metaphor used by Samuel Coleridge. In terms of the hyperverse, it is a grand hypertext publishing scheme that is commonly associated with Theodor Holm Nelson, a computer visionary who is perhaps most famous for coining the term hypertext. Nelson characterizes himself variously as a "rogue intellectual" with "maverick points of view" whose "ideas have a wide underground following." Conceptually provocative and occasionally seminal, his career has both soared and plummeted. Currently, he is attempting to revive a scaled-down version of the Xanadu vision.

To summarize a project as grand as Xanadu in a few words would be to do it an injustice. Nelson, however, provides a few succinct descriptions in the form of one-liners.

Xanadu is: "A distributed repository for worldwide electronic publishing." It is also "a mapping system between storage and virtual documents." And "a way of including anything in anything else."

People other than Nelson describe Xanadu as a paradigm that provides an ideal generalized model for all computer use extending beyond electronic publishing and includes all forms of operations with information. In short, Xanadu aspires to provide a unified system of order for all information. A big job.

ORGANIZATION MEMORY

Chapter 1 provided a brief overview of organization memory. This section reviews that material and provides additional details. As defined in Conklin (1992), organization memory indicates "the record of an organization that is embodied in a set of documents and artifacts." This is quite a general statement, and the implication is not simply maintaining the documentation or the data in an organization. Just as humans retain relationships and learning curves in their memories, the intention in supporting organization memory is on the *relationship between the documents, the reasoning behind the corporation's decision-making*, and the assumptions, values, experiences, and conversations that lead to and constitute the context and backgrounds of the artifacts. The "artifacts" are the documents, databases, reports, designs, and so on pertaining to the organization.

Thus, by "memory" the implication is not the archive of vast amounts of information. For one thing, office workers are already facing serious information overload problems. What needs to be captured and maintained are both the relationships between the various information objects (artifacts) as well as the reasoning that was applied in producing the information objects.

Chapter 2 discussed hypermedia systems. By and large, hypermedia represents "associative memory," and as such is ideal in capturing the semantic relationships between various documents and information in an organization. Human memory is associative in nature. People associate larger concepts with terms and have a "semantic" network of associations in their memories. Hypermedia more or less captures these nonlinear associations directly. Various anchors in a document are linked to other documents (or information objects) that provide additional details. These documents can themselves have hypermedia links, and thus the entire "knowledge base" in an organization can theoretically be arranged through a natural hierarchical structure. As discussed in Chapter 2 there are many types of links. Users can browse hypermedia documents at different levels of detail. Hypermedia links can be associated with various terms, figures, audio annotations, and video elements.

But maintaining the relationships (links) between documents or information objects is only part of organization memory. Although humans have associative memories, they can also maintain assumptions, values, and the overall reasoning sequences of conclusions. In an organization, the "conclusions" are the documents and information objects being produced. By its very nature, an organization involves multiple workers who are in many cases contributing to the culture, assumptions, values, and reasoning of the documents and information objects being produced and followed. These include corporate strategic decisions, the policies and procedures in the organization, the production strategies, the marketing strategies, and so on.

As organizations—like living organisms—grow and mature, they sometimes suffer from "amnesia." Decisions, policies, and procedures may be enforced while the reasons behind the decision-making are forgotten. Even governments suffer from this—U.S. law is filled with legislation that was relevant at some point in history but is no longer applicable today (and some of them are outright ridiculous). Thus, the reasoning and the background information that led to a conclusion is perhaps as important as the conclusion itself. This could apply to any department in an organization and to any type of decision (strategic, functional, administrative, project oriented).

The key point is that for organization memory to be effective, employees at any level in the organization should be able to ask: "Why are we using this administrative process?" or "How did we come to the conclusion that we need to concentrate on a particular market sector?" or "Why did we use a particular algorithm in our design and implementation of the product?" and be able to extract the decision-making logic that led to the decision. In a sense, these are special types of hyperlinks. The reasoning is "hyper"—attached to the conclusions. But hypermedia systems rarely provide direct support to organizational decision-making logic.

More recently, there have been some groupware systems that have attempted to address organization memory—especially those that capture discussions, reasoning, issues, assumptions, etc.—directly. In particular, two broad categories of systems have attempted to do this:

Topic discussions: As stated in Chapter 3, a number of advanced e-mail systems and other groupware products support discussion topic databases. Collabra Share from Collabra and Lotus Notes from Lotus are examples of such products. The idea is to maintain a hierarchically organized sequence of discussions. Electronic meetings and videoconferencing systems can also integrate components that keep track of the reasoning behind decisions, assumptions, and issues.

Capturing organization memory explicitly: Another category of products provide more direct support to organization memory. These systems are similar to topic databases that keep track of the thread of discussions for various conclusions. A good example is CM/1 from Corporate Memory Systems. This product allows users to pose questions or issues, and it keeps track of the discussion—pro and con—for the issue being raised. Various participants can make suggestions, observations, etc., and the system maintains graphically the positive as well as the negative arguments for the issue. In particular the system supports the following features:

1. Creating maps of discussions: Any user can start a "map" for a discussion (such as a question or a decision to be made) involving various participants.
2. For a particular "item" (question, suggestion, etc.) authored by a participant, there could be several responses. The responses could be positive or negative, and the system will explicitly indicate the positive and negative responses.

3. The CM/1 system also keeps track of who has seen an item. Besides the participant himself or herself, a user can also ask who has read an item.
4. Maps of discussions can be organized hierarchically—in the sense that an item can itself be another map of subdiscussion.
5. Finally, discussions usually have decisions, which also get recorded. The user can investigate the *line of reasoning* for a decision.

These powerful capabilities of CM/1 and other systems targeting organization memory allow organizations to remember the "intelligence"—reasoning—that went into the planning, decision-making, and implementation strategies.

SUMMARY

To recap, the following elements are necessary for any system designed to support collaboration in a community of knowledge workers:

- Collaborative dialogue
- Document development
- Production and control
- Research intelligence
- Community handbook development
- Computer-based instruction
- Meetings and conferences
- Community management and organization
- Specialized knowledge work by individuals and teams

Assumptions critical to the success of a CSCW system include:

- Coordinated set of user-interface principles
- Various grades of user proficiency
- Easy intradomain communication
- User programming capability
- People-support services; recognition of standards for information interchange and ranges of hardware
- Careful development of methodologies
- Coevolving roles, organization structure, and technologies

User-interface Principles

The first requirement is for a coherent and coordinated set of user interface principles. This does not mean a rigid interface for all purposes but rather the evidence of an underlying logic which coheres the various domains across an application suite. While the vocabularies may be unique for each specific area, the language and control structures should remain consistent throughout the tool environment.

Grades of Proficiency

A successful CSCW system must be able to accommodate various grades of proficiency. Even users who are most expert in certain domains of the collaborative environment are novices in other less familiar domains. A healthy environment is characterized by the ability to accommodate a spectrum of community abilities. The system should also encourage evolution within the environment by rewarding the accumulation of proficiencies with rich tool environments with advanced vocabularies and adequate opportunity for individual customization.

Ease of Communication Between Domains

No user should be trapped and bound to any isolated area within the environment, but must be able to move and communicate between domains easily.

User Programmability

Users should be able to add or interface new tools and, should the need arise, be able to extend the language.

People Support Services

Tools are insufficient by themselves. A human, informational interface must be available between the tools and the end-user community, for example, specialized professional services like designers, trainers, cataloguers, and so on.

Open Systems

At least relative independence from hardware, operating systems, and file format restrictions is highly desirable.

Development of Methodologies

In the words of Douglas Engelbart:

> The elements involved in augmenting communities of knowledge workers include the development of both "tool systems" and "human systems" (the set of skills, methods, languages, customs, procedures, training, and organiza-

tion structures needed for the effective use of tools). New technologies, even those such as CSCW that aim at improving group interaction, contribute directly only to the tool system. The cultural evolution that led to the current state of the human system took place with a very primitive tool system.

Coevolution of Roles, Organizations, and Technologies

The widespread availability of successful CSCW services will create the need for new organizational structures and roles. These structures and roles need to coevolve with the technologies. For example, there is a need for so-called knowledge-workshop architects to serve as "change agents" in introducing new technologies into their organizations.

To take advantage of the radical, emerging tool-system inventions associated with CSCW, it is inevitable that the evolution of the human system will begin to accelerate. The optimum design for either a tool system or a human system is dependent on the match it must make with the other. The high degree of mutual dependence implies that a balanced coevolution of both is necessary. The bind is that our society encourages and rewards progress in the technological and material sense and often ignores the human and social implications of that progress.

We must continuously reaffirm that all of our inventions, tools, systems, and structures should serve our human needs. It is tempting, especially in our technophiliac society, for us to adapt to our machines, structures, and conventional wisdoms. As tool builders we can create tools which fit our grasp and serve our diverse purpose.

7

Conclusions

In all living things there is a rhythm. The tide comes in and goes out. The sun rises and sets. Seasons come and go. Groups, large and small, come together and fall apart. Empires and corporations form a confluence of interest and then collapse into disarray, the residue becoming the raw material for the next aggregation of resources.

This simple rhythm of consolidation and decentralization is also evident in the evolution of computer technology. The monolithic mainframe and the monolithic mainframe maker, the once titanic IBM corporation, have both suffered decline as the social ethos turned to the '60s yearning for democracy and individual freedom, perhaps better expressed by the desktop microcomputer.

But the only constant is change, and technology is again trending toward the aggregation of resources. History, however, is not a circle but a spiral. Although the return is to the concept of hooking together computers either loosely through communications networks or intimately with LAN and a gamut of groupware products, the return is at a much higher level of sophistication, complexity, and power.

One of the most compelling visions for the millennium is of collaboration and teamwork. Cooperation, collaboration, democratization, empowerment, and teamwork is becoming essential to the survival of any viable business entity, from the independent contractor individual service vendor to restructured companies to virtual corporations to nations and entire trading blocks. One visionary, Paolo Soleri, the architect of Arco Santi in Phoenix, Arizona, considers that the electronically interlinked social mass forming around the globe is the culmination of the ancient prophecies that promised the second coming, the Messiah, but not as God made man as an individual incarnation but as the aggregate of the nations of the world coming together in consciousness as one, the Corpus Christus of humanity.

Whether the millennial visions and prophecies will come to pass remains to be seen. What is clear to many and becoming increasingly accepted as inevitable is the need to change how we organize ourselves as the nations of the world, as productive corporate beings, and as collaborative individuals.

THE SOCIAL IMPACT OF TECHNOLOGY

How technology changes the way we can organize ourselves and our resources is rarely mentioned or recognized today. The reason is that most of the interest for groupware products is from existing groups; groups that have already been formed. Typically, existing groups seek to enhance the performance of the group as constituted. Most companies are looking for ways of doing what they have already been doing, except more efficiently or more productively. Not surprisingly, they seek tools that can leverage existing systems.

Massive social changes are currently in motion and not yet resolved. The globalization of economies has forced businesses around the world to reorganize and redefine how they transact business. The approaching culmination of the industrial era and subsequent transition into an information economy is shifting the profit centers in existing business structures. While many enterprises strive to maintain a competitive balance in a fluid environment by downsizing and reengineering, other corporate behemoths are collapsing and fragmenting into smaller pieces not unlike the fragmentation of the Soviet empire. Some revolutionaries believe that it is futile to even attempt to retrofit corporate structures which have exhausted philosophies built into their very corporate genes, arguing instead that a pattern formed as an expression of an old paradigm is inherently unsuitable for a new paradigm. Tear down the old to make way for the new. Break down the obsolete into pieces from which the new can be formed. It is not yet clear which philosophy, that of the evolutionary reengineers or that of the revolutionary "infopreneurs" will hold sway.

In Southeast Asia, where many believe that the pendulum of economic destiny is swinging, another massive debate ensues. On the one side are those, such as Japan and Hong Kong, which would adopt the western socioeconomic model; on the other, are Singapore and mainland China, which would argue that capitalism need not be democratic, nor prosperity western. The philosopher-king of Singapore advocates a capitalist mercantile economy based on indigenous Asian values, and backs up his argument with an advanced information technology rich proof-of-concept: Singapore. While much of the argument, as politics tends to do, extends beyond mere economics and involves much renascent nationalism in the region and no small amount of Japan bashing, there is also genuine substantive debate about the shape of the world economies.

While some speak of the Pacific Rim as if the Pacific Ocean were as natural a trading medium as once was the Mediterranean, others prophesy a slow slide into trading blocs a la Orwell. How global politics will actually become resolved is, at this point, anybody's guess. What is crystal clear to all but the most obdurate ostrich is that the times are indeed changing. What this means in America is downsizing, outsourcing, and at the very least a reevaluation of business processes.

New Ways of Aggregating Resources

It could be argued that the form of indentured slavery characteristic of the agrarian economy of the pre-Civil War South was superseded by the notion of wage slavery favored in the industrial North on the basis of efficiency. It is cheaper to buy only those portions of a worker's life that directly contribute to the production imperative of the industrial process than it is to buy the entire worker. It also makes more sense to pay for the human resource as it is being consumed rather than paying for the asset before receiving any return.

Just so, the corporate culture of the Sloan industrial model is being superseded by the two-tiered corporate structure that many companies are evolving. Rather than wooing company employees with promises of lifetime security and a career path, many companies are downsizing to a flatter core competency group staffed by workaholic type 'A' personalities, and staffing up to strength on an as-needed project-by-project basis either by strategic alliances, temp agencies, outsourcing, vended services, or some combination of all of these options.

In a period of uncertainty, small and flexible is a survival characteristic. Companies that condense themselves into their core competencies not only can contain their costs and raise the median level of in-house productivity, but they can also compete on the basis of strength. Small, tightly integrated corporate structures can also turn more easily to catch the prevailing market trends. What is perhaps most cogent is that small specialized corporate units have tremendous flexibility. The same company could be the core of one enterprise for which it consumes vended services and outsources, or partners parts of that enterprise, while at the same time it might be a supplier of its specialized services to another corporate entity, sourcing goods and services for yet another commercial activity. The key is to work from a base of core competency in which that company is competitive.

Some believe that this period of turbulence is interim and that eventually all of the corporate enterprises will gel into one stable world (or trading bloc) economy. Those who hold this view believe that this period is a transient opportunity to stake out a piece of economic turf, not unlike the Middle Ages when after the collapse of the central authority of the Roman empire, warlords engaged in relatively small-scale local warfare for dominance before settling into an inbred and self-perpetuating aristocracy.

Others have a more creative and dynamic vision of a broad and deep pool of corporate competencies of various size which can come together in a number of ways. This vision of an opportunistic "erector set" economy promises tremendous flexibility and opportunity: a veritable reengineered business model. Vital to such a vision is, of course, some level of standardization and interoperability, especially at the level of the substance of collaboration which increasingly is becoming information.

Also key is groupware. Groupware could allow ad hoc groups to form, perhaps, with one team from one partner, another team from another partner, representatives from various suppliers and from marketing channels, and fleshed out by a contingent of specialist contractors, consultants, and service vendors. Groupware could be the glue that binds a diverse crew of talents, resources, and specialists who may also be variously distributed in space and in time into a transient and opportunistic, project-specific team.

It is in applications such as this that tools such as videoconferencing, which are truly difficult to justify on the basis of savings in travel expenses, become indispensable. Although a videoconferenced experience of a literal stranger is a pale surrogate for a real-time face-to-face meeting, it is also vastly superior to neutral e-mail and disembodied voices. While scarcely intimate, video does offer channels to experience each other in terms with which everyone is familiar.

This shift in how enterprises aggregate human resources can perhaps most easily be seen by considering the evolution of the movie business. Filmmaking evolved from the early days of the pioneer where dominant visionary personalities like Cecil B. de Mille and Henry Ford willed their visions into reality, through the assembly line studio systems with managed resources and controlled career paths through to the free agent entrepreneurial model of today. Zoetrope Studios, the corporation formed by Francis Ford Coppola, is comprised of a small core group of talent. On the strength of his reputation and personal wealth, Coppola, through Zoetrope, was able to aggregate a small army of human resources and additional talent for his "Apocalypse Now" project. Clearly, Zoetrope is a much more elastic structure than, say, Warner Brothers ever was. While this is an extreme example, and one that is contingent on a specific personality, it does nonetheless illustrate a fundamental shift in the nature of what is essentially a business enterprise.

The Nature of Enterprise

The nature of the corporation is changing from the static military model, which served the purposes of the industrial revolution, to more flexible models for the future. On the one hand, corporations are collapsing in on themselves, distilling their operations to core competencies. In a competitive global economy, the best investment of any endeavor is in whatever is the strongest point. On the other hand, many companies are fragmenting and flying apart. The very nature of enterprise is changing from the vertical model of tightly integrated conglomerates where everything is done internally to a more opportunistic and transient structure of temporary alliances and co-ventures.

Driving this trend in business is the reality of global competition. And what makes it possible is technology. That is what this book has been about: the technology that supports collaboration between individuals and groups, commonly called groupware. Groupware is an enabling technology for collaboration, human-computer interaction and human-human interaction through digital media. Groupware promises to bring orders of magnitude improvement and transformation to organizations, real and virtual.

GROUPWARE TECHNOLOGIES

Since groupware addresses the breadth of productive human enterprise, it encompasses many technologies and many markets. Analysts speculate that the groupware market will become one of the fastest growing industries of the decade. A conservative estimate is that groupware will become a $10 billion industry by 1999.

Groupware applications use and integrate other information technologies: graphical interfaces, communication and information sharing technologies, object-oriented technologies, and artificial intelligence. In general, think of groupware as the ultimate system for integrating existing and future software and hardware systems for collaborative work.

Most groupware applications include graphical user interfaces, multimedia, and object-orientation. Although currently limited and previously oversold, artificial intelligence, especially pattern recognition, figures in future generation groupware applications.

Technologies that enable routing, networking, communication, and concurrent sharing are also extremely important to groupware. As internetworked PCs and workstations demonstrate increasing advantage in terms of price/performance over mainframe systems, the words buzzing around organizations and rocking MIS departments are client/server architectures for downsized solutions.

Internetworked workstations, through client/server architectures and involving local as well as wide area connectivity servers (file servers, database servers, fax servers, messaging servers, and so on) provide resource and information sharing to network PCs and workstations acting as client nodes. Since groupware deals with connectivity and sharing, almost all groupware products are built on top of client/server architectures. Client/server is a concept so fundamental to groupware that an entire chapter (Chapter 3) of this book was dedicated to it.

Many products are characterized as groupware. Any system that helps co-workers collaborate or enhance teamwork efforts and achieve common goals can, in fact, be characterized as groupware. While groupware is in danger of becoming one of those hollow buzzwords so casually tacked onto products by overzealous marketers, the rush of freeloaders to jump onto any bandwagon is evidence of the strength of this trend. Still, the best advice is: buyer beware.

More to the point, remember that groupware of any sort is a tool used to implement a carefully thought out strategy, design, and plan. It is vital for the success of any groupware system to realistically assess organizational needs and to match the most appropriate groupware systems to the identified needs. One size does not fit all. Thorough research and preplanning are not easy or obvious but nonetheless, are critical. The wrong product can cause more harm than good.

GROUPWARE CATEGORIES: CHAPTER 1

Chapter 1 presented a number of taxonomies and categorization systems for groupware. First, document and forms-based groupware for collaboration and communication involving documents, application files, and forms were covered. This category includes e-mail, workflow, and document management.

Next, transaction-based groupware for communication and collaboration involving high volumes of record retrieval, or transaction based processing typically using high-performance DBMs, information retrieval, and document imaging systems were presented.

These categories are not discrete; for example, forms are almost always used with database management systems as well as with document imaging; nor are they definitive. Groupware is but an infant with a lot of growing up to do.

The distinction between the first two categories was clarified by the discussions of databases in Chapter 3, and workflow in Chapter 5. The third primary category, organizational communications groupware, deals with groupware applications that enhance organizational communication or collaboration such as group calendaring, videoconferencing, electronic meetings, and group authoring.

The Human Factor

As stated repeatedly, groupware enhances communication and collaboration among humans. This human organizational dimension is preeminent, and includes issues of organizational modeling, business process reengineering, and overall infrastructure and group dynamics in an organization. People make up the group part of groupware. Without people to use them, all of the products and wares are meaningless.

Groupware is more about people than it is about computers or networks. While technology might extend the notion of meetings and facilitate a subset of the genre, without people to meet, there is no such notion. This most vital component of any enterprise is often the most neglected. Although most companies pay lip service to the value of their employees, the relative scale of values becomes apparent whenever an economic crunch forces a choice between profits and employees. Throughout the industrial era, during which employees were rationalized into "cogs" on some planner's organization chart, management has, at least in the U.S., grown to regard its human resources to be as interchangeable as other commodity components of the industrial equation. To be sure, there have always been certain key personnel in any enterprise who were considered irreplaceable, but most of these people managed other, more fungible resources. This model is rapidly changing with the advent of the knowledge industries, but not because of any great resurgence of enlightened humanitarianism or impulse to social charity, instead because the most valuable productive component and processing unit for information is an empowered knowledge worker. Whereas skill might be interchangeable within limits, knowledge is much less so. Increasingly, the primary asset of knowledge is resident within the workers who constitute a company.

There is, of course, a crucial difference between information and knowledge. Knowledge is information within a context of understanding. It is in the area of this understanding that most of the value is added in the knowledge industries. It also is this understanding that differentiates so profoundly the knowledge worker from the information processor. The information processor is still within the framework of the industrial paradigm: bolting together pieces of information instead of steering assemblies, filling out forms instead of crimping pieces of sheet metal, but industrial nonetheless.

In the knowledge business, workers are not mere adjuncts to the machine; they *are* the machines that process the material that moves down the line. Indeed, in many cases, they are not only the units that process the information, but the sources that create and design the information and, perhaps more to the point, provide, on the basis of their training, education, and personal experience and study, the contexts within which the information becomes knowledge.

Remove the person and you risk losing the context that imbued the relatively neutral information with value. Change the context and you also change the knowledge. And knowledge is where the maximum value and hence the greatest profit potential is added in the information age. In a global marketplace where capital becomes increasingly fungible, the premium shifts to the human consideration.

Human elements of personal, organizational, and corporate cultures must now be considered as never before. Humans, however, tend to resist change, especially those that challenge well-established and well-deserved organizational hierarchies and vested interests. And few technologies challenge established hierarchies more than radical reengineering programs based on groupware. Even client/server architectures threaten established mainframe-based MIS departments.

Groupware also threatens corporate inertia. Perhaps the least secure are those in upper management. Traditionally, one of the primary functions of senior management has been to introduce cautious conservatism into an organization. Clearly, like opposing muscles in the human body that must work in concert, the balance of conservatism with iconoclastic innovation must be maintained. What must change is the point of balance.

Paradoxically, while the trend of technology is to consolidate human activities into collaborations, networks, and groups, the social forces are moving toward greater individual autonomy, empowerment, and accountability. Efficient implementations of groupware empower employees who can communicate between themselves, create options, make decisions, and assume roles traditionally reserved for corporate managers.

Evolution or Revolution?

Computers do simple things very quickly. They perform calculations at enormous speeds. This makes them ideal for automating routine calculations and repetitive tasks. Computers must, however, be programmed before they can do anything. As such they are clearly expressions of human intelligence, made in our own image, as it were. Despite ongoing refinement, sophistication, and fundamental paradigm shifts in programming models, most programs are written for some specific purpose and application.

The human brain, on the other hand, tends not to operate in the linear and sequential manner of the computer but rather in a parallel and fuzzy fashion with all sorts of inputs, emotional and intuitive, which are poorly understood at best. While work continues on fuzzy logic and artificial intelligence techniques, not very many of this research has found its way into real-world products. The result is that, there still are many things that computers don't do very well, from simple pattern recognition to matters of complex human interaction and organizational intelligence.

Today, in order to implement a useful groupware system, not only must the groupware tools that implement the repetitive and mechanical portions of a process be considered but so too the creative and discretionary portion of that process. For this the involvement of people is necessary.

Eventually, as processes abetted by groupware technologies that involve groups that may be dispersed in space and time become more familiar and formalized, and artificial intelligence programming techniques become more prevalent, more pieces of the corporate process may be relegated to the "ware" part of groupware.

As it is, information technologies enable collaborative computing as a means of organizing and communicating structured and unstructured digital information, displaying it in multimedia graphical user interface environments, and searching data warehouses.

First-generation Groupware

Remember, groupware is an infant. First-generation groupware extends existing networking, storage, graphical display (visualization), and information organization capabilities for collaborative computing. These are evolutionary products that extend the capabilities of various system components and applications including most of the basic technologies for easy access and management of information through distributed information technologies.

The focus of this book has been primarily on these first-generation groupware systems. These technologies are readily available in a variety of products with various degrees of complexity and robustness. Bear in mind, though, that as promising as these first-generation products are, the overall productivity or performance gains are not in the realm of orders of magnitude. This caution is intended to contain unrealistic expectations, not to discourage the adoption of groupware systems. As mentioned, perhaps the aspect of groupware with the greatest potential for productivity gains is the human component. The sooner organizations start to integrate groupware systems into their activities, the sooner they can start designing processes and procedures that can reap the benefits of tightly integrated collaborative teamwork.

Groupware systems are too interrelated and interdependent for casual implementation. Despite the promises of groupware marketers, the simple purchase and adoption of any single product or system will probably have negligible effect. The best advice, therefore, is to look before you leap into any particular system or strategy.

Despite obvious limitations, there is a real opportunity to bring about substantial improvements in productivity, quality, and cost reduction with these first-generation products. Successful implementation depends on the careful design and analysis of organization infrastructure, followed by a mapping of groupware product to corporate need. Reengineering is a three step process: first, careful analysis and planning; next, identification of available technologies and relevant features; and finally, adoption of the appropriate technology.

Second-generation Groupware

The potential for advances, research, and progress in this area of computer science is tremendous. Second-generation groupware technologies will employ artificial intelligence, pattern recognition, multimedia, networking, advanced user interfaces, and object-orientation, to name a few.

More revolutionary products and systems will be able to incorporate artificial intelligence capabilities to support group consciousness or the ability to learn. When "entities" are programmed to learn, they will be able to assist collaborative workers through active agents. "Agents" are programs that monitor the user and provide useful hints or suggestions to improve work; sort of like virtual guardian angels.

Whereas first-generation groupware provides structures to collect, maintain, and upgrade organizational memory, second-generation groupware products have the potential to learn from the organizational memory in a corporation. Intelligence, after all, deals primarily with an agent being conscious of its own existence. Next-generation groupware systems have the potential to participate and make proactive suggestions as intelligent agents.

Time and Place Dimensions for Categorizing Groupware

Recall the conventional taxonomy of groupware along the axes of time (synchronous versus asynchronous) and place (same place versus different places). Further recall some of the possible problems with adopting a groupware solution.

Same time/same place: The first category deals with face-to-face meetings and the various computer tools that can enhance generation of ideas. Groupware that supports meeting rooms and meeting facilitation fall in this category.

Same time/different places: This exciting category deals with products that support synchronous meetings, coauthoring, and collaborations over local and wide area networks. Synchronous coauthoring tools and videoconferencing are examples of products in this category.

Different times/same place: If the notion of "place" is extended to indicate not only a physical location—such as a meeting room—but electronic addresses as well, a number of products fall in this category. Actually, database management systems and document management systems that support check-out/check-in and even some aspects of e-mail and workflow fall in this category. Kiosks provide a more direct implementation of the different time/same place concept.

Different times/different places: This quadrant characterizes those products and systems that deal primarily with routing of information. For example, electronic mail indicates a collaborative work processing model where information flows between different places (the mailboxes) and at different times.

OBJECTS OF COLLABORATION: CHAPTER 2

Most knowledge work is performed on various objects to produce specific results. The objects shared by people working collaboratively in electronic environments may be as diverse as with single-user applications.

Objects created through collaborative efforts can be simple elements such as text documents, graphic objects, images, voice annotation, tables, spreadsheets, and so on. Simple elements may, however, be information rich and quite complex. Specifically, simple means that which is not composite or compound.

Objects may be single-application objects such as text documents, spreadsheets, or images, each with its own structure and behavior (such as an editor). Objects may also be hypermedia documents or compound objects that aggregate objects belonging to different applications. Earlier, objects were defined as:

$$Object = Structure + Behavior$$

Structure, typically the files that the user opens and edits, contains the data portion of the object. Generally, two components of the structure are stored in the same file: attributes or properties of the file and the content of the file. Behavior corresponds to the operations that can be performed on the objects, on different types of structure.

Every object of collaboration consists of data represented in a structure and various operations that capture the behavior of the objects. Everything in a collaborative computing environment can be reduced to operations on various objects.

Editing and Viewing Objects

The behavior of an object is composed of two parts:

$$Behavior = Viewing + Editing$$

Typically, an application vendor provide two utilities: one for editing an object and another for viewing. Two utilities are necessary because the consumption of information is different from the preparation of information.

There is a clear distinction between viewing an object and editing it. An application used to edit an object is usually much more complex than one used to view the object. On the other hand, more workers consume information by viewing, commenting on, and generally deriving meaning from the content of an object compared to the number of people who author, create, or design the object.

Portable Electronic Document Exchange Standards

Launchers and viewers make assumptions about the availability of application code or executables to either launch the application or viewer associated with the document or part of a document. Whether editing an embedded object, viewing an object pertaining to an application, or launching an application, there must be an executable available that has been provided by the publisher of the application—either a viewer, an executable that implements some application functionality, or the full application.

An alternative approach to launching or viewing through an application-specific viewer is to have common interchange formats for either the formatted electronic documents or for the multimedia elements (such as text, graphics, audio, video, etc.) which allow multiple applications to view or edit the multimedia elements without losing information.

Different applications may be able to read the same file formats. Many applications can read popular file formats such as Microsoft Word, Excel, WordPerfect, Lotus 1-2-3, dBASE, Photoshop, and others. These files can be converted into the active application's format and saved. Another approach is to write to a common and portable format supported either by U.S. or international standardization committees.

Apart from standards for multimedia elements within documents, there are standards such as Standard Generalized Markup Language (SGML) and Electronic Document Interchange (EDI) which specify the structure of formatted electronic documents.

Compound Documents

Graphical user interface platforms are migrating to document-centric environments, in contrast to the application-centric approach of the past decade. Although subtle, this transition is very significant, especially for groupware. Often these document-centric environments are based on compound document models and standards.

Compound documents are documents created from various components and applications, which follow certain procedural interfaces and standards supported by interoperability standards such as OpenDoc by CILabs or OLE 2 supported by Microsoft.

With applications developed within interoperability standards, users can drag and drop parts from these applications to construct the compound document containing all the relevant information. Users need not confine themselves to monolithic applications but can pick and choose applications for different parts of the compound documents.

Compound documents consist of parts that pertain to different types of applications. To edit the different parts, the user can launch an application or edit in place without leaving the context of the compound document. The disadvantage of launching specific applications for the various parts contained in the compound document is that the context is also changed and must be changed back in order to return to the original container document.

Hypermedia

A compound document that has parts and links between parts is a sort of nonlinear document or *hypermedia*. Compound documents can be containers with parts that can themselves be compound documents containing parts and so on. The user thus has "hyper" links from one compound document part to another. However, there are certain additional features of hypermedia that go beyond mere container models of compound or composite documents. Nevertheless, hypermedia documents, authoring systems, and environments are different from compound documents in a number of ways. For instance, with hypermedia, users have the ability to create anchors from one node to the other. Thus, in addition to the embedded or linked parts concepts of compound documents, users can select a term in text or an area/object in a graph and link it to another component or node. Also, with hypermedia products there are usually utilities to track and facilitate navigation through a hypermedia document to ameliorate the problem of disorientation within a nonlinear information space.

Hypermedia provides an associative way to browse through a set of documents. It complements the method of search and retrieval where the nature of a target document is specified and then a set of matches is returned. Hypermedia allows a user to find related information transparently without initiating further searches, and to form new links between documents. Hypermedia systems are more flexible than traditional information structuring methods because they allow information in a variety of forms (media) to be attached to nodes. Thus, a node in hypermedia may consist of a sound or picture, as well as text. Nodes in hypertext (hypermedia) can include icons, anchors, and/or buttons that provide links (send messages) to other nodes.

Through linking concepts from different authors, over possibly geographically distributed networks, hypermedia documents provide the associative model of an organization's memory. Already, World Wide Web servers on the Internet are providing associative navigation of the knowledge bases in various corporations. These servers, connected through hyperlinks, provide a *global* interconnected document of knowledge bases spanning corporations, universities, research centers, and even individuals.

Collaboration on Objects

A recurrent theme of this chapter and this book is that most groupware applications group-enable existing popular applications. Groupware products "enhance" application objects and compound documents; and the overall environment of the user is enhanced through various extensions. Four areas of communication and collaboration around object types include:

(a) Simple exchange of messages with attachments or enclosures: Message exchange through routing is a very important mechanism for sharing information.

(b) Commenting, approving, authorizing: Collaborative creation and development of an object includes a mechanism for group feedback in the form of comments and approval of the various components of the object being developed, either by marking up a document, writing a comment on the design object, or using a self-adhesive note, without actually modifying the object itself.

(c) Coauthoring: A sequence of messages interchanged between collaborating coworkers can easily be coauthored by means of the compilation and accumulation of messages.

(d) Information warehouses: Making information, in the form of structured records and electronic documents, available for collaborative access through a "library" model within a small team, an organization, or between organizations is also an act of collaboration. A good example of this is the Internet. An organization or company that allows its knowledge bases to be searched and accessed by its employees greatly enhances its organizational memory. This sharing of information and accessing information warehouses is an extremely important type of collaboration.

CLIENT/SERVER COLLABORATION: CHAPTER 3

Chapter 3 addressed one of the foundation technologies that enables workers to collaborate by searching for, organizing, and sharing information: the client/server architecture. Client/server is the hottest trend in advanced information systems. A client/server model is often mapped onto hardware platforms where servers are specialized network nodes that provide services, and clients are systems that provide the user with a graphical user interface to access the services of the server nodes.

Although client/server is often used as a synonym for using graphical user interfaces on client nodes to access relational databases and database servers, it is more. Client/server architecture exists whenever a client system makes requests of a server system. The system can be a module, a process, a program, or any other entity that could, in the case of clients, make requests, or, in the case of servers, respond to requests.

A significant advantage of client-server technology is the efficient utilization of hardware and software resources at both the front end (client application), and the back end database server which provides a centralized repository of shared database information. Client/server architectures of this type are constructed on top of wide and local area networks and operating systems.

LANs

A local area network—LAN—is a group of computers and workstations connected through cabling and covering a limited geographical area. The workstations can communicate with servers or network nodes and with each other. A LAN, therefore, enables a variety of independent devices—servers and clients—to communicate with one another over a shared cabling system.

The most crucial issues for local area networks include: bandwidth, or the network performance in terms of communication speeds; reliability, or the availability of the network and its ability to quickly restart following crashes; and bottlenecks, or points of congestion that affect the bandwidth and/or reliability of the network.

WANs

In contrast to local area networks, wide area networks (WANs) cover larger geographic areas. They can span city blocks, entire cities, even continents. Many different hardware/software components and new technologies are involved in constructing wide area networks. The technologies, protocols, and standards involved are quite different from those for local area networks. Therefore, designers of groupware applications should be aware of the underlying technologies and options for wide area networks.

File Servers

The file server was the original enticement that brought about the LAN revolution. As the number of personal computers in the office grew, so too did the need to exchange information between those computers. File servers were, as the name indicates, designed to provide file services to multiple users. Through file servers, users can concurrently share resources, the most prominent of which are the data and commonly used peripheral resources such as printers. File servers are also commonly used to share directories and files between users on a network.

Database Servers

With the growth of client/server computing, database servers have become an important part of the LAN environment. Database servers maintain the information base of the network, provide concurrent access to the information base, and maintain the consistency and validity of the data. Transaction control of database accesses is another key feature of the database server architecture.

In the most straightforward implementation, a database server is a separate node on the network that provides an interface to client nodes. The interface, which is often in the form of a library of functions, allows client applications to submit their requests to the database server and get back from the server the results of their queries.

A fundamental difference between a file server architecture and a database server architecture is that with a database server, the client workstation passes a "high-level" request, in message form, to the server. This is in contrast to the block I/O and file access requests in the case of a file server.

ELECTRONIC MESSAGING: CHAPTER 4

Electronic messaging is a very important enabling technology for groupware. The most vital requirement for collaborative work is the ability to share information and resources. In the broadest definition, electronic messaging is any messaging system that incorporates the electronic exchange of information and includes faxing, electronic fund transfer (EFT) systems, and Electronic Document Interchange (EDI). E-mail remains the most popular electronic messaging system that can interoperate with fax, voice messaging, EDI, and other electronic messaging standards.

Client/server architectures provide the context for sharing resources and information with various types of servers. One important category is messaging servers that are used to exchange electronic messages across local and wide area networks. With messaging, the goal is to exchange and to move information. Users and organizations must also, however, be able to locate, organize, filter, file, and otherwise manage their messages.

As just stated, the most popular mechanism for carrying collaborative work electronically over and between networks is e-mail. The availability and affordability of internetworking allows for the electronic interchange of messages at various proximities, from adjacent cubicles to across continents. If the same environment and products are used to interchange messages, then it is possible to relate to all e-mail collaborators as a single unified group through a consistent interface, whether between cubicles or continents. Interaction and discourse at a distance is no less immediate than with the closest neighbor. For the purpose of information-based collaborations, all collaborators are equally accessible.

There are three basic components or modules for e-mail services: transport services, directory services, and storage or e-mail database services. The transport module is responsible for actually moving the messages. E-mail systems use store and forward communication to send messages from one workstation or PC to another. The messages may go through several intermediate systems. Directory services maintain the physical locations of users, who can then be addressed physically or logically. These directories may be stored either as files or as databases. Entries in the directories contain at least the names of the users as well as their locations. Messaging typically contains the messages that are in the system: read messages, unread messages, message logs, information about the message originator, and attachments.

Different e-mail packages and products offer different solutions. It is rare to find all three components sold by the same vendor. Most e-mail packages offer alternative solutions that integrate with other modules such as directory services and transport services that may be offered by network operating system vendors.

In terms of products, e-mail applications provide the graphical front end to author and deliver messages, organize messages in in/out boxes, file messages in different folders, allow users to provide attachments to messages, forward messages, and so on. Currently, e-mail applications are the most commonly used network application in organizations of all sizes. In fact, e-mail has been described as the hottest technology in the past decade. The proliferation of local area networks and desktop-based electronic mail systems allows communication between users and other users, users and applications, and between applications. E-mail connectivity and networking through popular systems such as the Internet provide an electronic medium over which bulletin boards, forums, and interest groups regularly and frequently communicate.

As e-mail front-end and application programming standards become more accepted, the trend is for the proliferation of mail-enabled applications. Generally, mail-enabled applications treat e-mail as either a separate option or as a printer driver and allow the user to send the document to a target receiver list without leaving the application. In other words, the user could, while using an application such as a word processor or spreadsheet, select e-mail as an option.

E-mail and Organization Memory

An e-mail message could just as easily be sent to a group as to an individual. All the recipients get their messages quickly; recipients on the same network receive their messages almost instantaneously. But e-mail is more than messaging.

Typically, electronic mail systems involve e-mail "databases" which maintain histories of electronic interchanges for specified topics or subject categories. These interchange histories and mail databases enhance the organizational memory of an enterprise. The stored message threads of an interchange automatically trace and document the evolution of a discussion or issue. Message threads are self-documenting and become very useful for keeping track of the reasoning and development of discussion topics. Electronic mail systems, besides being a metaphor for posted mail, provide additional functionality which is feasible only because of the digital nature of the media. Users can, within mail-enabled applications, send mail directly from within their open applications.

If the structure of the message as well as the text content can be captured and maintained, and the e-mail system allows advanced querying and report generation capabilities, then the "message" database becomes an even more effective tool for tracking the evolution of the ideas and thoughts that form the corporate culture. Such a system can greatly enhance organizational memory from which group memories can be recalled from the mail database by queries on subject, participant, date, and so on.

WORKFLOW: CHAPTER 5

One of the most powerful paradigms for automating collaborative work processes in groupware technologies is workflow, or, as suggested, Computer-Supported Collaborative Work Processing (CSCWP).

Workflow systems are becoming increasingly popular in a host of applications. They attempt to capture the processes for "manufacturing" information in an organization. While current workflow products are first-generation, there is very real potential for productivity enhancement through workflow solutions if analyzed and implemented carefully.

Workflow organizes corporate processes into nodes which represent people, devices, applications, or other processes; and links which represent actions such as document routing, requests, instructions, and commands. Workflows may be designed either by scripting languages or graphical design tools. Scripting languages provide tremendous flexibility at the cost of a relatively steep learning curve. Graphical building block design tools provide ease of use at the cost of flexibility and customizability. Some workflow systems are narrowly based on some particular model or "religion" of human interaction, corporate organization, and work processing. Such narrowly bound solutions should be approached only with caution.

Three Types of Workflow

The industry often categorizes workflow in three groups: ad hoc, administrative, and production. With transaction or production workflow systems, there is usually a very involved and complex policy or procedure described and imposed by a corporation. The processes are usually complex, having evolved over time. Many tasks and activities are project-oriented, however, and do not use extensive processes and procedures. The production-based workflow systems deal with day-to-day tasks with more or less well-defined steps of the procedure. Ad hoc workflow applications have goals and deliverables, but the steps and the dynamics between users may be difficult to define in detail and to any degree of predictability.

The third type of workflow is administrative. Based primarily on e-mail systems and extensions of conventional e-mail capabilities, this type of workflow handles routine "administrative" tasks, as its name suggests. Most systems that deal with routing of forms are administrative workflow. The ideal workflow system supports all three types; unfortunately, current workflow products tend toward one or the other.

Workflow and Groupware

Early literature on the subject presented groupware as a computation and automation domain different from workflow. Workflow has been characterized as a means for automating formal policies and procedures that enable the reengineering of basic business processes. Groupware, on the other hand, is characterized as a means for facilitating informal group interactions by enhancing communications, coordination, and collaboration around task teams. Apparently, some people infer antithesis between the formal policy orientation of workflow and the informal collaborations of groupware.

Another stereotype has identified workflow closely with document imaging systems. This genre of workflow application had very distinct and sometimes rigidly prescribed steps within the information and task flow. Groupware, on the other hand, has typically been identified with either collaborative meeting systems, scheduling formal and informal meetings, or systems that help to maintain organizational memory.

Common examples of groupware include electronic meetings, videoconferencing, and collaborative authoring as well as groupware that supports collaborative business practice by enhancing organizational memory such as the next generation of e-mail systems that store and maintain a trace of topics and electronic conversations and provide messaging databases with querying and viewing capabilities. Lotus Notes is such a product.

Although groupware is associated with systems that encourage and nurture informal group interactions, there are groupware systems that encourage and enforce more formal interactions between team members: for example, shared calendars or scheduling systems. These systems allow team members to share calendars across a network and to schedule meetings and other events through a shared calendar database. Such systems help the team to arrange formal meetings in a fashion with specified forms of proposal, acceptance, counter-proposals, or rejection of proposals.

The "contradictions" between groupware and workflow arise from a somewhat academic definition of groupware as systems that assist the overall sharing of corporate memory and intelligence within a team. However, by defining groupware more generally as any system that assists collaborative work, workflow or Computer-Supported Collaborative Work Processing is really just another type of groupware.

Workflow Systems

Workflow systems provide a framework for automating and enhancing the flow of work or task activities between workers and processes. It does not need to be structured. The primary function of workflow is to facilitate the fulfillment of projects and deliverables by a team. It is a tool to empower individuals to manage business activities and events and an important part of this management is the collaboration and coordination between workers.

Workflow automation is a structure applied to the movement of information in order to improve the results of a business process. Workflow automation software manages the coordination of activities among people in general business processes. This aspect of coordination goes beyond merely communicating information through electronic media but also involves individuals within the organization who are working to accomplish a goal or implement a process.

Components of Workflow

Although there are many forms and variations in workflow products, there are three main elements which are common to most workflow systems:

The objective or the "case": Workflows are created and activated to accomplish an objective. Workflow systems typically allow the definition of the start and accomplishment (finish) of the objective. This typically is achieved by completing the "case" folder for the workflow's activation.

Participants or Participating Nodes: Nodes represent workers, process, or devices. For work to flow there needs to be senders and receivers; sources and sinks. A workflow definition specifies the participants and a workflow activation binds these to specific individuals, roles, groups, devices, or processes (including other workflows).

Flow or linking the participants: The third component is the linking or the flow of information, documents, and instructions between the participants of a workflow. There are many types of flow control that can be supported or implemented by a workflow system. The simplest is just routing a document or container.

Documents and forms being processed: In workflow, there is almost always *case data*, which represents the information being processed to get the job done. There are as many variations of case data as there are data types. Forms are quite common in processing cases.

ELECTRONIC MEETINGS (EMs): CHAPTER 6

The essence of groupware is the collaboration of workers. Groupware systems are designed to support and enhance the way people work together in groups. The two characteristics common to the groupware systems discussed in the preceding sections (and corresponding chapters in the book) are: asynchronous interactions between collaborating workers, which occur at different times; and incremental change, where existing technologies evolve and become group-enabled.

One consequence of asynchronous interactions is that relationships that are displaced in time tend to focus more on the content of the interaction and less on personal issues. For many types of interactions, this reduced intimacy is an asset; for others it is not. Indeed, the preponderance of daily business interactions revolve around "human" issues of social, political, and interpersonal concern. This is not to suggest that content is lacking, but that the content of the explicit communication is subsidiary to the metacommunication (also referred to as subtext) implicit in the interaction. Psychologists and communications professionals estimate that approximately 70 percent of a communication is carried out by relatively unconscious channels such as facial expressions, body posture, and manner of speech and presentation.

Of the previously discussed groupware systems, the penetration of e-mail and client/server architectures is larger by far than workflow. Furthermore, it is possible, by combining e-mail, client/server concurrent sharing, and other basic technologies such as rule-based e-mail and digital signatures, to implement many workflow scenarios.

Chapter 6 introduced a major new category of groupware products: support for electronic meetings. Although electronic meetings are not strictly limited to the same-time paradigm, most electronic meetings are usually synchronous.

Personal Information Managers and Group Calendaring Systems

Personal information managers (PIMs) are programs that organize appointments, scheduled events, notes, and to-do lists. Personal management tools include the calendars, to-do lists, alarms, tickler files, personal information managers, and contact managers. Appointment calendar schedules may be presented in a variety of views including, text, time-line, or GANT charts. Calendar views can be by the week, month, or year. One feature increasingly becoming accepted is the ability to share calendars, which raises the personal information manager into the realm of groupware. The benefits of interlinking time management tools within and across a group substantially increases the value of already valuable tools.

The value of calendars and scheduling increases with scope. A growing number of products permit time management for groups as well as individuals. Group schedulers may be resource-specific; for example, a scheduler that manages human resources would be called a project management application. Calendars based on a local area network permit a great deal of flexibility with scheduling groups, meetings, and assigning tasks. Tasks may be assigned and schedules set either by a manager/coordinator or by negotiation within a group.

When a suitable time has been found, the facilitator who is calling the meeting, uses the LAN-based software to enter a tentative time into everybody's calendar. Typically, the software will also follow-up with an e-mail message to all of the invited participants announcing the proposed meeting and include time, place, participants, assigned priority, and agenda.

Synchronous Meetings

Synchronous and colocated meetings fall into the same time/same place quadrant of groupware taxonomy. Modern technology has changed and continues to change the nature of real-time face-to-face meetings. Some of the devices and meeting support concepts that are currently popular include the following:

- Electronic copyboards
- PC and a projector
- Team rooms
- Group decision support systems

Synchronous same-place meetings may be one-to-one, one-to-many (a presentation), or many-to-many. The primary characteristic of this type of meeting is immediacy. Another characteristic is the expense required to negotiate distance and schedules. A consequence of this type of meeting is to lend a premium to several personal characteristics such as appearance, the ability to think on one's feet, and ease in public. Issues of eloquence and personal charisma may tend to dominate the session. The argument may go not to the most rational but to the most persuasive or politically potent. Clearly, certain personality types tend to predominate in this environment.

There is a growing proliferation of computer-enabled meeting rooms that are being made available for hire. Among the most well-known is the Decision and Planning Laboratory (DPL), a prototype electronic meeting room at the University of Arizona's College of Business and Public Administration. The DPL demonstrates how high-technology conference rooms can provide major productivity and time-saving benefits.

Distributed Meetings

A number of products offer support for the novel concept of distributed meetings. In the extreme, a distributed meeting is spread out over time sometimes to the extent that no one actually "meets" with anyone else at the same time. The concept of the distributed meeting is somewhere between a shared database bulletin board conference and a network chat session. Think of it as a structured and time-delimited bulletin board conference.

It is useful to stretch the concept of a meeting, and the new generations of groupware will help to evolve the range of available relationships that collaborating workers can maintain by means of electronic media. In practical terms, the concept of a distributed meeting is usually used to extend participation in electronic meetings to include transient members who drop in and out of ongoing meetings, perhaps limiting their participation to only those portions of a meeting that interest them, to do some research, or to capture the input of participants who are unable to attend.

Organization Memory

What does organization memory have to do with electronic meetings? First of all, almost all groupware products deal with organization memory in one form of another. Electronic mail databases that are filed and stored enhance organization memory, as do message threads and databases of topics that keep track of discussions on various topics and issues. The minutes of meetings, the comments of participants, and the resolutions of meetings are also part of the organization memory. In a sense, organization memory tries to tie all threads of groupware together—the corporate knowledge base, the corporate intelligence, the team rationale in arriving at various conclusions, and the overall memory of every decision, fact, and document.

EPILOG

Writing this book was an act of collaboration. Both authors live and work in the San Francisco Bay area. Setrag lives in Walnut Creek at the foot of Mount Diablo, northeast of the Santa Clara valley. Marek lives and works in the shadow of El Sombroso in the sleepy town of Los Gatos nestled in the Santa Cruz mountains on the southwest end of the valley. It is more than an hour's drive through heavy traffic to get together for a face-to-face meeting. Clearly, the situation required a groupware solution.

Many collaborative objectives can be achieved using existing technologies. This we did in a variety of ways. Perhaps the most useful technology was simple e-mail. However, essential to the successful implementation of any groupware system is the analysis of corporate culture, goals, and the subsequent design of a process that meet the situation requirements.

We had the advantage of having worked together before. The rapport and confidence that we developed in prior work activities were primary assets which shaped our work strategy.

Because of the logistics and commitments, this project required a loosely coupled collaboration. We didn't consult on detail but flagged items for peer reviews (different times/different places). Had our circumstances been different then so would our work strategy.

The most crucial lesson to draw from our experience is that it was designed around our respective individual and collaborative personalities and situations.

We offer our collaborative process not to suggest a model but to present an example. Our choice of tools and strategies is not an endorsement of any specific products. A tool is appropriate to the job at hand. We hope that this book will help you to choose wisely from the growing array of groupware tools.

References

Baecker, Ronald M. (1993). *Readings in Groupware and Computer-Supported Cooperative Work*. San Mateo, CA: Morgan Kaufmann Publishers.

Bellotti, Victoria, Dourish, Paul (1992). "Awareness and Coordination in Shared Work Spaces." *Proceedings of CSCW 1992*.

Bireman, B. (editor) (1994). *Workflow '94 Conference Proceedings*. Scottsdale, AZ: The Conference Group.

Bochenski, B. (1994). *Implementing Production-Quality Client/Server Systems*. New York, NY: John Wiley & Sons.

Bock, G. (1992). "Workflow As Groupware: A Case for Group Language?" *GroupWare '92*. David D. Coleman (editor). San Mateo, CA: Morgan Kaufmann Publishers.

Brockschmidt, K. (1994). *Inside OLE 2*. Redmond, WA: Microsoft Press.

Burns, N. (1994). "Workflow Automation: A Methodology For Change." *The Workflow CD-ROM Sampler*. Creative Networks.

Bush, V. (1945). "As we may think." *Atlantic Monthly*. 176.

Coleman, David D. (editor) (1994). *Groupware '94: The Workgroup Solutions Conference Proceedings*. Scottsdale, AZ: The Conference Group.

Conklin, J. (1992). "Capturing Organization Memory." *Groupware '92*. David D. Coleman (editor). San Mateo, CA: Morgan Kaufmann Publishers.

D'Alleyrand, Marc R. (1989). *Image Storage and Retrieval Systems*. New York, NY: McGraw-Hill.

Davidow, W.H., Malone, M.S. (1993). *The Virtual Corporation*. New York, NY: HarperCollins Publishers.

Dourish, P., Bellotti, V. (1992). "Awareness and Coordination in Shared Workspaces." *CSCW '92: Proceedings of the Conference on Computer Supported Cooperative Work*, J. Turner, R. Kraut (editors). Toronto, Canada.

Doyle, M., Strauss, D. (1976). *How To Make Meetings Work*. New York, NY: Berkley Publishing Group.

Engelbart, D., English, W. (1968). *A Research Center for Augmenting Human Intellect*. Greif, 1968.

Engelbart, Douglas (1988). "Working Together." *BYTE*, December, 1988.

Gray, P. (1987). "Group Decision Support Systems." *Decision Support Systems*, 1987.

Greif, Irene (editor) (1988). *Computer Supported Cooperative Work: A Book of Readings*. San Mateo, CA: Morgan Kaufmann Publishers.

Grohowski, R.B., McGoff, C., Vogel, D.R., Martz, W.B., and Nunamaker Jr., J.F. (1990). "Implementation of Electronic Meeting Systems at IBM." *MIS Quarterly,* 14, 4.

Grudin, J. (1989). "Why Groupware Applications Fail: Problems in Design and Evaluation." *Office Technology and People* 4(3).

Grudin, J. (1988). "Perils and Pitfalls." *BYTE,* December 1988.

Hammer, Michael, and Champy, James (1993). *Reengineering the Corporation: A Manifesto for Business Revolution*. New York: Harper Business.

Jessup, L.M., Valacich, J.S. (1993). "Group Support Systems." *New Perspectives*.

Johansen, R. (1988). *Groupware: Computer Support for Business Teams*. New York: The Free Press.

Jyachandra, Y. (1994). *Re-Engineering the Networked Enterprise*. New York, NY: McGraw-Hill.

Khoshafian, S. (1993). *Object-Oriented Databases*. New York, NY: John Wiley & Sons, Inc.

Khoshafian S., Baker, B., Abnous, R., Shepherd, K. (1992b). *Intelligent Offices*. New York, NY: John Wiley & Sons, Inc.

Khoshafian, S., Chan, A., Wong, A., and Wong, H.K.T. (1992a). *A Guide to Developing Client/Server SQL Applications*. San Mateo, CA: Morgan Kaufmann Publishers.

Koulopoulos, T. (1994). *The Workflow Imperative*. Delphi Consulting Group.

Kramer, J.L., King, J.L. (1988). "Computer-Based Systems for Cooperative Work." *ACM Computing Surveys,* 20(2), June 1988.

Langham, Don (1994). "The Commonplace MOO: Orality and Literacy in Virtual Reality." *Computer-Mediated Communication Magazine,* http://www.rpi.edu/ ~decemj/cmc/mag/current/toc.html, Volume 1, Number 3, July.

Marshak, R. N. (1994). "Workflow White Paper: On Overview of Workflow Software." *Workflow '94*. Bob Bierman (editor). San Jose, CA: The Conference Group.

Nelson, T. (1965). "The hypertext." *Proceedings of the World Documentation Federation*. 1965.

Nunamaker Jr., J.F., Vogel, D., Heminger, A., Martz, B., Grohowski, R., and McGoff, C. (1989). "Experiences at IBM with group support systems: A field study." *Decison Support Systems*, 5, 2 (1989).

Palermo, A.M., and McCreedy, S.C. (1992). "Workflow Software: A Primer." In *GroupWare '92* David D. Coleman (ed), Morgan Kaufman Publishers.

Parsaye, K., Chignell M., Khoshafian, S., and Wong H. (1989). *Intelligent Databases*. New York: John Wiley & Sons, Inc.

Saffo, Paul (1993). "The Future of Virtual Conferencing." *PC Computing,* January 1993.

White, Thomas E., and Fischer, Layna (editors) (1994). *The Workflow Paradigm*. Alameda, CA: Future Strategies Inc.

Winograd, Terry (1988). "Where the Action Is," *BYTE,* December 1988.

Winograd, T., and Flores, F. (1986). *Cognition Understanding Computers and Cognition.* Addison-Wesley.

Workflow Management Coalition (1993). *The Workflow Reference Model Version 0.6.* June 1993. Document Number SC001-1003. (This document gets periodically updated.)

Index

802.6 protocol, 134

ABORT, 148
abort log record, 148
abstract data types, 233
abstract data typing, 233, 234
Access, 91
access privileges, 79, 269
access privileges on objects, 112
access rights, 79, 130
accessibility, 52
accounting, 70
Action Technologies, 177, 219
action-coordination systems, 319–320
activations, 60, 230, 243
active feedback mechanisms, 312
active workflow, 246
activity network, 230
ad hoc workflow, 203, 223, 224
address bindings, 185
address book:
 attributes, 183
 duplication, 184
 directory services, 185
address books, 177, 182, 257
 e-mail, 182
 object-oriented, 183
 public, 182
address specification, 177
adjacency, 102
administration, 122
administrative workflow, 203, 223, 225
 encryption, 226
 notification, 226
 tracking, 226

admission control, 156
Advanced Program to Program Communications, 128
advanced electronic messaging, 193
advanced messaging capabilities, 175
Agenda, 280
agents, 10, 344
AIIM (Association of Imaging and Information Management), 15
alarm, 252
alarm function, 267
alarm, nudger, 267
alarm, tickler, 267
alarms, 264, 265, 270
Aldus Photo Styler, 95
ALL-IN-ONE, 163
allocation of logical data objects, 145
allocation strategies, 144
alpha, 253
AMD (Administration Management Domain), 180
America On Line (AOL), 165
AMI PRO, 69
amnesia, 41
amnesia, organization memory, 332
AMS, 197
analysis, 11
analysis of data flow of objects, 227
analysis of work, 227
Andrews Message Systems (AMS), 196
annotate contacts, 265
annotated document image, 214
annotated, objects can be, 266
annotating viewed documents, 198
annotation, 311
annotation film, 198

annotation tools, 214, 229
annotations, 203, 212, 233
anonymity, 288
anonymous meetings, 281
ANSI, 134
ANSI X12, 80
API (Application Programming Interface) specification, 176
API interfaces, 171
API, DSP, 307
API, messaging, 172
APIs, common mail, 171
Apocalypse Now, 339
APPC, 128
Apple, 59, 86, 96, 120, 176, 177, 219
Apple DigiSign, 203
AppleScript, 89
AppleTalk, 314
application items, 177
application models:
 component, 31
 compound, 31
 container, 31
application nodes, 222
application programming interface, 254
application servers, 257
application-centric environments, 114
applications:
 based FAX services, 157
 evolutionary, 9
 message aware, 173
 message enabled, 173
 message-based workgroup, 173
appointment calendar, 265
approval processes, 248
approving, 62

361

arbitrary graph structured complex objects, 235
arbitrary graph structured composite objects, 235
arbitration registry, 89
architectural models, 267
architecture, OLE 2, 91
archives, 41
Arco Santi, 336
arcs, 246
Arizona Room, 274
ARPANET, 128
artificial intelligence, 2, 10
assembly line-like processing of work, 245
assignment of responsibilities and authorities, 246
assisting work processing, 226–227
associative memory, 331
associative structures, 27, 100
ASTRO.MOO, 329
Asymetrix, 69
asymmetric cryptoalgorithms, 200
Asynchronous Transfer Mode, 132
asynchronous, 11
asynchronous and co-incident, 44, 48–49
asynchronous and displaced, 44, 49–50
asynchronous collaborative authoring system, 311
asynchronous editor, 312
asynchronous groupware systems, 259
asynchronous meetings, 261
At Work, 279
AT&T, 173, 186
AT&T Bell Labs, 289
ATM (Asynchronous Transfer Mode), 17, 47, 132, 155, 160
  connection circuits, packet mode transfers, 133
  connection services, circuit mode transfers, 133
  features:
    cell relay, 132
    cell-based protocol, 132
    transfer rates, 132
  networks, 17, 121
  virtual circuits, 132
    nonswitched Permanent Virtual Circuits (PVC), 133
    Switched Virtual Circuits (SVC), 133
atomic commitment, 147
attachments, 12, 176, 189
attribute types, process definition, 237
attribute types, process instances, 237
attribute values of objects, 247
attribute-based, 212
attributes, 57, 64, 214, 233, 235, 237
  address book, 183
  built-in, 65
  custom, 65
  object, 65
audit trail of hiring candidates, 252
audit-trails, 254
Augment, 29
Augmentation Research Center (ARC), 6, 260
augmenting collaboration, 260

author, 231
authoring, environment, 103
authoring systems, hypermedia, 100
authoring, shared, 313
authorization, 130
authorizing, 62
automate, 226
automated information flow, 212
automatic dialing, 265
automatic notice, 252
automatic time picking feature, 271
automation, 221
automation primitives, 226
avant guard corporations, 221
AVI, 61
awareness context, 311
awareness, group, 310
awareness information, 311
awareness mechanisms, 313
awareness, self, 310

back-end database server, 116
back-end e-mail server, 167
back-end service, 172
back-end service vendors, 171
back-end services, 171
backbone system connectivity, 116
backlinking, 263
balancing microphones, 303
bandwidth, 121
Banyan, 129, 163, 170, 173
Banyan Vines, 196
Banyan Systems Incorporated, 196
base table, 75
BCC, 162, 189
behavior, 57, 114, 233, 234, 237, 345
Bell Atlantic, 186
Bell Labs, 304
Bellcore, 134, 181, 311
beta, 253
BeyondMail, 163, 195, 196, 247
bifurcated application logic, 267
binary predicates, 194
binary representation of objects, 84
bindery, 131
binding, 93
binding part handlers, 89
bit mapped images, 71
bitmap-oriented paint program, 309
blind carbon copies, 162
block size, 156
blueprint of re-engineered business processes, 240
BMP, 61
Borenstein, Nathaniel, 181
Borland, 176
bottom-up integration, 144
Brainstorming, 280
brainstorming, 30, 38, 288
Brainwriting, 282
bridges, 27, 141
British Telecom, 289
broad band intelligent digital network, 121
bug tracking processes, 253
building a NOS, 129

built-in terms, 218
Bull, 211
bulletin boards, 39, 204
bus architecture, 137
bus structure topology, 125
business practice, 261
business procedures and policies, 243
business process re-engineering, 6, 7, 11, 20
business process reengineering, 209
business processes, 6, 216, 253
business rules, 243
buttons, 74

C compiler, 217
C libraries, 217
C++, 231
cabinets, 191
cable bandwidths:
  coaxial, 123
  twisted-wire pair, 123
cable television, 123, 302
cable types, 122
cabling, 121, 123
caching mechanisms, 155
CAD, 71
Cairo, 92
calendar views, 266
calendaring software, 262
calendars, electronic, 264
call timer, 265
callback mechanisms, 167
calling procedures, 234
CALS, 61
capturing attributes, 225
carbon copy receivers, 162
card readers, 24
cartography systems, 103
case, 245
case data, 229, 254
case documents, 245
case folder, 245, 248
case object, 245
case status, 246
case workflow, 245
Cashman, Paul, 29
casting director, 324
categories of information technologies, 2
categories, groupware applications, 4
categorization systems, 4
CC, 162, 189
cc:Mail, 163, 177, 186, 206, 240
CCIR 601, 294
CCITT, 186
CD-ROM, 58
cell switching, 17
cellular modems, 121
central backbone communications line, 125
centralized architecture, 124
CERN (European Particle Physics Laboratory), 165
certified mail, 199
challenges to, 7
change agents, 335
change bars, 318
change management, 121, 148

Index

changes in object states, 248
channel coding, 304
check object back in, 231
check-in/check-out, 63
check-out
　by identifier, 152
　by selection criteria, 152
　/check-in, 121
　/check-in mechanisms, 191
　/check-in model, 34, 159
　/check-in of objects, 150
　/check-in process, 152
　/check/in model, 111
　/check-in client/server model, 231
checks, 22
checksum, 203
children, 141
CILabs, 59, 84, 85, 114
CILabs, 120
ciphertext, 200
class behavior, 233
class instance, 233
class object, 237
class:
　collection of operations, 233
　name, 233
　representation, 233
classes, 233
　documents, 233
　folders, 233
　office peripherals, 233
　workflow participants, 233
　workflow queues, 233
　workflow templates, 233
clerical workers, 223
client application, 167
client buffer, 155
client nodes, 2, 7, 23, 34, 115, 122, 167
client platform, 210
client/server, 267
client/server architecture, 2, 16, 115, 118, 167, 340
　defined, 115
client/server collaboration, 348
client/server computing, 231
client/server e-mail, 166
client/server model, defined, 115
closed systems, 219
clustering, 140
clusters, 140
CM/1, 6, 332
CMC, 51
CMC platforms, 174
co-authoring, 62
co-authors, 231
co-incident meetings, 261
co-routine threads, 156
co-routines, 156
coarse grained, 116
coarse grained client/server, 121
coarse grained client/server architecture, 113
coauthoring, 344, 347
coaxial cable, 123
code, 234
code reusability, 234

code sharing, 234
CODEC, 290
codecs, digital video, 292
coders, parametric, 305
coders, source, 305
Cogger, Richard, 297
Cognitech Corp, 264
cognitive process, 33
CoLab, 260
Coleridge, Samuel (Taylor), 29, 330
collaboration(s), 31, 62, 259, 261, 285
collaborations over networks, 344
collaborations, tightly coupled, 270
Collaborative technologies, 282
collaborative access, 111
collaborative authoring, 207, 285
collaborative authorship, 287
collaborative computing, 4, 9, 85, 167
collaborative computing environment, 57
collaborative dialog, 262
collaborative knowledge work, 261
collaborative meeting systems, 207
collaborative work processing, 231
collaborative work processing system, 211
collaborative workers, 210, 231
Collabra, 205, 206, 332
Collabra Share, 332
Collage, screen capture, 300
Collage, screen capture window, 301
Collage, text editor, 301
Collage, white board, 300
collection objects, 191
collection of work activities, 254
collection types, 105
collections, 74–75, 106
collections types, 227
colocal meetings, 273
colocated meetings, 273
color bitmap images, 176
COM, 91, 92
combining predicates in expressions, 194
commenting, 62, 231
commercial DBMS, 220
COMMIT, 148
commodity, information as, 263
Common Messaging Calls (CMC), 174
Common Object Request Broker Architecture, 121
common APIs, 171
common application programming interface, 172
common e-mail services interface, 171
common interfaces, 253
common library, 231
common mail APIs, 171
common messaging API, 171
common service provider interface, 172
common set of standards, 254
common space, 287
common time availability, 267
communication, 31, 161, 171
community handbook, 263
Compaq, 136
Compel, 69
Component Integration Laboratories (CILabs), 86

Component Object Model, 84, 91
component, 83
component application model, 31
component based architectures, 225
component computing, 119
component object models, 239
component software, 83
components, 57, 105
components of a workflow system, 240
components of workflow, 240
composite, 56
composite containment information objects, 238
composite document models, 198
composite objects, 238
composite or compound documents, 187
compound, 56
compound application model, 31
compound document(s), 57, 58–60, 83–94, 98, 100, 105, 113, 114, 230, 231, 238, 239, 346
compound document model, 32, 84
compound object spaces, 235
compound objects, 57
compression, 213
compression, Delta-based, 292
compression, pulse code modulation, 290
compression, run length encoding, 291
compression, video, 290
CompuServe, 165, 205
computation and automation domain, 207
computational model, 115
Computer Aided Design, 113
Computer Aided Manufacturing, 113
Computer Aided Software Engineering, 113
Computer Integrated Telephone (CIT), 301
Computer Supported Collaborative Work Processing (CSCWP), 207
Computer Supported Cooperative Work, 17, 29
Computer Supported Cooperative Work, 260
computer aided engineering tools, 209
computer based instructional tools, 263
computer enabled meeting rooms, 274
computer mediated communication, 51
computer networks, 336
computer supported cooperative work (CSCW), 11
computer supported environment, 210
computer-supported, 210
computer/human interaction, 10, 94, 219
computer/human interaction models, 223
computerized environment, 210
computing environments, alphanumeric, 33
computing environments, multimedia, 33
concept index, 99
conceptual links, 100
concurrency, 70
concurrency control, 24, 38, 111
concurrency control strategies, 159
concurrent access(es), 34, 150, 111
concurrent sharing, 67, 89, 111, 113, 114, 226, 257
concurrently shared e-mail database, 192

364 ■ Index

concurrently shared objects, 226
condition nodes, 222
condition routing, 221
conditional links, 102
conditions, 247
conference calls, 277
conferencing groupware, 260
conferencing systems, 45
confidentiality, 200
confirmation, 253
connection oriented protocol, 128
connection types, 243
connectionless integrity, 200
connectionless service, 201
connectivity, 2, 122, 211, 254
consensus, 261
consensus seeking, 281
constant data rates, 156
consultants, 338
contact lists, 265
contact manager scheduler, 267
contact managers, 264
contacts, annotate, 265
contacts, document, 265
container application model, 31
container types, 105
containers, 86, 98, 105,108, 109, 230
containers of parts, 230
containment, 114
content, 57
content based model, 86
content model, 87
content objects, 87
content-based indexing, 212
contractors, 338
control flow, 240
control flow diagrams, 227
control mechanisms, 316
controlling work flow, 227
controls, 22
conventional taxonomies, 345
conversation architecture, 319
conversation-commitment-action model, 219
cooperation, 285
cooperative work processing, 231
coordination of activities, 209
coordinator force, 148
Coppola, Frances Ford, 339
CORBA, 84, 86, 121, 231
core competency, 338
core small teams, 221
Cornell University's Information Technology department (CIT), 297
Cornell Video CuSeeMe, 297
Corporate Memory Systems, 332
corporate bulletin boards, 206
corporate bulletin boards, 206
corporate culture, 6, 261, 337
corporate database access, 38
corporate database management system, 70, 39
corporate databases, 70
corporate e-mail systems, 206
corporate identity, 42
corporate inertia, 342

corporate intelligence, 43
corporate memory, 39
corporate structures, tightly integrated, 338
corporation reengineer, 216
corporation, hollow, 325–327
corporation, nature of, 339
cost benefit, 214
cost estimates, 249
cost of attending meeting, 264
cost/performance advantages, 16
CPUs, RISC-based, 301
Credit Research Foundation, 80
criteria for notification, 199
cryptoalgorithms, 200
cryptographic algorithms, 201
cryptography, 200
CSCW (Computer Supported Cooperative Work), 17, 19, 29, 210, 211, 230, 260
CSCWS, 260
cultureware, 328
cursor collisions, 315
Curtis, Pavel, 329
CuSeeMe, 297
custom forms, 175
customization, 21, 64, 66
cyberspace, 329
cyberworkers, 51
cycle, 156

D-SOM, 219
Dalrina, 72
DARPA, 289
DASD storage, 156
data, 57
data compression standard, 293
data conferencing, 299, 303
data digest, 203
data entry, 224
data flow diagrams, 227
data independence, 144
data integrity, 267
data manipulation, 213
data objects, 144
data origin authentication, 200
data portion, 233
data replication, 148
data transport protocols, 127
data type, application files, 229
data type, forms, 70
data type, images, 229
data type, multimedia, 229
data types, 229
database front-end tools, 70
database interfaces, 172
database management systems, 4, 14, 71, 111, 210
database models, 25, 33
database server node functions, 139, 140
database servers, 23, 24, 115, 121, 138, 154, 159, 349
database schemata, 6
database server back-end, 70
database standards, 172
database tables, 75

database'd workflow, 220
database, concurrently shared e-mail, 192
database, private, 193
databases, e-mail, 193
databases, multi-user, 49
databases, quality assurance, 253
databases, topics, 206
datagram, 127, 128
datagram-based protocol, 128
DaVinci, 163
day-timer, 271
day-to-day tasks, 224
dBASE, 61
DBMS (database management system), 113, 141, 220, 257
deadlines, 225
deadlock avoidance, 146
deadlock detection, continuous, 146
deadlock detection, periodic, 146
deadlocks, 93–94
debates designer, 139
DEC, 78, 86, 163, 173
Decision and Planning Laboratory (DPL), 274
Decision Support Systems, 30
decision making, 7, 276
decision support tools, 262, 280
declarative rules, 218
decryption key, 201
decryption technology, 200
dedicated leased lines, 164
Defense Advanced Research Projects Agency, 289
defining workflow, 254
deliverable(s), 225, 230, 238, 256
delivery rate, 155
Delphi Consulting, 223
Delrina, 220
delta based compression, 292
department of defense (DOD), 128
dependencies between data objects, 299
design business process, 254
design specifications, 231
design step, 209
design-fill-approve cycle, 80
designating proxies, 270
designing workflow, 254
desktop metaphors, 211
desktop teleconferencing, 48, 278
desktop videoconferencing, 37, 289
development environment, 256
development process, 231
developing distributed databases, 142, 144
diagramming graphics tool, 240
diagramming tool(s), 240, 241, 243
diagramming workflow software, 249
Dial Tone Multiple Frequency, 279
dial-up account, 164
Dick Tracy, 294
difference between architecture, file server, and database server, 138
difference between document models, 32
difference between information and knowledge, 341
differences, linked object and embedded object, 93

Index ■ 365

different times/different places, 44, 49–50, 73, 273
different times/same place, 44, 48–49
Digital Equipment Corporation, 321
digital frames, 134
digital image, 214
digital media, 1, 339
digital network, 135, 289
digital signal processor, 302–307
digital signatures, 162, 193, 200, 202, 203, 206, 220
digital structured form, 214
digital video, 290
digitized documents, 212, 214
direct inward dialing (DID), 157
directory information base (DIB), 186
directory servers, 253
directory service(s), 168, 170, 240, 257
directory services, address book, 185
discussion groups, 39
discussion maps, 332
disk access, 156
disk I/O scheduling, 156
disorientation problem, 103
displaying a part, 87
distance education, 289
distinguished name, 177
distributed architecture, 125
distributed collaborative environment, 85
distributed computing, 85
distributed concurrency control, 146
distributed database construction, 159
distributed database prototypes, 142
distributed database systems, 145
distributed databases, 25, 141, 159
distributed electronic conferences, 282
distributed enterprises, 210
distributed meeting(s), 282–284, 344, 355
distributed networks, 220
distributed object managers, 219
distributed object standards, 231
distributed object support, 93
distributed object system, 94
distributed objects, 90
distributed transaction, 147
distributed transaction management, 146
distributed transaction processing, 148
distributed whiteboards, 309
distribution of control, 145
document, 57:
    annotate, 58
    approve, 58
    comment, 58
    parts, 86
    parts, root, 86
document annotations, 197
document-based groupware, 4
document-based model, 86
document conferencing tools, 262
document contacts, 265
document container, 90
document description language, 61
document drafts, 90
document feeder, 213
document Imaging, 211
document Imaging systems, 211, 214

document imaging applications, 212
document imaging systems, 4, 15, 71, 76, 198, 207, 215, 341
document imaging terminology, 78
document interchange, 62
document management, 340
document management systems, 14, 38, 121, 191
document management tools, 208
document manager scheduler, 267
document region, defined, 103
document sharing, concurrent, 48
document structure, 61, 227
document type definition, 61
document views, 312, 313
document-centric environments, 114
document-centric model of information, 231
documentation, 41
documents, 78
documents, tree-structured, 312
DOE (Distributed Object Everything), 121
Dorcey, Tim, 297
Domain Name System, 180
domains, 181
DOMF (Distributed Object Management Facility), 121
DOS, 129
download data, 266
downloading files from source archives, 165
downsized corporation(s), 7, 221
downsized re-engineered corporation, 221
downsized solutions, 2
downsizing, 16, 21, 321, 337
DS1, 134
DS3, 134
DSOM (Distributed System Object Model), 90, 120
DSP API, 307
DSP resource manager, 307
DSPs, 299, 302
DSS (Decision Support Systems), 30, 276
DTD, 61
DTMF, 158, 279
DTMF international support, 158
dual-tone multifrequency decoding (DTMF), 157
dumb terminals, 24
Dungeons and Dragons, 329
Dynamic Linked Libraries, 93
dynamic decision making at run time, 256

e-fax, 262
e-mail, 6, 20, 27, 38, 39, 111, 161, 231, 340, 350
    address books, 182
    address syntax, 185
    advanced features, enclosures, 27
    annotations:
        embedded documents, 198
        image documents, 198
    attachments, 189
    client applications, 167
        client tool, 240
        connectivity standards, CCITT X.400, 169
    Novell MHS, 169

database, 171
database server, 158
database services, 168
databases, 162, 193
directory services, 158, 170
enclosures, 190
gateways, 182
graphics objects, 197
industry, 240
message database, 163, 171
message exchange, 166
messaging transport engines, 257
querying, 163
report generation, 163
security, 200
security services, 200
service modules, directory services, 168
    e-mail database services, 168
    storage, 168
    transport services, 168
services, 167
services engine API (Application Programming Interface), 171
software:
    Internet based, 163
    LAN-based, 163
    mainframe and minicomputer, 163
standards, 171
transport services, 158, 169, 253
e-mail system support:
    annotations, 203
    digital signature, 203
    message threads, 203
    notifications, 203
e-mail systems, 161, 225, 253
    advanced features, attachments, 27
    advanced features, rules, 27
    advanced features, workflow, 27
    interoperability, 27
e-mail view, 192
e-mail workflow support, 203
e-mail-based applications, 253
e-mail based workflow, 220, 226, 253
e-mail-enabled applications, 253
e-mail server component(s), 168, 171
e-mail server, transport standards, 177
eEasyLink, 165
echo-cancelled modem, 304
Eden Corp, 282
EDI (Electronic Document Interchange), 346
EDI, 61-62, 80
edit cursor, 315
editing, 213
editing a part, 87
editing objects, 58
editor, asynchronous, 312
editor, multi-user, 312, 314
editor, synchronous, 314
editor, text, 314
editor, synchronous, 312
educational programming, 154
EIES, 23
electro-magnetic interference, 123
Electronic Document Interchange (EDI), 61, 62, 80-83

Electronic Meeting Support, 284
electronic calendar, 264
electronic communication, 6, 39
electronic copyboards, 273
electronic customer support, 165
electronic data interchange, 167
electronic document processing, 212
electronic encryption, 112
electronic environment, 56, 94
electronic environments, alphanumeric, 94
electronic environments, multimedia, 94
electronic form(s), 83, 108, 212
electronic fund transfer (EFT), 349
electronic highlighters, 231
electronic interchange mechanisms, 215
electronic interchange of messages, 161
electronic key, 79
electronic Kiretsu, 326
electronic mail, 27
electronic mail systems, 160, 208
electronic meeting room(s), 46, 278
electronic meeting support systems, 275, 284
electronic meetings, 6, 207, 210, 259, 341, 353
electronic message, 167
electronic messaging, 160, 349
electronic messaging, scope, 171
electronic notepad, 270
electronic passwords, 216
electronic post-it notes, 266
electronic publishing, 29
electronic signature, 79
electronic voting, 280
electronic-pencil products, 240
electronic-supported conversations, 287
electronically supported meetings, 285
element, 238
EM, 259
embedded documents, 198
embedded object(s), 60, 93, 256
embedded parts, 86, 87
embedding objects, 92
employee empowerment, 186
empowering users, 221
empowering workers, 21, 22
EMS, 284
enabling technology, 1
encapsulated business process, 221
encapsulation, 90
enclosures, 12, 190
encrypted data, 200
encrypted digest, 203
encryption, 201, 226
encryption keys, 200, 201
Engelbart, Douglas, 6, 28, 260, 334
engine, 118
entering appointments into PIM, 264
entering data, 78
Enterprise Wide Group Scheduling, 284
enterprise, 39
enterprise re-engineering, 308
enterprise wide group scheduling, 267
enterprise, knowledge based, 261
enterprise-wide calendar connectivity, 264
enterprise-wide networking, 129
entity-relationship diagramming tools, 241

envelope fields, 178
environment, computer supported, 210
environment, computerized, 210
environment, homogeneous, 210
erector set economy, 338
ethernet, 17, 125
ethernet speed, 125
evaluation sample products, 165
event dispatcher, 89
evolution, computer technology, 336
evolutionary applications, 9
evolutionary reengineers, 337
eVote, 280
Excel, 60, 61
Excel for Windows, 91
exception handling capability, 221
exchange information between applications, 61
exchange of messages, 347
exchanging messages, 62
explicit role assignment, 312
exported process definition, 254
Extended Industry Standard Architecture (EISA), 137
Extended MAP, 175
Extended MAPI, 174
extensibility, 219, 234
extensible object-oriented environment, 241
extension, 65
extension mechanism, 66
extensions, 225

face-to-face meetings, 46, 280, 282
FAQs: Frequently Asked Questions, 205
fast ethernet, 155
fast packet cell switching technology, 134
FAX, 119
FAX printer paradigm, 157
FAX servers, 24, 121, 157, 159
FAX servers, LAN-based multi-user, 157
FAX servers, mainframe transaction processing, 157
FAX services, 157
FAX-board, 157
fax-mail, 279
FAX-modem, 157
FAXing, 222
faxmail, 279
FDDI, 47
FDDI-II, 155
feedback loop, 280
Fiber Distributed Data Interface (FDDI) standard, 123
fiber optic cable, 123
fiber-optic networks, 121
fiber-optic transmission systems, 134
field level security, 226
field or attribute values, 214
fields, 74
fields, 233
file format conversion, 61
file messages, 12
file names, 235

file server buffering, 138
file server caching, 138
file server, 23, 24, 121, 136, 154, 155, 159, 349
    dedicated, 136
    non-dedicated, 136
file storage, 257
FileNet, 211
filing cabinets, 78
filing messages, 192
filmmaking, 339
filtering, 194
filters, 194
final release, 253
fine grained, 116
fine grained client/server architecture, 118
first generation groupware, 10, 343
First-In-First-Out, 245
flat-bed scanner, 212
flattened organization, 221
flattening effect of groupware, 14, 22, 52
flow, 230
flow capabilities, 220
flow controls, 229
flow diagrams, 230
flow graph, 222
flow of information, 229
flow of work, 227
flow schematic, 230
flow system, 231
flowcharting tools, 241
flowcharts, 240
folder, 105–107, 191
Ford, Henry, 325, 339
foreign keys, 235
forgeries, 201
form, 253
form applications, 220
form attributes, 227
form based indexing, 214
form based indexing, automatic, 214
form based indexing, manual, 214
form based systems, 6
form design editing, 73
form designer, 72
form editor, within e-mail system, 198
form entry, 224
form flow, 80
form recognition technologies, 214
FormFlow, 72
Formflow, 220
form processing, 225, 226
forms, 4, 67, 68, 69, 70, 71–80, 162, 229
forms based groupware, 4
forms based packages, 71
forms, features:
    access rights, 79
    e-mail, 80
    electronic authorization, 79
    electronic signatures, 79
    front-ends to databases, 79
    workflow, 80
forms, processing, 12, 34, 70, 80
forms, recognition, 9
forms, routing, 212
forms, buttons, 74

forms:
    collections, 74–75
    fields, 73–74
    graphics, 74
    lists, 74–75
    records 75
    tables, 74–75
forms-based groupware, 340
forum, 205
forums, 204
forwarding cases, 230
forwarding primitives, 191
fragment integrity, 145
fragmentation of logical data objects, 145
fragments, 144
frame relay connection services, Private Virtual Circuits (PVC), 134
frame relay connection services, Switched Virtual Circuits (PVC), 134
frame relay service, 133
frames, 88
frames, video, 290
Free Time Search capability, 268
free agent entrepreneurial model, 339
front-end client applications, 178
front-end client GUI, 115
Frontier Systems, 280
FRS, 134
full content retrieval systems, 14
Fully-Sorted Scheduling, 156

game-playing, 288
Gantt charts, 249, 265
garbage-in-garbage-out, 210
gateways, 27 141 145 171 182
GDSS, 30
General Instruments, 302
general purpose architecture, 167
general purpose programming environment, 218
generalization, 144
generic operations, 236–237
Genie, 165
geographically displaced meetings, 277
GIGO, 210
global competition, 339
global conceptual schema, 144
global connectivity, 160
global economy, 339
global schema, 144
goal directed meeting, 276
granule of access privilege, 112
granule of security, 112
graph structured object spaces, 234, 235
Graphic Image Format (GIF), 181
graphical design tool, 256
graphical diagramming tools, 240
graphical editor, 214
graphical front-end, 243
graphical node-and-link editor, 254
graphical user interface(GUI), 220
graphical user interface constructs, 218
graphical user interface platforms, 114
graphical user interfaces, 10, 115, 231
graphical workflow definition, 240

graphical workflow editor, 214
graphics, 74
graphics objects, 197
graphics packages, 71
Greif, Irene, 29
Grohowski, 275
Group Decision Support Systems, 30 276
Group Support Systems, 275
Group Systems, 280
group authoring, 6 341
group calendaring, 6, 9, 39, 341
group calendaring systems, 354
group co-authoring, 39
group communication, 208
group coordination, 272
group decision support systems, 273
group dynamics, 6
group enabling, 6
group membership, 246
group schedulers, 266, 267
group-authoring, distributed, 46
group-authoring, face-to-face, 46
group-enabling applications, 67
    defined, 65
    objects, 4
groups, 246
GroupSystems, 274, 282
groupware, 1, 17, 275, 338
groupware:
    asynchronous, 259
    categories, 4
    challenges, 50
    collections, address books, 107
    concept of, 259
    corporate databases, 106
    database, 171
    document-based, 4
    failure, 14
    first generation, 9
    forms based, 4
    high-volume data, 4
    history, 23
    information management, 4
    information types, 113
    organization communications, 6
    resistance to, 52–53
    roots, 23
    second generation, 10
    small team, 39
    system documents, 113
    taxonomy, 11
    track exchanges, 107
    transaction based, 4
GROVE, 312
Grove, Andy, 326
Grudin, Jonathan, 313
GSS (Group Support Systems), 205
guaranteed continuous rate, 154
guest availability, 271
GUI (Graphical User Interface), 162
Gupta Technologies, 78

H.32P, 294
hackers, 200
handle, 152

handwriting recognition, 9
hard interrupt, 20
hardware infrastructure, 301–307
Harvard Business School, 23
hash value, 203
HDTV, 294
heterogeneity, 145, 210
heterogeneous distributed database, 25, 144
heterogeneous e-mail systems, 171
Hewlett-Packard, 86, 173
hierarchical change management, 150
hierarchical containment storage structure, 84
hierarchical structured storage, 93
high level predicate, 231
high performance DBMSs, 341
high value production, 223
high volume transaction based applications, 4
high-end scan station, 213
high-tech conference rooms, 274
high-volume data, groupware, 4
hiring process, 250
hollow corporation, 325–327
home pages, 100
home shopping, 154
homogeneous distributed databases, 25
homogeneous environment, 210
Hopland, Jan, 321
horizontal applications, 249
host-based applications, 267
hot linking with other data and applications, 231
hot links, 100, 165
html (hyper text markup language), 61, 165
human communication theories, 219
human considerations, 6 342
human factor, 308–333, 341
human intelligence, 342
human interaction, 1, 9, 342
human issues, 259
human resources, how enterprises aggregate, 339
human systems, 334
human-computer interaction, 1, 33, 339
human-human interaction, 1, 3, 339
HyperCard, 103
hyperlinks, 28, 100
hypermedia, 27, 57, 98–105, 114, 165, 346
    applications, 100
    document views, 100
    glossary, 99
    navigation, 98
    node anchors, 98
hypermedia authoring systems, 100
hypermedia document model, 32
hypermedia document systems, 100
hypermedia document, 57, 100, 103, 105
    link types, 102
    node types, 100
        destination, 102
        source, 102
hypermedia linking strategies, 102, 103
hypermedia nodes, 103
hypermedia processing, 103
hypermedia publishing system, 165

Index

hypermedia system, 311, 331
 containers, 105
 documents on networked environments, 103
 iterative authoring, 105
 linking concepts, parts, and text, 103
 tracing knowledge, 103
hypermedia views, 102
hypertext, 27, 101, 103, 330
hypertext markup language, 61
HyTime, 61

IBM, 59, 78, 84, 86, 90, 120, 127, 128, 133, 137, 163, 176, 177, 186, 219, 306
IBM Logical Unit 6.2, 128
IBM's MWAVE, 306
IDC/Avante Technology Inc., 223
idea buckets, 281
idea evaluation, 282
ideal workflow implementation, 221
identification of technologies, 11
identifier keys, 234
identify addresses by attributes, 193
identity, 235
identity, databases, 234
identity, programming languages, 234
IDraw, 310
image documents, 198
image editing tools, 71
image editors, 70–71
imaging applications, 215
imaging industry, 214
imaging peripherals, 224
imaging systems, 78
implementation primitives, 226
implementing a corporate database, 64
import and export, 254
imposition of belief, 219
in-place editing, 59, 60, 88
incoming FAX, 157
Indeo, 292
indexed manually, 214
indexing, 78, 140, 141, 213
indexing stations, 78
Indigo Magic, 295
industrial paradigm, 341
industrial revolution, 339
industries, fastest growing industries, 340
Industry Standard Architecture (ISA), 137
industry analyst, 252
information domains, 31
Information Model, 31
information, 263, 281
information age, 30
information and task flow, 207
information chunks, 312
information consumption, 58
information flow, 7, 214, 230
information management, 71
information management groupware, 4
information model, 31–33, 214, 227, 240, 241
information objects, 238
information overload, 40
information preparation, 58

information processor, 341
information servers, 160
information sets, 263
information sharing, 111
information sources, 40
information superhighway, 121
information technology, 9, 231, 339
information ticklers, 266
information types, 41
information warehouses, 63, 348
information, as environment, 30
information, substance of our collaboration, 338
informational meetings, 285
Informix, 78
infra-red technologies, 121
inheritance, 102, 233, 234, 237
inheritance class hierarchies, 234
inheriting representation, 234
initialize video stream, 156
inks, 246
InPerson Desktop Conferencing, 295
InPerson Shared Shelf, 295
InPerson Whiteboard, 295
InPerson, Silicon Graphics, 295
instance structure and operations, 243
instance variables, 233, 234, 234
instances, 230, 310
instances of workflow classes, 235
Integrated Services Digital Network (ISDN), 135, 290
integrity constraints, 139, 144
Intel (Corp.), 137, 302, 306, 326
intelligence, 10
intelligent address books, 184
intelligent agents, 10
intelligent e-mail, 203
intelligent groups, 184
intelligent groupware systems, 10
intelligent office, 146
intelligent office worker, 195
intelligent workflow systems, 221
intensity adjustment, 212
Inter Process Communication Environment, 181
inter-application information exchange, 187
inter-application messaging, 171
inter-organization communication, 171
inter-transaction concurrency, 146
interaction mechanisms, routing, 204
Interactive Multimedia Association (IMA), 306
interactive communications, 304
interactive editors, 286
interactive TVs, 122
interchange formats, 61
interchange information case data, 254
interconnecting e-mail systems, 182
interface, 231, 235
interfaces, database, 172
internal communication, 164
International Standards Organization (ISO), 125, 179, 293
International Telecommunications Union, 294

International Telephone and Telegraph Consultive Committee (CCITT), 135, 179
Internet, 39, 163, 165, 180, 200, 205, 297, 347
Internet address, 164
Internet message, 180
Internet, domain, 164
Internet, local part, 164
Internet, mailbox name, 164
Internetwork Packet Exchange, 127
internetworked architecture, 211
internetworked client/server systems, 200
internetworked LAN architecture, 141
internetworked LANs, 167
internetworked WANs, 167
internetworked workstations, 340
internetworking, 161
internetworking technologies, 17
interoperability, 122, 171, 182, 188
interoperability between applications, 253
interoperability between workflow products, 258
interoperability platform, 83
interoperability platforms, 225
interoperability specification, 91
interoperability standards, 120, 219, 231
interoperability through message exchange, 253
interpretability, 31
InterViews, 310
intra-organization communication, 171
intruders, 200
investment transaction workflows, 253
IP, 128, 134
IPCE, 181
IPX, 127
IRIX, 295
ISDN 2B+D interface, 135
ISDN, 135, 155, 181, 290
ISDN Basic Rate Interface (BRI), 135
ISDN Primary Rate Interface (PRI), 136
ISDN, defined, 135
ISIS toolkit, 310
ISO standard, 61
ISO/IEC Draft International Standard, 293
issues, time-critical, 277
iteration, 249
ITU Study Group 15, 294

Johnson-Lenz, Peter and Trudy, 23
Joint Photographic Experts Group, 293
JPEG, 61

key exception points, 221
key, encryption, 200
key, private, 200
key, public, 200
Keyfile, 211
killer multimedia application, 303
kiosk, 49, 344
Kiretsu, 326
knowledge base, 205, 251
knowledge business, 341
knowledge industries, 308

Index

knowledge worker(s), 221, 222, 223, 225, 263, 341
knowledge-based workflow, 223
knowledgebases, 21, 42, 43, 331

LAMBDA.MOO, 330
LAN (Local Area Networks), 15, 122, 160, 343
  bandwidth, 122
  bottlenecks, 122
  performance, 122
  reliability, 122
  response time, 122
LAN based FAX server, 157
LAN based schedulers, 268
LAN Manager, 129
LAN topologies, 123, 124, 125
LAN-to-LAN bridges, 158
LAN-to-LAN connections, 160
LAN-to-WAN bridges, 158
LAN-to-WAN connections, 160
Langham, Don, 330
language independence, 90
LANMAN, 130
LANs, 116
Laser Data, 211
launchers, 60, 345
launching, 61
launching an application, 59
Lawrence Berkley Labs, 309
legal contracts, 201
Lehtman, Harvey, 260
level of groupware functionality, 12
level of programming, 217
librarian, 252
library model, 63
light emitting diodes (LEDs), 123
limited set of primitive, 219
linked components, 103
linked nodes, 103
linked object, 93
linking, 88, 93, 103
linking case data, 256
links, 105, 229, 230, 331
links of active workflows, 243
lists, 74–75
lists, contact, 265
LLC, 134
loading part handlers, 89
Local Area Networks, *see also* LAN, 16, 121, 122, 210
local time, 188
local users, 211
locality, 155
locate node authors, 104
location independence, 92
location transparency, 109
lock and check-out, 231
locking, 152, 191, 226
locks, 145
logical databases, 141
login ID, 171
looney tunes, 265
Lotus, 50, 123, 171, 176
Lotus Notes, 49, 50, 132, 205, 332

LotusVIM, 171
low end scan station, 212
LU6.2, 128

MAC, 134
Macintosh Apple, 103, 125, 129, 161, 174, 176, 186, 240, 297, 303, 314
Mackay, Harvey, 264
MacProject, 225, 249
magnetic disk drives, 156
mail address syntax, 181
mail enabled applications, 162, 187, 198
mail enabled OpenDoc documents, 89
mail enabling, 187
mail engine, 172
mail transport protocols, 187
mail-enabled applications, 167
mailbox management, 172
mailboxes, 171
mainframe, 336, 24
MAN, 134
manage objects, 266
managers, personal information, 264
manual indexing, 78
many-to-many assignment of tasks, 245
many-to-one, 245
map, discussion, 332
MAPI, 171, 172
MAPI architecture, 172
MAPI client applications, 174
MAPI dynamic-link libraries (DLLs), 172
MAPI spooler, 172
MAPI-SPI compliant mail engine, 172
mapping systems, 103
market size, 2
marking ink, 288
massaging transport protocol, 210
master database, 148
master/slave model, 148
maximum number of streams, 156
MCI Communications, 186
MCI Mail, 165
MediaMail, 295
medium range scan station, 213
Meeting Maker, 269
Meeting Manager, 280
Meeting Room, 282
meeting categories, 273
meeting facilitation, 276
meeting facilitator, 276
meeting notification message, 271
meeting room support, 273
meeting rooms, 344
meeting tools, 282
meeting, distributed, 344
meeting, goal directed, 276
meeting, information-sharing, 277
meetings, 6, 261
  anonymous, 281
  asynchronous, 261
  coincident, 261
  colocal, 273
  colocated, 273
  cost of attending, 264
  distributed, 274, 282

  electronic, 259
  electronically enhanced, 259
  electronically supported, 285
  face-to-face, 46, 280
  face-to-face meetings, 39
  geographically displaced, 277
  information centered, 281
  informational, 285
  minutes, 41
  real time, 274
  same time/different place, 277
  scheduling of, 264
  status, 264
  synchronous, 259, 261, 273, 276
  synchronous and local, 263
  synchronous and remote, 277
memex, 28
memo fields, 184
memory, associative, 331
memory, organization, 331-333
Message Application Programming Interface, 172
Message Handling Service, 27
Message Handling System (MHS), 179
Message Store (MS), 179
Message Transfer Agent (MTA), 179
Message Transfer System (MTS), 179
Message User Agent (MUA), 179
message aware application, 173
message based workflow, 220
  enhanced e-mail, 220
  mail-enabled, 220
message containers, 177
message content, 188
message database, 171
message database handling services, 171
message enabled application, 173
message integrity, 201
message response hierarchy, 205
message spooler, 172
message structure, 188
message thread, 162
message threads, 162, 203, 204, 205
message type(s), 188, 198
message, meeting notification, 271
message-based workgroup application, 173
messager handling standards, MHS, 27
messager handling standards, X.400, 27
messages, active, 192
messaging API, 172
messaging based workflow, 162
messaging between applications, 171
messaging databases, 177, 207
messaging servers, 121, 158, 159, 160
messaging services, 34
messaging standard, 179
messaging system, 111
messaging transport, 253
messaging transport mechanism, 111
meta activities, 264
meta information, 254
Metafiles, 176
methods, 233
metropolitan area networks, 121
MHS, 27, 177, 196, 240
MHS file, 178

MHS mailbox, 178
MHS server, 177, 178
MHS standard, 178
MHS-compliant application, 178
Micro channel Architecture (MCA), 137
microcode, 213
microprocessor, 302
Microsoft, 24, 59, 61, 69, 84, 85, 90, 92, 114, 120, 129, 171, 172, 177, 205, 219, 301, 302
Microsoft At Work, 279
Microsoft AVI format, 96
Microsoft Corp, 279
Microsoft LAN Manager, 129, 163
Microsoft Mail, 91, 163, 186
Microsoft MAPI, 171
Microsoft Office, 60, 91
Microsoft Project, 225, 249
Microsoft WAV, 95
Microsoft Windows, 174
Microsoft Windows Messaging System (WMS), 172
Microsoft Windows print subsystem, 172
Microsoft Word, 61, 69, 190
microwave, 121
MIDI, 95
mind set, 261
minicomputers, 24
mission critical data, 200
mission critical documents, 193
mixed-media conferencing, 303
mixed-media modems, 303
mobile computing, 160
model, information, 31
modeling primitive, 235
models, 120, 148
models, check-out/check-in, 34
models, collaboration, 11
models, database, 32
models, object representation, 11
models, routing, 34
models, client/server, 34
modem connections, 160
monikers, 93
monitoring, 243
monitoring the progress of workflows, 248
Morton, Scott, 276
Motion JPEG, 292
Motion Picture Experts Group (MPEG), 181
movement of information, 209
movies on-demand, 154, 156
MPEG, 61, 292
MPEG I, 293
MPEG II, 294
MPEG III, 294
MPEG IV, 292, 294
MS-DOS, 174
Mscrawl, 309, 310
muddlers, 329
MUDS, 329
Multi User Dungeons, 329
multi-gateway switches, 182
multi-part documents, 88
multi-platform interface, 174
multi-threaded operating systems, 94

multi-user databases, 49
multi-user drawing editor, 310
multi-user editor, 312
multi-user FAX services, 158
multi-user text editor, 314
multicast protocol, 310
MultiDraw, 309, 310
multiMedia objects, 94
multimedia, 10, 12, 33, 196, 206, 231
multimedia applications, 71
multimedia authoring tools, 58
multimedia conferencing, 303
multimedia data types, 94, 95, 96, 98, 193
multimedia element, 197
multimedia information, 212
multimedia object editors, 71
multimedia objects, 94
Multiple User Dimensions, 329
multiple databases, 141
multiple documents, 231
multiple parent objects, 235
multiple servers, 17
Multipurpose Intenet Mail Extension (MIME), 181
multitasking DSP operating systems, 306
Musical Instrument Digital Interface, 95
mutual consistency, 146
mutual exclusion primitive, 156
MWAVE, 306

name specification, 177
National Association of Credit Management, 80
National Center for Supercomputing Applications, 299
National Science Foundation, 298
navigation tools, 272
NCSA Collage, 299-301
NCSA Mosaic, 165
near-line storage, 156
Nelson, Ted, 29, 330
nested workflows, 253
NET BIOS, 128
Net frame, 136
Netcom, 164, 165
netcruising software, 165
NetWare, 24, 129
NetWare bindery, 170
Network Basic Input/Output System, 128
network access control, 216
network architecture, 121
network control center, 48
network directory services, 170
network nodes, 121
network of commitments, 219
network operating system, 128, 210
    directory, 170
network operating system functions, 128
network packets, 156
networked DLLs, 93
networked project manager, 231
networking, 10, 121
networking protocols, 125
networks, 121
neural networked pattern recognition, 9

newsgroups, 39
NewsNet, 204
NeXT, 86, 121
next generation e-mail application, 220
next generation e-mail systems, 193, 226
next generation electronic mail systems, 193
next generation global enterprises, 219
next generation workflow system, 258
next-generation CPUs, 301
Nippon Electric Corporation (NEC), 289
NLM (Nether Load Modules), 138
NLM (NetWare Loadable Module), 177
NLS, 29
node and link representation, 101
nodes and links, 240
nodes of active workflows, 243
non-preemptive co-routines, 156
non-real time standard file system interface, 157
North American Directory Forum (NADF), 186
NOS, 128
note attachments, 231
note part, 176
notepads, 266
Notes, 177, 206
notification and receipt, 193
notification, rules, 203
notifications, 12, 34, 49, 191, 199, 203, 226, 243, 247, 252
notifiers, 270
Novell, 24, 27, 120, 127, 138, 140, 169, 173, 176, 177, 182, 205
Novell bindery, 131
Novell File Server, 177
Novell NetWare, 129, 163, 182
Novell NetWare directory structures, 170
nudger alarm, 267
Nunamaker, Jay, 280

Object Broker specification, 86
Object Linking and Embedding, 172
Object Representation vs Collaboration, 33
Object Request Broker standard, 121
object attribute, equation, 65
object attributes, 65, 114
object embedding, 90
object granule, 152
object handle, 153
object identity, 233, 234, 235, 238
object interaction, 119
object levels, 152
object linking, 90, 93
object orientation, 63–68, 114, 118, 218, 231, 233
object orientation, equation, 233
object representation, 30
object representation models, 11
object sharing, concurrent, 108
object sharing, referential, 108
object space, 111
object:
    defined, 57
    equation, 63, 233

extension, 65
specialization, 65
structure, 57, 64
object-orientation, 10
object-oriented address books, 183
object-oriented analysis, 240
object-oriented analysis and design tools, 227 241
object-oriented databases, 111, 145, 204
object-oriented DBMS, 257
object-oriented design, 240
object-oriented drawing program, 309
object-oriented environments, 209
object-oriented language, 235
object-oriented programming, 90
object-oriented programming languages, 233
object-oriented system, 235
object-oriented workflow, 231, 235, 238
object-relational databases, 145
object-server, 140
objects, 55, 63 118, 121 234
  annotations, 239
  cabinets, 191
  of collaboration, 31 57 345
  folders. 191
  group-enabling, 4
ObjectVision, 73
OCR, 119 214, 223
OCR error rate, 158
OCR processing, 214
ODBC, 172
off-line, work, 271
Office Automation, 113
office, 55 71
office environment, 212, 221
office repository, 153
office workers, 55, 214
Office.IQ, 198 214
OLE 2, 32, 59, 60, 84, 86, 90–94, 114, 120, 197, 198, 219, 225, 231, 240, 346
OLE 2, distributed objects, 93
OLE 2 storage model, 92
OLE, 172
OLE DLLs, 93
OMG (Object Management Group), 84, 86, 121
OMI (Object Messaging Interface), 176
On Technology, 269
oN Line System (NLS), 6, 29, 260
on-line banking, 165
on-line services, 164
on-line shopping, 165
Open Scripting Architecture, 89
Open Systems Interconnection Reference Model (OSI), 125
open architecture, 235
OpenDoc, 32, 59, 60, 84, 86–90, 114, 120, 197, 198, 219, 226, 231, 240, 346
OpenDoc architecture, 87, 88
OpenDoc container document, 239
OpenDoc run-time, 89
OpenDoc storage, 88
OpenDoc user interface, 88
operating system messages, 167
operating systems, 57
operations, 233

Optical Character Recognition (OCR), 9, 119, 157, 214, 223
optical disk servers, 24
optical jukebox, 155, 156
optical storage jukeboxes, 156
Oracle, 24, 78
organization amnesia, 332
organization character, 42
organization communications groupware, 6
organization memory, 6, 11, 162, 331–333, 350, 356
organization structure, flattened, 7
organizational communications groupware, 341
organizational intelligence, 9, 342
organizational memory, 10, 30, 41–43, 207
organizational modeling, 6
organizational structure, traditional, 7
organizational theory, 219, 223
organizing messages, 191
origin authentication, 201
OSI layers, 126, 127
OSI model, 127, 128
OSI presentation layers, 127
OS/2, 108, 129, 174
OS/2 Server, 24
outsourcing, 337
override, 234
ownership, 102

Pacific Bell, 186
pager alarms, 265
Palo Alto Research Center, 260
paper-based business processes, 215
paper-based information flow, 212
paperless office, 71
parallel routing, 221
parametric coders, 305
parent, 108
part boundary, 87
part display, 87
part editors, 88
part handlers, 87, 88
part viewers, 88
participatory design (PD), 287
partnering, 321
parts, 86, 105
password key, 112
password protection, 130, 269
passwords, 130, 171
pattern recognition, 2, 9, 10
Pave, Cal, 23
PC, 161
PC-LAN, 128
PCS 100, 296
PCX, 61
PCX format for FAX, 176
PD, 287
peer-to-peer, 267
peer-to-peer architectures, 121
peer-to-peer PHY, 134
Pentium, 307
performance barrier, 155
performance bottlenecks, 121
performance gains, 12

period of turbulence, 338
persistence and concurrency control capabilities, 257
persistent information about users, 171
persistent reference, 88
persistent space, 318
persistent storage, 88, 89
personal assistant, 279
personal computer, 260
personal computer revolution, 260
personal database management, 69
personal databases, 69
personal digital assistants, 122
personal information managers, 211, 264, 354
personal management support tools, 272
personal privacy, 269
personal time manager, 264
Pert charts, 249
philosophy of language, 320
photo-detector, 123
physical database design, 144
physical databases, 141
PICT, 176
Picturephone, 289
PictureTel Corporation, 296
PictureTel LIVE, 296
PictureTel System 1000, 296
PIM features, 264, 265, 266
PIMS, 264
pixels, 95
place, defined for groupware, 45
place, physical location, 45
place, virtual location, 45
plaintext, 200
platform, client, 210
platform, server, 210
play back, 197
PLV, 292
point-and-click GUI, 205
pointers, 235
points of congestion, 122
polling, 125, 167
portable electronic document exchange standards, 346
portable electronic exchange standards, 345
portable format, 61
Portal, 164
ports, 179
post offices, 267
post-it notes, electronic, 266
posting upgrades, 165
POTS bandwidth limitation, 304
PowerPC, 301, 307
PowerPoint, 69, 91
PPP (Point-to-Point-Protocol), 164, 165
PR (Purchase Requisition) form, 251
predecessor routes, 248
predefined notification primitives, 203
predicate expressions, 231, 247
predicates, 194, 247
predictable response time, 156
PREP, 312
preplanning, 4
prescribed time frame, 248
presentation packages, 69

prevalence, 14
PRI, 136
printer servers, 24
printing support, 266
priorities, 12
private database, 193
private key, 200, 203
private windows, 314, 315
privilege, 226
privileges, 38
PRM: Privacy Enhanced Mail, 200
PRMD (Private Management Domain), 180
Pro Share, 298
problem domain, 227
problem solving in real time, 260
process, 230, 235
process definition, 230, 235, 236, 243
process facilitation, 282
process instances, 235, 236
  activated, 230
  named, 230
  tracked, 230
process templates, 254
process work, 230
processing checked-out objects, 231
processing work, 230
Prodigy, 165
product space, 11
production based workflow, 223
production based workflow systems, 224
production workflow, 223, 249
production workflow subsystems, 4
productivity gains, 10
Professional Office System (PROFS), 163
programmatic object, 88
programming language, 218, 231
project management, 247, 249
project management systems, 225
project manager scheduler, 267
properties, 57, 64
propogation delay, 267
proprietary DBMS, 220
Protocol Data Unit (PDU), 134
protocol, 233
protocol, massaging transport, 210
proxy feature, 270
public address book, 182
public communication, 164
public communications service providers, 164
public e-mail service, 164
public key, 200, 203
public key cryptography, 203
publishing codec, 293
pulse code modulation, 291
purchase requisitions, 251
purchasing, 252
purge operation, 150

QBE, 75
quality assurance databases, 253
queries, 231
Query By Example, 75
query, 71

query language, 75
query optimization, 24
query optimizers, 140
query translation, 145
query-by-forms, 71, 75
queue of activities, 254
queue tasks, 245
queue worker, 245
QuickCam, 297
QuickMail, 163
Quicktime, 96, 292, 298
Quilt, 311, 313

R* (ref), 142
RAM-based DSP, 303, 307
range of programming, 218
read permission, 239
real time communication link, 267
real time logic, 156
real time meetings, 274
Real-Time E-Conferencing, 295
real-time interactive communications, 304
real-time scheduler, 156
real-time stream API function calls, load video, 156
real-time tools, 260
receipt notification, 199
receipts, 199
receivers, 229
receivers, Blind Carbon Copy, 189
receivers, Carbon Copy, 189
receiving messages, 177
recognition, forms, 9
recognition, handwriting, 9
recognition, neural networked pattern, 9
recognition, optical character, 9
recognition, pattern, 9
record retrieval, 4
records, 75
recovery from crashes, 122
redundancy, 267
reengineered corporation, 223
reengineering, 7, 21, 321, 209
reengineering industry, 327–329
referential sharing, 108, 191
referential sharing of objects, 238
relational databases, 115, 142
relational DBMS, 257
relationship links, 102
reminders, 272
remote users, 211
rendezvous, 248
rendezvous point, 248
replica consistency, 145
replicated databases, 148
replication of logical data objects, 145
reporting, 243
reports, 69
representation, 31, 57, 234
rerouting, 247
research, 4, 252, 253
resistance to change, 6
resistance to groupware, 52-53
resistance, CEO, 7
resource tables, 249

restricting representation of existing classes, 234
resume tracking, 250
retraction, 247
reusability, 234
reusable components, 234
revolutionary infopreneurs, 337
RFCs, 181, 263
Rich Text Format, 61
rich message types, 193
rigidity, 219
RLE, 291
role assignment, 247
role attribute, 246
role restrictive CSCW, 314
roles, 246
roles, explicit, 314
Roman empire, 338
root part, 86
rotational latency time, 156
routing, 6, 34, 49, 67, 89, 218, 230
routing based on content, 222
routing information, 191
routing mechanism, 240
routing model, 34, 49
routing of forms, 225
routing of information, 49
RTF, 61
RTV, 292
rule support, 193
rules, 194, 206, 247
rules in workflow, 247
run length encoding, 291
run-time environment, 254
runtime storage, 89

Saffo, Paul, 329
same time/different places, 44, 47–48, 273
same time/different places interactions, 277
same time/same place, 30, 44, 46, 273
satellite connectivity, 121
satellite transmission, ATM transfer rates, 17
scalability, 255
scan station, 78, 212
  high-end, 213
  low end, 212
  medium range, 213
Scandinavian approach, 287
scanned documents, 214
scanned forms, 76
scanned images, 212, 223
scanner control card, 213
scanner servers, 24
scanner, flat-bed, 212
scanning, 213
schedules, 249
scheduling, 225, 263
scheduling a meeting, 207, 271–272
scheduling features:
  alarms, 270
  archive, 268
  download schedule, 269
  export schedules, 269
  import schedules, 269
  lists, 270

Index   373

multiple views, 268
notes, 270
notifiers, 270
proxy, 270
scheduling of meetings, 264
scheduling software, 262, 284
scheduling systems, 208
scheduling tools, 264
schema manager, 141
schema translation, 145
Scientific Atlanta, 302
scope of collaboration, 211
script, 89
scripting environment, 256
scripting language, 89, 214
scripting language systems, 218
scripting language, 4th generation, 256
scripting languages, 226
SCSI disk arrays, 155
SCSI overhead, 156
SCSI raid, 156
search capability, 69
second generation groupware, 344
security, 78, 122, 130, 193, 200, 226, 269
security control, 38
security database, 131
security levels, 231
security service, 201
security service, confidentiality, 201
seek time, 156
semaphores, 137, 267
semi-synchronous systems, 318
senders, 229
sending messages, 234
Sequenced Packet exchange, 128
sequential delivery, 263
server based workflow, 220
server operating systems, 210
server platform, 210
servers, 118, 121, 122
service, 118
service vendors, 338
services, messaging, 34
session level connection, 128
session level protocol, 128
set of primitives, 218
set-top box, 302
settlement of the trade, 253
SGML (Standard Generalized Markup Language), 61, 346
share information, 160
share resources, 160
shared authoring, 313
shared calendering, 208
shared data, 160
shared document, 315
shared e-mail databases, 193
shared environment, 272
shared feedback, 314, 316, 317, 318, 319
shared file, 267
shared information spaces, 30
shared resources, 156
shared space, 287, 314
shared windows, 314, 315
shared workspace, 309, 315–318
shared workspace program, 310

sharing, 2
sharing, code, 234
sharing, structure, 234
Sharkware, 264
shielded twisted pair, 123
Show Me, 298
ShrEdit, 314
Sigma, 211
sign-off, 12, 216
signature, 216
Silicon Graphics, 278, 295
Simple MAPI, 174
simple administrative workflow, 249
simple elements, 56
Singapore, 337
single application objects, 56
single frame accuracy, 293
single-site applications, 144, 145
sinks, 229
Sloan, Alfred P., 325
SLIP (Serial Link Interface Protocol), 164, 165
slope, 12
small teams, 210
Smalltalk, 231
smart cable converter, 302
smart compound documents, 231
smart container, 231
smart e-mail, 193, 210
smart e-mail applications, 193
smart e-mail system, 199
smart folders, 231
smart forms, 175
smart hubs, 155
smart mail, 206
smart servers, 302
smart telephones, 122
SMDS, 134, 155
SMDS protocol, 134
SMDS router, 134
SMF, 177
SMPTE time code, 287
SMTP (Simple Mail Transport Protocol), 178, 180, 181
SMU Decision Room, 30, 276
sneaker net, 136
snooze interval, 270
soft interrupt, 20, 166
software system, 210
software, calendaring, 262
software, component based, 240
software, scheduling, 262, 284
software, specialized, 240
Soleri, Paolo, 336
SOM (System Object Model), 84, 120
SOM/DSOM, 85
SONET, 134
SONET signal, 134
SONET transmission standard, 134
sorting, on date received, 194
sorting, on priority, 194
sorting, on sender, 194, 194
sorting, on subject, 194
source code, 231
source coders, 305
sources, 229

Southeast Asia, 337
space overhead for still images, 95
space, common, 287
space, shared, 287
spatial database, 103
specialization, 65
specialization, 237
specializing classes, 234
speech acts, 319
speech compression, 304
speech-act theory, 320
SPI compliant back-end service, 172
SpigotVDIG, 298
spreadsheet, 69
SPX, 128
SQL, 75, 140
SQL Server, 24, 29
SRI, 260
Stakeholder Identification, 280
Standard Generalized Markup Language, 61
Standard Image File, 293
standard application programming interfaces (APIs), 171
standard data format for forms, 83
standard DSP API, 307
standard format, 254
standard optical interface, 134
standard, X.500, 170, 186
standardization effort(s), 240, 253, 254
standardization for workflow, 253
standardized workflow systems, 258
standards, 120, 253
standards for interoperability, 254
standards to store and retrieve, 254
standards:
    CALS, 61
    CORBA, 86
    database, 172
    e-mail, 171
    EDI, 61
    interoperability, OLE 2, 32
    interoperability, OpenDoc, 32
    ISO, 61
    portable electronic document exchange, 60
    SGML, 61
    X.400 API Association (XAPIA), 174
Stanford Research Institute (SRI), 6, 29, 260
Stanford University, 305
state information, 88
state of an object, 248
state transitions, 235
state-transition diagram, 320
states, 237, 247
static diagram, 240
static military model, 339
statistics, 243
status, 243, 249
status and progress reports, 254
status information, 240
status meeting, 264
status of workflow, 42
steps, 230
storage, 168

storage capacity, 154, 155
storage manager DBMS module, 141
storage representation standard, 84
store and forward, 171, 267
store and forward strategy, 169
store-and-forward linking, 187
storing a part, 87
strategic business evaluation, 209
stream formats, 176
StreetTalk, 170
structural, 235
structure, components, 57
structure, 57, 114, 233, 345
structure of content, 64
structure of objects, 114
structure sharing, 234
structure, document, 61
structure, forms, 70
structure, object, 64
Structured Query Language, 75
structured database, 163
structured information, 214
structured storage, 92
sub-components, 256
sub-object, 235
sub-workflows, 239
subclass, 234
submission authentication, 263
subworkflows, 253
SUN, 86
Sun Microsystems, 121, 298
super servers, 136
superclass, 234
superdocument, 263
superset, 234
superset of notification in e-mail systems, 247
suspense, 248
Switched multi-megabit data service, (SMDS), 132, 134
switches, 182
switching, cell, 17
switching, packet, 17
Sybase, 78
Sybase SQL Server, 130
symmetric cryptoalgorithms, 200
symmetric multi-processing, 129
synchronization, 264
synchronize activities, 262
synchronizing network directories, 184
Synchronous Optical Network (SONET), 134
Synchronous Payload Envelope (SPE), 135
Synchronous Transport Signal 1 (STS-1), 134
Synchronous Transport Signal frame, 135
synchronous, 11
synchronous and co-incident, 44, 46
synchronous and displaced, 44, 47-48
synchronous editor, 312
synchronous group-authoring, distributed, 46
synchronous group-authoring, face-to-face, 46
synchronous local meetings, 263, 272
synchronous meetings, 259, 261, 273

synchronous meetings, 355
synchronous text editor, 314
synchronous, multi-user text editor, 314
syntax, e-mail address, 185
syntax, mail address, 181
System 7, 57, 108
System Network Architecture (SNA), 127
System Object Model (SOM), 84, 90
system, asynchronous collaborative authoring, 311
system, database management, 210
system, network operating, 210
system, server operating, 210
system, software, 210
systems:
    asynchronous groupware, 259
    database management, 4
    document imaging, 4, 211
    electronic mail, 208
    human, 334
    hypermedia, 311, 331
    semi-synchronous, 318
    timesharing, 260
    tool, 334

T1 transmission rates, 17, 131, 134
T2 transmission rates, 17, 131
T3 transmission rates, 17, 131
table, 75
tables, 74–75
tagged, objects can be, 266
Taligent, 219
targets, 229
task, 55
task assignment and retraction, 247
task group, 264
task lists, 266
task processing capability, 221
task queues, 245
task teams, 207
tasks, 235
tax preparation, 70
taxonomies, 4
taxonomies for groupware, 340
taxonomies of workflow systems, 214
TCP, 128
TCP/IP, 128, 165
TCP/IP based network, 165
team, 55
team rooms, 273
team work, 30
teams, 7
teams, 160
teamwork, 1
technical architect, 231
technical section, 231
technology mapping, 11
telecommunications, 277
telecommunications, impact of, 47
telecommuters, 51
teleconferencing, 277, 303
Telephone Application Program Interface (TAPI), 302
telephone, impact of, 47
term frequency calculation, 214

terminal adapters (TAs), 136
text editor, synchronous and multi-user, 314
text messages, 12
textual representation, 254
thread context switch, 156
threading, 204
threads, 39, 156
tickler alarm, 267
tickler files, 264
ticklers, 263
TIFF, 61
tight coupling, 145
time and place dimensions, 344
time critical issues, 243
time lines, 249
time management, 263, 284
time management systems, 249
time management tools, 264
time manager, personal, 264
time stamps, 162
time-critical information, 243
time/place interactions, 11, 44–50
TimeLine, 249
timesharing, 16
timesharing systems, 260
timing constraint, 248
to-do list, 264, 270
to-do list window, 272
token, 125
token passing, 125
token ring, 125
tool systems, 334
tool, Agenda, 280
tools that empower individuals, 209
tools, 262
    brainstorming, 280
    computer based instructional, 263
    decision support, 262
    decision support, 280
    diagramming, 241
    document conferencing, 262
    document management, 208
    entity-relationship diagramming tools, 241
    flowcharting, 241
    idea consolidation tools, 280
    issue evaluation, 280
    meeting, 282
    object-oriented analysis and design, 241
    personal management, 272
    real-time, 260
    scheduling, 264
    stakeholder Identification, 280
    task automation, 7
    time management, 264
    voting, 280
top-down distribution, 144
topical index, 99
topics, 204
topics databases, 39, 205, 206
total isolation, 146
total quality management, 253
trace, 162
traces, 107
tracking, 226, 243, 263
trade posting, 253

Index ■ 375

trading, 252
trading transaction, 253
trails, 107
transaction based groupware, 4
transaction based processing, 4, 341
transaction based workflow, 223
transaction coordinator, 147
transaction management, 111
transaction workflow, 223
transaction-based groupware, 340
transactions, 138
Transmission Control Protocol/Internet Protocol, 128
transmission medium, 121
transmission rates, T1, 17
transmission rates, T2, 17
transmission rates, T3, 17
transmission speed, 16
transport engines, 220
transport mechanism, 177
transport mechanism, 240
transport module, 177
transport services, 168, 169, 177
Transportation Data Coordinating Committee, 80
traversed, 246
tree-structured documents, 312
triggers in relational databases, 248
Tru Motion, 292
turnaround time, 251
TV cabling, 121
two phase commit, 147
two phase commit protocol, 147
type of notification, 199
type of participant, 229

U.S. Postal Service, 186
UDP, 310
ultimate system for collaborative work, 340
unary predicates, 194
understanding, context of, 341
uniform interface, 171
unique identifier, 177
University of Arizona, 274, 280
University of Arizona's College of Business and Public Administration, 274
University of Essex, 329
UNIX, 108, 125, 129, 161, 164, 165, 174, 182
UNIX workstations, 240
unshielded twisted pair, 123
user interface standard, 84
user interfaces, 10
user perception, 235
user specified names, 234
users, 130
using generic group scheduler, 271
UUNET, 164

v-mail, 278
V.34, 294
Van Jacobsen, 309
VAR, 235
VCOS operating system, 306

Vendor Independent Messaging, 176
Ventana Corporation, 274, 280
version control, 78
version management tree, 150
versioning, 42, 89, 121, 159
versioning primitives, 38
Vertical Application developers, 235
vertical applications of workflow, 249
Very Large Scale Integration, 289
Video for Windows, 292
video, 285
video archive, 157
video clips, 197
video compression, 290
video conferencing, 6
video frames, 290
video mail, 278
video server API, 156
video server, data storage, 155
video server, data throughput, 155
video server, response time, 155
video servers, 121, 154, 159
video streams, 156
video telephones, 289
videoconferencing, 47, 121, 133, 207, 273, 288–294, 303, 341, 344
videoconferencing rooms, 289
videoconferencing, desktop, 289
view common format, 61
view portable format, 61
viewers, 60, 190, 345
viewing components, 93
viewing objects, 58
ViewStar, 211
VIM, 171, 176
  address specification, 177
  distinguished name, 177
  message containers, 177
  messaging databases, 177
  name specification, 177
  note part, 176
  receiving messages, 177
  unique identifier, 177
VIM API specification, 176
VIM application items, 177
VIM attachments, 176
VIM Interface, 176
VIM stream formats, 176
Vines OS, 129
Virtual Corporation, 7
virtual canvas, 71
virtual circuits, 133
virtual corporation, 219, 321–326
  cons, 324
  pros, 322, 323
virtual meeting rooms, 48, 278
virtual offices, 160
virtual space(s), 30, 108, 329
virtual table, 75
Visio, 240
VisionQuest, 282
Visual SQL, 75
VL-EISA, 155
VLSI, 289
Vocorders, 305
voice annotation, 197

voice coding, 304
voice gateway, 278
voice mail, 278
voice mail threads, 278
voice mail, Germany, 279
voice mailbox, 279
voice messaging, 278
VoiceSpan, 304
voting, 281
voting tools, 280
voting, electronic, 280

wait-for cycle, 94
WAN, 15, 131, 132, 348
Wang, 211
wasting asset, information as, 263
Wave Guide technology, 305
wb, 309
Web servers, 165
weight evaluation techniques, 214
the Well, 164
While I am Out rule, 195
whiteboard, 287
Widcom, 289
Wide Area Networks (WANs), 17, 121, 131, 160
wide area communication networking technologies, 339
wide area connectivity servers, 340
Wide-Fast SCSI, 155
Windows 3.1, 125, 130
Windows, 57, 176, 186, 240
Windows NT, 130
Windows Open Services Architecture, 172
Windows Program Manager, 266
Windows WinBeep, 270
windows, private, 314, 315
windows, shared, 314, 315
Windows-based standards, DSP, 306
Winograd and Flores, 219
wireless communication, 160
wireless local area networks, 122
wireless networking, 121
wireless networks, 160
WMC standardization committee, 230
WMC, activity, 230
WMC, process definition, 230
WMC, process instance, 230
Word, 60, 61
Word for Windows, 91
word processor, 69
WordPerfect, 61, 69, 120, 173, 190
work, 30, 55, 210, 230
work modes, asynchronous, 318
work modes, synchronous, 318
work off-line, 271
work processing, 210, 211, 230
work processor, 221
work queues, 245
work-list, 254
worker(s), 22, 246, 251
workers, collaboration between, 259
Workflow Management Coalition (WMC), 230, 253

workflow, 6, 34, 38, 198, 340, 351–353
workflow activations, 254
workflow applications, 222
workflow architecture in client/server environment, 258
workflow automation, 209
workflow client nodes
workflow activation tool, 256
workflow design tool, 256
workflow tracking - status, 256
workflow concepts:
   case, 258
   groups, 258
   iteration, 258
   project management, 258
   retraction, 258
   roles, 258
   work queues, 258
   workflow rules, 258
   workflow status, 258
   workflow tools, 258
workflow database, 256
workflow devices, 222
workflow enactment services, 254
workflow engine, 220, 235, 240, 256
workflow engine functionality, 220
workflow engines, 254
workflow examples:
   hiring process, 250
   purchase requisitions, 251
   quality assurance and production, 253
   securities trading, 252
workflow for hiring a candidate, 250
workflow instance(s), 238, 254
workflow management engines, 254
workflow manager, 257
workflow manager scheduler, 267
workflow meta-data, 240
workflow model, 219
workflow notification, 248
workflow process(es), 238, 246
workflow processing, 218
workflow processing system, 214
workflow scripting language, 254
workflow server:
   database management system, 257
   messaging, transport, and communication services, 257
   workflow manager services, 256
workflow services manage, 256
workflow status, 246
workflow status information, 243
workflow status management tool, 256
workflow system, 207, 210, 214
   DBMS component, 257
   e-mail transport services interface, 257
   taxonomies, 214
workflow system elements, 229
workflow systems assist processing of work, 226
workflow systems automate processing of work, 226
workflow systems control processing of work, 226
workflow systems with e-mail backbone, 226
workflow template, 254
   activations, 243
   behavior, 243
   structure, 243
workflow:
   ad hoc, 34
   ad-hoc, 223, 258
   administrative, 34, 223, 258
   integrated with information model, 220
   knowledge-based, 223
   message based, 220
   production, 34, 223, 258
   production based, 223
   server based, 220
   transaction based, 223
workgroup community, 51
workgroup system integration, 272
working, new ways of, 261
workspace, 20
World Wide Web, 61, 100, 165, 347
WORM, 150
WOSA, 172
write permission, 238
WWW (World Wide Web), 165
WWW home pages, 100
WYSIWYG, 58

X-window, 310
X.25 packet switching, 17
X.400, 27, 179, 186
   addresses, 180
      Mnemonic Originator/Recipient, 180
      Numeric Originator/Recipient, 180
      Postal Originator/Recipient, 180
      Terminal Originator/Recipient, 180
   API Association (XAPIA), 174
   delivery service, 279
   domains, 180
   MHS, 179
      Message Store (MS), 179
      Message Transfer Agent (MTA), 179
      Message Transfer System (MTS), 179
      Message User Agent (MUA), 179
   private service, 180
   public domains, 180
   public service, 180
X.500, 170
   product, 240
   standard, 186
Xanadu, 29, 330
XAPIA, 174
Xerox, 260
Xerox Liveboard, 287
Xerox Network Standard (XNS) packet protocol, 127
Xerox PARC, 329
Xspy, 309, 310

yellow pages, 186

Zoetrope Enterprises, 339